LINCOLN CHRISTIAN U
P9-CQY-790

A HISTORY OF THE JEWISH PEOPLE
IN THE TIME OF JESUS

EMIL SCHÜRER

A HISTORY OF
The Jewish People
IN THE TIME OF JESUS

EDITED AND INTRODUCED BY
NAHUM N. GLATZER

SCHOCKEN BOOKS · NEW YORK

This volume is an abridgement of the First Division of Schürer's work. The English rendition of the work was first published in 1886-1890 by T. & T. Clark, Edinburgh.

First SCHOCKEN PAPERBACK *edition 1961*

Fifth Printing, 1975

Copyright © 1961, by Schocken Books, Inc.

Printed in the United States of America

Library of Congress Catalogue No. 61-8195

PREFACE

This new and abridged edition of Emil Schürer's monumental work presents the political history of Palestine, from B.C. 175 to A.D. 135, i.e. the "First Division" of the original work, in the authorized English translation. Not included in the present version is the excursus on the "Valuation Census of Quirinius" and the two sketches of the history of Syria; the latter have been replaced by a concise chronological summary. In place of the bibliographical lists of the original text (§§ 1-3), this new version includes a chronological guide to the period and genealogies of the Asmoneans and of the House of Herod, originally printed as appendices VII and VIII. Other appendices have been replaced by a bibliography of selected works in the field written in the last decades. The footnotes have been revised to include only essential information. Wherever possible, misprints have been corrected. The translator's peculiar spelling of names (influenced by Schürer's German spelling) has been retained.

132100

CONTENTS

FIRST PERIOD.

FROM ANTIOCHUS EPIPHANES DOWN TO THE CONQUEST OF JERUSALEM BY POMPEY.

THE RISE OF THE MACCABEES AND THE PERIOD OF FREEDOM, B.C. 175–63.

SECOND PERIOD.

FROM THE CONQUEST OF JERUSALEM BY POMPEY TO THE HADRIAN WAR.

THE ROMAN-HERODIAN PERIOD, B.C. 63–A.D. 135.

INTRODUCTION

Schürer's History

The interest of the general historian in Jewish history of post-Old Testament times, that is to say, the period of the Second Temple, or Second Commonwealth, is of comparatively recent origin. It arose when students of Early Christianity realized that the life and activity of Jesus cannot be understood as an isolated phenomenon but must be studied within the context of the contemporary history of Israel. This emphasis on the historic background of early Christianity is commonly associated with the research of Albrecht Ritschl (1822-89), his school, and its organs, the *Theologische Literaturzeitung* (founded in 1876) and *Zeitschrift für Theologie und Kirche* (founded in 1891). Hebrew literary sources of the Second Commonwealth and early rabbinic times had been accorded scholarly attention for some time, as for example by the Christian theologians Johann David Michaelis (1717-91) and August Friedrich Gfrörer (1803-61), and the Jewish historian Leopold Zunz (1794-1886). But the man who first attempted a political, religious, and literary history of Judaism in the centuries preceding the rise of Christianity, was Emil Schürer, a member of the Ritschl school.

Schürer approached his gigantic task with the conviction that an understanding of Christianity presupposes a knowledge of Israel's history, with which it is "inseparably joined by innumerable threads. No incident in the New Testament story . . . is intelligible apart from its setting in Jewish history." Knowledge of the Old Testament, he postulated, is not sufficient background for the history of primitive Christianity; on the contrary, the New Testament is "much more closely connected with its immediately contemporary surroundings."

There existed several histories of the New Testament era when Schürer commenced his work, but he did not follow the path established in these works. In their respective presentations, Adolf Hausrath and Matthias Schneckenburger combined analysis of Jewish religious history with description of the religious world of paganism. Feeling that such a combination must lead to arbitrary selection of issues and materials, Schürer concentrated on the "native soil of the sacred history." But, while imposing this restriction on the presentation of religion, he considered it essential to expand one's view of political history. Schneckenburger and Hausrath began their discourses with Pompey's conquest of Jerusalem in 63 B.C.; Schürer went back to the period of the Maccabean battles against Antiochus IV Epiphanes in 175 B.C. and the Judean struggle for independence from the rule of the Seleucid kings of Syria who succeeded Alexander the Great. He realized that it was then that "the spiritual life of Israel took a form it still maintained in the New Testament period."

Pharisaism, which in increasing measure characterized the following period, had, according to Schürer, its origin in the conflicts of the Maccabean age.

Political and spiritual crises in Jewish life determined the starting point of Schürer's history. Similarly, they determined its termination with the Bar-Cochba rebellion under Hadrian (132-135). The suppression of this revolt marked "the complete abolition of Jewish national freedom" which Judea had preserved in some measure even under Roman rule. Intellectual life, too, underwent a decisive change after the destruction of Jerusalem and the fall of Bethar (Bethther). This change Schürer found exemplified in the commitment to writing of the traditional law that had hitherto

been communicated only orally,—a process that "laid the
foundation of the Talmudical code." The period in Jewish
history in which Pharisaism "in consequence of the overthrow of the Jewish commonwealth became a purely spiritual
and moral power," was outside Schürer's immediate concern.

Separation of the political development of Judea 175
B.C. to 135 A.D. from the presentation of its internal conditions was a matter of some concern to Schürer. While available sources of information allowed him a clear view of the
political situation created by the Maccabean rebellion and,
later, by Roman domination, he found himself on less solid
ground in approaching cultural and religious material. With
typical scholarly caution, he spoke of "the necessity of ap-
pending to the outline of the political history a description
of the inner condition of the people in a separate division."

In his analysis of religious life in the Judaism of the
period, Schürer tried to interpret "the life under the Law"
as cultivated by the Pharisees. In his view, the prophetic
idea of the covenant between God and Israel was apprehended
by the Pharisees in a purely juridic sense; the concept of
precise recompense had replaced a deeper piety; life had
turned into a series of accurate, conscientious performances,
fulfillments of legal requirements, without any inward motive, indeed empty of religious content. The result was "an
incredible externalization of religious and moral life," so
that "all free moral action was crushed under the burden of
numberless separate statutory requirements." Schürer went
into great detail to demonstrate how "ethics and theology
were swallowed up in jurisprudence" and "the moral point
of view superseded by the legal and formal one."

This narrow, lopsided view of Jewish piety was already
noted and refuted in Schürer's lifetime. His failure to see
the non-legal, decidedly internalized aspects of Jewish piety,
prevented him from fulfilling his projected aim: to give an
objective, factual account of the "inner condition" of Ju-

daism. The researches of R. Travers Herford and George Foot Moore (to mention only Christian scholars) have done much to restore a balanced, comprehensive, and more just view of Pharisaism.

While the intellectual history of ancient Judaism, recounted in the "Second Division" (i.e. §§22-34) of Schürer's work, would require far-reaching rectification, and is therefore omitted from this edition, the political history of the period, constituting the "First Division," stands out as an example of reliable scholarship. Recent years have opened up new vistas; new source materials have increased our knowledge of the period, but it is Schürer's work that has provided the entire discipline with a solid foundation. It is not difficult to agree with Adolf von Harnack who said (in 1910) that he knew of no other segment in the entire realm of history for which there existed a manual as exhaustive as Schürer's work on the history of the Jewish people.

Emil Schürer was born in 1844 in Augsburg, Germany. He studied Theology at the Universities of Erlangen, Berlin, and Heidelberg; his doctoral dissertation (1868) dealt with the concept of religion in Schleiermacher. In 1869 he joined the Department of Theology at the University of Leipzig; in 1878 he became professor of New Testament at the University of Giessen; in 1890 he was called to Kiel, and in 1895 to Göttingen. Schürer died in 1910. Among his writings are *De controversiis paschalibus* (1869); *The Community Constitution of the Jews in Rome* (Die Gemeindeverfassung der Juden in Rom, 1879); *The Preaching of Jesus Christ and its Relationship to the Old Testament and to Judaism* (Die Predigt Jesu Christi im Verhältnis zum Alten Testament und zum Judentum, 1882); and *The Messianic Consciousness of Jesus* (Das messianische Selbstbewusstsein Jesu, 1903). From 1876 on, he edited the influential *Theologische Literaturzeitung*. However, Schürer's lasting fame is bound up with his monumental *History of the Jewish People in the Time of Jesus Christ.*

Very early in his career, Schürer freed himself from the theological systems of his masters. While acknowledging his indebtedness to Schleiermacher, Richard Rothe, and F. C. Baur, he insisted on independent pursuit of his religious views and methods of historic research. Theological romanticism was foreign to him; the sobriety of the Kantian concepts was closer to his heart. In his works we meet a master of keen, thorough research, and of lucid, well-balanced presentation.

The first edition of the *History* appeared under the title *Lehrbuch der neutestamentlichen Zeitgeschichte* (Leipzig 1874); a second, revised edition was published in 1886 (vol. II) and 1890 (vol. 1) under the title *Geschichte des jüdischen Volkes im Zeitalter Jesu Christi.* This title was used in all subsequent editions. In 1898-1902 the third and fourth edition of the first volume and the third edition of the second and third volumes appeared; the last two volumes were issued in a fourth edition in 1907-1911; in 1920 the first volume came out in a fifth printing, a re-issue of the text of the third and fourth edition. An authorized English translation, by John Macpherson (vols. I-II) and Sophia Taylor and Peter Christie (vols. III-V) appeared in Edinburgh, 1886-90, based on the second German edition of the work. The last of the eleven re-issues of the translation came out in 1924.

To transform the original textbook for students (Lehrbuch) into a full-fledged history, Schürer took a leave of several years from the administration of his *Literaturzeitung,* entrusting this task to his colleague, Adolf von Harnack. Into his new, thoroughly revised edition Schürer incorporated much additional material derived from recent scholarship by himself and others, so that the section on the political history of the period grew from 364 to 589 pages. While a planned revision of the chapter on Messianism was not effected, there was added a discussion of the priesthood and the Temple worship.

Thematically, the work was organized into two "divisions," the first, comprising volumes I and II of the English edition ("Political History of Palestine, from B.C. 175 to A.D. 135"); the second, consisting of volumes III to V ("The Internal Conditions of Palestine, and of the Jewish People, in the Time of Jesus Christ"). An index volume accompanied both German and English editions.

SOURCES AND LITERATURE

An important key to the author's success in presenting so vivid a picture of the political structure of the period is his sense for the historically original among his sources, and his acute ability to discriminate between conflicting and contradictory elements.

We shall quote the sources of this material as Schürer listed them at the head of each chapter, (referred to as paragraph by the author). Schürer used *First and Second Maccabees* (especially the first) and Josephus' *Antiquities* XII, 5 through XIII, 7, for the discussion of the Maccabean rebellion and the activities of the Maccabean brothers (§§ 1-7). In relating the story of the Hasmonean rule (§§ 8-14), he used *Antiquities* XIII, 8 through XIV, and *Wars* I, 2-18:3. For the rule of Herod the Great (§ 15), he consulted *Antiquities* XV through XVII, 1-8, and *Wars* I, 18-33. The background material for the account of the sons of Herod and the Roman procurators (§§ 16-19), was obtained from *Antiquities* XVII, 9 to the end of the book, and from *Wars* II, 1-14. Schürer also used New Testament sources for the Chapter on Herod Antipas (§ 17b), and for the chapter on Archelaus (§ 17c), Philo's *Embassy to Gaius*. The story of the "Great War with Rome" (§ 20) is based on *Wars* II, 14 to the end of the book, and Josephus' *Life*. (The summaries of Josephus' history as recorded by the twelfth-century Byzantine historian Zonaras were consulted throughout.) Finally Schürer presents the rebellions under Trajan and Hadrian according to the accounts of Dio Cassius, Eusebius *(Church History* and *Chronicle)*, and Orosius. In many parts of his work Schürer, an ardent student of the Mishnah, consulted Rabbinic material of historical significance, using the collection of such sources in Joseph Derenbourg's *Essai sur l'histoire et la géographie de la Palestine d'après les Thalmuds et les autres sources rabbiniques* (Paris, 1867).

Historic information drawn from inscriptions and coins were given special attention. For non-Jewish Greek and Latin inscriptions from Palestine and neighboring countries Schürer used the *Corpus Inscriptionum Latinarum* (vol. III, 1873). He also made use of the discoveries of Wetzstein and Waddington, and the collection of Nabatean inscriptions by De Vogüé (1868) and Eutiny (1885). Hebrew inscriptions, collected by Daniel Chwolson, Jewish inscriptions in Greek and Latin, mostly epitaphs on tombstones, and Roman inscriptions referring to Jewish history from Vespasian to Hadrian (published by James Darmesteter in 1880) offered auxiliary information. Schürer himself collected inscriptions referring to the Herodian princes. Inscriptions on coins were helpful in illustrating the history of the Seleucid rulers, the government of Phoenician and Hellenistic cities, and certain aspects of Jewish history. For the latter subject Schürer used the then classical work, *Coins of the Jews,* by Frederic W. Madden (London, 1881), and a host of other collections.

The listing of "Literature" at the head of each chapter, and the wealth of footnotes show Schürer's familiarity with most of the histories, scholarly monographs and periodical literature available at the time. Among other works, he lists the older *Histoire des Juifs* by Jacques Basnage, *Seleucidarum imperium* by Foy-Vaillant, the *Annales compendiarii regum etc.* by Froelich; the more recent *History of Israel* by Heinrich Ewald, I. M. Jost's *Geschichte des Judentums,* Heinrich Graetz's *Geschichte der Juden* and Levi Herzfeld's *Geschichte des Volkes Israel,* Ferdinand Hitzig's work by the same name, *Lectures on the History of the Jewish Church* by Arthur P. Stanley, and *Die Pharisäer und die Sadducäer* by Julius Wellhausen. He mentions the works of Félicien de Saulcy and Volkmar and refers to the researches of James Darmesteter and Joseph Derenbourg. He quotes articles from the *Monatsschrift für die Geschichte und Wissenschaft des Judentums, Revue des études juives,* Hamburger's *Real-Encyclopaedie für Bibel und Talmud,* and Ersch and Gruber's *Encyclopaedie.* He makes use of the various Lexica, Bibel dictionaries, cyclopaedias and atlasses (Herzog, Pauly, Schenkel, Smith, Winer, Menke). For the history of Rome he quotes Ferdinand Gregorovius, the fifth volume of Theodor Mommsen's *Römische Geschichte,* and B. G. Niebuhr's *Vorträge über alte Geschichte.* For the history of early Christianity: *The Life and Words of Christ* by Geikie, *History of New Testament Times* by Adolf Hausrath, K. T. Keim's liberal *Geschichte Jesu von Nazara,* Matthias Schneckenburger's *Vorlesungen über Neutestamentliche Zeitgeschichte,* Lewin's *Fasti sacri,* a key to the chronology of the New Testament, and the works of Ernest Renan. While many of these works are now forgotten and some are of use to specialists only, Schürer's work has retained its appeal for the intelligent reader and is indispensable to the historian.

From his sources and subsidiary material Schürer reconstructed the Jewish history of the period, placing it within the context of the history of the Seleucid, and later, of the Roman realm. Seen against this background, the Maccabean struggle for liberty, the expansion of the Hasmonean Kingdom, Herod's power, the rebellion of the Jewish patriots against Rome, and, finally, the heroic defense of Jerusalem and the last fortresses of Judea assume the proportions of a classical drama. This effect is achieved and enhanced by Schürer's scholarly detachment, objectivity, and scrupulous attention to detail.

As time progressed, interest in the period presented by Schürer grew in scope and intensity. There is today a stronger awareness of the part played by the Second Jewish Commonwealth in the ancient world. Much attention is directed toward the understanding of Hellenism and the place of Judaism in Hellenistic civilization by such scholars as Elias Bickerman and Victor Tcherikover. Closer study of Flavius Josephus by H. St. John Thackeray and Solomon Zeitlin, and the incisive analysis of Philo by Harry A. Wolfson have opened new avenues of thought. The discovery of the writings of the Qumran sect have intensified study of both the historic background of the sectarian development and the relationship between the teachings of the Qumran group and the early Christian community. Among the many scholars who have written on this subject are Karl Georg Kuhn and Krister Stendahl. Finally, the rebirth of the State of Israel and archaeological discoveries in the area (the most recent being the so-called Bar Cochba letters) have focused attention on the period of the Second Jewish Commonwealth. These concerns augment the theological inquiry into the background of the New Testament for the sake of which Schürer undertook to write his work.

Brandeis University.   NAHUM N. GLATZER

A HISTORY OF THE JEWISH PEOPLE
IN THE TIME OF JESUS

§ 1. POLITICAL HISTORY
OF PALESTINE

40	Invasion of Syria and Palestine by the Parthians; Hyrcanus II taken prisoner; Herod in Rome; designated king of Judea
40-37	Antigonus, son of Aristobulus II, high priest and king
39-38	Parthians driven out of the country; Herod lands at Ptolemais
37-4	Herod the Great: *see* Chronological Summary, pp. 121-128
31	Battle of Actium
30 B.C.-14 A.D.	Augustus
4 B.C.-6 A.D.	Archelaus, son of Herod, ethnarch of Judea, Samaria, and Idumea
4 B.C.-39 A.D.	Herod Antipas, son of Herod, tetrarch of Galilee and Perea
4 B.C.-34 A.D.	Philip, son of Herod, tetrarch of Batanea, Trachonitis, and Auranitis
A.D. 6-41	Judea, Samaria, and Idumea, a Roman province, governed by procurators, residing in Caesarea. Coponius, first procurator
6	Census of the population, taken by Quirinius, legate of Syria
14-37	Tiberius, emperor
26-36	Pontius Pilate, procurator
29	Execution of John the Baptist
30	Crucifixion of Jesus
32-37	A. Avillius Flaccus, governor of Egypt
37-44	Herod Agrippa I, grandson of Herod the Great, king over the territory of Philip; from 41 on, over the former realm of Herod the Great
37-41	Caligula, emperor
38	Anti-Jewish riots in Alexandria
40	Embassy of Alexandrian Jews (headed by Philo) to Caligula
44-66	The Roman procurators Herod marries Mariamme, granddaughter of Hyrcanus II

44-?	Cuspius Fadus, procurator
ca.45	Conversion of King Izates of Adiabene and his mother Helena
?-48	Tiberius Alexander, nephew of Philo, procurator
50	Agrippa II, son of Agrippa I, becomes king of Chalcis, later king of the territory of Philip and Lysanias
52-60	Felix, procurator; rise of Zealots and Sicarii; the Jewish prophet from Egypt; imprisonment of the Apostle Paul at Caesarea
54-68	Nero, emperor
60-66	Festus, Albinus, Gessius Florus, procurators
66	(Spring) Outbreak of the revolutionary movement against Rome
	(October) Victory of the Jews over Cestius Gallus, legate of Syria, near Beth-horon
	(November) Organization of the Jewish defence: Joseph, son of Gorion and high priest Ananus (Jerusalem); Jesus, son of Sapphias and Eleasar, son of Ananias (Idumea); (Flavius) Josephus, son of Matthias (Galilee)
67	Vespasian arrives; the war in Galilee
	(July) Fall of fortress Jotapata; Josephus surrenders to Vespasian and joins the Roman camp
	(end) The entire north of Palestine in Roman hands; John of Gischala, Galilean Zealot, escapes to Jerusalem
67-68	(Winter) Civil war in Jerusalem between the Zealots led by John of Gischala, and the men of order, led by high priest Ananus; flight of the Christian community from Jerusalem
68	(March to June) Vespasian's conquests in Perea, western Judea and Idumea
	(June) Death of Nero; suspension of war operations
69	(January) Murder of Galba, successor of Nero
	(April) Simon Bar-Giora, rival war leader in Jerusalem
	(June) Resumption of the war; all Palestine except Jerusalem and three fortresses subjected to Vespasian

	(July) Vespasian proclaimed emperor; Jewish war committed to Titus; Titus prepares for attack
69-79	Vespasian, emperor
70	(April) Titus arrives before the walls of Jerusalem
	(May) Romans subdue first and second wall; Josephus appeals to the city to surrender; John of Gischala and Simon Bar-Giora destroy Roman earthworks
	(July) Cessation of the daily sacrifices; fall of the fortress Antonia; preparations for a siege of the Temple site
	(August) Temple gates burn down (9th of Ab); conflagration of the Temple (10th of Ab)
	(September) Fall of the city
71	Titus and Vespasian celebrate triumph in Rome; execution of Simon Bar-Giora; John of Gischala imprisoned for life; Lucilius Bassus attacks strongholds of Herodium and Machaerus
73	(April) Masada, last fortress, defended by Eleasar, son of Jair, conquered by Flavius Silva
	Jewish uprisings in Alexandria and Cyrene; closing of the Onias temple in Leontopolis
75	Agrippa II and his sister Berenice arrive in Rome
79-81	Titus, emperor
81-96	Domitian, emperor
96-98	Nerva, emperor
98-117	Trajan, emperor
100	d. Agrippa II; his kingdom incorporated into the province of Syria
115-117	Jewish rebellions in Egypt, Cyrene, Cyprus and Mesopotamia ("The War under Trajan"); Lusius Quietus, Roman general, appointed governor of Palestine
117-138	Hadrian, emperor
132-135	The great rebellion under Hadrian; Bar-Cochba, Jewish leader; Julius Severus, Roman general
135	Fall of Beth-ther; Jerusalem converted into a Roman colony (Aelia Capitolina).

§ 2. THE RULERS OF SYRIA

The Last Century of the Seleucid Dynasty

B.C. 175-164   Antiochus IV Epiphanes

164-162   Antiochus V Eupator

162-150   Demetrius I Soter

150-145   Alexander Balas

145-138   Demetrius II Nicator (145-?, Antiochus VI; ?-138, Trypho)

138-128   Antiochus VII Sidetes

128-125 (or 124)   Demetrius II Nicator (a second time); 128-122(?), Alexander Zabinas

125 (or 124)   Seleucus V

125 (or 124)-113   Antiochus VIII Grypos

113-95   Antiochus IX Cyzicenos; 111-96, Antiochus VIII Grypos

95-83   Conflicts among the five sons of Antiochus Grypos

83-69   Tigranes, King of Armenia

69-65   Antiochus XIII Asiaticus

65   Pompey abolishes the Seleucid dynasty

Syria as a Roman province

65-48   Under the influence of Pompey (More important governors: A. Gabinius, 57-55; M. Licinius Crassus, 54-53)

47-44   During the time of Caesar (Sextus Caesar, 47-46; Caecilius Bassus, 46)

44-42   Under the administration of Cassius (C. Cassius Longinus, 44-42)

41-30   Under the rule of Marc Antony (Decidius Saxa, 41-40; Ventidius, 39-38; C. Sosius, 38-37)

30 B.C.-14 A.D.   Under Octavianus Augustus (M. Tullius Cicero, 28 (?); Varro, down to 23; M. Agrippa, 23-13; P. Sulpicius Quirinius, 3-2(?); C. Caesar, B.C. 1-A.D. 4 (?); P. Sulpicius Quirinius, A.D. 6 ff.)

A.D. 14-37   Under Tiberius (Cn. Sentius Saturninus, 19-21; L. Pomponius Flaccus, 32-35 (?); L. Vitellius, 35-39)

37-41   Under Caligula (P. Petronius, 39-42)

41-54   Under Claudius (C. Cassius Longinus, 45-50)

54-68   Under Nero (C. Cestius Gallus, 63-66; C. Licinius Mucianus, 67-69)

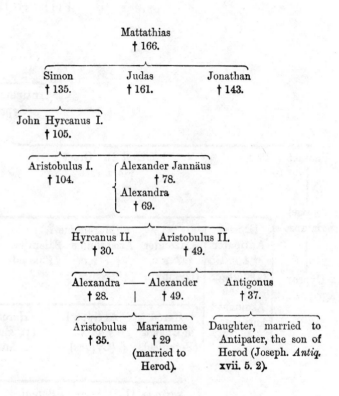

An

Antipater † 43
(Cypros).

Phasael † 40 B.C.   Herod the Great   Joseph
† 4 B.C.

Phasael
(Salampso).

Cypros
(Agrippa I.).

(Doris)
Antipater
† 4 B.C.
(Daughter
of the
Asmonean
Antigonus).

(Mariamme I.)
Alexander   Aristobulus   Salampso   Cypros.
† 7 B.C.   † 7 B.C.   (Phasael).
(Glaphyra).   (Berenice).

Herod   Agrippa I.   Herodias
of Chalcis   † 44 A.D.   (1. Herod.
(Berenice).   (Cypros).   2. Antipas).

Agrippa II.   Berenice
† 100 A.D.   (1. Herod von Chalcis.
        2. Polemon of Cilicia).

tipas.

Joseph † 34
(Salome).

† 38. Pheroras † 5 B.C. Salome † about 10 A.D.
(1. Joseph † 34.
2. Costobar † 25.
3. Alexas).

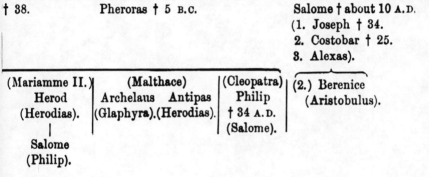

(Mariamme II.) (Malthace) (Cleopatra) (2.) Berenice
Herod Archelaus Antipas Philip (Aristobulus).
(Herodias). (Glaphyra).(Herodias). † 34 A.D.
  (Salome).
Salome
(Philip).

Drusilla
(1. Azizus.
2. Felix).

Proofs of the greater number of the details will be found in the following places :

1. *Antiq.* xiv. 7. 3 ; *Wars of the Jews*, i. 8. 9 (parents and brothers and sisters of Herod).
2. *Antiq.* xvii. 1. 3 ; *Wars of the Jews*, i. 28. 4 (wives and children of Herod).
3. *Antiq.* xviii. 5. 4, xix. 9. 1 ; *Wars of the Jews*, ii. 11. 6 (the descendants of Mariamme).

11

FIRST PERIOD

FROM ANTIOCHUS EPIPHANES DOWN TO THE CONQUEST OF JERUSALEM BY POMPEY.

THE RISE OF THE MACCABEES AND THE PERIOD OF FREEDOM, B.C. 175–63.

———◆———

§ 4. RELIGIOUS DESTITUTION

AND REVIVAL

Since the conquests of the Assyrians and Chaldeans, the Jewish people had lost their political independence. The northern kingdom of the ten tribes had been overthrown by the Assyrians, the southern kingdom of Judah by the Chaldeans. The sovereignty had passed from the Chaldeans to the Persians, and from the Persians, after a supremacy of two centuries, to Alexander the Great. In the wild commotions of the Diadochean period, Palestine formed a main object of strife between Ptolemy Lagus and his opponents, and was therefore sometimes under one, sometimes under another master. With short intervals it continued throughout the third century under the sway of the Ptolemies. But in the beginning of the second century, Antiochus the Great succeeded in permanently securing possession of Phoenicia and Palestine. In place of the Ptolemies, the Seleucidae now became the suzerains of the Jewish people.

13

Even in the beginning of the Persian domination the Jews
had resolved to organize themselves anew as a religious and
political community.   But the form in which the Jewish
commonwealth was restored after the exile was essentially
different from that which prevailed before.   It was from this
time forward a government of priests.   As they were pre-
eminently religious interests that had given the impulse to
the reconstruction, so also the form of the new commonwealth
was more that of a religious than of a political association.   The
priests had in it a predominating influence, at least from the
time of Ezra.   Indeed, a priest stood at the head of the
political organization.   For the so-called high priest was not
by any means simply the supreme director of worship, but
was at the same time also the supreme head of the State, in
so far as civil authority was not exercised by the great king
and his officers.   The rank of high priest was held for life,
and was hereditary.[1]   Alongside of him, probably even during
the Persian period, and in any case from the beginning of the
Greek domination, stood a council of elders, the γερουσία,
with the high priest at its head as its executive organ.   How
far administration and legislation lay in the hands of this
native board, and how far these were exercised by the Persian
and Greek suzerains, cannot now be determined with any
certainty.   Under the Greek suzerains the political independence of the Jewish people could not be less, but probably
greater, than it had been before.

The extent of the Jewish commonwealth, which still
possessed a relatively considerable measure of independence,
was probably limited to Judea proper, that is, the province
lying south of Samaria, which in its range corresponded nearly
with the kingdom of Judah of earlier days.   All the coast
cities were excluded from it, for these were mainly occupied
by a heathen population, and formed independent communities
by themselves (see § 23. 1).   How far those Gentile districts

extended inland may be seen from this, that even Ekron and Gazara did not belong to Judea. Ekron was first united with the Jewish domain and Judaized in the time of Jonathan (1 Macc. x. 88, 89), Gazara first in the time of Simon (1 Macc. xiii. 43–48). On the situation of these towns, see below under § 6 and 7. Also the whole of the land east of the Jordan was excluded from the Jewish territory. We find there partly Hellenistic communities (see § 23. 1), partly independent tribes, under native rulers.[2] In the country west of the Jordan, towards the end of the third and the beginning of the second century, "Judea" and "Samaria" formed each a separately administered province alongside of "Coele-Syria" and "Phoenicia."[3] Galilee was not reckoned as a distinct province, and so it belonged to one of the four above named, but scarcely to Judea, toward which it did not conveniently lie. Now the Pseudo-Hecataeus, indeed, expressly affirms that Alexander the Great gave to the Jews Samaria as a district free from tribute.[4] But even if this statement were more credible than it is, it could not by any means apply to the period of the Seleucid rule, since even under the Maccabean high priest Jonathan it is related as a proof of the special favour of King Demetrius II., that he took three νομοί from Samaria and united them with Judea, and made over this whole district to the Jews free of tribute.[5] Ordinarily, therefore, the territory of the Jewish high priest embraced only Judea. And that, too, Judea in the narrower sense, without Galilee, for this is evidently the meaning of the passages quoted from the First Book of Maccabees.[6]

The spread of the Jewish population was by no means limited to the bounds of Judea in the political sense. Even the circumstance that during the Maccabean age stress was laid upon the union with Judea of the three southern districts of Samaria (1 Macc. xi. 34; Ephraim, Lydda, and Ramathaim), leads to the conjecture that the population within those

districts was mainly Jewish,—in other words, that they had
not with the schismatical Samaritans offered sacrifices on Mount
Gerizim, but in Jerusalem, and that they had maintained
religious fellowship with the Jews there.[7]   But also in the
province of Galilee, and even in Gilead, in the country east
of the Jordan, at the beginning of the second century, a
considerable number of Jews must have resided, who maintained religious intercourse with Jerusalem ; for it was one of
the first acts of the Maccabee brothers, after the restoration
of the Jewish worship, to bring help to their brethren in the
faith in Galilee and Gilead who had been oppressed by the
heathen : Simon went to Galilee, Judas to Gilead (1 Macc. v.
9–54).   The manner in which they afforded this help shows
us, however, on the other hand, that then the general mass of
the population of those districts was no longer Jewish.   For
neither Simon nor Judas took the provinces as such under
Jewish protection.   But after Simon had defeated the heathen
in Galilee, he led all the Jews away out of Galilee and
Arbatta (properly עֲרָבוֹת, the lower districts of the Jordan),
together with their wives and children and all their possessions,
into Judea, in order that there he might keep them in safety
(1 Macc. v. 23).[9a]   In precisely the same way Judas dealt
with those Jews that lived in Gilead, after he had overthrown
the heathen there (1 Macc. v. 45–54).   It therefore seems
quite evident that the Jews in Galilee and Gilead formed
then a " dispersion " among the heathen ; and the first Maccabees made no sort of attempt to Judaize those provinces, but,
on the contrary, withdrew from them their Jewish population.
It was John Hyrcanus, or one of his successors (probably not
before Aristobulus I.), who first introduced that policy.

The internal development of Judaism from the time of
Ezra to that of the Maccabees, or even down to the compilation
of the Talmud, can be sketched only in very general outlines.
The starting-point, indeed, is known to us in fuller detail—

the priestly law introduced by Ezra in the fifth century before
Christ; and then, again, the culmination: the codification of
the Jewish law in the Mishna in the second century after
Christ. Between these two points lies a period of six
centuries. What stage of development had Judaism reached
at the outbreak of the Maccabean revolution? We can only
say, it was already on the way to those results which are set
before us in the Mishna; and the Maccabean age was simply the
period of the greatest crisis through which it was called to pass
during that whole era. The attempt was made to overthrow
the foundations of its earlier development, to convert the
Jewish people to heathenism. The result was that the
foundations laid before by Ezra were now strengthened, and
the theoretical elaboration of the law and its practical appli-
cations were prosecuted with glowing enthusiasm. The law
which Ezra had introduced was essentially a ceremonial law.
The religion of Israel is there reduced to strictly legalized
forms, in order that it may be made more secure against the
influences of heathenism. In the form of a law given by
God Himself, the Jew was told what he had to do as a
faithful servant of Jehovah, what festivals he should celebrate, what sacrifices he should offer, what tribute he should
pay to the priests who conduct the services, and generally
what religious ceremonies he should perform. Precision in
the observance of all these prescribed rites was to be made
henceforth the gauge and measure of piety. And in order to
make this precision as exact as possible, it was necessary that
an authentic interpretation be supplied. A special order
under the name of " Scribes " devoted themselves to the study
of the law as a profession, and engaged upon a subtle and
refining exposition of it. But the pious considered it to be
their chief business to fulfil with zeal and conscientiousness the
law as thus expounded. That very considerable progress in
this direction had been made even in the second century

before Christ, is distinctly proved by the history of the Maccabean revolution.   There was a religious party which inter-
preted the Sabbath command so strictly, that they would
rather surrender without a struggle than infringe upon the
observance of the Sabbath by wielding the sword (1 Macc. ii.
32–38).   It also belonged to the ideal of piety, which even
the author of the book of Daniel had already set before the
eyes of his comrades in the faith as an essential condition,
that they should not defile themselves with the eating of the
food of the heathen (Dan. i.).

But alongside of this legalistic tendency there were operating in Palestine, from the time of Alexander the Great,
influences of an altogether different kind, which proved the
more decidedly and dangerously hostile to the interests of
the law and its promoters the longer they existed.   These
were the Hellenizing tendencies.   It had been the fond dream
of Alexander to found a universal empire, which would be held
together not merely by the unity of the government, but also by
the unity of language, customs, and civilisation.   All the Oriental
races were to be saturated with Hellenic culture, and to be
bound together into one great whole by means of this intellectual
force.   He therefore took care that always Greek colonists
should directly follow in the steps of his army.   New cities
were founded, inhabited only by Greeks, and also in the old
cities Greek colonists were settled.   Thus over one half of Asia
a network of Greek culture was stretched, which had as its
object the reducing under its influence of the whole surrounding
regions.   The successors of Alexander continued his work ; and
it is a striking testimony to the power of Greek culture, that
it fulfilled in large measure the mission which Alexander had
assigned it.   All Western Asia, in fact, if not among the wide
masses of the population, yet certainly among the higher
ranks of society, became thoroughly Hellenized.   Even in
Palestine about the beginning of the second century this

movement was in full progress. It cannot indeed be proved that all those cities, which we have come to reckon during the Roman period as Hellenistic cities (see § 22. 2 and § 23. 1), had been already Hellenized in the beginning of the Maccabean period. But this may safely be assumed in regard to the majority of them. Many had Hellenic institutions introduced by Alexander the Great himself, others by his successors, and everywhere Greek influence and Greek ideas were promoted.[8] Even in the pre-Hellenic age, Gaza, as its coins prove, had lively commercial intercourse with Greece; from the time of its conquest by Alexander it was a Macedonian arsenal and residence for troops; and Josephus describes it as a πόλις Ἑλληνίς.[9] Anthedon by its very name betrays its Greek origin. In Ashkelon coins of Alexander the Great were stamped.[10] Ashdod on its coins, which date from the age of the Diadochae or even earlier, makes use indeed of the Hebrew language, but writes the letters in Greek characters (ΙΡ ΑΣΔΩΔ ΑΣΙΝΑ). Joppa is the old site of the myth of Perseus and Andromeda, and was in the age of the Diadochae a Macedonian garrison town. Apollonia is manifestly a foundation of the Greek times. Straton's Tower has indeed a Greek name, but was really founded at an earlier date by the Sidonians. On the other hand, Dora was possibly even in the fifth century before Christ put under tribute by the Athenians. In Acre, afterwards Ptolemais, as early as the times of Isaeus and Demosthenes, there was a Greek trading colony. The coins impressed there with the name of Alexander were already very numerous, and in the age of the Diadochae it was an important garrison town. The real Hellenizing and refounding of it as Ptolemais was probably the work of Ptolemy II. Philadelphus. —Along with these coast towns we must also include a number of inland cities. We know certainly of Samaria that it was colonized by Alexander. Scythopolis is met with bearing this Greek name as early as the third century; and

even earlier we have Paneion, the grotto at the source of the
Jordan, as the sanctuary of Pan. Along with Scythopolis,
Polybius (v. 70) makes mention of an important city not
otherwise known, Philoteria on the Lake of Gennesaret, in the
time of Antiochus the Great, B.C. 218, which, like the
similarly named city in Upper Egypt, had its name probably
from a sister of Ptolemy II. Philadelphus.[11]—Of the cities of
the countries east of the Jordan, Hippus and Gadara were
distinctly reckoned πόλεις Ἑλληνίδες.[12] Pella and Dium are
denominated Macedonian cities, and were founded perhaps by
Alexander the Great, and at latest during the Diadochean age.
The derivation of the name Gerasa from the γέροντες, the
veterans of Alexander the Great, is probably nothing more than
an etymological fancy. This, however, is certain, that the old
capital of the Ammonites was Hellenized by Ptolemy II.
Philadelphus under the name of Philadelphia. And finally,
the Second Book of Maccabees speaks generally of πόλεις
Ἑλληνίδες within the boundaries of Judea (2 Macc. vi. 8).

Within the encircling network of Hellenistic cities the
small province of Judea kept itself clear of the influence of
Greek customs and ways. There, too, Hellenism encroached
more and more. The indispensable requirements of daily life
obliged the Jews to make use of the universal language of the
Greeks. How otherwise would commercial intercourse with
foreign lands have been possible? But with the language
came also the manners and customs, and indeed the whole
culture of Greece. In the beginning of the second century the
progress of Hellenism in Palestine must have already become
quite observable. For only thus can we explain how a
section of the people, including the upper classes and the
educated, readily gave their consent to the Hellenizing projects of Antiochus Epiphanes, and even went beyond him in
carrying them out.[13]—Had this process been allowed to go on
in its natural and peaceful course, then the Judaism of Pales-

tine would probably have in time assumed a form in which it would be scarcely recognisable,—a form even more syncretistic than that of Philo. For it belonged to the very essence of Hellenism that it should dominate and colour the modes of religious worship, and at least clothe them in Grecian garments. We find it so in Syria as well as in Egypt. Nor would it have happened otherwise in Judea, if matters there had been permitted to take a smooth course. But the more perfect that legalistic Judaism had become on the one hand, and the more thoroughly developed the central principle of Hellenism had grown upon the other, the more decided and irreconcilable did the opposition between the two appear. Within the circle of the Jewish people itself there now arose two antagonistic parties: the party friendly to the Greeks and the party of "the pious" (חֲסִידִים, ᾿Ασιδαῖοι, 1 Macc. ii. 42, vii. 13), who held stoutly by the strict ideal of the scribes. But the whole preliminary history of the Maccabean revolution makes it evident that already the adherents of the former party were in the majority. Everything seemed conspiring to present before Hellenism an open door. It appeared as if nothing else was now left for "the pious" but to form themselves into a sect. But just then a powerful reaction set in, brought about by the attempt of an unintelligent despot, Antiochus Epiphanes, prematurely and with rude violence to force upon them Hellenic institutions. The Jewish worship was to be completely abolished, purely Greek rites were to be introduced, all Jewish ceremonies were all at once to be forbidden. It was just the extreme and radical character of this attempt that saved Judaism. For now not only the strict party of *Chasidim*, but the whole mass of the people, was roused to do battle for the old faith. And the further development of events led to the complete expulsion of Hellenism from Jewish soil, at least in matters of religion. So far as our information reaches, this is the only example of an Oriental religion completely emancipating itself from the influence of Hellenism.

Antiochus IV. Epiphanes, son of Antiochus the Great, had succeeded his brother Seleucus IV. in the government of Syria, after that king had been murdered by his minister Heliodorus, and held possession of the throne from B.C. 175 till B.C. 164. He was by nature a genuine despot, eccentric and undependable, sometimes extravagantly liberal, and fraternizing with the common people in an affected manner; at other times cruel and tyrannical, as he showed himself in his treatment of Judea. The picture drawn of him by Polybius describes him under the more pleasing aspect. This is the sketch he gives: [14] —

"Sometimes he would slip away from the palace and would appear at one time here, at another time there, in the city, sauntering along in company with one or two. Very often he was to be found in the workshops of the silversmiths and goldsmiths, where he would chat away with the moulders and other workmen, and seek to impress them with his love of art. Then he would condescend to familiar intercourse with any sort of people he chanced to come across, and would carouse with the meanest strangers who might happen to be present. But when he learned that young folks anywhere were to have a drinking bout, he would appear among them unexpectedly with horn and bagpipe, so that most, through sudden fright, would rush precipitately away. Often, too, he laid aside his royal robes, and, dressed in a toga, would go to the forum as a suppliant for an office. He would then seize some by the hand, others he would embrace, and entreat them to give him their vote, sometimes for the office of aedile, sometimes for that of tribune of the people. If he succeeded in obtaining the office, and was seated according to Roman custom in the ivory chair of state, he would take into consideration the cases that were to be adjudicated upon in the forum, and give his decisions with much earnestness and conscientiousness. Rational people, therefore, were at a loss what to think about him. Some regarded him as a simple and homely man, others looked upon him as crazed. He acted in a similar manner in the bestowal of his gifts. To some he gave bone dice, to others dates, to others gold. But if perchance he should meet any one whom he had never seen before, he would give him unexpected presents. But in the sacrifices which he had offered up in cities, and in the honours which he gave to the gods, he went beyond all other kings. As a proof of this we may point to the Temple of Zeus at Athens, and the images around the altar at Delos. He was wont also to bathe in the public baths, when they were quite full of their habitual visitors, where vessels of the most costly perfumes would be brought to him. When somebody once said to him: 'Happy art thou, O king, since thou hast such perfumes and givest forth such fragrance;' he went on the following day, without having said anything to the man, to the place where he bathed, and showered upon his head the contents of a large vase of that most precious ointment called *stacte*; whereupon all made a rush forward in order to wash themselves with the ointment. But on account of the slipperiness of the pavement many fell, amid shouts of laughter, the king himself joining in the mirth." — Thus far Polybius. Diodorus and Livy give similar accounts. They give special prominence to his love of pomp and his munificence. Brilliant spectacles, magnificent buildings, kingly presents, these were the sort of things in which he delighted.[15] But in everything he was inclined to rush to extravagant extremes, so that Polybius already styled him ἐπιμανής rather than ἐπιφανής.[16]

Such being the character of the man, we need not trouble ourselves seeking to discover any very deep motives for his proceedings against Judea. Tacitus has, upon the whole,

given a fair estimate of them when he said: Antiochus strove
to overthrow the superstition of the Jews and to introduce
among them Greek customs, but was prevented by the war
with the Parthians "from improving the condition of this
most detestable race." [17]   His endeavour was to advance
everywhere the lustre of Greek culture.   In Judea a section
of the people declared in favour of his plans.   He was
naturally prepared to give that party his support, and to make
over to it the government of Judea.   But when the Jewish
people organized an opposition to these schemes, this roused
the capricious humour of the despot.   He first of all chastised
the refractory people by plundering the rich treasures of their
temple, which must have been very enticing to the king, now
sorely in need of money.   Then, as the opposition still continued, he proceeded to radical and sweeping measures.   The
Jewish worship was completely suspended, all Jewish ceremonies were strictly forbidden, and with rude violence a
thoroughgoing Hellenizing process was attempted.

At the head of the party in Judea attached to the old faith
at the time when Antiochus Epiphanes ascended the throne,
stood the high priest of that day, Onias III.   The leader of
the party friendly to the Greeks was his own brother Jesus,
or, as he is better known under his Greek name, Jason.[18]   In
Jerusalem the inclination in favour of Greek customs was
already so strong that the friends of the Greeks could venture
upon the attempt to seize the government for themselves, and
to carry out their plans by force.   Jason promised the king a
great sum of money,—whether as a gift bestowed once and for
all, or as a regular tribute, is not very clear,—if he would
transfer to him the high-priesthood, permit him to erect a
gymnasium and an ephebeion, and finally allow " the inhabitants of Jerusalem to be enrolled as Antiocheans," τοὺς ἐν
Ἱεροσολύμοις Ἀντιοχεῖς ἀναγράψαι, that is, grant them the
title and privileges of citizens of Antioch.[22]   Antiochus was

quite ready to concede all this. Onias was driven out, and Jason was installed as high priest.[19] The Hellenizing process was now carried on with energy. There is indeed no mention of any attack having been made upon the Jewish religion. But in every other direction he put down " the institutions that were according to the law, and brought up new customs against the law " (2 Macc. iv. 11). A gymnasium was erected below the castle ; the young men of Jerusalem exercised themselves in the gymnastic arts of the Greeks. The very priests forsook their service at the altar and took part in the games of the palaestra. The contempt for Jewish customs went so far that many sought artificially to remove the traces of their circumcision.[20] With a latitudinarianism of a genuinely Hellenistic type, Jason sent a contribution to the sacrificial festival of Hercules at the games celebrated every fourth year at Tyre. This, however, was so offensive to the Jews entrusted with the carrying of it, that they entreated that the money should be applied to building ships.[21]

For three years, from B.C. 174 to B.C. 171, Jason administered his office after this fashion. Then he fell, through the machinations of a rival, who continued his work in a manner still more contemptible. Menelaus, by promising still larger gifts of money, was able to bring about Jason's overthrow, and to secure the transference to himself of the high priest's office.[22] He roused against himself the bitter animosity of the people by appropriating the treasures of the temple. He also was the instigator of the murder of the former high priest Onias III., who had sought the asylum of the sanctuary at Daphne, from which, however, he was decoyed and treacherously murdered.[23]

Meanwhile Jason had not abandoned his claims to the high-priesthood. In B.C. 170, when Antiochus was engaged upon his expedition against Egypt, he succeeded by a sudden stroke in making himself master of Jerusalem, and forcing his rival to betake himself for protection to the castle. This success of Jason was, according to the representation of the Second Book of Maccabees, the occasion that led to the king's direct interference against Jerusalem. Antiochus looked upon the proceeding as a slight to his majesty, and resolved to chastise the rebellious city.[24]

When, toward the end of B.C. 170, he had returned from Egypt,[25] he marched against Jerusalem in person with his army, and there gave direction for a terrible massacre, and plundered the enormous treasures of the Jewish temple, in which he is said to have received assistance from Menelaus himself. All the valuable articles, among them the three great golden pieces of furniture in the inner court of the temple, the altar of incense, the seven-branched candlestick, and the table of shewbread, he carried away with him to Antioch.[26]

The cup of sorrow and humiliation for the believing Israelites, however, had not yet been completely drained, and the worst was yet to come. Two years later, in B.C. 168, Antiochus undertook another expedition against Egypt. But this time the Romans took the field against him. The Roman general, Popilius Laenas, had sent him a decree of senate, in which he was required, if he were to avoid being regarded as an enemy of Rome, to abandon once for all his schemes against Egypt; and when Antiochus answered that he wished time to consider the matter, Popilius gave him that well-known brief *ultimatum*, describing a circle round about him with his staff and addressing him with a determined " ἐνταῦθα βουλεύου." Antiochus was thus compelled, whether he would or not, to yield to the demands of the Romans.[27] The result of this blasting of his plans with regard to Egypt was that Antiochus directed his energies immediately to a war of extermination against the Jewish religion.[28] Since nothing more could be done in Egypt, he would carry out all the more determinedly his schemes in Judea. He sent a chief collector of the tribute to Judea (his name is not given in 1 Macc. i. 29, but in 2 Macc. v. 24 he is called Apollonius), with orders to Hellenize Jerusalem thoroughly.[29] The Jewish population which would not yield was treated with great barbarity; the men were killed, and the women and children sold into slavery. Whoever was able escaped from the city. In place of the Jewish population thus destroyed, strangers were brought in as colonists. Jerusalem was to be henceforth a Greek city.[30] In order that such measures might have enduring effect, the walls of the city were thrown down; but the old city of David was fortified anew and made into a powerful stronghold, in which a Syrian garrison was placed. This garrison remained in possession of the citadel during all the subsequent struggles of the Maccabees, and maintained the supremacy of the Syrian kings amid all changes. Simon was the first, twenty-six years after this, in B.C. 142–141, to gain possession of the citadel, and so to vindicate the independence of the Jews.[31]

The destruction of the Jewish population of Jerusalem was only a means towards the chief end after which Antiochus was striving. Throughout the whole land the Jewish religion was to be rooted out, and the worship of the Greek gods introduced. The observance of all Jewish rites, especially of the Sabbath and circumcision, was forbidden on the pain of death; the Jewish mode of worship was abolished. In all the cities of Judea sacrifices were to be offered to the heathen deities. Officers were sent into all the districts, charged with the duty of seeing that the commands of the king were strictly obeyed. Wherever any one showed reluctance, obedience was enforced with violence. Once a month a rigorous search was instituted: if a copy of the book of the law were found in the possession of any one, or if any one had had his child circumcised, he was put to death. In Jerusalem, on the 15th Chisleu of the Seleucid year 145, that is, in December B.C. 168, at the great altar of burnt-offering a pagan altar was built, and on 25th Chisleu, for the first time, a sacrifice was offered upon it (1 Macc. i. 54, 59 ; this is "the abomination that maketh desolate," שִׁקּוּץ מְשֹׁמֵם or שִׁקּוּץ שֹׁמֵם, LXX.: βδέλυγμα τῆς ἐρημώσεως, of which the book of Daniel speaks, Dan. xi. 31, xii. 11). This sacrifice, according to the account given in the Second Book of Maccabees, was rendered to the Olympic Zeus, to whom the temple of Jerusalem has been dedicated. The Jews were also compelled to keep the Dionysiac festival, crowned with ivy, marching in procession as devotees of Bacchus.[32]

The Second Book of Maccabees relates wonderful stories of the bright martyr courage with which a certain section of the people firmly adhered to the ancient faith. With considerable rhetorical extravagance it tells how an old man ninety years of age, called Eleasar, was tortured ; and then also seven brothers, one after another, suffered before the eyes of their mother, who at last herself likewise met a martyr's death.[33] The question of the accuracy of these details must be left undecided. The fact is that a large circle of the people, notwithstanding all the violent measures of the persecutors, remained true to the faith and customs of their fathers. For their encouragement an unknown author, under the name of Daniel, published a hortatory and consolatory treatise, in which he set before his fellow-believers, for stimulus and incitement, stories culled from the history of earlier times, and with confident assurance of faith represents the speedy overthrow of the heathen rule, and the downfall of the worldly oppressors of the people of God (Div. ii. vol. iii. p. 44 ff.). The effect of such a work we can easily conceive must have been very great.

The passive resistance thus shown was soon succeeded by

open revolt,—viewed from a human point of view, a foolhardy enterprise; for how could the small nation of the Jews
secure any permanent advantage over the forces of the king?
But religious enthusiasm waits not to ask about possibilities
of success. The excitement broke forth into revolution in
the town of Modein, at the call of a priest of the order of
Joarib, named Mattathias, and his five sons, John, Simon,
Judas, Eleasar, and Jonathan.[34] When the king's officer had
entered that place, in order to insist upon the presentation of
the heathen sacrifice, Mattathias refused to obey the command. "Though all the nations," said he, "that are under
the king's dominion obey him, and fall away every one
from the religion of their fathers, and give consent to his
commandments, yet will I and my sons and my brothers walk
in the covenant of our fathers. God forbid that we should
forsake the law and the ordinances." When he saw a Jew
preparing to offer sacrifice, he rushed forward and slew him
upon the altar. He also killed the king's commissioner, and
levelled the altar to the ground.[35]

He then fled along with his sons into the mountains.
But soon a terrible disaster proved to him that mere flight
meant nothing less than utter destruction. Multitudes of
like-minded men had now withdrawn into hiding-places in
the desert. There they were sought after by a detachment
of the Syrian garrison of Jerusalem, and an attack was made
upon them on a Sabbath day; and since they declined to
offer any resistance because of the Sabbath, they were
remorselessly hewn down to the last man, along with their
wives and children.[36] To the vigorous, strong-minded
Mattathias such a martyrdom seemed a poor way of con-
tributing to the cause of God. He and those about him
resolved to proceed to action, and, in case of necessity, not
even to scruple engaging in battle upon the Sabbath day.
And now the "Pious," Ἀσιδαῖοι, חֲסִידִים, attached themselves

to him ; that is, those who proved faithful in their observance
of the law, who had hitherto showed their resolution simply
in endurance.[37]　Mattathias then gathered together all the
men fit for battle, who were ready to fight for their faith,
passed with them up and down through the country, over-
turned the altars, slew the apostate Jews, circumcised un-
circumcised children, and gave encouragement to all to
engage in open hostility to the heathen persecutors.[38]

The work thus begun he was not to be permitted long to
carry on.　Soon after the beginning of the revolt, in B.C.
167–166, in the Seleucid year 146 (1 Macc. ii. 70),
Mattathias died, after exhorting his sons to continue the
work, and recommending Simon as a man of counsel, and
Judas as best qualified to act as leader in battle.　Amid
great lamentations he was buried at Modein.[39]

And thus now Judas came to the front as head of the
movement.　His surname, ὁ Μακκαβαῖος, from which the
whole party has received the name of Maccabees, was probably intended to designate him as the vigorous, sharp-
beating warrior, from מַקָּבָה, "the hammer."　"In his acts
he was like a lion, and like a lion's whelp roaring for his
prey."　Thus the First Book of Maccabees (iii. 4) characterizes him a hero of chivalry, bold and powerful, not
waiting to ask about the possibility of success, but enthusias-
tically sacrificing his goods and his blood in a noble cause.[40]
The triumphs which he achieved could indeed, in presence of
such a terrible array of hostile forces, only be temporary.
The cause which he represented must certainly have been
lost if it had to depend only on the sword.

In its earliest stage the movement had a course of
singularly good fortune.　In one battle after another Judas
won brilliant victories, which resulted in the restoring of the
Jewish worship on Zion.　A Syrian battalion, under Apollonius, probably the same of whom mention has already been

made at page 206, was cut down by Judas, and Apollonius himself was slain. The sword which he took from him as spoil was the one which Judas from this time forth always himself used in battle.[41] Also a second Syrian army, which Seron, "the prince of the army of Syria," whom Judas went forth to meet, was completely routed by him at Beth-horon, north-west of Jerusalem.[42]

The king found it necessary to take vigorous measures in order to suppress the revolt in Judea. While he himself, in B.C. 166–165 (1 Macc. iii. 37 gives the Seleucid year 147), went forth upon an expedition against the Parthians,[43] he sent Lysias back to Syria as imperial chancellor and guardian of the minor Antiochus V., and gave him orders to fit out a large army against Judea to quell the rebellion there.[44] Lysias sent three generals, Ptolemy, Nicanor, and Gorgias, with a large body of troops against Judea. The defeat of the Jews seemed so certain, that foreign merchants accompanied the Syrians in order to purchase as slaves the expected Jewish captives.[45]

Meantime, however, Judas, and those adhering to him, had not been inactive. Now that Jerusalem had been wrested from the heathens, Judas collected his fighting men in Mizpah, the ancient stronghold of Israel in the times of the Judges, not far from Jerusalem.[46] It no longer consisted merely of a small group of enthusiasts, but was a regular Jewish army, which he had there organized according to military rules; he "ordained captains over the people, even captains over thousands, and over hundreds, and over fifties, and over tens." By prayer and fasting he prepared himself for the unequal struggle. In the province of Emmaus, west of Jerusalem, at the entrance into the hill country, the armies encountered one another.[47]

While the main body of the Syrian army remained in camp at Emmaus, Gorgias endeavoured with a strong detachment to engage the Jewish army. When Judas heard of this he circumvented him, and got between him and the main body lying at Emmaus. His brave words of encouragement aroused such enthusiasm among the Jews, that the Syrian troops were completely overpowered. When the detachment under Gorgias returned, they found the camp already in flames, and the Jews quite prepared to join with them in battle. Without venturing on such a conflict, they at once fled into the Philistine territory. This victory of the Jews, in B.C. 166–165, was complete.[48]

In the following year, B.C. 165–164, and indeed, as further details show, in autumn of B.C. 165, Lysias himself led a new and still more powerful army against Judea. He did not make his attack directly from the north, but came against Judea from the south by the way of Idumea (1 Macc. iv. 29). He must therefore have fetched a compass round about Judea; it may have begun, as Hitzig conjectures, p. 393, on the east, round about the Dead Sea, or, what is more probable, on the west, since he had marched along the Philistine coast and round about the hilly region. At Bethzur, south of Jerusalem, on the road to Hebron,[54] the contending forces met. Although the Syrian army greatly exceeded in numbers, Judas this time again won so complete a victory that Lysias found himself obliged to return to Antioch in order to collect new forces.[49]

After these two brilliant and decisive successes, Judas again took possession of Jerusalem, and directed his attention to the restoration of the services of divine worship. The citadel of Jerusalem was indeed still held by Syrian troops, but Judas kept them continually in check by his people, so that the works of the temple could not be destroyed by them. Thus protected, the work was proceeded with. Everything impure was carried out from the temple. The altar of burnt-offering, which had been polluted by heathen sacrifices, was

wholly taken down and a new one built in its place.[50] The
sacred garments and furniture were replaced by new ones;
and when everything was ready, the temple was consecrated
anew by the celebration of a great feast. This took place,
according to 1 Macc. iv. 52, on 25th Chisleu, in the Seleucid
year 148, or December B.C. 165, or precisely the same day
on which three years before, for the first time, the altar had
been desecrated by the offering up of heathen sacrifices.[51] The
festivities lasted for eight days, and it was resolved that
every year the memory of those events should be revived by
the repetition of the festival observance.[52]

The reconsecration of the temple forms the first era in the
history of the Maccabean revolt. Hitherto the struggles of
the heroes of the faith had been invariably crowned with
success. Judas had led his followers on from one victory to
another. The future must now prove whether their power
was elastic enough, and their enthusiasm enduring enough, to
keep permanent possession of what had thus in so rapid a
course been won.

§ 5. THE TIMES OF JUDAS

MACCABAEUS, B.C. 165-161

During the next year and a half after the reconsecration of the temple down to the summer of B.C. 163, Judas remained master of Judea. The central government of Syria took no concern in the movements there, for its attention was wholly taken up elsewhere. Hence Judas was able unhindered to arrange for the strengthening of his position. The temple mount was furnished with stony fortifications. On the southern frontier of Judea, Beth-zur, which constituted the key to Judea, was strongly fortified and garrisoned with Jewish troops.[1] And also throughout all the border districts military raids were made, partly in order to protect the Jews dwelling there, partly for the establishment of their own dominion. The Edomites, the Bajanites (a tribe otherwise unknown), and the Ammonites, all of whom had shown themselves hostile, were sharply chastised one after another.[2]

Complaints soon came from Gilead, east of the Jordan, and from Galilee, of persecutions which the Jews dwelling there had been subjected to on the part of the heathens. It was resolved that help should be sent to both. Simon went to Galilee with three thousand men, Judas to Gilead with eight thousand men.[3] In neither case was there any idea of making a permanent conquest of the territory in question. But after Simon had won many battles against the heathen in Galilee, he gathered together the Jewish residents, with their women, children, and goods, and led them amid great rejoicing to Judea, where they would be kept secure.[4]   Judas acted in a similar manner in Gilead.   In a series of successful engagements, especially in the north of the country east of the Jordan, he subdued the native tribes, whose leader was one Timotheus, then gathered together all the Israelites in Gilead, great and small, women and children, with all their possessions, and led them carefully, after he had been compelled to fight a passage for himself by Ephron, a town of the east Jordan country otherwise unknown, through Bethsean or Scythopolis to Judea.[5]

During the period when Simon and Judas were absent from Judea, the direction of affairs there had been assigned to certain men called Joseph and Asariah.   These two, in direct opposition to the orders of Judas, undertook a military expedition against Jamnia, but were driven back with considerable loss by Gorgias, who since his defeat had remained at Emmaus in Philistine territory.   The First Book of Maccabees does not fail, in recording this incident, to call attention to the fact that it was by the hand of the family of the Maccabees that salvation was to be wrought for Israel.[6]

But Judas carried his military expedition farther a-field. He went out again against the Edomites, besieged and destroyed Hebron ; then passed through Marissa (for thus we are to read in place of Samaria in 1 Macc. v. 66) into the land of the Philistines, overthrew Ashdod, cast down the altars there and the idols, and returned back to Judea with rich spoil.[7]   The object now quite evidently was no longer the protection of the Jewish faith, but the strengthening and extending of the Jewish power.

Meanwhile a change had taken place in the affairs of Syria.   Antiochus Epiphanes, in his undertakings in the eastern parts of the empire, had been no less unfortunate than his generals had been in Judea. He had advanced into the province of Elymais, but after making an unsuccessful attempt to appropriate the rich treasures of the temple of Artemis there, he had been compelled to retire back upon Babylon, and on the way, in the Persian town of Tabä, he died in B.C. 164, or, according to 1 Macc. vi. 16, in the Seleucid year 149, that is, B.C. 164–163.[8] Before his end he appointed one of his generals, Philip, to be imperial chancellor, and tutor to his son Antiochus V. Eupator during his minority. But instead of him Lysias secured possession of the person of the young king, and obtained absolute sovereign power in the empire.[9]

The revolted Jews might not perhaps have been interfered with for a long time had not pressing appeals been made to Antioch directly from Judea. Judas now laid siege in B.C. 163–162, the Seleucid year 150 (1 Macc. vi. 20), to the Syrian garrison in the citadel of Jerusalem. Some of the garrison, notwithstanding the siege, escaped, and in company with representatives of the Greek party among the Jews, betook themselves to the king in order to urge upon him the necessity of his interfering. The representatives of the Greek party, in particular, complained of how much they had to suffer from their hostile fellow-countrymen, so that many of them had been slain and had their possessions taken from them.[10]

It was this that first again roused those in Antioch to take active measures. Lysias himself, in company with the youthful king, went forth at the head of a powerful army and marched against Judea. He once more made his attack from the south, and began with the siege of Beth-zur. Judas was obliged to raise the siege of the citadel of Jerusalem, and to go forth to meet the king. At Beth-Zachariah, between Jerusalem and Beth-zur, the armies met.[11] It soon appeared that over against the vigorous onslaught of the Syrian troops the Jews with all their valour could not secure any decisive or lasting victory. They went forth boldly to the conflict. Judas's own brother Eleasar distinguished himself above all the rest. He thought that he had discovered the elephant on which the young king was seated ; he crept forward, stabbed the elephant from below, and was crushed under the weight of the falling animal. His self-immolation and all the efforts of the Jews, however, were in vain. The Jewish army was beaten, and that so completely, that the king's army soon appeared before the walls of Jerusalem, and laid siege to Zion, the temple mount.[12]

Beth-zur also was obliged to yield and to receive a Syrian garrison. Those besieged in Zion, however, soon began to suffer from want of the means of life, since owing to the Sabbatical year no provision had been made beforehand.[13] The utter discomfiture of the Jews now seemed imminent, when suddenly Lysias, on account of events occurring in Syria, found himself compelled to treat with the Jews for peace under favourable conditions. That same Philip whom Antiochus Epiphanes had nominated as imperial chancellor and tutor of his son Antiochus V. during his minority, had marched against Antioch in the hope of securing the power to himself. In order to have a free hand against him, Lysias granted to the Jews that which had hitherto been the occasion of the war, the liberty freely to celebrate their own religious ceremonies. It was henceforth to be permitted them to " observe their own institutions as formerly." On this condition those besieged in Zion capitulated ; its strongholds were reduced, contrary to the promise sworn to by the king. The subjugation of the Jews was accomplished, but only after that had been granted to them on account of which the Syrian government had declared war against them five years before.[14]

The understanding with the Jews at which Lysias and Antiochus V. in their own interests had arrived, was not interfered with by any of the following kings. None of them resorted again to the foolish attempt of Antiochus Epiphanes forcibly to introduce pagan culture and ceremonies among the Jews. The Jewish worship, which had been restored by Judas Maccabaeus amid all the changeful circumstances of the age, continued to be observed in essentially the same way. This deserves to be specially noted in order that a correct estimate may be formed of the conflicts which followed. The end aimed at in the struggle was now different from that previously before them. It had to do no longer with the preservation of religion, but, just as we have already seen in the preliminary history of the Maccabean revolt, with the question whether the friends of the Greeks or the national party within the Jewish nation itself should have the supremacy. It was essentially a Jewish internecine war, in which the Syrian superiors took part only in so far as they supported and put at the head of the provincial government sometimes the one, sometimes the other, of these two Jewish parties. To a certain extent, indeed, religious interests did come into consideration. For the Greek party were inclined to go farther in the way of favouring Greek institutions, while their nationalist opponents seemed more attached to the religion of Israel. But the fundamental points were no longer in dispute.[15]

In consequence of the events of the previous year, the party in Judea friendly to the Greeks were driven out of the government, and were indeed for the most part persecuted. Judas stood practically at the head of the Jewish people.[16] It may be readily supposed that the opposition party did not quietly submit to this arrangement, but made vigorous efforts on their part to obtain again the governing power. But they succeeded in their efforts only after a change had occurred in the occupancy of the throne. Antiochus V. and Lysias had, indeed, after a short struggle overcome that Philip who had contended with them for the supremacy.[17] But they them-

selves were soon driven out by a new pretender to the crown.
Demetrius I., afterwards distinguished by the cognomen Soter,
the son of Seleucus IV. Philopator, therefore nephew of
Antiochus Epiphanes and cousin of Antiochus Eupator, who
had previously lived as a hostage at Rome, and had vainly
entreated from the Roman senate permission to return home,
succeeded in secretly making his escape, and landed at
Tripolis on the Phoenician coast.[18]   He was able soon to
gather around him a considerable number of followers;[19]
indeed the very bodyguard of King Antiochus deserted him
and his guardian Lysias, and joined Demetrius.   By the orders
of Demetrius both were murdered, and he himself proclaimed
king in B.C. 162.[20]   The Roman senate was at first in con-
sternation over the flight of Demetrius, but by and by Demetrius managed on his part to induce the Romans to recognise
him as king.[21]

Soon after Demetrius had entered upon the government,
the leaders of the Hellenistic party, with a certain Alcimus
at their head, or as his Hebrew name properly reads, Jakim,[22]
made representations to the king with reference to their
oppression under the party of Judas.   Judas and his brothers
had meanwhile slain the adherents of the king, or expelled
them from the country.   Demetrius was naturally readily
impressed by such a statement.   Alcimus was appointed
high priest, and at the same time a Syrian army under the
command of Bacchides was sent to Judea, in order to instate
Alcimus by force, if need be, in his office.[23]

The further development of affairs is highly characteristic
of the struggles of the Maccabees.   The opposition to Alcimus
on the side of the strict Jewish party was by no means
engaged in by all its adherents.   In consequence of quieting
assurances which he gave, he was immediately acknowledged
by the representatives of the strictest section of the scribes
and the " pious " ('Ασιδαῖοι, 1 Macc. vii. 13), as the legiti-

mate high priest of the family of Aaron. Only Judas and his adherents persevered in their opposition. They did not trust the promises of Alcimus, and considered that their religious interests could only be secured if they got the government into their own hands.[24]

Results showed that they were not wrong. One of the first acts of Alcimus was to order the execution of sixty men belonging to the party of the Asidaeans. This struck fear and trembling into the hearts of the people, but had also the effect of arousing more determined opposition. Bacchides now thought that his presence in Judea was no longer necessary. Leaving behind a military force in Judea for the protection of Alcimus, he himself returned to Syria. Then Alcimus and Judas had practically an opportunity of measuring their strength and testing their own resources against one another. The open war between the two parties which now began seemed to tend more and more in favour of the Maccabees, so that Alcimus found it necessary to go to the king and to entreat of him further support.[25]

Demetrius sent now against Judea another general, Nicanor, with a great army. Nicanor sought first of all through stratagem to obtain possession of the person of Judas. But Judas got information of this plot, and so the scheme miscarried. An engagement thus took place at Capharsalama,[26] which resulted in the defeat of Nicanor. He then advanced upon Jerusalem, and wreaked his vengeance on the innocent priests. While they greeted him respectfully, he treated them with scorn and ridicule, and threatened that if they did not deliver up to him Judas and his army, he would on his victorious return set their temple on fire.[27]

Therefore he returned to the district of Beth-Horon, north-west of Jerusalem, where he waited for reinforcements from Syria. Judas lay encamped over against him in Adasa.[28] On 13th Adar, B.C. 161, a decisive conflict was engaged in which resulted in the utter defeat of the Syrians. Nicanor himself fell in the tumult. When his people saw this, they threw their weapons away, and betook themselves to hasty flight. The Jews pursued them, surrounded them, and cut them down to the last man; so, at least, the First Book of Maccabees affirms. The victory must certainly have been overpowering and complete. For from this time the 13th Adar, corresponding roughly to our March, was annually observed as a festival under the name of " Nicanor's Day." [29]

Judas was thus once more master of the situation. Josephus assigns to this period the death of Alcimus, and from this time reckons the priesthood of Judas. But the death of Alcimus, according to the First Book of Maccabees, occurred considerably later; and that Judas exercised generally the functions of the high priest, is extremely improbable.[30]

There is, however, this element of truth in the statement of Josephus, that Judas now actually stood at the head of the Jewish commonwealth. And it was his determined plan to maintain himself, or at least his party, in that position. But the events which had occurred taught him that this was possible only after they had completely freed themselves from the Syrian yoke. The king of Syria had indeed showed his inclination to secure the supremacy in Judea to the opposition party by force of arms. The resolve was therefore made to shake off once and for all every sort of subordination to the Syrians. In order to accomplish this purpose, Judas applied to the Romans for help. The rulers of the Western empire, ever since their conflicts with Antiochus the Great, between B.C. 192 and B.C. 189, had taken the liveliest interest in matters that affected the Syrian empire, and looked closely into everything that occurred with watchful eyes. They repeatedly interposed their authority to decide upon the affairs of Syria.[31] All centrifugal movements in that quarter might therefore count upon their support. It was thus very natural

that Judas should make the attempt with the help of the
Romans to secure permanently that freedom which had been
temporarily wrung from their enemy.   In grand pictorial
style the First Book of Maccabees describes how Judas had
heard of the deeds and might of the Romans, and how this
led him to endeavour to obtain their aid.   Even the inaccuracies which are mixed up in this story serve to set
before us very strikingly the measure of the knowledge of the
Romans, which was then current in Judea.   Judas therefore
sent two men of his party as ambassadors to Rome, Eupolemus
son of John, and Jason son of Eleasar, the former perhaps
identical with that Eupolemus who is known to us as a
Hellenistic writer, see Div. ii. vol. iii. pp. 203–206.   The
end which he had in view in so doing was avowedly the
throwing off of the Syrian yoke (1 Macc. viii. 18 : τοῦ
ἆραι τὸν ζυγὸν ἀπ᾽ αὐτῶν).   The Roman senate readily
granted an audience to the Jewish embassy, and a treaty of
friendship was made of which the principal provisions were
that the Jews should give help to the Romans and the
Romans to the Jews in times of war (συμμαχία), but not on
precisely equal terms, and in every case just as circumstances
required (1 Macc. viii. 25, 27 : ὡς ἂν ὁ καιρὸς ὑπογραφῇ).
It therefore practically depended on the pleasure of the
Romans how far they should consider themselves bound by
the agreement.[32]

About the same time as this treaty was concluded the
Romans issued a missive to Demetrius, wherein they ordered
him to desist from every sort of hostile proceeding against
the Jews, who were the allies of the Romans.[33]   Their inter-
position of authority came too late.   Demetrius proceeded so
rashly and energetically, that the overthrow of Judea had
been already completed before there was any possibility of
interference on the part of the Romans.[34]   Immediately after he
had received news of the death and defeat of Nicanor, he sent

a great army under Bacchides to Judea, which appeared in the neighbourhood of Jerusalem as early as the first month of the Seleucid year 152, that is, in April B.C. 161 (1 Macc. ix. 3), only about two months after the fall of Nicanor. Bacchides encamped beside Berea, Judas beside Elasa (written also Eleasa and Alasa).[35] The superiority of the Syrians was so evident, that even in the ranks of Judas there no longer remained any hope of victory. His followers deserted in large numbers. With a few faithful men Judas ventured with the wild courage of despair on the hopeless conflict. The result was just what had been clearly foreseen : the troops of Judas were hewn down, and he himself fell in the battle. To his brothers Jonathan and Simon were granted the sad privilege of burying him in the grave of his father at Modein.[36]

With the overthrow of Judas it was finally and definitely proved that it was a vain endeavour on the part of the Jewish nationalists to measure swords with the mighty forces of Syria. Brilliant as the earlier achievements of Judas had been, he was largely indebted to the recklessness and self-confidence of his opponents. Continuous military success was not to be thought of if only the Syrian authorities seriously roused themselves to the conflict. The following age cannot show even one conspicuous victory of the kind by which Judas had won renown. What the Maccabean party finally reached, it won through voluntary concessions of claimants of the Syrian throne contending with one another, and generally in consequence of internal dissensions in the Syrian empire.

§ 6. THE TIMES OF JONATHAN,

B.C. 161-143

THE power of the Jewish national party was quite anni-
hilated by the defeat and death of Judas. The party friendly
to the Greeks, with the high priest Alcimus at their head,
was able now unhindered to carry on the government committed to it by the king. Wherever any opposition was
offered, it was at once vigorously suppressed. The friends
of Judas were sought out and brought to Bacchides, who
"took vengeance on them." The "unrighteous" and the
"ungodly," as the opponents of the Maccabees are designated
in the First Book of Maccabees, had now the rule in Judea.[1]

But the friends of Judas were by no means disposed to
abandon all sort of resistance. They elected Jonathan, the
brother of Judas, as their leader, "in order that he might
direct the conflict."[2] No regular or serious undertakings
indeed were at first to be thought of. They required first of
all gradually to gather together their forces and wait a favourable opportunity. The earliest incidents of this period
which we have, represent the doings of Jonathan more in the
light of the raiding of a freebooter than the acts of a religious
party. When their personal property was no longer secure
in Judea, they sent it under the guardianship of John, a
brother of Jonathan, over into the country of the friendly
Nabathaeans. While so engaged, John, along with his bag-

44

gage, was attacked by a robber tribe of the sons of Ambri, near
Medeba, in the country east of the Jordan, and slain.   In
order to avenge his death, Jonathan and Simon crossed the
Jordan and fell upon the sons of Ambri when these were
engaged in great festivities in connection with a wedding
celebration.   Many were slain, and the rest fled into the
mountains.   On their return Jonathan and his followers were
met at the Jordan by Bacchides and a Syrian army, and were
in great jeopardy, but saved themselves by swimming across
the Jordan.[3]

Bacchides now took measures to secure that the subjection
of Judea under the Syrian rule should be more decided than
hitherto.   He fortified the cities of Jericho, Emmaus, Beth-
Horon, Bethel, Thamnatha, Pharathon, Tephon, and occupied
them with Syrian garrisons.   He likewise gave orders that
the fortifications of Beth-zur, Gazara, and the citadel of
Jerusalem should be strengthened.   Finally, he took the sons
of distinguished Jews as hostages, and put them in ward in
the citadel of Jerusalem.[4]

About this time, in the second month of the Seleucid year
153, that is, in May B.C. 160 (1 Macc. ix. 54), the high priest
Alcimus by his ungodly conduct caused great offence to those
who adhered strictly to the observance of the law.   He threw
down the walls of the inner court, and "so destroyed the works
of the prophets."   In his death, which speedily followed, they
beheld God's righteous judgment on such wickedness.[5]   The
office of the high priest does not seem to have been again
filled.[6]

Soon after the death of Alcimus, Bacchides returned to
Syria, believing that the subjugation of Judea was now complete.[7]   There follows a period of seven years, B.C. 160–153,
about which the First Book of Maccabees says almost nothing.
But these seven years must have been of very great importance for the reinvigorating of the Maccabean party.   For at

the close of that period it stands forward as the one party really capable of forming a government and as actually having Judea under its control, so that the Syrian kings in their contentions with one another are found eagerly seeking to secure its devoted adherence. Only by one episode is light shed upon the darkness of this era in the record of the First Book of Maccabees. Two years after the retirement of Bacchides, that is, in B.C. 158, the dominant party of the Jews favourable to the Greek customs made urgent representations to the king's government about the resuscitation of the Maccabean party. The consequence of this was that Bacchides went again with a still larger army in order to utterly destroy Jonathan and his adherents. But his following had already become so strong that Bacchides could not so easily be done with them. A portion of them entrenched themselves under Simon's leadership in the wilderness at Bethbasi, a place not otherwise known, and was there laid siege to by Bacchides in vain. With another portion Jonathan went forth on a plundering expedition into the country. When Bacchides observed how difficult the task assigned to him was, very much against the will of the Graeco-Jewish party which had brought him into such difficulties, he made peace with Jonathan and returned again to Syria.[8]

The Jewish parties appear now to have made an attempt to come to terms with one another. The result of this seems to have been that Jonathan more and more secured again to himself the leadership. " The sword was now at rest in Israel, and Jonathan dwelt at Michmash ; and he began to judge the people, and drove out the ungodly from Israel." With this laconic notice the First Book of Maccabees passes over the following five years.[9] This can only mean that Jonathan, while the official Sanhedrim of Jerusalem was still filled by those friendly to the Greeks, established at Michmash a sort of rival government, which gradually won the position of main influence in the country, so that it was able even to drive out (ἀφανίζειν) the ungodly, that is, the Hellenizing party. The Hellenistic or Greek favouring party had no root among the people. The great mass of the Jews had still the distinct consciousness that Hellenism, even if it should tolerate the religion of Israel, was irreconcilable with the ideal of the scribes. So soon, then, as pressure from above was removed, the great majority of the people gave themselves heart and soul to the national Jewish movement. The Maccabees, therefore, had the people soon again at their back. And this is the explanation of the fact that during the struggles for the Syrian throne now beginning, the claimants contended with one another in endeavouring to secure to themselves the good-will of the Maccabees. The Syrian kings were no longer in a position to force upon the people a Hellenistic government, but were obliged to do all in their power to conciliate and win the favour of the Jews. But this they could have only under the sway of the Maccabees. The concessions they made, however, furthered at the same time those tendencies which actually brought about the dissolution of the Syrian empire.

In the Seleucid year 160, or B.C. 153–152, and indeed, as the sequel shows, as early as B.C. 153 (1 Macc. x. 1, 21), Alexander Balas, a youth of mean extraction, and merely a tool of the kings leagued against Demetrius, made his appearance as a claimant of the throne. The despotic Demetrius was himself no favourite in the country, and so all the greater was the danger threatening him from the forces of the confederate kings. It was even feared that the Jews might go over to his opponent if he should be inclined to promise to set up among them a national government. Demetrius now sought to meet this danger by himself granting concessions to Jonathan. He gave him full authority to summon together an army in order to support the king, and for this purpose agreed to the liberation of the Jewish hostages who were still detained in the citadel of Jerusalem. Jonathan then went to Jerusalem invested with full power. The hostages were, in fact, set free, and given back to their parents. But Jonathan now formally seized possession of Jerusalem, and fortified the city and the temple mount. Also the Syrian garrisons of most of the fortresses built by Bacchides were sent away. Only in Beth-zur and in the citadel of Jerusalem did these garrisons remain.[10]

But Demetrius was not sufficiently liberal in his concessions to Jonathan. He was immediately far outbidden by Alexander Balas. He appointed Jonathan high priest of the Jews, and sent him, as a badge of princely rank, the purple and the diadem. Jonathan was not slow to grasp these new offers. At the Feast of Tabernacles of the Seleucid year 160, in the autumn of B.C. 153, he put on the sacred vestments.[11] He had thus all at once, even formally, become the head of the Jewish people. The Greek party was driven out of the government in Judea, and never again regained power, for Jonathan succeeded in maintaining his position amid all the changes of the following year. Favoured by circumstances, he was able to attain to that which Judas, with all his bravery, had never been able to reach.

When Demetrius heard that Jonathan had gone over to the party of Alexander Balas, he endeavoured by yet more liberal promises to win him back to his side. The gracious offers which he now made the Jewish leader were indeed too good to be credited: the tribute was to be remitted, the citadel of Jerusalem given over to the Jews, the Jewish territory to be enlarged by the addition of three districts of Samaria, the temple to be endowed with rich presents and privileges, the expense of building the walls of Jerusalem was to be defrayed out of the royal treasury.[12]

Jonathan was prudent enough not to yield to these tempting offers.   It was quite foreseen that Demetrius would succumb to the superior strength of his opponent.   But even should he go forth conqueror, it was not to be expected that he would fulfil such extravagantly liberal promises.   Jonathan therefore remained on the side of Alexander Balas, and never had occasion to regret his doing so.   Demetrius was conquered by Alexander and his confederates in B.C. 150, and lost his own life in the battle.   Alexander was crowned king.[13]

In the same year, however, B.C. 150 (1 Macc. x. 57, Seleucid year 162), an opportunity was afforded Alexander of showing marked respect to Jonathan, and loading him with honours.   Alexander had treated with King Ptolemy Philometor of Egypt for the hand of his daughter Cleopatra. Ptolemy had promised her to him, and the two kings now met together in Ptolemais, where Ptolemy himself gave away his daughter to Alexander, and the marriage was celebrated with great magnificence.   Alexander also invited Jonathan to be present, and received him with marked respect.   The deputies of the Hellenistic party in Judea, who made accusations against Jonathan, were indeed also there.   But the king gave them no audience, but only showed his favour toward Jonathan the more conspicuously.   He had him clothed in the purple and seated beside him, and appointed him στρατηγός and μεριδάρχης, presumably for the province of Judea, and thus the political privileges already actually exercised were now formally confirmed.[14]

During the next year Jonathan was exposed to no danger from any side in maintaining the position which he had reached.   The Greek party had been thoroughly silenced. Alexander Balas was an incapable ruler, who abandoned himself to sensual gratifications, and never thought of restricting the concessions that had been made to the Jewish high priest. The Syrian suzerainty continued indeed to exist.   But since

Jonathan and his party ruled in Judea, the aims hitherto striven after by the Maccabees were reached. Soon, however, the revolutions about the Syrian throne brought new dangers, but at the same time a new opportunity for the extension of political power. We see Jonathan now as a political partisan, sometimes of one, sometimes of another claimant of the Syrian throne, and using in a clever manner the weakness of the Syrian empire for the purpose of obtaining advantages to the Jewish people. But the aims of the Maccabean movement pointed higher than this. It no longer seemed enough that the party of Jonathan ruled unopposed in internal affairs. The troubles of the Syrian empire were made use of for the purpose of widening the boundaries of the Jewish territory— partly by donation, partly by conquest at their own hand, and finally with a dogged determination to accomplish the complete emancipation of the Jewish nation from the Syrian empire.

In B.C. 147 (1 Macc. x. 67, Seleucid year 165), Demetrius II., son of Demetrius I., set himself up as rival king in opposition to the contemptible weakling Alexander Balas. Apollonius, the governor of Coele-Syria, took his side, while Jonathan continued faithful to Alexander. Consequently hostilities were commenced between Apollonius and Jonathan, in which Jonathan was victorious. He drove out a garrison of Apollonius' from Joppa, then defeated an army under the command of Apollonius in the neighbourhood of Ashdod, destroyed Ashdod and the temple of Dagon in that city, and returned to Jerusalem with rich spoils.[15] In acknowledgment of this support, Alexander Balas bestowed upon him the city of Ekron and its territory.[16]

But Jonathan was the only one who stood by Alexander in opposition to Demetrius. The inhabitants of Antioch, and Alexander's own soldiers, declared in favour of Demetrius.[17] Even his own father-in-law, Ptolemy, ranged himself on the side of Alexander's opponent, took Cleopatra back from Alexander, and gave her to the new candidate for the throne as his wife.[18] Ptolemy also led a strong army against Alexander, with which he attacked him at the river Oenoparas, on the plains of Antioch. Alexander fled to Arabia, where his life was put an end to by the hand of an assassin. Immediately afterward Ptolemy also died of wounds received in the battle.[19] Thus Demetrius became king in B.C. 145 (1 Macc. xi. 19, Seleucid year 167).

As the confederate of Alexander Balas, Jonathan had occupied a hostile attitude toward Demetrius. It would appear that he now felt himself strong enough to make the attempt to secure by force emancipation from the Syrian empire. In a regular manner he laid siege to the citadel of Jerusalem, in which a Syrian garrison still lay. Here again, as so often happened in similar cases, it was the opposition party in his own nation, the ἄνδρες παράνομοι and ἄνομοι, as they are called in 1 Macc. xi. 21, 25, who called the attention of the Syrian king to these revolutionary measures. In consequence of these reports, Demetrius summoned Jonathan to Ptolemais to answer for his conduct. But Jonathan was daring enough boldly to claim concessions from Demetrius. He allowed the siege still to proceed, betook himself with rich presents to Ptolemais, and demanded of Demetrius the cession to Judea of three provinces of Samaria, and immunity from tribute for this whole district. These were some of the most essential points in the concessions which Demetrius I. had made to Jonathan. Demetrius did not venture to refuse these demands. He agreed to add to Judea the three Samaritan provinces of Ephraim, Lydda, and Ramathaim, made over this enlarged Judea to Jonathan free from tribute, and confirmed him in all dignities which he had previously enjoyed. Of the citadel of Jerusalem no mention whatever was then made. Evidently these concessions were the price on account of which Jonathan agreed to raise the siege.[20]

Such a receding on the part of the Syrian king before the

Jewish demands ten years previously would not have been thought of for a moment. But now the power of the Seleucidae was broken. None of the kings of Syria was henceforth sure of his throne. And Jonathan knew how to make use of this weakness, and skilfully to turn it to his own advantage. The next years gave him abundant opportunities for carrying out his policy of annexation. Demetrius had scarcely made these concessions, when he found himself obliged to make new promises in order to secure the support of Jonathan in circumstances of serious difficulty. A certain Diodotus, surnamed Trypho, of Apamea,[21] a former general of Alexander Balas, managed to get hold of the person of the youthful son of Alexander, called Antiochus, who had been brought up by an Arab Imalkue, and set him up as rival king in opposition to Demetrius.[22] The situation was fraught with extreme peril to Demetrius, since his own troops deserted, and the inhabitants of Antioch assumed a hostile attitude. In face of these dangers, he promised to surrender to Jonathan the citadel of Jerusalem and the other fortresses of Judea, if Jonathan would place at his disposal auxiliary troops. Jonathan soon sent three thousand men, who just arrived at the right moment in order to afford powerful aid to the king in suppressing the revolt that had now broken out in Antioch. It was admittedly by their assistance that the rising in the city was crushed. With the thanks of the king, and with rich booty, the Jewish troops returned to Jerusalem.[23]

But Demetrius did not fulfil the promise which he had made. It also soon appeared that he must yield before the new claimant to the throne. With the help of the troops that had deserted from Demetrius, Trypho and Antiochus made themselves masters of the capital Antioch, and in this way secured the sway in the centre of the empire. Without delay they sought also to win over Jonathan to their side. Antiochus confirmed him in possession of all that Demetrius had granted him.   At the same time his brother Simon was appointed military commander for the king, from the ladder of Tyre down to the borders of Egypt.[24]

In view of the faithlessness and weakness of Demetrius, Jonathan regarded it as justifiable as well as useful to pass over to the side of Antiochus.   He therefore joined his party, and undertook, in connection with his brother Simon, to reduce the provinces of the empire lying next to Judea under the rule of the new claimant.   A beginning was made in those districts over which Simon had been appointed military commander.   So Jonathan, at the head of Jewish and Syrian troops, went out against the cities of Ascalon and Gaza.   The former readily declared its submission to Antiochus; the latter yielded only after Jonathan had recourse to forcible measures.   He compelled the city to give hostages, and took them with him to Jerusalem.[25]   Then Jonathan proceeded to northern Galilee, and offered battle in the valley of Hazor to the general of Demetrius, which at first went against him, but at last resulted in a victory.[26] At the same time Simon laid siege to the fortress of Beth-zur in the south of Judea, where still a garrison adhering to Demetrius lay.   After a long siege he compelled them to surrender the citadel, and placed in it a Jewish garrison.[27]

While taking those steps toward the establishment of his power, Jonathan did not forget to strengthen his position still further by diplomatic negotiations with foreign nations. He sent two ambassadors, Numenius and Antipater, to Rome, in order to renew the covenant with the Romans that had been concluded in the time of Judas.[28]   These ambassadors were also bearers of letters from the high priest and Jewish people to Sparta and other places, in order to open up and secure friendly relations with them.[29]   From these documents we also learn that such relations between the Jews and foreign peoples were not wholly without example in earlier times. In the letter to the Spartans, Jonathan refers to the fact that King Areus of Sparta had addressed a friendly communication to the high priest Onias.[30]

The conflict between Jonathan and Demetrius meantime continued, and was so conducted by him that he not only served the interests of Trypho and Antiochus, but also advanced his own. Soon after the defeat which the troops of Demetrius sustained in the valley of Hazor, Demetrius sent a new army to attack Jonathan. But this time the Jewish leader withdrew farther to the north, into the district of Hamath, north of Lebanon. No decisive engagement had taken place, when the Syrian army was recalled.[31] Jonathan then turned his forces against the Arabian tribe of the Zabadeans, then against Damascus, and then, again, he directed his course southwards. When he had returned to Jerusalem he saw to the strengthening of the fortifications of the city, and by the erection of a high wall cut off the Syrian garrison from all intercourse with the city.[32] Even before Jonathan's return Simon had placed a Jewish garrison in Joppa. He now also fortified Adida in the "Sephela," that is, in the lowlands in the west of Judea.[33]

All these operations were avowedly carried on by Jonathan and Simon in the interests of the young king Antiochus and his tutor-regent Trypho. But the latter seems to have regarded with considerable misgivings the increase of the Jewish power. And not without reason. For the more the power of the Jews themselves increased, the greater became the danger of their shaking themselves free of the Syrian dominion altogether. It may therefore be quite easily understood how Trypho, so soon as Demetrius allowed him a free hand, turned against Jonathan. According to the First Book of Maccabees, this came about because Trypho wished himself to assume the crown, while Jonathan would not allow it.

This may indeed have been so, only the motives by which Jonathan was actuated were not so much moral as political.[34]

Trypho went therefore with an army to Palestine, in order to reduce within moderate limits the increasing Jewish power. At Beth-sean or Scythopolis he met Jonathan. The interview was at first of a friendly nature, although Jonathan had with him as large an army as that of Trypho. Trypho sought to remove the suspicions of Jonathan by heaping upon him tokens of respect. He represented to him that a great army was superfluous, since they did not occupy toward one another a warlike attitude. If Jonathan should follow him with a small select company to Ptolemais, he should give over to him that city and "the rest of the fortresses and troops," meaning those between the Ladder of Tyre and the borders of Egypt, over which Simon had been appointed military commander. Jonathan actually allowed himself to be deceived by those promises. He dismissed his army, and followed Trypho to Ptolemais with only a thousand men. But scarcely had he reached that place when he was put in prison, and his people murderously cut down.[35]

The news of this faithless proceeding of Trypho caused great excitement throughout Judea. It was natural that Simon, the last survivor of the five brothers of the Maccabees, should place himself at the head of affairs. By the decree of a popular assembly he was formally chosen leader. His first acts were the acceleration of the works on the fortifications of Jerusalem, and taking definite possession of Joppa. The latter place had never hitherto belonged to the Jewish territory. But in the exercise of his own official authority as military commander over the coast districts, Simon had placed there a Jewish garrison. The Gentile inhabitants were now expelled from Joppa, the city was Judaized and united with the Jewish territory.[36]

Trypho, now carrying Jonathan as prisoner with him, went

against Judea with a great army. At Adida, Simon obstructed his march into the interior by opposing him with his troops. Thereupon Trypho sent ambassadors to Simon and let him know that he kept Jonathan prisoner only for this reason, that he had failed to pay the money due for the offices that had been conferred upon him. If the money should be paid, and as a guarantee of future fidelity, the sons of Jonathan delivered up as hostages, he would then set him free. But although Simon now sent all that was demanded, Jonathan was not liberated. Trypho sought rather by going round about the mountains, to push on to Jerusalem over Adora in Idumaea from the south. When he was prevented from accomplishing this by a heavy snowfall, he marched his troops on to Gilead, that is, through the country east of the Jordan, caused Jonathan to be murdered at Bascama, and returned back to Syria.[37]

Simon now actually entered into his brother's place as high priest of the Jews. He had the remains of Jonathan carried from Bascama, and buried him beside his parents and three brothers, at their native Modein. Over their common sepulchre, Simon, at a later period, erected a magnificent monument, which could be seen from the sea.[38]

§ 7. SIMON, B.C. 142—135 [1]

By the heroic deeds and successes of Jonathan, the Maccabean party had passed out far beyond its original aims. It had not at first intended to strive for anything more than the restoration of the Jewish worship, and the securing of the free exercise of the Jewish religion. But even Judas, when he had attained this end, did not rest satisfied therewith. He and his party then wished also to gain the supremacy in the control of home affairs. In the time of Jonathan this end was completely won. By Jonathan's appointment as high priest the ruling power was placed in the hands of the Maccabean party, and the Hellenistic party was driven out. But even this no longer seemed sufficient. Favourable circumstances—the weakness of the Syrian empire—tempted them to strive after thorough emancipation from the Syrian suzerainty. The last acts of Jonathan were important steps in this direction. The significance of the reign of Simon consists in this, that it completed the work of Jonathan, and made the Jewish people wholly independent of the Syrian empire.

In Syria, Demetrius and Trypho, as tutor-regent for the young king Antiochus, still occupied a position of antagonism to one another. Trypho, who had hitherto appeared only as representative of his youthful *protégé*, about this time or not much later, let fall the mask, secured the assassination of Antiochus VI., and had himself crowned king.[2]

After the last hostile proceeding on the part of Trypho, it was clear that Simon would unhesitatingly attach himself to Demetrius. But he did this only after he had exacted the promise that Demetrius would recognise the freedom of the Jews. While he continued eagerly to proceed with the building of the fortresses of Judea, he sent an embassy to Demetrius " to secure for his country exemption from tribute." Since Demetrius had actually no longer any power in the south of the empire, it was in his interest to act the part of the munificent, and to guarantee to the Jews all that they desired. He therefore not only granted remission of all out-standing taxes, but also perfect exemption from all paying of tribute in the future.[3] Thus was the political independence of Judea recognised. " The yoke of the Gentiles," as the First Book of Maccabees expresses it, " was taken away from Israel." In order to give expression to this fact, they now adopted a mode of reckoning of their own, beginning with the Seleucid year 170, or B.C. 143–142. Documents and treatises were dated according to the year of Simon as high priest and prince of the Jews.[4]

With this statement of the First Book of Maccabees we ought to combine a fact derived from a study of numismatics. There are Jewish shekel and half-shekel coins which, in the opinion of most numismatists, were stamped in the time of Simon. They bore on the one side the inscription ירושלם קדשה or ירושלים הקדושה, on the other side, according to their weight, either שקל ישראל, Israel's shekel, or חצי השקל, half-shekel. On the whole shekel and on the half-shekel the number of the year was impressed, and there are specimens of both coins with the year numbers ד, ג, ב, א (1, 2, 3, 4), and one specimen of a whole shekel with the date ה or 5. The era here used is held to be the era of Simon referred to in

the First Book of Maccabees. Now these coins, if indeed
they were stamped in the time of Simon, are not to be considered properly as coins of Simon, but as coins of the civic
commune of Jerusalem, for after the fashion of the Hellenistic
communes Jerusalem is regarded as in a position of authority
over all Judea (compare § 23, I. and II.). Also the number
of the year on the coins does not designate the year of
Simon's reign, but the year of a civil era of Jerusalem; as
also other cities of Phoenicia, such as Tyre, Sidon, Ascalon,
had begun toward the end of the second century before
Christ, in token of the freedom which they had obtained, to
adopt a cycle of their own. But even were it possible that
the era used upon the coins was identical with " the years of
Simon " spoken of in the First Book of Maccabees, the first
year of Simon is just the same as the first year of Jewish
freedom. But a difficulty is presented by the fact that up
to the present time out of the great number of specimens of
shekel coins only one piece is found bearing the mark of the
year 5 ; and that no higher numbers are found, whereas the
era of Simon, according to 1 Macc. xiii. 41, 42 and xiv. 27,
began in the Seleucid year 170, and Simon did not die
before the Seleucid year 177 (1 Macc. xvi. 14), so that coins
of his time might have been expected at least with the years
6 and 7. Merzbacher has therefore assumed that the era
of Simon had been made in the First Book of Maccabees
to begin two years too early. Its actual starting-point was
the third year of Simon, the Seleucid year 172, or B.C.
141–140, in which Simon was pronounced by a popular
decree hereditary high priest (1 Macc. xiv. 25–49). Then,
too, for the first time did Demetrius confer the privileges
that have been mentioned upon the Jews. But the author
of the First Book of Maccabees has erroneously used the
official " first " year of Simon as interchangeable with his
actual first year.[5] The reasons for this hypothesis are set

forth by Merzbacher with acuteness and skill of combination,
but on closer examination they do not prove convincing.
The plain and distinct statement of the First Book of Maccabees, that a beginning was made in the Seleucid year 170 to
number the years of Simon (xiii. 41, 42; compare xiv. 27),
cannot be thus set aside.   Also Merzbacher's theory is set up
simply in order to overcome the difficulty above referred to
which the year numbers on the shekel occasion.   But besides
this difficulty there are still other considerations which tell
against the supposition that the shekel was issued under
Simon.[6]   It cannot therefore be regarded as by any means
certain, though indeed most numismatists are in favour of the
idea.[7]

The charter of Demetrius conferred privileges which,
indeed, Demetrius had it not in his power to give away.   It
was Simon's policy rather to emphasize and give effect to these
in face of the power of Trypho, which was more perilous to
him.   In order to confirm his position, Simon sought above all
to get possession of two of the fortresses that would be of
chief value to him—the city of Gazara and the citadel of
Jerusalem; and in both cases he had the good fortune to be
successful.   Gazara, the old Geshur, not far from Emmaus-
Nicopolis in a westerly direction, at the base of the mountains,
had been up to that time a Gentile city.   Possession of it
was of importance to the Jews, because it was one of the
places which commanded the passes of the mountains, and
the holding of it was thus absolutely necessary in order to
maintain connection between Jerusalem and the port of
Joppa, which had been already annexed by the Jews.   Simon
opened against the city a skilfully directed siege, conquered
it, expelled all Gentile inhabitants from it, and settled it
with "men who observed the law." [8]   Simon's son John
was appointed governor of Gazara.[9]

Soon after the conquest of Gazara, Simon compelled the
Syrian garrison of the citadel of Jerusalem to capitulate

through famine. The national struggles of the Maccabees had long been directed to the attainment of this object, for so long as the citadel was in the hands of the Syrian kings the Jews were really their subjects. Now at last Simon succeeded in making himself master of this stronghold. On the 23rd day of the second month of the Seleucid year 171, that is, in May B.C. 142, he entered with great pomp and ceremony into the citadel.[10]

Since the Syrian kings were not in a position to be able to give any attention to proceedings in Judea, several years passed of undisturbed prosperity and peace for the Jews. As such a period the reign of Simon is generally characterized in the First Book of Maccabees. The securing of Joppa as a harbour, and the conquest of Gazara, Beth-zur, and the citadel of Jerusalem, are there represented as the chief services rendered by him.[11] Also express mention is made of his care for the spiritual and material wellbeing of the country, for strict administration of justice and the re-establishment of the Jewish law. "Then did they till their ground in peace, and the earth gave her increase, and the trees of the field their fruit. The ancient men sat all in the streets, communing together of good things, and the young men put on glorious and warlike apparel. He provided victuals for the cities, and set in them all manner of munition, so that his honourable name was renowned unto the end of the world. He made peace in the land, and Israel rejoiced with great joy: for every man sat under his vine and his fig-tree, and there was none to fray them: neither was there any left in the land to fight against them: yea, the kings themselves were overthrown in those days. Moreover he strengthened all those of his people that were brought low: the law he searched out; and every contemner of the law and wicked person he took away. He beautified the sanctuary, and multiplied the vessels of the temple."[12]

In these words of the First Book of Maccabees expression

is given to the feeling of satisfaction which the majority of
the people had in Simon's reign. The ultimate aims of the
Maccabean struggles had been secured. The government was
in the hands of the national party ; the country was emancipated from the suzerainty of the Syrians. Thus Simon now
reaped the full fruit of the common labours of the Maccabees : the formal legitimizing on the part of the people of
their family as the ruling sacerdotal family. It had, indeed,
been an act of usurpation by which the son of Mattathias
attained unto the supremacy. Up to the outbreak of the
Maccabean revolt the office of high priest had been hereditary in another family. In the course of events that family
had been driven out of its place. The Maccabean brothers
had undertaken the leadership of the national party, and the
Syrian king had transferred to them the high-priestly rank.
For the maintenance of Simon's government it was of supreme
importance that the legitimacy of his rule should be expressly
recognised by a popular decree as affecting his own person
and that of his descendants. Such an act was successfully
carried out in the third year of Simon's reign. On the 18th
Elul of the Seleucid year 172, that is, in September B.C. 141,
it was resolved in a great assembly " of the priests, and the
people, and the princes of the people, and the elders of the
land," that Simon should be high priest and military commander and civil governor of the Jews (ἀρχιερεύς, στρατηγὶς
and ἐθνάρχης), and that " for ever until there should arise a
faithful prophet " (1 Macc. xiv. 41).[13] By the last phrase
it was meant that this popular decree should remain in force
until an authentic communication from God should make
some other enactment. Henceforth therefore Simon's official
rank was regarded as " for ever," that is, hereditary. The
significance of this popular resolution lies not so much in the
fact that it conveyed to him any new dignity, but rather in
this, that it legitimized and pronounced hereditary those

dignities which he already had. In this way a new high-priestly and princely dignity was founded, that of the Asmoneans.[14] The terms of the popular decree were engraved on brazen tablets, and these were set up in the court of the temple.[15]

The legitimizing on the part of the people was soon followed by recognition on the part of the Romans. Just about the time when that popular decree was issued, Simon sent an embassy, under the leadership of Numenius, to Rome, which carried as a present a golden shield weighing a thousand minas, and treated about the renewal of the covenant. The embassy was courteously received by the senate, and obtained a decree of senate, which guaranteed to the Jews unrestricted possession of their own territory. Information regarding the contents of the decree of senate was sent to the kings of Egypt, Syria, Pergamum, Cappadocia, and Parthia, and to many of the smaller independent states and communes of Greece and Asia Minor; while, at the same time, they were charged to deliver up to the Jewish high priest any evil-doers who might have fled to them from Palestine.[16] The terms of the decree of senate is given us probably in the *Senatus consultus* communicated by Josephus, *Antiq.* xiv. 8. 5, which Josephus, however, assigns to the time of Hyrcanus II. The relations presupposed in this document are precisely the same as those of 1 Macc. xiv. 24 and xv. 15–24: Jewish ambassadors, of whom one is named Numenius, carried as a present a golden shield, with a request for the renewal of the covenant; and the senate concluded in consequence of this to insist upon the autonomous cities and kings respecting the integrity of the Jewish territory. The session of senate referred to took place, according to Josephus, εἰδοῖς Δεκεμβρίαις, that is, on the 13th December, under the presidency of the praetor Lucius Valerius. This president may possibly be the same as "Consul Lucius," who, according to 1 Macc. xv. 16, sent

out the circular letter to the kings and cities. It is, however, also possible that by this term is intended L. Calpurnius
Piso, one of the consuls for B.C. 139, who, according to the
correct reading of Valerius Max. i. 3. 2, has the praenomen,
not of Cneius, but of Lucius. In any case, the arrival of the
Jewish ambassadors at Rome must be assigned to B.C. 139,
for they returned to Palestine in the Seleucid year 174, that
is, B.C. 139–138 (1 Macc. xv. 10, 15). Without doubt,
therefore, the statement of Valerius Maximus about the
establishment of a Jewish propaganda at Rome in B.C. 139
has reference to the proceedings of these ambassadors.[17]

Meanwhile the government of Simon seems not to have
been going on so smoothly as it had hitherto. He became
once more involved in Syrian affairs. Just about this time
Demetrius II. had been temporarily withdrawn from the
scene of Syrian politics. He had allowed himself to be
entangled in a tedious war with the Parthian king Mithridates I., which ended by Demetrius being taken prisoner by
the Parthians in B.C. 138.[18] In place of Demetrius, his father
Antiochus VII. Sidetes now took up the struggle against
Trypho. Like all Syrian pretenders, who had first of all to
win their throne by conquest, Antiochus hasted to secure
the aid of the Jews by flattering promises. He had heard in
Rhodes of the imprisonment of Demetrius. Even before his
landing on the Syro-Phoenician coasts, "from the islands of
the sea" he wrote a letter to Simon, in which he confirmed
to him all the privileges granted by former kings, and
expressly gave him the right of coining money.[19] Soon
thereafter, in the Seleucid year 174, or B.C. 139 – 138
(1 Macc. xv. 10), Antiochus landed in Syria, and quickly
gained the victory over Trypho. The latter was obliged to fly
to Dora, the strong fortress on the Phoenician coast, and was
there besieged by Antiochus.[20] Trypho, indeed, succeeded
in effecting his escape from that place. He fled by Ptole-

mais and Orthosias [21] to Apamea. But there he was again besieged, and in the siege lost his life.[22]

No sooner had Antiochus gained some advantage over Trypho than he assumed another attitude toward the Jews. Even during the siege of Dora, Simon sent him two thousand auxiliary troops, and besides, silver and gold and weapons for their equipment. But Antiochus declined to accept what was offered, repudiated all his former promises, and sent one of his confidants, Athenobius, to Jerusalem in order to obtain from Simon the surrender of the conquered cities of Joppa and Gazara and the citadel of Jerusalem, as well as of all places outside of Judea that had been taken possession of by the Jews. If Simon should be unwilling to restore them, then he was to pay for them altogether the sum of a thousand talents, to be, as it was made to appear, once for all the sum of acquittance. The demands were justified by the plea that for their conquests the Jews had not been able to show any legal title. But Simon refused to yield to these terms, and declared that he would pay only one hundred talents. With this answer Athenobius returned to the king.[23]

Antiochus had resolved to enforce his claims by violent measures. While he himself was still engaged in conflict with Trypho, he appointed his general Kendebäus to conduct the campaign against Simon. Kendebäus made Jamnia his headquarters, fortified Kedron,—a place not otherwise known, probably in the neighbourhood of Jamnia,—and made raids upon Judea.[24] Simon was prevented by his age from personally taking the field. He sent, therefore, his sons Judas and John with an army against Kendebäus. Both justified the confidence placed in them by their father. In a decisive engagement Kendebäus was utterly defeated. When Judas was wounded, John undertook the pursuit, and chased the enemy to Kedron and down into the territory of Ashdod. He returned as conqueror to Jerusalem.[25]

So long as Simon lived, the attack was not repeated on the part of Antiochus.

It thus seemed as if Simon were to be allowed to end his days in peace. But it was not so to be. Like all his brothers, he too died a violent death. His own son-in-law Ptolemy, who was military commander over the plain of Jericho, entertained bold and ambitious schemes. He wished to secure to himself the supreme power, and so plotted by what stratagem he could put Simon and his sons out of the way. When, therefore, in the month Shebat of the Seleucid year 177, that is, in February B.C. 135 (1 Macc. xvi. 14), Simon, on a tour of inspection through the cities of the land, visited Ptolemy in the fortress of Dok near Jericho, Ptolemy made a great feast, during which he had Simon and his two sons who were with him, Mattathias and Judas, treacherously murdered.[26]

Thus was the last of the sons of Mattathias gathered unto his fathers.

§ 8. JOHN HYRCANUS I, B.C. 135-105[1]

Seeing that the high-priestly and princely offices had been declared hereditary in the family of Simon, his third son still surviving, John Hyrcanus, who had held the post of governor of Gazara, was nominated his successor.[2] Against him, therefore, were first directed the attacks of the pretender Ptolemy, who had murdered his father and his two brothers. Immediately after the bloody deed the assassin Ptolemy sent to Gazara in order to do away also with John. That prince, however, had meanwhile been warned by friendly messengers, and so he had the murderers apprehended immediately upon their arrival. Then he hasted to Jerusalem, which he was fortunate enough to reach before Ptolemy. When the latter arrived, he found that the city was already in the power of Hyrcanus.[3]

Ptolemy then retired to the fortress of Dagon, identical probably with that of Dok, near Jericho. There he was besieged by Hyrcanus; and undoubtedly the city would soon have been conquered, and the murderer given over to his well-deserved doom, had not Hyrcanus been restrained by affection for his mother. She had fallen into the power of Ptolemy. And so often as Hyrcanus threatened to storm the fortress, Ptolemy had her led out upon the walls, and threatened to hurl her down unless Hyrcanus would abandon his project.

This caused him to hesitate in his proceedings. And so the siege was protracted, until at length the return of the Sabbatical year necessitated its abandonment. Ptolemy was thus set free ; but nevertheless he had the mother of Hyrcanus murdered, and then fled.[4]

Thus through Ptolemy had Hyrcanus lost both his parents and his two brothers, without having been able to take vengeance upon him.

An evil fate, however, overtook the murderer. Antiochus VII. Sidetes had hitherto made no further attempt upon Judea. We know not the reason of this, but it was perhaps because the home affairs of Syria were occupying all his attention. He was, however, by no means disposed to forget the demands which he previously made of Simon. In the first year of John Hyrcanus, B.C. 135–134, he invaded Judea, devastated the whole country, and finally laid siege to Hyrcanus in his capital, Jerusalem. He surrounded the whole city with a rampart and a trench, and cut off the besieged from all egress from the city. Hyrcanus on his part sought to harass the besiegers by sallies. In order to make the victuals last longer, he sent the non-combatants out of the city. But Antiochus would not let them pass, and drove them back again, so that they were obliged to roam about between the circle of the besiegers and the city, and many of them perished of hunger. It was not till the Feast of Tabernacles that Hyrcanus received them again into the city. For the celebration of this feast he had begged of Antiochus an armistice for seven days. Antiochus granted not only this, but sent also gifts for sacrifice into the city, which they were to present in the temple. This generous act raised the spirits of Hyrcanus, and he now hoped, by timely capitulation, to obtain favourable terms. He sent therefore an embassy to Antiochus to treat for conditions of peace. After protracted negotiations an understanding was at last come to.   The terms of the arrangement were that the Jews should deliver up their arms, pay tribute for Joppa and the other towns lying outside of Judea which they had conquered, give hostages, and besides pay 500 talents.   The conditions were indeed by no means satisfactory.   Yet in the circumstances Hyrcanus was indeed very glad even at this price to obtain the raising of the siege and the withdrawal of the Syrian army.   The walls of the city too were thrown down.[5]

The remarkable moderation of Antiochus had perhaps other reasons than those assigned for it by the historians. In a decree of the Roman senate, which Josephus communicates in *Antiq.* xiii. 9. 2, it is assumed that a King Antiochus had taken from the Jews in war, Joppa, Gazara, and other towns (πολεμῶν ἔλαβεν Ἀντίοχος), on account of which a Jewish embassy had gone to Rome with the prayer that the senate should order Antiochus to restore these towns. This Antiochus can have been no other than Antiochus VII. Sidetes, for under no earlier Antiochus were the Jews in possession of the towns of Joppa and Gazara, and of the later kings there was none able to usurp any authority worth mentioning over the Jews.   Evidently Antiochus, as is indeed in itself most probable, had in that war, before advancing to the siege of the capital, seized upon and taken from the Jews Joppa, Gazara, and the other towns that had been conquered by them.   But then it is hardly credible that of his own accord, by a peaceful treaty, he would have left the Jews in possession of these cities, and only have imposed on them a tribute for the holding of them.   The mild conditions are to be accounted for rather by the interference of the Romans.   The senate certainly did not at first, in the decree referred to, formally accede to the prayer of the Jews, but rather put off any final decision.   It appears, however, that very soon afterwards a second Jewish embassy went to Rome, which did secure the result desired.   In a subsequent passage, *Antiq.* xiv. 10. 22, a decree of the Roman senate is given by Josephus, erroneously inserted in a decree of the Pergamenes, which evidently refers to the matters now under discussion. In consequence of an embassy sent by Hyrcanus, a command is issued to King Antiochus that he must restore all the cities taken by him from the Jews, and in particular that he must withdraw the garrison from Joppa (τὴν ἐν Ἰόπῃ δὲ φρουρὰν ἐκβαλεῖν). The king is there indeed called "Antiochus, son of Antiochus," instead of "son of Demetrius," but he can scarcely be any other than Antiochus Sidetes. For if the Jews, since the conclusion of peace with him, obtained possession again of Joppa by the payment of tribute, it can scarcely be supposed that any of the weak successors of Sidetes could have again placed a garrison there. In any case, the Jews would have had no occasion to call in the help of the Romans against such an adversary. It may therefore be conjectured that the decree of senate in question preceded the conclusion of peace with Antiochus Sidetes, and was pre-eminently the means of securing for the Jews such mild and favourable conditions. —If these combinations are correct, we must assume that the war continued for more than a year.

The conflicts which took place during those first years of Hyrcanus, gave new proofs that the small Jewish state could maintain its freedom from Syrian suzerainty only so long as the Syrian empire was internally weak. Before the first vigorous onslaught of Antiochus, the freedom that had previously been won by Simon was again lost. Hyrcanus' dependence on Antiochus VII. also obliged him to take the field with the Syrian monarch against the Parthians in B.C. 129. But he was not involved in the disaster that overtook Antiochus.[6]

The death of Antiochus in the Parthian campaign, in B.C. 128, was for Hyrcanus a favourable occurrence.[7] His place upon the Syrian throne was taken by the weak Demetrius II., who had previously been released from imprisonment by the Parthians. He was immediately involved in a civil war, which obliged him to seek to win the favour of the Jews.

Hyrcanus as soon as possible turned to account the altered circumstances. Without troubling himself about Demetrius, he began to seize upon considerable districts in the neighbourhood of Judea, to the east, to the north, and to the south. First of all he marched into the land east of the Jordan, and conquered Medaba after a six months' siege.[8] Then he turned to the north, took Shechem and Mount Gerizim, subdued the Samaritans, and destroyed their temple. Finally, he went south, took the Idumean cities Adora and Marissa, and compelled the Idumeans to submit to circumcision, and to receive the Jewish law.[9] The policy of conquest, which had been already inaugurated by Jonathan and Simon, was carried out vigorously by Hyrcanus. The purely worldly character of his policy, however, is shown conspicuously in this, that first among the Jewish princes he no longer conducted the war by means of Jewish soldiers, but called in the aid of foreign mercenaries.[10]

This independent procedure on the part of Hyrcanus was possible only on account of the internal weakness of the Syrian empire. Demetrius II., after his restoration to the throne, was again guilty of the folly of waging war with Ptolemy VII. Physcon, king of Egypt. The Egyptian monarch therefore set up over against Demetrius a pretender to the throne, in the person of a young Egyptian, whom he gave out to be an adopted son of Antiochus Sidetes, who was, however, according to others, a son of Alexander Balas.[11] This pretender was named Alexander, and was surnamed by the Syrians Zabinas, i.e. "the purchased." Conquered by this Alexander at Damascus, Demetrius was obliged to retire to Ptolemais, and to take ship from thence to Tyre, where as soon as he landed he was murdered, in B.C. 125 or 124.[12]

Alexander Zabinas, however, had on his part to contest the sovereignty with the son of Demetrius, Antiochus VIII. Grypos. So he was not forced by necessity to live in peace and friendship with Hyrcanus.[13]

After some years, somewhere about B.C. 122, Alexander Zabinas was subdued by his opponent. Antiochus VIII. Grypos conquered him, and had him executed; while, according to others, he brought his own life to an end by poison.— There now followed a long period of quiet. For eight years Antiochus VIII. Grypos held undisputed sway in Syria.[14] Nevertheless even he made no attempt against Hyrcanus. He had no longer the ambition to restore to Syria its ancient dimensions. In B.C. 113 he was driven out by his cousin and step-brother, Antiochus IX. Cyzicenos, who ruled Syria for two years, and then, when Antiochus Grypos again secured possession of the greater part of Syria in B.C. 111, he took up his residence in Coele-Syria, the part adjoining Palestine, and made it his headquarters.[15]

Of Antiochus IX. Cyzicenos, who ruled in Coele-Syria from B.C. 113 to B.C. 95, Diodorus gives the following description:[16] "So soon as he attained the throne, Antiochus Cyzicenos gave way to drunkenness and shameful sensuality, and to habits most unbecoming in a king. He took great delight in theatrical displays and the performance of comedies, and generally in all sorts of showmen, and tried to learn their art. He also zealously promoted the exhibition of marionettes, and sought to fabricate in silver and gold animals five ells long that would move of themselves, and other such arts. On the other hand, battering-rams and engines of war, which would have brought him great advantage and renown, he did not make. He also was passionately fond of adventurous expeditions; and often through the night, without the knowledge of his friends, accompanied only by two or three servants, he would go out into the country to hunt lions,

panthers, and boars. In such escapades he often engaged to
the extreme peril of his life in foolhardy encounters with wild
beasts."

We see here traditions of an earlier Antiochus IV. imitated
again after a baser fashion. From such a ruler, who was
taken up with such pursuits, Hyrcanus had nought to fear.
And so it came about that from the death of Antiochus
Sidetes, in B.C. 128, Judea had been able to keep itself
absolutely independent of Syria. The taxes laid upon Judea
by Antiochus Sidetes were not paid to any of the following
kings. "Neither as their subject nor as their friend did he
longer pay them any regard."[17]

In the last years of his reign Hyrcanus undertook an
expedition for the conquest of the neighbouring districts.
After having previously subdued the borders of Shechem and
Mount Gerizim, he now directed his attack against the city
of Samaria, whose inhabitants had given him occasion to
complain. He had them enclosed by a wall and a trench,
and then transferred the conduct of the siege to his sons
Antigonus and Aristobulus. The Samaritans in their straits
called in the aid of Antiochus Cyzicenos, who went indeed
very willingly, but was driven back by the Jews. So then
a second time Antiochus sought to bring them help by
means of Egyptian auxiliary troops, which Ptolemy Lathurus
supplied, and by their help devastated the Jewish territory,
without, however, securing any decided advantage. After
sustaining great loss, Antiochus withdrew from the scene of
conflict, leaving his generals, Callimander and Epicrates, to
carry on the campaign to its close. Of these the one was
defeated by the Jews and lost his life, while the other,
Epicrates, also achieved nothing, but treacherously gave over
Scythopolis to the Jews. Thus Samaria, after a year's siege,
fell into the hands of the Jews, and was utterly razed to the
ground.[18]—The Jewish legends relate that on the day of the

decisive victory of Antigonus and Aristobulus over Antiochus Cyzicenos, the occurrence was made known to Hyrcanus by a voice from heaven, while he was presenting a burnt-offering in the temple.[19]

What has now been told is all that is known to us as to the external events of what seems to have been the truly brilliant reign of Hyrcanus. The record is scanty enough. But even still more fragmentary is the reports which have come down to us regarding the internal affairs of that government. Something may first of all be gained from the inscriptions on the coins. These, in common with the coins of the immediate successors of Hyrcanus, bear the inscription—

יהוחנן הכהן הגדל וחבר היהודים

or: יהוחנן הכהן הגדל רֹאשׁ חבר היהודים

The reading of this last word is doubtful. Probably it is to be read : *cheber hajjehudim ;* and by *cheber*, which literally means fellowship, association, is to be understood, not the γερουσία, but rather the assembly of the whole body of the people. The inscription would therefore run thus : " Jochanan the high priest and the congregation of the Jews," or " Jochanan the high priest, head of the congregation of the Jews." This official title shows us that John Hyrcanus regarded himself as in the full sense still high priest. As in the pre-Maccabean age, so also still the Jewish commonwealth was a government of priests, and the chief priest standing at its head was not an autocrat, but simply the chief of the congregation. The coins, at least those of the first order, were not only stamped in his name, but also in that of the congregation. On the other hand, it is a proof of the increasing prominence given to the possession of princely prerogatives, that John has had his name engraven on the coins. He is the first of the Jewish princes who did so. Then from

the coins of the second order the name of "the congregation" disappears altogether, and instead thereof he is himself
designated under his twofold title of rank as "High Priest,"
and as "Chief of the Congregation of the Jews."

In reference to the internal policy of Hyrcanus, during his
thirty years' reign, one fact at least is well established, and
that one of the greatest importance: his breaking away from
the Pharisees, and attaching himself to the Sadducees. These
two parties now appear for the first time under those names
upon the arena of history. Their beginnings lay far back;
their consolidation under those names seems to have been a
consequence of the Maccabean movement.[20] The Pharisees
are nothing else but the party of strict zealots for the law:
essentially the same circles as we meet with in the beginning
of the Maccabean movement under the name of the Pious or
Chasidim. Diametrically opposed to them were those who in
the most extreme fashion favoured everything Greek, who
even went beyond the Hellenizing movement of Antiochus
Epiphanes by opening the door to Hellenism, not only in
the domain of social life, but also in that of religious worship.
These extreme Grecianizers, who were found specially in the
ranks of the higher priesthood, had been swept away before
the blast of the Maccabean revolution. Ideas of this sort
could no longer be allowed to find expression in the league
of the Jewish commonwealth. But the foundations on which
that type of thought had grown up had still continued to
exist there. It was the essentially worldly spirit of the
higher priesthood, opposed to any kind of religious enthusiasm.
They wished to maintain their position on the basis of the
Mosaic law. But whatever therein transcended the mere
letter, they rejected with a lofty assumption of superiority.
They had far heartier interest in the affairs of this life
than in those of the time to come. The spirit which among
the higher priests was represented pre-eminently by "the

sons of Zadoc," was now called that of the Zadocites or Sadducees.

The Maccabees belonged properly neither to the Pharasaic nor to the Sadducean party. The zeal for the law, which had led them to take the sword in their hand, associated them indeed with the Chasidim, who also at the outset took part in the war of independence. But soon the two went their several ways, and as time advanced they parted farther and farther from one another. The Chasidim had no interest in political supremacy and political freedom. With the Maccabees this was the point of most vital importance. They did not indeed at a later period abandon their original aim, the preservation of the religion of their fathers. But as time wore on they became more and more deeply involved in other political schemes. In this way they were brought into closer relations with the Sadducees. As political up-starts, the Maccabees could not venture to ignore the influential Sadducean nobility. And it may be taken for granted that in the γερουσία of the Maccabean age, the Sadducean party was represented.—But in spite of all this, in religious sympathies the Maccabees originally stood far nearer to the Pharisees than to the Sadducees. They were the conservers of their fathers' faith and their fathers' law. It may be unhesitatingly stated, even in regard to Hyrcanus, that in the earlier years of his reign, in regard to the observance of the law, he held the doctrines of the Pharisees. For it was his abandonment of the traditions of the Pharisees which formed the chief accusation brought against him by the stricter Jews.[21]

The interests and activities of the Maccabees were thus going forth in two different directions, the religious and the political, and this explains to us the change of front which took place during the course of Hyrcanus' reign. The more the political interests were brought into the foreground by him, the more were the religious interests put in abeyance.

And just in proportion as this policy was carried out, Hyrcanus was obliged to withdraw from the Pharisees and associate himself with the Sadducees. Any close and hearty relationship with the Pharisees could not possibly continue while he wrought out the devices of his purely worldly policy. Hence it was just what might have been expected, that he should openly break with the Pharisees and cast in his lot with the Sadducean party.

The ostensible occasion of the breach between Hyrcanus and the Pharisees is described by Josephus and the Talmud in a similar manner as follows. Hyrcanus once made the request, when many Pharisees were with him at dinner, that if they observed him doing anything not according to the law, they should call attention to it, and point out to him the right way. But all present were full of his praise. Only one, Eleasar, rose up and said : " Since thou desirest to know the truth, if thou wilt be righteous in earnest, lay down the high-priesthood and content thyself with the civil government of the people." And when Hyrcanus wished to know for what cause he should do so, Eleasar answered : " We have heard it from old men that thy mother had been a captive under the reign of Antiochus Epiphanes." But this statement was incorrect. On account of it Hyrcanus was incensed against him in the highest degree. When then Hyrcanus laid before the Pharisees the question as to the punishment which Eleasar deserved, they made answer, " stripes and bonds." Hyrcanus, who believed for such an offence nothing less than death was due, became now still more angry, and thought that Eleasar had given expression to a sentiment that was approved of by his party. Forthwith he separated himself entirely from the Pharisees, forbade under penalties the observance of the laws ordained by them, and attached himself to the Sadducees.[22]

The story indeed, in its anecdotal form, bears on it the imprint of a thoroughly legendary character, and is even by

Josephus given only as a tale derived from oral tradition. Nevertheless it may be accepted as a fact that Hyrcanus did turn away decidedly from the party of the Pharisees and abolished the Pharisaic ordinances. For it was a conscious reaction against the policy.pursued from the time of Hyrcanus, when Alexandra returned again to the observance of the Pharisaic institutions.[23] Two of the particular ordinances set aside by Hyrcanus are mentioned in the Mishna. But in view of the thoroughgoing opposition of Hyrcanus to every sort of Pharisaic ordinance, the cases referred to in the Mishna are spoken of as being only unimportant matters of detail.[24]

On a review of Hyrcanus' government Josephus passes a favourable verdict upon him, saying that "he was esteemed of God worthy of the three privileges—the government of his nation, the dignity of the high-priesthood, and prophecy." Upon the whole, the reign of Hyrcanus seems to the Jewish historian a pre-eminently happy one.[25] He is quite right, if political power is regarded as the measure of prosperity and success. After Hyrcanus' predecessors had already enlarged the Jewish territory to the sea-coast by the addition of Joppa and Gazara and other conquests in the west, Hyrcanus, by new conquests in the east, south, and north, and by making still more secure his independence of Syria, built up a Jewish state such as had not been from the time of the overthrow of the ten tribes, perhaps not even since the partition of the kingdom after the death of Solomon.

Among the great sepulchral monuments in the neighbourhood of Jerusalem, that of " the high priest John " is frequently referred to by Josephus in his *Wars of the Jews.*[26]

§ 9. ARISTOBULUS I, B.C. 105-104

JOHN HYRCANUS left five sons.[1] But according to his will,
the government was to pass to his wife,[2] while only the high-
priesthood was to go to his eldest son Aristobulus. The
young prince, however, was not satisfied with this arrangement. He put his mother in prison, where he allowed her to
die of hunger, and assumed the government himself.[3] Also
all his brothers, with the exception of Antigonus, he cast into
prison. Only in the latter had he such confidence that he
assigned to him a share in the management of the kingdom.
But this very pre-eminence proved the occasion of disaster to
Antigonus. It aroused the jealousy of many whose intrigues
were at last successful in making Aristobulus the murderer of
his favourite brother. It was represented to him that Antigonus was endeavouring to secure the supreme power to
himself. Aristobulus in consequence became suspicious, and
gave orders to his bodyguard, that if Antigonus should come
to him armed, they should cut him down. At the same time
he commanded his brother to come to him unarmed. But
the enemies of Antigonus bribed the messengers, so that they
should announce to him that Aristobulus desired him to
obtain new weapons and new armour, and commanded him
that he should come clad in armour in order that he might
see his new equipment. Antigonus acted accordingly, and

was cut down by the bodyguard when he, suspecting nothing, entered the citadel. After the deed was done, Aristobulus is said to have bitterly repented, and his sorrow seemed to have accelerated his death.[4]

The whole domestic tragedy, if it can be taken as historical, presents the character of Aristobulus in a very dark light. His whole concern was with the civil government. All considerations of piety were sacrificed to that one end. In other directions also Aristobulus was estranged still more completely than his father from the traditions of the Maccabees. The monarchical selfish spirit led him to assume the title of king, which his successors maintained down to the time of Pompey.[5] The Greek culture, against the introduction of which the Maccabees had first taken a stand, was directly favoured by him. Whether he assumed the title of $\Phi\iota\lambda\epsilon\lambda\lambda\eta\nu$ is not with absolute certainty to be concluded from the words of Josephus.[6] As already his father Hyrcanus had given his sons purely Greek names (Aristobulus, Antigonus, Alexander), it may be taken for granted that he was inclined to those tendencies afterwards openly avowed by Aristobulus.

On the coins Aristobulus has made use neither of his royal title nor of his Greek name. He calls himself on them, "Judas, high priest." For the coins with the inscription—

יהודה כהן גדול וחבר היהודים

belong, as Cavedoni was the first to point out, to one Aristobulus, whose Hebrew name was Judas.[7]—How thoroughly Aristobulus, notwithstanding his Greek leanings, still occupied the Jewish standpoint, is shown us by the most important occurrence which is recorded of his short reign : the conquest and Judaizing of the northern districts of Palestine. He undertook a military expedition against the Itureans, conquered a large portion of their land, united that to Judea, and compelled the inhabitants to allow themselves to be circumcised and to live according to the Jewish law.[8] The Itureans had their residence in Lebanon. As Josephus does not say that Aristobulus subdued "the Itureans," but only that he conquered a large portion of their country and judaized it; and as Galilee had not hitherto belonged to the territory of the Jewish high priest, the conquests even of John Hyrcanus extending northwards only as far as Samaria and Scythopolis; and as, yet again, the population of Galilee had been up to that time more Gentile than Jewish,—the conjecture has good grounds that the portion conquered by Aristobulus was mainly Galilee, and that the actual judaizing of Galilee was first carried out by him.[9] In any case, he extended the Jewish power farther northward, as Hyrcanus had toward the south.

Aristobulus died of a painful disease after a reign of one year.[10] Seeing that the judgment passed upon him by Gentile historians is a favourable one,[11] we cannot avoid entertaining the suspicion that the cruelties which he, the Sadducee and friend of the Greeks, is said to have inflicted upon his relatives, are calumnious inventions of the Pharisees.

§ 10. ALEXANDER JANNÄUS

B.C. 104-78

WHEN Aristobulus was dead, his widow Salome Alexandra released from prison the three brothers of Aristobulus, whom he had placed in confinement, and raised the eldest of them to the throne and the high-priesthood,[1] while at the same time she gave him her hand in marriage.[2]

Alexander Jannäus, B.C. 104–78,[3] was, during his reign of twenty-six or twenty-seven years, almost constantly involved in foreign or in civil wars, which for the most part were provoked by his own wilfulness, and resulted by no means invariably in his favour.

First of all he took the field against the citizens of Ptolemais, besieged them, and surrounded the city. The inhabitants applied for help to the Egyptian prince Ptolemy Lathurus, who, driven from the throne by his mother Cleopatra, was then exercising rule in Cyprus. Ptolemy arrived with an army, and Alexander through fear of him raised the siege.[4]— He sought, however, by guile to get rid of Ptolemy, for he openly concluded peace and a friendly treaty with him, but secretly called his mother to his help against him. Ptolemy was at first disposed to enter into a mutual agreement. But when he heard that Alexander had secretly summoned his mother to his aid, he broke the truce and went forth with his army against Alexander. He conquered and plundered

the city of Asochis in Galilee,[5] and thus put himself in
position against Alexander at Asophon on the Jordan.[6] Alexander had a standing army, fairly well equipped. That of
Ptolemy was not nearly so well armed, but his soldiers were
experienced, and had thorough confidence in the tactical skill
of their general Philostephanus. The two armies now lay
on either side of the river. The Egyptian troops began to
cross. Alexander allowed them peacefully to accomplish this,
because he hoped more completely to destroy them when
once they had all come over. On both sides they fought
bravely, and at first the army of Alexander gained some
advantage. But then the Egyptian general managed by a
clever manœuvre to cause a part of the Jewish army to
retreat, and when once a part fled, the rest could no longer
hold their ground. The whole Jewish army took to flight;
the Egyptians pursued them, continuing the massacre without
intermission, " and slew them so long that their weapons of iron
were blunted, and their hands quite tired with the slaughter." [7]

The whole country now lay open before Ptolemy. But
now Cleopatra sent an army to Palestine, in order to check
in time the increasing power of her son. While this army
operated in Palestine, Ptolemy succeeded in pressing forward
into Egypt. But he was driven out of it again and obliged
to return to Gaza, and Cleopatra took possession of the whole
of Palestine. When she had the power in her hands, some
of her counsellors advised her to unite the land of the Jews
again with Egypt. But the representations of her Jewish
general Ananias prevailed in getting their scheme set aside, and
in inducing her rather to conclude a treaty with Alexander.
Ptolemy could no longer maintain his position in the Jewish
territory, and so he returned to Cyprus. Cleopatra also withdrew her army from Palestine, and Alexander was again ruler
of the country.[8]

He was now in a position to make preparations for other

conquests. He began these on the east of the Jordan, for he took Gadara[9] and the strong fortress of Amathus on the Jordan.[10] The former he succeeded in taking only after a two months' siege. Then he turned his attention to the land of the Philistines, conquered Raphia, Anthedon, and finally the city of Gaza, so celebrated in days of old. For a whole year Alexander lay before that city, and at last he obtained the mastery only through treachery, whereupon he plundered it and set it on fire.[11]

The conquest of Gaza must have taken place in B.C. 96, for it was about the same time that Antiochus VIII. Grypos died.[12]

No sooner was peace secured with those outside of the nation than conflicts arose within. The incurable dissension of parties which had already cast its shadows over the reign of Hyrcanus, became productive of strife and turmoil during Alexander's reign, especially in matters of internal government. The rabbinical legends tell of disputes between the king and the chiefs of the schools of the Pharisees which were of a very harmless kind, childish wranglings rather than serious contendings. But their tales are so utterly worthless from a historical point of view, that they can find a place here only as evidence of the peculiar lusts and equally peculiar morals of Talmudic Judaism. The hero of these tales is Simon ben Shetach, the celebrated Pharisee, reputed to be a brother of Alexander's wife Salome. Of his doings at court the following are told.[13] There came once 300 Nazarites to Jerusalem in order to present there the prescribed sacrifices. Simon found ways and means to relieve them of the one-half of their burden. But with the other half he could not do so, and therefore he petitioned the king that he should bear the cost, pretending that he himself would bear the expense of the other half. The king agreed to this. But when he discovered that Simon had deceived him he was exceedingly angry, and Simon was obliged to go into hiding in order to escape his wrath. Some time thereafter Parthian ambassadors arrived at the king's court and wished to see the distinguished rabbis. The king turned to the queen, who knew Simon's place of concealment, and urged her to induce her brothers to bring him forth. The queen obtained from him a promise that no injury would be done the high priest, and then urged him to come. No sooner was the agreement come to than Simon entered in and seated himself between the king and the queen, whereupon the following conversation took place between him and the king. The king: "Wherefore didst thou flee?" Simon: "Because I heard that my lord and king was angry with me." The king: "And why didst thou deceive me?" Simon: "I did not deceive thee. Thou didst give thy gold, and I my wisdom." The king: "But why didst thou not tell this to me?" Simon: "If I had told thee, thou wouldest not have given it me." The king: "Wherefore hast thou taken thy place between the king and the queen?" Simon: "Because it is written in the book of Sirach, Exalt wisdom, and it will exalt thee among princes" (Sirach xi. 1).—Thereupon the king ordered to set wine before him, and called upon him to invoke the blessing at table. Simon began: "Thanks be unto God for the nourishment which Jannai and his companions have enjoyed." "Thou dost ever continue stiff-necked," said the king; "I have never before in any grace at table heard the name of Jannai." "Could I say," retorted Simon, "we thank Thee for that which we have eaten, when I as yet have received nothing?" The king then gave orders that they should set food before Simon; and when he had partaken of it, he said: "Thanks be unto God for that which we have eaten."

The real conflicts between Alexander on the one hand, and the Pharisees and those of the people who sympathized with them on the other, were of an entirely different and wholly

tragic character. The deeper foundations of this strife lay in
the general course of development taken by the internal affairs
of the nation since the establishment of the Asmonean
dynasty. Among the people the Pharisees gained power and
influence more and more. The policy of the Asmoneans
separated them always farther and farther from the popular
movements, and brought them at last into direct antagonism
with the nationalist party. It could only be with deep-
seated resentment that pious Jews could look on and see a
wild warrior like Alexander Jannäus discharging the duties
of high priest in the holy place, certainly not with the conscientious and painstaking observance of the ordinances
regarded by the Pharisees as divine. Even while he was
discharging his priestly office it is said that for the first time
they broke out in open rebellion. During the Feast of Tabernacles, when every one taking part in it was required to
carry a palm branch (לוּלָב φοῖνιξ) and a citron fruit (אֶתְרוֹג
κίτριον) as a festal emblem, Alexander was once, as he
stood beside the altar about to offer sacrifice, pelted by the
assembled people with the citrons. At the same time they
insulted him by calling out that he was the son of a prisoner
of war, and was unworthy of the office of sacrificing priest.
Alexander was not the man to bear this quietly. He
called in the aid of his mercenaries, and 600 Jews were
massacred.[14] The bitterness of feeling created thereby among
the people was so great, that only a favourable opportunity
was waited for in order to break off the hated yoke.

By his love of war Alexander was soon again involved in
further complications. He went forth against the Arab
tribes which dwelt east of the Jordan, and of these he made
the Moabites and Gileadites tributary. But Amathus, which
had once previously been conquered but never very securely
held, was now utterly destroyed. He then began hostilities
against the Arabian king Obedas; but during the conflict

with him in the neighbourhood of Gadara,[15] Alexander fell into an ambuscade, in which he was so sore pressed that he narrowly escaped with his bare life. He went as a fugitive to Jerusalem. But there a poor reception awaited him. The Pharisees took advantage of the moment of Alexander's political weakness to break down his power and influence at home. There was a general rebellion against him, and Alexander had for six full years to fight against his own people with mercenary troops. No less than 50,000 Jews are said to have perished during this period in these civil conflicts. When Alexander's power had been established he held out the hand of peace. But the Pharisees wished to turn the state of affairs to account so as to secure a victory to their party. When therefore Alexander inquired what they wanted from him, and under what conditions they would agree to maintain the peace and yield obedience, they said that they wanted only his death. At the same time they called to their aid Demetrius III. Eucärus, a son of Antiochus Grypos, and at that time governor of a portion of Syria,[16]—somewhere about B.C. 88.

Demetrius arrived with an army. The Jewish national party united themselves with him at Shechem. Alexander was completely beaten, lost all his mercenary troops, and was obliged to flee to the mountains.[17] But now it seemed as if among many of the Jews who now attached themselves to Demetrius, the national feeling had again wakened up. They would rather, in a free Jewish state, be subject to an Asmonean prince than be incorporated into the empire of a Seleucid ruler. Six thousand Jews went over to Alexander, and Demetrius was in consequence under the necessity of withdrawing again into his own land. The rest of the Jews who still continued in revolt had no other object than to get rid of Alexander. But they were by him defeated in many battles, and many of them were slain. The leaders of the rebellion at last fled to Bethome or Besemelis, where [18] they were besieged by Alexander. After the overthrow of the city, Alexander carried them as prisoners to Jerusalem, and there within the city, at least according to the account of Josephus, while he along with his mistresses gave himself up to debauchery, he had somewhere about 800 of the prisoners crucified in his own presence, and while they were yet alive caused their wives and children to be slain before their eyes. His opponents in Jerusalem were by these atrocities so paralysed with terror, that they fled during the night to the number of 8000, and during his lifetime kept away from the land of Judea.[19]

From this time forward Alexander, throughout his whole reign, enjoyed peace at home. It was not so in the matter of his relations with those outside.

The empire of the Seleucidae then, indeed, lay in its death-throes. Its last convulsions, however, were the occasion of again putting Judea into commotion. Antiochus XII., the youngest of the five sons of Antiochus Grypos, was at this time at war with his brother Philip and the king of the Arabians. When once he resolved to take his way to Arabia through Judea, Alexander Jannäus endeavoured to prevent that by constructing a great wall and trench from Joppa to Capharsaba, and fortifying Joppa with a wooden tower. But Antiochus laid everything low with fire, and made his way through it all.[20]

When Antiochus met his death in battle against the king of the Arabians, and that monarch, whose name was Aretas, extended his rule to Damascus, he became from this time forth the most powerful and the most dangerous neighbour of the Jews. On the south and the east Palestine was bounded by districts which lay under the dominion of the Arabs. Very soon Alexander Jannäus also began to have experience of their power. He was obliged by an attack of Aretas to retreat to Adida, within the boundaries of Judea, where he suffered a rather serious defeat, and could only by making concessions purchase the withdrawal of the Arabian king.[21]

More fortunate were the results of the campaigns which Alexander Jannäus during the next three years, B.C. 84–81, carried on in the country east of the Jordan, in order to extend his power in that direction. He conquered Pella, Dium, Gerasa, then advanced again northward and took Gaulana, Seleucia, and at last the strong fortress of Gamala. When, after these exploits, he returned to Jerusalem, he was then received by the people in peace.[22]

Not long after this, as the result of a drunken debauch, he became sick, and this sickness continued throughout the last three years of his life, B.C. 81–78. He did not, however, abandon his military expeditions until at last, amid the tumult of war, during the siege of the fortress Ragaba he succumbed to his sickness and exertions in B.C. 78.[23] His body was brought to Jerusalem, where he was buried with great pomp.[24]

Of the coins issued by him, those are of special interest which bear the inscription in two languages—

יְהוֹנָתָן הַמֶּלֶךְ ‖ ΒΑΣΙΛΕΩΣ ΑΛΕΞΑΝΔΡΟΥ.

They were known even to the earlier numismatists; but first de Saulcy stated the correct and now generally accepted view regarding them, that the Hebrew inscription supplies us with the Hebrew name of Alexander. Jannai is therefore a contraction for Jonathan, not, as was formerly supposed, for Jochanan. But if undoubtedly Alexander's name was Jonathan, then the coins of the high priest are to be ascribed to him which bear the inscription

יהונתן הכהן הגדל וחבר היהדים (or ינתן).

These high-priestly coins are of the same type as the coins

of John Hyrcanus and Aristobulus. The bilingual royal coins are a novelty introduced by Alexander.

By the conquests of Alexander the boundaries of the Jewish state had now been extended far beyond the limits reached by John Hyrcanus. In the south, the Idumeans had been subdued and judaized. In the north, Alexander's dominion reached as far as Seleucia on the Lake Merom. The sea-coast, on which Joppa had been the first conquest of the Maccabees, was all now completely under Jewish rule. With the single exception of Ascalon, which had been able to maintain its independence, all the coast towns were conquered by Alexander, from the borders of Egypt as far as Carmel.[25] But also the country east of the Jordan, from the Lake Merom to the Dead Sea, was wholly under his sway; among them a number of the more important towns, which had previously been centres of Greek culture, such as Hippos, Gadara, Pella, Dium, and others.[26]

This work of conquest, however, proved at the same time a work of destruction. It did not lead, as once the conquests of Alexander the Great had done, to the furtherance, but to the extinction of Greek culture. For in this respect Alexander Jannäus was still always a Jew, who subjected the conquered territories, as far as they went, to Jewish modes of thought and manners. If the cities in question would not consent to this, they were laid waste.[27] Such was the fate that befell the great and hitherto prosperous coast towns, and the Hellenistic cities on the east of the Jordan. The Romans, Pompey and Gabinius, were the first to rebuild again those ruins, and reawaken in them a new prosperity.

§ 11. ALEXANDRA, B.C. 78-69

ACCORDING to the latest expression of Alexander's will, the succession of the throne went to his widow Alexandra, who again nominated her eldest son Hyrcanus high priest.[1] Alexandra, or, as her Hebrew name runs, Salome, B.C. 78–69, was in all respects the direct antithesis of her husband.[2] While he hated the Pharisees, and was hated by them, she befriended them, and committed to them the helm of government. While he was a despot of the real Oriental type, she was a God-fearing ruler, according to the very ideal of the Pharisees. Her rule, measured by the Pharisaic standard, was faultless.

Alexander, upon his deathbed, is said to have advised his wife to make peace with the Pharisees.[3] This may be true, or it may not; this at least is a fact, that Alexandra, from the beginning of her reign, took her stand unhesitatingly on the side of the Pharisees, lent an ear to their demands and wishes, and in particular gave legal sanction again to all the Pharisaic ordinances abolished since the time of John Hyrcanus. During these years the Pharisees were the real rulers in the land. "She had indeed the name of regent, but the Pharisees had the authority; for it was they who restored such as were banished, and set such as were prisoners at liberty, and to say all at once, they differed in nothing from lords."[4] To this period of Pharisaic reaction we may also assign a series of triumphs of the Pharisees, of which a report is given in the rabbinical traditions. But the authentic accounts which are given of these in the Festival-Calendar (*Megillath Taanith, i.e.* the list of the joyous days of thanksgiving on which fasting was not to be practised) are so brief and enigmatical, that they afford no satisfactory historical basis. And the quite modern Hebrew commentary thereon gives purely worthless fancies.[5] Also the statement of the Mishna, that Simon ben Shetach had once caused eighty women to be hanged in Ascalon, cannot be used for this reason, that that celebrated rabbi had no connection with Ascalon.[6] Historical information is therefore wholly to be derived from Josephus. And the picture of this queen with which he presents us, in respect of vividness leaves nothing to be desired. The Pharisees, conscious of their power, went so far as to cause the execution of the former counsellors of King Alexander who had advised him to massacre the 800 rebels. This despotic proceeding did not involve in ruin the aristocracy of Jerusalem. An embassy representing them, including Alexandra's own son Aristobulus, approached the queen, and besought her to put a stop to the scheme of the Pharisees; and the queen was obliged, whether she wished it or not, to consent thereto.[7]

In her foreign policy Alexandra showed circumspection and energy.[8] There are, however, no very important political events to be recorded during her reign. The most important was a military expedition of her son Aristobulus against Damascus, which, however, ended without result.[9] The Syrian empire was then in the hands of the Armenian king Tigranes. He assumed a threatening attitude toward the end of the reign of Alexandra. The danger, however, that thus hung over Judea was arrested, partly by Alexandra purchasing peace by bestowing rich presents, partly and mainly by the Romans having just then made a descent under Lucullus upon the empire of Tigranes, which obliged him to abandon his plans in regard to Judea.[10]

Upon the whole, Alexandra's reign was looked upon by the people as one of prosperity. There was peace abroad as well as at home. The Pharisees were satisfied; and since they had the people at their bidding, all expressed themselves in favour of the God-fearing queen. In the Pharisaic tradition the days of Alexandra are naturally represented as a golden age, in which even the soil of the land, as if blessed on account of the piety of the queen, enjoyed a truly miraculous fruitfulness. "Under Simon ben Shetach and Queen Salome rain fell on the eve of the Sabbath, so that the corns of wheat were as large as kidneys, the barley corns as large as olives, and the lentils like golden denarii; the scribes gathered such corns, and preserved specimens of them in order to show future generations what sin entails." [11]

But the Pharisees were not yet so exclusively in possession of power that the queen, without risk, could depend upon their support alone. The influence of the Sadducean nobles was not altogether broken. And the discontent of this circle was all the more considerable, from the fact that at its head stood Alexandra's own son Aristobulus. The queen must herself have felt, toward the close of her life, on what a shifting foundation she had built. When, in her seventy-third year, she fell sick of a serious complaint, and intended to bestow the succession to the throne upon her elder son Hyrcanus, Aristobulus thought that the time had now arrived for unfurling the standard of revolt. He succeeded in getting the strongest fortresses into his possession. As the number of his adherents rapidly grew, the elders of the people and Hyrcanus became sorely distressed, and made representations to the queen that it was necessary to adopt measures against him. The queen granted the necessary authority for this, but died even before the war broke out, in B.C. 69.[12]

§ 12. ARISTOBULUS II, B.C. 69-63

THE star of the Asmoneans was now hasting to its setting. After Alexandra's death a war immediately broke out between the brothers Aristobulus II. and Hyrcanus II., which, after a few years, ended in the Romans taking from the Jews that freedom which they had wrested from the Syrians. Alexandra had died just at the critical moment -when the idea had taken possession of her son Aristobulus to grasp for himself the government by force. Her legitimate successor was her eldest [1] son Hyrcanus, who had been already, during the reign of his mother, invested with the office of high priest. He also began to exercise civil government. But his brother Aristobulus was by no means disposed to acquiesce in his plans. He advanced against Hyrcanus with an army. Near Jericho they engaged in a battle, in which many of the soldiers of Hyrcanus went over to Aristobulus, and thus secured for him the victory. Hyrcanus fled to the citadel of Jerusalem, but was obliged there to surrender to Aristobulus. A truce was now concluded between the two brothers, according to the terms of which Hyrcanus, who undoubtedly was a weak and indolent character, was to renounce the royal and high-priestly rank, and to resign both to his brother Aristobulus. In return, he was to be left in the undisturbed enjoyment of his revenues.[2]

By all this the state of affairs had been by no means improved. For now the Idumean Antipater or Antipas, the
father of him who was afterwards King Herod, joined in the
game.[3] His father, who was also called Antipater, had by
Alexander Jannäus been appointed governor, στρατηγός, of
Idumea, and his son had now, as it seems, stepped into his
place. But the younger Antipater saw clearly that he could
assert his position much better under the government of the
weak and unmanly Hyrcanus, than under the warlike and
active Aristobulus. He therefore set all plans in motion for
overturning Aristobulus and restoring again Hyrcanus to the
head of affairs. First of all, he managed to win to himself
adherents from the most distinguished of the Jews, representing to them that Aristobulus, against all right and fairplay, had
seized upon the throne, while Hyrcanus was the legitimate ruler.
Then he turned to Hyrcanus, made it appear to him that his
life was in danger so long as Aristobulus held the reins of
government, and that at once, for his own sake, he must seek
his overthrow. The indolent and easy-minded Hyrcanus at
first gave him no hearing. But at last Antipater's endeavours
were successful. He had also secured the confederacy of the
Arabian prince Aretas, who promised that if Hyrcanus fled
to him, he should receive him as a friend. Now at length
Hyrcanus was induced to listen to the representations of
Antipater. In company with him, he fled by night from
Jerusalem, and betook himself to Petra, the capital of Aretas.
To him he gave the promise that, after he had won again the
sovereignty, he would restore to him the twelve cities which
Alexander Jannäus had taken from the Arabians; while Aretas,
on the other hand, undertook to lend him his support in
recovering the throne.[4]

In fulfilment of this promise Aretas went forth against
Aristobulus with an army, and conquered him in a battle. In
consequence of this victory a great part of the army of Aristo-

bulus went over to Hyrcanus, and indeed the people as a whole attached themselves to their old king. Only a few remained faithful to Aristobulus, so that he was obliged to withdraw to the temple mount, where he was besieged by Aretas and Hyrcanus. Of the period of this siege Josephus relates certain episodes which are highly characteristic of the Jewish piety of that time. On the side of Hyrcanus there was a certain Onias, who had attained unto a great reputation by having prayed to God for rain during a great drought, and having had his prayer immediately answered. They wished to make use of this man, or rather of the irresistible power of his prayers, to secure the destruction of the besieged. They conducted him into the camp, and insisted that he should solemnly invoke God's curse upon Aristobulus and his adherents. But instead of doing so, Onias went forth into the middle of the camp and said : " O God, the King of the whole world, since those that stand now with me are Thy people, and those that are besieged are also Thy priests, I beseech Thee that Thou wilt neither hearken to the prayers of those against these, nor bring to effect what these pray against those." But the people were so little in sympathy with this spirit of brotherly love in Onias that they immediately stoned him to death.[5] In connection therewith Josephus relates also another incident which places the besiegers in a by no means favourable light. The Passover festival came round,[6] at which the priests who were among the followers of Aristobulus wished at any cost to offer the appointed sacrifices. But they had no animals for sacrifice, and they knew of no other way of procuring such but by obtaining them for payment from the people of Hyrcanus. A thousand drachmas were demanded for the supply. The price was indeed preposterously extravagant. Yet, notwithstanding, the besieged consented to the terms, and passed out the money through an opening in the wall. The besiegers, however, after accepting of the money, still kept the animals to themselves. For this wickedness, as Josephus thinks, retribution soon came upon them. A violent storm burst forth which destroyed all the fruits of the field, so that the *modius* of wheat cost eleven drachmas. [7]

While this was going on, Pompey had meanwhile begun his victorious campaign in Asia. He had conquered Mithridates in B.C. 66, and had in the same year received the voluntary submission of Tigranes. While he himself now pressed on farther into Asia, he sent Scaurus to Syria in B.C. 65. When that general arrived at Damascus he heard of the war between the brothers in Judea, and pushed forward without delay to see how he might turn to account this strife between the rival princes. He had scarcely reached Judea when ambassadors presented themselves before him, both from Aristobulus and from Hyrcanus. They both sought his favour and support. Aristobulus offered him in return four hundred talents; and Hyrcanus could not be behind, and so promised the same sum. But Scaurus trusted Aristobulus rather because he was in a better position to fulfil his engagement, and so decided to take his side. He ordered Aretas to withdraw if he did not wish to be declared an enemy of the Romans. Aretas did not venture to show opposition. He therefore raised the siege, and thereupon Scaurus returned to Damascus. But Aristobulus pursued Aretas on his way homeward, and inflicted upon him a crushing defeat. [8]

But the Roman favour which Aristobulus had so exerted himself to secure, under the protection of which he believed himself to be safe, soon proved fatal to his wellbeing and that of his country. He himself left no stone unturned in order to win the goodwill of Pompey as well as of Scaurus. He sent Pompey a costly present, a skilfully wrought golden vine worth five hundred talents, which Strabo found still on view at Rome in the temple of Jupiter Capitolinus. [9]   But all this could not save Aristobulus, whenever Pompey found it to be for his advantage to withdraw his favour and take the side of Hyrcanus. In the spring of B.C. 63, Pompey proceeded from his winter quarters into Syria,[10] subdued the greater and smaller princes in the Lebanon,[11] and advanced by way of Heliopolis and Chalcis upon Damascus.[12] There he was met at one and the same time by representatives of three Jewish parties. Not only did Aristobulus and Hyrcanus appear, but the Jewish people also sent an embassy. Hyrcanus complained that Aristobulus, in defiance of all law, had violently assumed the government; Aristobulus justified his conduct by pointing out the incapacity of Hyrcanus. But the people wished to have nothing to do with either, asked for the abolition of the monarchy and the restoration of the old theocratic constitution of the priests.[13] Pompey heard them, but cautiously deferred any decision, and declared that he would put all things in order when he had accomplished his contemplated expedition against the Nabateans. Till then all parties were to maintain the peace.[14]

Aristobulus, however, was by no means satisfied with this arrangement, and betrayed his discontent by suddenly quitting Dium, whither he had accompanied Pompey on his expedition against the Nabateans.[17] Pompey grew suspicious, postponed his campaign against the Nabateans, and marched immediately against Aristobulus. He passed by Pella and crossed the Jordan near Scythopolis, and at Corea entered the territory of Judea proper.[15] Thence he sent messengers to Alexandrium, to which Aristobulus had fled, and ordered him to surrender the fortress. After long delay and manifold negotiations, Aristobulus did this, but at the same time went to Jerusalem in order that he might there prepare for resistance.[16] Pompey pursued him through Jericho, and soon appeared in the neighbourhood of Jerusalem. But now Aristobulus lost heart. He betook himself to the camp of

Pompey, gave him further presents, and promised to surrender
to him the city if Pompey would suspend hostilities. Pompey
was satisfied with this, and sent his general Gabinius to take
possession of the city, while he retained Aristobulus in the
camp. But Gabinius returned without having obtained his
object, for the people in the city had shut the gates against
him. Pompey was so enraged at this that he put Aristobulus
in prison, and immediately advanced against the city.[17] In
Jerusalem opinions were now divided. The adherents of
Aristobulus had no wish for peace, and resolved to defend
themselves to the utmost. The adherents of Hyrcanus, on
the other hand, regarded Pompey as their confederate, and
wished to open the gates to him. The latter were in the
majority, and succeeded in carrying out their purpose. The
city was surrendered to Pompey, who sent in his legate Piso,
and without drawing sword took possession of it. But the
war faction gathered together on the temple mount and there
prepared themselves for resistance.[18]

The temple mount was then, as afterwards, the strongest
point in Jerusalem. It presented to the east and the south a
sheer precipice. Also on the west it was separated from the
city by a deep ravine. Only on the north was there a
gradual slope; but even there approach was made almost
impossible by the construction of strong fortifications. In
this fortress, well-nigh impregnable, the adherents of Aristobulus had now taken refuge, and Pompey, whether he would
or not, had to engage upon a regular siege. It was quite
evident from the nature of the ground that the north side
must be the point of attack. A rampart was thrown up, and
on it were placed the great battering-rams and engines of war
which they had brought with them from Tyre. For a long
time the powerful walls withstood the shock of their blows.
At length, after a three months' siege, a breach was made in
the wall. A son of the dictator Sulla was the first to make

way through it with his troops.   Others quickly followed.
Then began a frightful massacre.   The priests, who were then
engaged offering sacrifice, would not desist from the execution
of their office, and were hewn down at the altar.   No less
than 12,000 Jews are said to have lost their lives in this
general butchery.   It was towards the close of autumn of the
year B.C. 63, under Cicero's consulship, according to Josephus
on the very day of atonement, according to Dio Cassius on a
Sabbath, that this holy city bowed its head before the Roman
commander.[19]

Pompey himself forced his way into the Most Holy Place,
into which only the feet of the high priest had ever before
entered.   But he left the treasures and precious things of
the temple untouched, and also took care that the service
of God should be continued without interruption.   On the
besieged he passed a severe sentence.   Those who had
promoted the war were beheaded ; the city and the country
were made tributary (τῇ χώρᾳ καὶ τοῖς Ἱεροσολύμοις ἐπι-
τάττει φόρον).[20]   The boundaries of the Jewish territories
were greatly curtailed.   All the coast towns from Raphia to
Dora were taken from the Jews ; and also all non-Jewish
towns on the east of the Jordan, such as Hippos, Gadara,
Pella, Dium, and others ; also Scythopolis and Samaria, with
the regions around them.   All these towns were immediately
put under the rule of the governor of the newly-formed
Roman province of Syria.[21]   The contracted Jewish territory
was given over to Hyrcanus II., who was recognised as high
priest, without the title of king.[22]

After Pompey had made these arrangements for the
government of Palestine, he sent Scaurus back as governor of
Syria, while he himself hasted away again to Asia Minor, and
first of all to Cilicia.   He took Aristobulus along with him
as a prisoner of war.   He had with him also his two daughters
and his sons Alexander and Antigonus, the former of whom

contrived almost immediately to make his escape.[23]—When, in B.C. 61, Pompey celebrated his triumph in Rome with great magnificence and display, the Jewish priest-king, the descendant of the Maccabees, was made to march in front of the conqueror's chariot.[24] Besides Aristobulus and his family, Pompey also had with him a great number of Jewish prisoners, who, at a later period being set at liberty, formed the original stock of the Jewish community at Rome, which quickly rose to a position of importance.[25]

With the institutions of Pompey the freedom of the Jewish people, after having existed for scarcely eighty years, if we reckon it as beginning in B.C. 142, was completely overthrown. Pompey, indeed, was acute enough to insist upon no essential change in the internal government of the country. He suffered the hierarchical constitution to remain intact, and gave the people as their high priest Hyrcanus II., who was favoured by the Pharisees. But the independence of the nation was at an end, and the Jewish high priest was a vassal of the Romans. This result, indeed, was inevitable from the moment the Romans set foot in Syria. For their power was altogether of a different sort from that of the Seleucidae. And even the most powerful of the princes, and one most loved by the people, would have been utterly unable to withstand the continued pressure of the superior forces of the Romans. But the work of conquest was made light to their Western assailants by the fact that the country was torn with internal strifes, and that the contending parties were so blind to their own interests as to seek protection and help from the strangers. There was no longer any trace left of that spirit which had led the people on to victory a hundred years before.

SECOND PERIOD.

FROM THE CONQUEST OF JERUSALEM BY POMPEY TO THE WAR OF HADRIAN.

THE ROMAN-HERODIAN AGE, B.C. 63–A.D. 135.

———•———

§ 13. HYRCANUS II. (63-40), ANTIPATER,

PHASAEL, AND HEROD

OWING to the meagreness of the sources, it is difficult to give an exact account of the position which Palestine at this time occupied in reference to the Romans. This much is certain, that it was tributary (Josephus, *Antiq.* xiv. 4. 4 ; *Wars of the Jews*, i. 7. 6), and lay under the general oversight of the Roman governor of Syria. But the question is, whether it was immediately incorporated or not with the province of Syria. In favour of the latter supposition might be alleged the statement of Josephus, that by the enactment of Gabinius, who divided Palestine into five sections, the country was now freed from monarchical rule: ἀσμένως δὲ τῆς ἐξ ἑνὸς ἐπικρατείας ἐλευθερωθέντες τὸ λοιπὸν ἀριστοκρατίᾳ διῳκοῦντο (*Wars of the Jews*, i. 8. 5). Hyrcanus therefore had stood at the head of the government of the country, and was subordinate only to the supervision of the Roman governor.

After the campaign of Pompey there followed for Palestine some years of peace. Scaurus as well as his two successors, Marcius Philippus and Lentulus Marcellinus, had still indeed some skirmishes with the Arabians.[1] But these had no influence upon the fortunes of Palestine. In A.D. 57, however, Aristobulus' son Alexander, who had escaped from his keepers on his way to Rome, sought to secure to himself the government of Palestine. He succeeded in collecting an army of 10,000 heavy-armed soldiers and 1500 horsemen, and got into his power the fortresses of the Alexandrium, Hyrcania, and Machaerus.[2] Gabinius, who had just then arrived as proconsul in Syria, sent against him, first of all, his lieutenant M. Antonius, afterwards the well-known triumvir, and soon followed with the main body of his troops. Alexander was defeated in an engagement near Jerusalem, and withdrew into the stronghold of the Alexandrium. Here he was besieged by Gabinius, and was compelled to surrender; but it would seem that, on condition of his yielding up the fortresses which were in his possession, he was allowed his freedom.[3] At this time, too, Gabinius made an important change in the political relations of Palestine. He assigned to Hyrcanus only the care of the temple, but took from him the political administration; for he divided the country into five districts (σύνοδοι, συνέδρια), with Jerusalem, Gazara, Amathus, Jericho, and Sepphoris as their capitals.[4] What is to be understood by those five σύνοδοι or συνέδρια is not altogether clear. They may be regarded as either customs, districts, or circuits, making the jurisdiction of law courts (conventus juridici).[5] The term συντελεῖν (Wars of the Jews, i. 8. 5: οἳ δ᾽ ἵνα συντελῶσιν εἰς Ἀμαθοῦντα) favours the former view; the term σύνοδοι (Wars of the Jews, i. 8. 5) favours the latter. Possibly the one view may not exclude the other. At least this measure of Gabinius took away the remnant of political independence which Palestine had hitherto enjoyed. Pompey having already deprived Hyrcanus of the title of king, the next step was to strip him of all political prerogatives and to restrict him to his priestly functions. The country was parted into five divisions, which were " delivered " from the dominion of Hyrcanus, *i.e.* were incorporated in the province of Syria. This arrangement was not indeed of long duration. By the ordinances of Caesar it was again wholly set aside.

Soon after this, in A.D. 56, the country was anew involved in a revolution by Aristobulus and his son Antigonus, who had both escaped from their Roman imprisonment. Aristobulus so completely failed to learn caution from the abortive attempt of his son Alexander, that he made himself a similar endeavour in that direction in which his son had failed. But he himself had no better fortune. A detachment of the Roman army attacked him, and the little band which he had gathered was, without much difficulty, driven across the Jordan. He attempted to defend himself in Machaerus; but was obliged after a two years' siege to yield, and was sent again as a prisoner to Rome. His children, however, were set at liberty by the senate.[6] Just then Gabinius, against the will of the senate, undertook the Egyptian campaign, in order to set up Ptolemy Auletes again as king.

When he returned from thence, in A.D. 55, he had once again to deal with a revolt in Judea. Alexander had made a fresh attempt to secure the sovereignty, and had won over to his side at least a part of the people. His proceedings, however, were also this time again brought to a speedy end.[7]

In A.D. 54 the triumvir, M. Licinius Crassus, went to Syria as proconsul in place of Gabinius. While Gabinius had already sorely oppressed the country by his exactions, Crassus at once began to indulge in open robbery. Pompey, upon the taking of the temple, had left its rich treasures untouched. Crassus now laid hold for himself of all these : in pure gold alone, 2000 talents; of other articles of value, 8000 talents.[8] Palestine was soon indeed delivered from his rapacity, for he met his death in A.D. 53 in the war against the Parthians.

During the period B.C. 53—51 C. Cassius Longinus, the quaestor of Crassus, held the supreme authority in Syria. He had not only to be on his guard against the Parthians, but also to suppress the revolutionary elements that were still always present in Palestine. Aristobulus, indeed, was detained in his Roman imprisonment, and his sons had for the time no wish to risk anew sharing his fate. But a certain Pitholaus now undertook to play their role, and gathered together the malcontents. He did not indeed succeed in his aim any better than those who had tried before. For the final issue of his undertaking was this, that he himself was slain, and 30,000 of the disturbers of the peace were sold as slaves.[9]

With the year B.C. 49 begins the period of the civil wars, disastrous for Italy as well as for the provinces, but peculiarly disastrous for the provinces, inasmuch as they were obliged to find the enormous sums which the contesting parties required for carrying on their operations. During these twenty years, from Caesar's crossing the Rubicon down to the death of Antony, B.C. 49—30, the whole Roman history was reflected in the history of Syria and also in that of Palestine. Every change and turn in the Roman history was answered by a corresponding movement in Syrian history, and during this short period Syria and Palestine changed sides and owned new masters no less than four times.

When, in the beginning of the year B.C. 49, Pompey and the party of the senate had fled from Italy, and Caesar had established himself in Rome, Caesar and his friends wished to make use of the prisoner Aristobulus for their own ends. And so they released him from prison and gave him two

legions, in order that with these he might fight in Syria
against the party of Pompey.   But the adherents of Pompey
who still remained in Rome put a stop to the enterprise by
ridding themselves of Aristobulus by poison.   At the same
time also one of Aristobulus' sons, Alexander, fell a victim to
the party strifes of the civil war.   He too had made his
appearance as an adherent of Caesar, and so he was now, at
the express command of Pompey, beheaded at Antioch by Q.
Metellus Scipio, Pompey's father-in-law, who was then proconsul for Syria.[10]

After the battle of Pharsalia, on 9th August B.C. 48, and
Pompey's death, on 28th September of the same year,
Hyrcanus and his old friend Antipater immediately attached
themselves to Caesar's party.[11]   They clearly perceived that
their safety depended wholly upon his grace, and therefore
they hastened to prove their capacity for serving him.
Caesar, after his landing in Egypt, in October B.C. 48, had
become involved in a war with King Ptolemy.   Mithridates
started from Pergamum in the spring of B.C. 47 to go into
Egypt with an auxiliary force.[12]   When he encountered
obstacles at Pelusium, Antipater went to his help, at the
command of Hyrcanus, with 3000 Jewish troops, which had
been indeed collected for this very purpose, and he had also
arranged that the neighbouring powers should contribute
auxiliaries.   With these Jewish troops Antipater rendered
most important service to Mithridates, not merely in the
capture of Pelusium, but also throughout the whole of the
Egyptian campaign.   Not less important was the aid rendered
by Hyrcanus in seeing to it that the Egyptian Jews ranged
themselves upon Caesar's side.[13]

When, therefore, Caesar, at the conclusion of the Alexandrian war, in the summer of B.C. 47, went to Syria and
rewarded, by proofs of his clemency, the governing families
that had favoured him,[14] Hyrcanus and Antipater were

treated in the most generous manner. Antigonus indeed appeared before Caesar as the only remaining son of Aristo-bulus, complained that Hyrcanus and Antipater had violently thrust themselves forward, and sought to show that his claims were older and better.[15]   But Caesar estimated the trust-worthiness and usefulness of Hyrcanus and Antipater more highly than the professions of Antigonus, ignored the claims of the latter, and showed favour exclusively to the other two. Even before the intervention of Antigonus, Hyrcanus seems to have been established as high priest, and upon Antipater the right of Roman citizenship and immunity from tribute had been conferred.[16]   Hyrcanus was now appointed ἐθνάρχης of the Jews, i.e. he was reinstated in the political authority that had been taken from him by Gabinius; but Antipater was made procurator, ἐπίτροπος, of Judea, and so confirmed in the authority with which he had been already invested.   At the same time permission was given to rebuild the walls of Jerusalem.[17]

We obtain further details with respect to the proceedings of Caesar from documents communicated by Josephus, Antiq. xiv. 10. 2–10, which, however, are so slight and fragmentary that in regard to many particulars no certain conclusion can be reached.   This, at least, is unquestionable, that the letter of Caesar to the Sidonians, Antiq. xiv. 10. 2, was written in the year B.C. 47, and that the formal decree of Caesar appointing Hyrcanus was issued in that same year.[18] According to this document, Hyrcanus was appointed hereditary ἐθνάρχης and ἀρχιερεύς of the Jews, with all the rights and privileges which belonged to him as high priest according to the Jewish law, and jurisdiction in all Jewish matters was conceded to the Jews.   Hyrcanus also, for himself and for his children, was declared the "confederate" of the Romans, and it was stipulated that the Roman troops should not seek winter quarters in his territory, nor should levies of

money be exacted.[19] It is uncertain whether some of the
other documents belong to this same year or not, but it is
certain that Hyrcanus, not long before Caesar's death, somewhere about the end of the year B.C. 45, sent an embassy to
Rome, which procured a decree of senate granting new concessions to the Jews. The beginning of this decree of senate,
under Caesar's fourth dictatorship and fifteenth consulship, *i.e.*
B.C. 44, is given in Josephus, *Antiq.* xiv. 10. 7. Its date is
probably correctly preserved in *Antiq.* xiv. 10. 10 : πρὸ
πέντε εἰδῶν Φεβρουαρίων, *i.e.* 9th February. As it was not
immediately put down in the tables of the treasury, a new
decree of senate was passed, after Caesar's death, during the
consulship of Antony and Dolabella, τῇ πρὸ τριῶν εἰδῶν
'Απριλλίων, *i.e.* 11th April B.C. 44, by which the recording
of the former decree of the senate in the tables of the
treasury was now ordered (*Antiq.* xiv. 10. 9–10). Since the
new decree is of a purely formal character, we gain no information from it regarding the contents of the claims conceded
to the Jews. Also, the fragment of the earlier decree preserved in *Antiq.* xiv. 10. 7 contains only the formal introduction. It is extremely probable, however, that other portions
of it are contained among the fragments in Josephus, *Antiq.*
xiv. 10. 3–6. Yet it is just here that the difficulties of the
investigation begin. The question arises as to what pieces
belong to the decree of senate of B.C. 44 and what to former
years, such as B.C. 47 or other years. Owing to the corrupt-
ness of the text, no certain result can ever be reached.[20] The
chief portion of the passage peculiarly rich in material,
Antiq. xiv. 10. 6, belongs most probably to B.C. 44. Among
the concessions there said to have been secured to the Jews,
the most important are these: that Joppa, " which the Jews
had originally, when they made a league of friendship with
the Romans," was made over to them ; that also the villages in
the great plain, which they had previously possessed, should

be restored to them ; and that, finally, also still other places "which belonged to the kings of Syria and Phoenicia, the confederates of the Romans," should now be given to them.[21] It may be assumed that these were merely possessions that had been taken away from them by Pompey. Of the places thus restored, Joppa, as affording a harbour, was the most important.

The Jews also, through Caesar's favour, obtained important privileges beyond the limits of Palestine. The Alexandrian Jews gained protection by having the privilege of Roman citizenship conferred upon them ;[22] and the Jews of Asia Minor were guaranteed the undisturbed exercise of their religion.[23] It was in accordance with the general course of Caesar's policy to keep the provincials contented, so as to secure the interests of the empire. But by none of the foreign peoples was so great a lamentation made over his death as by the Jews.[24]

The weak Hyrcanus, who had been installed in Palestine as "Ethnarch" of the Jews, held the government only in name. This was exercised in reality by the crafty and active Antipater. He now even appointed his two sons, Phasaël and Herod, governors, στρατηγοί, the one in Jerusalem and the other in Galilee.[25] Herod, whom we meet with here for the first time, was then a young man twenty-five years of age.[26] But even as early as this he gave proofs of that energy which brought him afterwards to the throne. In Galilee a robber chief named Hezekiah, with his numerous band, made the country insecure. Herod gained possession of his person, and had him executed along with many of his followers.[27] They were little accustomed in Jerusalem with such summary procedure. The aristocracy of that city regarded Herod's conduct as an infringement of the privileges of the Sanhedrim, to which tribunal alone it belonged to pass a death sentence ; and they therefore insisted that Hyrcanus

would call young Herod to answer for what he had done.
Hyrcanus yielded to their request, and summoned Herod
before the Sanhedrim at Jerusalem. Herod indeed appeared,
not, however, as became an accused person, in mourning
garments, but decked in purple, and attended by a bodyguard. When he thus entered the presence of the Sanhedrim,
complaints were hushed, and he would undoubtedly have
been exculpated, had not the celebrated Pharisee Sameas
(Shemaiah ?) arisen and aroused the conscience of his colleagues. They were now disposed to insist upon their
prerogatives and condemn Herod. But Hyrcanus had
received orders from Sextus Caesar, governor of Syria, to
secure Herod's acquittal. When he therefore perceived that
things were taking a dangerous turn, he suspended the
sitting, and advised Herod to withdraw secretly from the
city. Herod did so; but he soon returned with an army
against Jerusalem in order to avenge himself for the insult
that had been given him. Only the most urgent representations of his father Antipater succeeded in appeasing his
wrath, and restraining him from open violence. He then
returned to Galilee, comforting himself with the reflection
that he had at least given an exhibition of his power, and put
a wholesome terror upon his opponents.—During this conflict
with the Sanhedrim Herod was appointed, by Sextus Caesar,
governor of Coele-Syria, στρατηγὸς τῆς Κοίλης Συρίας.[28]

All this happened in B.C. 47, or in the beginning of
B.C. 46. In the spring of B.C. 46, while Caesar had to be
away fighting against the adherents of Pompey in Africa, one
of Pompey's party, Caecilius Bassus, succeeded in making
himself master of Syria by getting Sextus Caesar put out of
the way by the hand of an assassin. He was afterwards
besieged in Apamea by the Caesarian party, under the command of C. Antistius Vetus, in the autumn of the year
B.C. 45 To the forces of Vetus were also added the

troops of Antipater, which, as a new proof of his serviceableness to Caesar, he had sent to the aid of the Caesarian party.[29] The struggle of the two parties meanwhile continued without yielding any decisive result; and even the new governor, L. Statius Murcus, who arrived in Syria in the beginning of B.C. 44, and was supported by Marcius Crispus, the governor of Bithynia, obtained no decided advantage over Caecilius Bassus.

Meanwhile, on the 15th March B.C. 44, Caesar was murdered. Marc Antony resolved to avenge his death and continue his work. And it was only the fact that just then the fortunes of the party were in a rather backgoing condition that prevented the conspirators from also taking immediate steps in their own interest. It was only after Antony had proceeded against them in an openly hostile manner that the leaders of the conspiracy went to the East in order to collect their forces there : M. Brutus to Macedonia, L. Cassius to Syria. When Cassius, in the end of the year B.C. 44, arrived in Syria, Caecilius Bassus was still besieged by Statius Murcus and Marcius Crispus in Apamea. Although Murcus and Crispus had hitherto belonged to Caesar's party, they now placed their army at the service of Cassius, and Statius Murcus even offered his own personal aid. The legion of Caecilius Bassus also went over to Cassius. Thus did Cassius become master of Syria, and gained possession of a considerable fighting force. But for the support of the large and now further increasing army immense sums of money were necessary. And to this even the small Jewish land must contribute its share. It was laid by him under an arrestment of 700 talents, in the collection of which Antipater and his son Herod showed themselves particularly useful. For, with the same zeal with which they had once secured to themselves Caesar's favour, they now sought to win the goodwill of Cassius.

How useful this zeal was, some frightful examples in Judea itself showed. The inhabitants of the towns of Gophna, Emmaus, Lydda, and Thamna, because they could not contribute their share, were sold by Cassius as slaves.[30] But young Herod, as a reward for services rendered, was appointed by Cassius, as he had previously been by Sextus Caesar, governor (στρατηγός) of Coele-Syria.[31]

About this time, B.C. 43, Antipater became the victim of personal enmity. A certain Malichus endeavoured, just as Antipater had done, to gain an influential position in Judea. But Antipater, more than any one else, stood in the way of his realizing his ambition. He must therefore, if he was to gain his end, rid himself of that man. By bribery he won over the cupbearer of Hyrcanus, who put Antipater to death by poison as he was one day dining with Hyrcanus.[32]

Herod undertook to avenge the death of his father. While, therefore, Malichus was busying himself in the endeavour to carry out his ambitious plans and secure to himself the government of Judea, he was murdered in the neighbourhood of Tyre by hired assassins, whom Herod, with the connivance of Cassius, had sent.[33]

After Cassius had departed from Syria, in B.C. 42, still harder fortunes befell the province. Cassius had indeed wrung from it the most exorbitant sums, but now that the province was left to itself affairs fell into such a state of utter anarchy that there was no law but the will of the stronger. During this period Antigonus also made an attempt, with the assistance of Ptolemy the son of Mennaeus of Chalcis, to secure the sovereignty of Palestine. Favoured by fate and fortune, Herod indeed frustrated this attempt, but he was not able to prevent Marion, tyrant of Tyre, from snatching to himself certain portions of Galilean territory.[34]

A new crisis arose in Palestine, and especially in the

fortunes of the two Idumeans Phasael and Herod, when, late in autumn of the year B.C. 42, Brutus and Cassius were defeated at Philippi by Antony and Octavian. With this one stroke all Asia fell into the hands of Antony. The situation was all the more critical for Phasael and Herod, after an embassy of the Jewish nobility appeared before Antony in Bithynia about the beginning of B.C. 41, and made complaints against these two princes. Yet Herod succeeded by personal explanations in neutralizing for the time being the effect of these charges.[35] Soon after this, while Antony lingered in Ephesus, an embassy from Hyrcanus appeared before him asking that Antony should give orders for the emancipation of the Jews sold into slavery by Cassius, and for the restoration of the places that had been conquered by the Tyrians. Antony readily assumed the role of the protector of all rights and privileges, and issued the orders prayed for, with violent denunciation of the lawless proceedings of Cassius.[36]—Some time afterwards, in the autumn of B.C. 41, when Antony had gone to Antioch, the Jewish nobles renewed their charges against Phasael and Herod. But neither at this time did they lead to any result. Antony, when he was serving in Syria under Gabinius in B.C. 57-55, had been for many years the intimate friend of Antipater. That friendship he did not now forget. And since, besides, Hyrcanus, who had also gone to Antioch, gave a favourable account of the two brothers, Antony appointed Phasael and Herod tetrarchs of the country of the Jews.[37] Hyrcanus was then stripped of his political authority. He did not indeed mourn over the loss, for he had for a long time possessed political authority only in name.

The period of Antony's residence in Syria was for the province a time of sore oppression. His luxurious style of living consumed enormous sums of money, and these the provinces were required to provide. Thus, wherever Antony went exorbitant taxes were invariably imposed; and Palestine was not by any means allowed to escape.[38]

In the year B.C. 40, while Antony was during part of the time held in thrall by Cleopatra in Egypt, and during another part occupied with the affairs of Italy, the great invasion of the Parthians occurred, who overran all Further Asia with their wild hordes.   And in consequence of this occurrence Antigonus succeeded, for a while at least, in securing the end for which he had been striving.

As the Parthians under Pacorus and Barzapharnes, the former the son of King Orodes, the latter a Parthian satrap, had already occupied Northern Syria, Antigonus succeeded in persuading them, by great promises, to aid him in securing possession of the Jewish throne.   Pacorus marched along to the Phoenician coast, Barzapharnes advanced into the interior of the country toward the south.   Pacorus sent to Jerusalem a detachment under the leadership of the king's cupbearer, whose name was also Pacorus.   Before that company arrived at the city, Antigonus had already succeeded in gathering around him a company of adherents from among the Jews, and had with it advanced upon Jerusalem, where the battle was waged daily between him on the one hand and Phasael and Herod on the other.[39]   In the meantime the Parthian troops under Pacorus arrived.   The Parthian gave out that he desired to settle terms of peace, and demanded of Phasael that he should go to the camp of Barzapharnes in order that he might put an end to this strife.   Although Herod earnestly warned his brother, Phasael walked into the snare, and went along with Hyrcanus and Pacorus, the cupbearer, to the camp of Barzapharnes.   A small detachment of Parthian horsemen remained behind in Jerusalem.[40]   In the Parthian camp the mask was soon thrown aside, and the two princes, Phasael and Hyrcanus, were put in irons.[41] When Herod was told of this, not being strong enough to offer open opposition, he resolved to escape from Jerusalem by flight. Without attracting the attention of the Parthians, he had the female members of his family and the children carried out of the city and brought to the fortress of Masada, which he put under the charge of his brother Joseph.[42] Meanwhile, on the spot where at a later period he built the fortress Herodium, he had to fight with the Jews, who were still hostile to him. He was able, however, successfully to repel their attack. After he had thus secured all belonging to him in a stronghold, he continued his flight farther southward, and went first of all to Petra in Arabia.[43]

Their friendship for Antigonus did not restrain the Parthians from plundering the country round about the capital. Phasael and Hyrcanus were now placed at the disposal of Antigonus. The ears of Hyrcanus were cut off, so that he might no longer be eligible for the office of high priest. Phasael, on the contrary, escaped the hands of his enemies by dashing his head upon a rock after he had received the joyful tidings of the fortunate flight of his brother.

Afterwards the Parthians carried away Hyrcanus with them as a prisoner, and set up Antigonus as king.[44]

§ 14. ANTIGONUS, B.C. 40-37

ANTIGONUS, or, as he was called according to the evidence of the coins by his Hebrew name, Mattathias, had thus by the help of the Parthians reached that position after which his father and brother had vainly striven. After the example of his forefathers, from the time of Aristobulus I., he assumed the rank and title of "king" and "high priest" (on the coins: *BACIΛEΩC ANTIΓONOT*, מתתיה הכהן הגדל).

The hopes of Herod rested simply and wholly on Roman aid. Without going to Petra — for the Arabian prince Malchus had forbidden him to visit his country—he proceeded to Alexandria, and thence took ship for Rome, although already the autumn storms had begun. After passing through various dangers, he managed to reach Rome by Rhodes and Brundusium, and immediately upon his arrival he laid his sad complaint before Antony.[1] Herod knew how to win favour, whenever that had to be gained, by means of money. And so it happened that he, after having secured also the goodwill of Octavian, was declared at a formal session of the senate to be king of Judea. The appointment was celebrated by a sacrifice at the capitol and a banquet by Antony.[2]

From the appointment to the actual possession of the office was now indeed a longer and a more difficult step.

For the time being the Parthians, and their *protégé* Antigonus, still maintained their authority in the country. The
Parthians were indeed driven out of Syria in the year
B.C. 39 by Ventidius, the legate of Marc Antony. But
from Antigonus, Ventidius only exacted a heavy tribute,
and left him otherwise undisturbed. And Silo also, his
lieutenant, pursued a similar policy after the departure of
Ventidius.[3]

This was the state of matters when Herod, in B.C. 39,
landed at Ptolemais. He quickly collected an army; and
as now Ventidius and Silo, at the command of Antony,
supported him, he soon made progress. First of all Joppa
fell into his hands. Then also he gained possession of
Masada, where his relatives had hitherto been besieged.
As he succeeded, the number of his adherents increased,
and he could even venture to go to Jerusalem and lay
siege to it. He made nothing, however, of this attempt at
the time, for the Roman troops of Silo, which were to have
supported him, assumed a stubborn and defiant attitude, and
insisted upon withdrawing into winter quarters.[4]

In the spring of the year B.C. 38, the Parthians renewed
the attack upon Syria. While thus Ventidius and Silo
had to go forth to fight against them, Herod sought to
subdue the country wholly under him, and to rescue it out
of the hands of many adventurers. Vast bands of brigands
concealed themselves, especially among the inaccessible
caverns in the mountain gorges of Galilee. But even of
these Herod knew how to gain possession, for he let down
his soldiers in large chests (λάρνακες) from the lofty rocky
peak, and thus secured for them an entrance into the
caves.[5]

Meanwhile, however, the Parthians were conquered by
Ventidius on 9th June B.C. 38. And that general then
turned his attention against Antiochus of Commagene, and

laid siege to him in his capital of Samosata. During the
siege Antony himself arrived at Samosata. Herod could
not let this opportunity escape of speaking to his patron;
for he had good grounds for complaining of the way in
which support had been withheld from him. He therefore
now proceeded to Samosata in order to pay his respects to
Antony. He received him very graciously, and as the
surrender of Samosata soon afterwards took place, Antony
instructed Sosius, the successor of Ventidius, to afford efficient
assistance to Herod.[6]

In Palestine, during the absence of Herod, matters were
in a bad way. Joseph, the brother of Herod, to whom he
had in the meantime transferred the chief command, had
been attacked by an army of Antigonus, and was himself
slain in the battle, and Antigonus had ordered his head to
be struck off. In consequence of these events, the Galileans
had seized the opportunity to rise again against Herod, and
had drowned his adherents in the lake of Gennesareth.[7]

A full report of all these proceedings reached Herod at
Antioch, and he now hastened to avenge the death of his
brother. Galilee was without difficulty reconquered. At
Jericho he encountered the army of Antigonus, but did not,
it would seem, venture upon any decisive engagement. It
was only when Antigonus divided his forces, and sent a
portion of his troops under Pappus to Samaria, that Herod
courted a regular contest. Pappus and Herod came together
near Isana. The first attack was made by Pappus, but he
was utterly defeated by Herod, and driven into the city,
where all who had not managed to save themselves by
flight were ruthlessly cut down. Pappus himself there met
his death. With the exception of the capital, all Palestine
thereby fell into the hands of Herod. Only the coming on
of winter hindered him from beginning immediately the siege
of Jerusalem.[8]

In the spring of B.C. 37, so soon as the season of the year admitted of it, Herod laid siege to the capital, and began by the erection of military engines of assault. When these were ready for operating, he left the army for a little while and went to Samaria, in order there to celebrate his marriage with Mariamme, a granddaughter of Hyrcanus, to whom he had been engaged for five years. This engagement had been entered into in B.C. 42 (*Antiq.* xiv. 12. 1; *Wars of the Jews*, i. 12. 3).[9]

After the celebration of the marriage he returned again to the camp. Sosius also now appeared before Jerusalem with a great army; and Herod and Sosius made a joint attack upon the city. They made their onslaught, as Pompey had done, from the north. On this side mighty ramparts were raised, and against these the battering-rams began to play. Forty days after the beginning of these operations, the first rampart was taken; after fifteen days more the second also fell. But the inner court of the temple and the upper city were always still in the hands of the besieged. At last these too were stormed, and the besiegers now went on murdering in the city all whom they could lay their hands upon. Antigonus himself fell at the feet of Sosius and entreated of him mercy. The Roman looked upon him with scorn, called him Antigone, and had him bound in fetters. It was now Herod's greatest care to rid himself as soon as possible of his Roman friends. For the murdering and plundering that was going on in what was now again his capital could not possibly be pleasing to him. By means of rich presents he succeeded at last in inducing Sosius and his troops to take their departure.[10]

In this way was Herod, almost three years after his appointment, enabled to enter on the actual possession of his sovereignty. Antigonus was carried away by Sosius to Antioch, and there, in accordance with the wish of Herod, he was by Antony's orders led to the block.   It was the first time that the Romans had executed such a sentence on a king.[11]

The rule of the Asmonean dynasty was thus brought to an end.

§ 15. HEROD THE GREAT, B.C. 37-4

B.C.	A.U.C.	
37	717	Conquest of Jerusalem, some time in July. Executions, Josephus, *Antiq.* xv. 1. 2 ; compare xiv. 9. 4, *fin. ; Wars of the Jews,* i. 18. 4.
36	718	Hyrcanus II. returns from the Parthian imprisonment, *Antiq.* xv. 2. 1–4.
35	719	Beginning of the year : Aristobulus III., brother of Mariamme, is at the instigation of his mother Alexandra nominated high priest by Herod, *Antiq.* xv. 2. 5–7, 3. 1.[2]
		End of the year : Aristobulus III. is by Herod's order, soon after the Feast of Tabernacles, drowned in the bath at Jericho, τὴν ἀρχιερωσύνην κατασχὼν ἐνιαυτόν, *Antiq.* xv. 3. 3 · *Wars of the Jews,* i. 22. 2.
34	720	Herod is summoned by Antony to Laodicea to answer for the death of Aristobulus, but is dismissed with Antony's favour, *Antiq.* xv. 3. 5 and 8. 9.[3]
34	720	Joseph, the husband of Herod's sister Salome, is executed, *Antiq.* xv. 3. 9.
		Antony presents to Cleopatra the Phoenician coasts, with the exception of Tyre and Sidon,

B.C.	A.U.C.	
		and portions of Arabia and Judea; the region around Jericho being specially excepted, *Antiq.* xv. 4. 1–2; *Wars of the Jews*, i. 18. 5.[4]
		Cleopatra with Herod in Jerusalem, *Antiq.* xv. 4. 2; *Wars of the Jews*, i. 18. 5.
32	722	War of Herod with the Arabians, after the out-break of hostilities between Antony and Octavian, *Antiq.* xv. 5. 1; *Wars of the Jews*, i. 19. 1–3.
		Earthquake in Palestine, *Antiq.* xv. 5. 2; *Wars of the Jews*, i. 19. 3 : κατ' ἔτος μὲν τῆς βασιλείας ἕβδομον, ἀκμάζοντος δὲ τοῦ περὶ ῎Ακτιον πολέμου, ἀρχομένου ἔαρος.[5]
32	722	Herod conquers the Arabians, *Antiq.* xv. 5. 2-5; *Wars of the Jews*, i. 19. 3–6.
		After the battle at Actium on 2nd September, Herod attached himself to the party of Augustus, for he supported Didius in the struggle with Antony's gladiators; compare *Antiq.* xv. 6. 7; *Wars of the Jews*, i. 20. 2. Also above, p. 345.
30	724	Spring: Hyrcanus II. executed, *Antiq.* xv. 6. 1–4; *Wars of the Jews*, i. 22. 1; πλείω μὲν ἢ ὀγδοήκοντα γεγονὼς ἐτύγχανεν ἔτη, *Antiq.* xv. 6. 3.[6]
		Herod visits Augustus at Rhodes, and is by him made king, *Antiq.* xv. 6. 5–7; *Wars of the Jews*, i. 20. 1–3.
		He attaches himself to Augustus on his march to Egypt at Ptolemais, *Antiq.* xv. 6. 7; *Wars of the Jews*, i. 20. 3.
		Autumn: Herod visits Augustus in Egypt, and gets Jericho back from him, as also Gadara, Hippo, Samaria, Gaza, Anthedon, Joppa, Straton's Tower, *Antiq.* xv. 7. 3; *Wars of the Jews*, i. 20. 3.

B.C.	A.U.C.	
		End of the year : he accompanies Augustus on his return from Egypt as far as Antioch, *Antiq.* xv. 7. 4.
29	725	End of the year : Mariamme executed, *Antiq.* xv. 7. 4–6 ; *Wars of the Jews,* i. 22. 3–5 (*Antiq.* xv. 7. 4 : ἤ τε ὑποψία τρεφομένη παρέτεινεν ἐνιαυτοῦ μῆκος, ἐξ οὗ παρὰ Καίσαρος Ἡρώδης ὑποστρέφει).
28 ?		Alexandra executed, *Antiq.* xv. 7. 8.
25	729	Costobar, the second husband of Salome, and the sons of Babas, executed, *Antiq.* xv. 7. 10. The date is discovered from the statement of Salome : ὅτι διασώζοιντο παρ᾽ αὐτῷ χρόνον ἐνιαυτῶν ἤδη δώδεκα, that is, after the overthrow of Jerusalem in B.C. 37.
?		The four years' contendings begun. Theatre and amphitheatre built in Jerusalem, *Antiq.* xv. 8. 1.
?		Conspiracy against Herod, *Antiq.* xv. 8. 3–4.
27	727	Samaria rebuilt and named in honour of Augustus Sebaste, *Antiq.* xv. 8. 5 ; *Wars of the Jews,* i. 21. 2.
25	729	Famine and pestilence (κατὰ τοῦτον μὲν οὖν τὸν ἐνιαυτόν, τρισκαιδέκατον ὄντα τῆς Ἡρώδου βασιλείας = B.C. 25–24, from Nisan to Nisan), *Antiq.* xv. 9. 1. The famine continues also into the following year, B.C. 24–23, *Antiq.* xv. 9. 1, when Petronius was governor of Egypt, *Antiq.* xv. 9. 2.
25	729	Herod sends 500 men as auxiliaries to the expedition of Aelius Gallus against Arabia, *Antiq.* xv. 9. 3 ; compare Strabo, xvi. 4. 23, p. 780 : συμμάχων, ὧν ἦσαν Ἰουδαῖοι μὲν πεντακόσιοι.— The campaign ended in the following year, B.C.

B.C.	A.U.C.	
		24, disastrously, and without any appreciable results.[7]
?		Herod builds for himself a royal palace, and marries the priest's daughter, Mariamme, *Antiq.* xv. 9. 3 (the name: *Wars of the Jews*, i. 28. 4, 29. 2, 30. 7).
		The building of Caesarea is begun, *Antiq.* xv. 9. 6. Since the building after twelve years' labour was completed in B.C. 10, the works must have been begun in B.C. 22.
23	731	The sons of the first Mariamme, Alexander and Aristobulus, are sent to Rome for their education, *Antiq.* xv. 10. 1.
		Augustus bestows upon Herod the provinces of Trachonitis, Batanaea, and Auranitis, *Antiq.* xv. 10. 1; *Wars of the Jews*, i. 20. 4 (μετὰ τὴν πρώτην Ἀκτιάδα).[8]
22	732	Herod visits Agrippa in Mytilene in Lesbos, *Antiq.* xv. 10. 2.[9]
20	734	Augustus comes to Syria and bestows upon Herod the territory of Zenodorus, *Antiq.* xv. 10. 3: ἤδη αὐτοῦ τῆς βασιλείας ἑπτακαιδεκάτου παρελθόντος ἔτους (the seventeenth year of Herod extended to 1st Nisan at the end of the year B.C. 20); *Wars of the Jews*, i. 20. 4: ἔτει δεκάτῳ πάλιν ἐλθὼν εἰς τὴν ἐπαρχίαν (also reckoned from the end of the year B.C. 30).—Dio Cassius, liv. 7, places the visit of Augustus to Syria in the consulship of M. Appuleius and P. Silius, A.U.C. 734.—Also Dio Cassius, liv. 9, makes mention of that presentation.
		Pheroras appointed tetrarch of Perea, *Antiq.* xv. 10. 3; *Wars of the Jews*, i. 24. 5; compare i. 30. 3.

B.C.   A.U.C.

Herod remits one-third of the taxes, *Antiq.* xv.
10. 4.

Begins the temple building, *Antiq.* xv. 11. 1 : ὀκτω-
καιδεκάτου τῆς Ἡρώδου βασιλείας γεγονοτος
ἐνιαυτοῦ = B.C. 20–19.[10]

18 or 17 | Herod fetches his sons Alexander and Aristobulus
home from Rome : the first Roman voyage of
Herod,[11] *Antiq.* xvi. 1. 2.—Since Herod met
Augustus in Italy, and as Augustus did not
return to Italy before˛ the summer of B.C. 19,
the journey of Herod must be placed at the
earliest in the middle of the year B.C. 19, and
at latest before the summer of B.C. 16, since
Augustus was in Gaul from the summer of B.C.
16 till the spring of B.C. 13.

15   739 | Agrippa visits Herod in Jerusalem, *Antiq.* xvi.
2. 1 (Philo, *Legat. ad Cajum*, § 37, ed. Mangey,
ii. 589).—He left Judea again before the end
of the year : ἐπιβαίνοντος τοῦ χειμῶνος.

14   740 | Herod with Agrippa in Asia Minor, *Antiq.* xvi. 2.
2–5 (ἔαρος ἠπείγετο συντυχεῖν αὐτῷ).   Compare
also : *Antiq.* xii. 3. 2 ; Nicolas of Damascus
in Müller, *Fragment. Hist. Graecor.* iii. 350.

After his return he remits a fourth part of the
taxes, *Antiq.* xvi. 2. 5.

Beginning of quarrels with the sons of Mariamme,
Alexander and Aristobulus.—Antipater brought
to the court, *Antiq.* xvi. 3. 1–3 ; *Wars of the
Jews*, i. 23. 1.

13   741 | Antipater is sent with Agrippa to Rome that he
might be presented to the emperor, *Antiq.* xvi.
3. 3 ; *Wars of the Jews*, i. 23. 2.

12   742 | Herod goes with his sons Alexander and Aristo-
bulus to Rome in order to accuse them before

B.C.	A.U.C.	
		the emperor. Herod's second Roman journey. He meets the emperor at Aquileia. Augustus reconciles the discord.—Antipater returns back with them to Judea, *Antiq.* xvi. 4. 1–6 ; *Wars of the Jews*, i. 23. 3–5.
10	744	The celebration of the completion of the building of Caesarea fell εἰς ὄγδοον καὶ εἰκοστὸν ἔτος τῆς ἀρχῆς = B.C. 10–9, *Antiq.* xvi. 5. 1 ; after it had been twelve years in building, *Antiq.* xv. 9. 6 : ἐξετελέσθη δωδεκαετεῖ χρόνῳ (xvi. 5. 1 says : ten years, which is certainly wrong). On the building, compare also *Wars of the Jews*, i. 21. 5–8.
?		The quarrel in Herod's family becomes more and more bitter and complicated, *Antiq.* xvi. 7. 2–6 ; *Wars of the Jews*, i. 24. 1–6.
?		Herod by torturing Alexander's dependants seeks to fasten guilt upon him ; Alexander is cast into prison, *Antiq.* xvi. 8. 1–5; *Wars of the Jews*, i. 24. 7–8.
10 ?		Archelaus, king of Cappadocia, Alexander's father-in-law, effects once more a reconciliation between Herod and his sons, *Antiq.* xvi. 8. 6 ; *Wars of the Jews*, i. 25. 1–6.
		Herod's third journey to Rome, *Antiq.* xvi. 9. 1.
9 ?		Campaign against the Arabians, *Antiq.* xvi. 9. 2.
8 ?		Herod in disfavour with Augustus, *Antiq.* xvi. 9. 3.
		Herod having extorted by torture damaging statements against Aristobulus and Alexander, has them cast into prison, and accuses them to Augustus of high treason, *Antiq.* xvi. 10. 3–7 ; *Wars of the Jews*, i. 26. 3, 27. 1.

B.C.	A.U.C.	

7 ?   Augustus, having again become favourable to Herod through the good offices of Nicolaus of Damascus (*Antiq.* xvi. 10. 8–9), gives him full power to deal with his sons according to his own discretion, *Antiq.* xvi. 11. 1 ; *Wars of the Jews*, i. 27. 1.

Alexander and Aristobulus condemned to death at Berytus, and strangled at Sebaste (Samaria), *Antiq.* xvi. 11. 2–7 ; *Wars of the Jews*, i. 27. 2–6.

Antipater all - powerful at Herod's court, *Antiq.* xvii. 1. 1, 2. 4 ; *Wars of the Jews*, i. 28. 1, 29. 1.

Executions of suspected Pharisees, *Antiq.* xvii. 2. 4.

6 ?   Antipater goes to Rome, *Antiq.* xvii. 3. 2 ; *Wars of the Jews*, i. 29. 2.

First testament or will of Herod, in which he named Antipater, or if he should die before himself, Herod, the son of the second Mariamme, his successor, *Antiq.* xvii. 3. 2 ; *Wars of the Jews*, i. 29. 2.

5   749   Beginning of the year : Pheroras, Herod's brother, dies, *Antiq.* xvii. 3. 3 ; *Wars of the Jews*, i. 29. 4.

Herod discovers Antipater's hostile designs, *Antiq.* xvii. 4. 1–2 ; *Wars of the Jews*, i. 30. 1–7.

Antipater returns again to Judea, *Antiq.* xvii. 5. 1–2 ; *Wars of the Jews*, i. 31. 3–5 ; seven months after Herod had made that discovery, *Antiq.* xvii. 4. 3 ; *Wars of the Jews*, i. 31. 2.

Antipater on his trial ; seeks in vain to justify himself, and is put in chains, *Antiq.* xvii. 5. 3–7 ; *Wars of the Jews*, i. 32. 1–5.

Herod reports the matter to the emperor, *Antiq.*

B.C. A.U.C.

xvii. 5. 7–8 ; *Wars of the Jews*, i. 32. 5.

Herod is ill and makes his second testament, in which he appoints his youngest son Antipater his successor, *Antiq.* xvii. 6. 1; *Wars of the Jews*, i. 33. 5.

4   750   Revolt of the people under the rabbis Judas and Matthias rigorously suppressed by Herod, *Antiq.* xvii. 6. 2–4; *Wars of the Jews*, i. 33. 1–4.

Herod's illness becomes more severe, *Antiq.* xvii. 6. 5 ; *Wars of the Jews*, i. 33. 5.

Antipater, after leave had been obtained from the emperor, is executed, *Antiq.* xvii. 7; *Wars of the Jews*, i. 33. 7.

Herod again changes his will, for he appoints Archelaus king, and Antipas and Philip tetrarchs, *Antiq.* xvii. 8. 1; *Wars of the Jews*, i. 33. 7.

Herod dies five days after the execution of Antipater, βασιλεύσας μεθ᾽ ὃ μὲν ἀνεῖλεν Ἀντίγονον, ἔτη τέσσαρα καὶ τριάκοντα, μεθ᾽ ὃ δὲ ὑπὸ Ῥωμαίων ἀπεδέδεικτο, ἑπτὰ καὶ τριάκοντα, *Antiq.* xvii. 8. 1 ; *Wars of the Jews*, i. 33. 8.

Herod   was born to be a ruler.   Blessed by nature with a powerful body capable of enduring fatigue, he early inured himself to all manner of hardships.   He was a skilful rider, and a bold, daring huntsman.   He was feared in pugilistic encounters.   His lance was unerring, and his arrow seldom missed its mark.[12]   He was practised in the art of war from his youth.   Even in his twenty-fifth year he had won renown by his expedition against the robbers of Galilee.   And then again, in the later period of his life, when over sixty years of age, he led in person the campaign against the Arabians.[13]

Rarely did success forsake him where he himself conducted any warlike undertaking.

His character was wild and passionate, harsh and unbending. Fine feelings and tender emotions were strange to him. Wherever his own interests seemed to demand it, he carried matters through with an iron hand, and scrupled not to shed streams of blood that he might reach his object. Even his nearest relatives, even his most passionately loved wife, he could not spare, so soon as the wish arose in him.

He was, besides, cunning and adroit, and rich in devices. He understood thoroughly what measures should be taken to suit the circumstances of each changing day. Hard and unpitying as he was toward all who fell into his power, he was cringing and servile before those that were high in place. His glance was wide enough in its range, and his judgment sufficiently keen to perceive that in the circumstances of the world at that time nothing was to be reached except through the favour and by the help of the Romans. It was therefore an unvarying principle of his policy to hold firmly by the Roman alliance under all circumstances and at any cost. And he knew how to carry out this principle happily and cleverly.

Thus in his composition were linked together cunning and energy.

But these most conspicuous characteristics of his nature were set in motion by an insatiable ambition. All his devices and endeavours, all his plans and actions, were aimed directly toward the one end: the extending of his power, his dominion, his glory.[14] This powerful lever kept all his powers in restless activity. Difficulties and hindrances were for him so much greater inducement to put forth more strength. And this indefatigableness, this unwearied striving, continued to characterize him in extreme old age.

Only by a combination of all these characteristics was it

possible to attain to such greatness, as he unquestionably reached, amid the perilous circumstances of his times.

His reign falls into three periods. The first period, which reaches from B.C. 37 to B.C. 25, is the period of the consolidation of his power. He has still to contend with many hostile powers, but goes forth at last from the conflict victorious over them all. The second period, from B.C. 25 to B.C. 13, is the period of his prosperity. The friendship of Rome has reached its highest point. Agrippa visits Herod in Jerusalem. Herod is repeatedly received by the emperor. It is at the same time the period of great buildings, pre-eminently the work of peace. The third period, from B.C. 13 to B.C. 4, is the period of domestic trouble. Everything else now passes out of view in presence of the disturbances in Herod's own house.

I.

In the first period of his reign Herod had to contend with many powerful adversaries : the people, the nobles, the Asmonean family, and—Cleopatra.

The people, who were wholly in the hands of the Pharisees, tolerated only with deep aversion the dominion of the Idumean, half-Jew and friend of the Romans.[15] It must have been Herod's first care to secure their obedience. By the utmost rigour he was able to reduce the rebellious elements ; while he won the more pliant by bestowing on them favours and honours. Even of the Pharisees themselves two performed good services for Herod — Polio (Abtalion) and his scholar Sameas (Shemaia or Shammai). They saw in the dominion of the foreigner a judgment of God, which as such they were under obligation patiently to bear.[16]

Among the nobles of Jerusalem there were numerous

adherents of Antigonus. Herod delivered himself from them
by executing forty-five of the most wealthy and the most
prominent of their number. By confiscating their property
he gained possession of abundance of money, which he
employed so as to secure a firmer hold upon his patron
Antony.[17]

Of the members of the Asmonean family, it was particularly Alexandra, Herod's mother-in-law, the mother of
Mariamme, who pursued him with unremitting enmity. The
aged Hyrcanus had indeed returned from his Parthian
exile;[18] but he was before that time on good terms with
Herod. And this good understanding still continued undisturbed. Since he could not, owing to his physical
mutilation, enter again on the high priest's office, Herod
chose as high priest an utterly unknown and insignificant
Babylonian Jew of the sacerdotal family called Ananel.[19]
But even this was considered by Alexandra an infringement
of Asmonean privileges. According to her view, it was her
young son Aristobulus, brother of Mariamme, who alone was
entitled to the high priest's office. She therefore set every
wheel in motion in order to secure her rights. In particular,
she applied to Cleopatra, urging her to exert her influence
upon Antony, so as to force Herod to appoint Aristobulus
high priest. Mariamme also pressed her husband with
petitions in favour of her brother. Thus Herod at last
felt himself obliged to set aside Ananel (which was unlawful,
inasmuch as the high priest held his office for life), and in
the beginning of B.C. 35 made young Aristobulus high priest,
who was now only in his seventeenth year.[20]

The peace, however, was not of long duration. Herod
saw, and not without reason, in all the members of the
Asmonean family his natural enemies. He could not rid
himself of suspicion and distrust, especially in regard to
Alexandra, and he kept a careful watch upon her proceed-

ings. This constant espionage Alexandra found intolerable,
and thought to escape such supervision by flight.   The
coffins were already prepared in which she and her son
Aristobulus were to have had themselves carried out of the
city and thence to the sea-coast, so as to fly to Egypt to
Cleopatra.   But their secret was betrayed, and so their
scheme proved futile, and thus it only served to increase
the suspicions of Herod.[21]—When, moreover, the people, at
the next Feast of Tabernacles, in B.C. 35, made a public
demonstration in favour of young Aristobulus while he officiated
as high priest, Herod became thoroughly determined to rid
himself, without delay, of Aristobulus as his most dangerous
enemy and rival.   Soon an opportunity for doing so was
given him.   Herod had been invited to Jericho to a feast by
Alexandra.   And after the meal, as young Aristobulus along
with others was refreshing himself in the bath, he was
pushed under the water as if in sport by some of those with
him who had been bribed by Herod, and kept down so long
that he was drowned.   After the affair was done Herod
pretended the most profound grief, and shed tears, which,
however, nobody regarded as genuine.[22]

Alexandra, who clearly perceived the true state of matters,
agitated again through Cleopatra, so that Herod was summoned to make answer before Antony for the deed.   Antony,
who since the spring of B.C. 36 had been again residing in
the East, and under the spell of Cleopatra, was just then, in
the spring of B.C. 34, undertaking a new expedition to the
West, ostensibly against the Parthians, really against the
Armenian king Artavasdes.   When he had now reached
Laodicea, that is, Laodicea by the sea, south of Antioch,
Herod was summoned to meet him there,—for Alexandra
had, through Cleopatra, actually obtained her wish,—to give
an account of his conduct.   Herod did not dare to refuse,
and, no doubt with a heavy heart, presented himself before

Antony. But it may be readily supposed he did not go empty-handed. This circumstance and his clever representations soon prevailed in dispelling all clouds. He was pronounced innocent, and returned to Jerusalem.[23]

His absence was the occasion of fresh disturbances. He had on his departure appointed his uncle Joseph, who was also his brother-in-law, for he had married his sister Salome, as his viceroy, and had committed Mariamme to his care. And as he considered his going before Antony as dangerous, he had commanded Joseph, in case he should not return, to kill Mariamme, for his passionate love for her could not brook the thought that any other should ever obtain his beloved. When, then, he did return, Salome calumniated her own husband, charging him with having himself had unlawful intercourse with Mariamme. Herod at first gave no heed to the calumny, as Mariamme maintained her innocence. But when he learned that Mariamme knew about that secret command, which the chattering old man had told her as a proof of the peculiar love of Herod, Herod thought that he had in this a confirmation of those charges, and caused Joseph to be executed, without affording him an opportunity of being heard.[24]

The fourth hostile power during this first period of Herod's reign was Cleopatra. She had even previously, by her combination with Alexandra, been the means of giving troubled days to Herod. It was still more unfortunate for him that she now sought to use her influence with Antony to obtain an increase of territory. Antony at first gave no heed to her demands. But at length, during that same expedition against Armenia, in B.C. 34, he was induced to bestow upon her the whole of Phoenicia and the coast of the Philistines south of Eleutherus, with exception only of Tyre and Sidon, and besides, a part of the Arabian territory, and the fairest and most fertile part of the kingdom of

Herod, the celebrated district of Jericho, with its palm trees and balsams.[25] Opposition on the part of Herod was not to be thought of, and he was now obliged to take his own land in lease from Cleopatra.[26] He had indeed to accept the disagreeable with as good a grace as possible, and to receive Cleopatra with all honour and with royal munificence when she, on her return from the Euphrates, to which point she had accompanied Antony, paid a visit to Judea. But when she sought to draw him also into her net, he was cunning enough not to commit himself any more into her power.[27]

Thus Herod's first four or five years were spent amid various struggles for his own very existence. The outbreak in B.C. 32 of the war between Antony and Octavian caused fresh anxieties. Herod wished to hasten with a powerful army to the help of Antony; but at the instigation of Cleopatra he was instead ordered by Antony to fight against the Arabian king. That prince had latterly failed to pay regularly his tribute to Cleopatra, and was now to be punished for that fault. And Cleopatra wished that the war should be committed to Herod, in order that the two vassal kings might naturally weaken and reduce one another. And thus Herod was sent against the king of Arabia rather than against Octavian. But as Athenio, Cleopatra's commander, went to the help of the Arabians, he suffered a crushing defeat, and found himself obliged to stop the great war, and rest satisfied with mere robber raids and plundering expeditions.[28]

Then again in the spring of B.C. 31 a new calamity befell him, for a terrible earthquake visited the country, by which 30,000 men lost their lives. Herod now wished to treat for peace with the Arabians; but these slew his ambassadors and renewed their attack. Herod required to use all his eloquence in order to induce his dispirited troops again to enter into the engagement. But this time his old fortune in war returned to him. He drove before him the Arabian army in utter rout, and compelled its remnants, which had sought refuge in a fortress, soon to surrender. Proud of this brilliant success, he returned home.[29]

Soon thereafter, on 2nd September B.C. 31, the decisive battle at Actium was fought, by which Antony finally lost his power. It was at the same time a sore blow to Herod. But with that adroitness which was characteristic of him, he passed over at the right time into the camp of the conqueror, and soon found an opportunity for proving his change of mind by action. In Cyzicus there was a troop of Antony's gladiators, who held themselves in readiness for the games, by which Antony had intended to celebrate his victory over Octavian. When these now heard of the defeat and flight of Antony, they wished to hasten to Egypt to the assistance of their master. But Didius, the governor of Syria, hindered their departure, and Herod afforded him in this zealous and efficient aid.[30]

After he had given such a proof of his disposition, he could venture to present himself before Augustus. But in order to secure himself against any miscarriage, he contrived to have the aged Hyrcanus, the only one who might prove a dangerous rival, as nearer to the throne than himself, put out of the way. That Hyrcanus was condemned to death for conspiring with the Arabian king, as was affirmed in Herod's own journals, is highly improbable when we consider the character and the extreme age of Hyrcanus. Other contemporary writers have expressly declared his innocence. For Herod in his critical position, the mere existence of Hyrcanus was sufficient motive for the bloody deed. Thus fell the last of the Asmoneans, a memorial of past times, an old man more than eighty years of age, a sacrifice to the jealousy and ambition of Herod.[31]

Herod now set out to meet Augustus, who had passed the winter, B.C. 31–30, for the most part in Samos.[32] He met him in the spring of B.C. 30 in Rhodes. At the meeting he played his part skilfully. He boasted of his friendship with Antony, and of the service which he had rendered him, and wished in this way to prove how useful he might be to any one whose party he might join. Augustus was not inclined to give too much heed to this speech, but found it to his advantage to win over to himself the crafty and energetic Idumean who had been the steady friend of the Romans. He was very gracious to him, and confirmed him in his royal rank. With this joyful result Herod returned to his own home.[33]

Soon thereafter, in the summer, Augustus left Asia Minor and touched at the Phoenician coast on his way to Egypt, and Herod failed not to receive him with all pomp at Ptolemais, and took care that during that hot season of the year his army in its march should want for nothing.[34]

After Augustus in Egypt had done with Antony, who, as well as Cleopatra, had committed suicide in August B.C. 30, Herod again visited Augustus, undoubtedly with the intention of wishing him success, and securing for himself as great a reward as possible. In this latter object he was completely successful. Augustus now gave him back, not only the district of Jericho, but also Gadara, Hippos, Samaria, Gaza, Anthedon, Joppa, and Straton's Tower.[35]—In proof of his gratitude, Herod gave his patron, on his return from Egypt in the end of B.C. 30, the pleasure of his company as far as Antioch.[36]

While thus he had exchanged his outward dangers for good fortune, Herod had nothing but confusion and strife in his own house. Even when he had gone away to Rhodes, he had committed the guardianship of Mariamme to a certain Soemus, and to him again he had given the same command as before to Joseph.[37] Mariamme had also this time again come to know it, and gave to Herod on his return proofs of her aversion.[38] The mother of Herod, Cypros, and his sister Salome, who had both for a long time been disaffected toward the proud Mariamme, were greatly gratified at this misunderstanding, and they knew how to inflame the quarrel by giving currency to the most scandalous calumnies. At last Salome managed to bribe the king's cupbearer, and got him to declare that Mariamme had given him a poison draught in order that he should give it to Herod. When Herod heard this, he had Mariamme's eunuch examined by torture in reference to this matter. This servant indeed knew nothing of the poison draught, but confessed that Mariamme hated her husband on account of the command which he had given to Soemus. When, now, Herod heard that Soemus, as well as Joseph, had betrayed the secret of his command, he saw again in this a proof of unlawful intercourse, and cried out saying that he had now evidence of his wife's unfaithfulness. Soemus was immediately executed; Mariamme, after a judicial investigation, was condemned, and then executed in the end of B.C. 29.[39]

In Herod's relations with Mariamme were revealed all the savagery and sensuality of his nature. Ungovernable and passionate as his love for her was, such was also his hatred so soon as he thought himself deceived by his wife. But equally ungovernable and passionate was also his yearning over his beloved whom he himself had murdered. In order to drown the pangs of remorse, he sought relief in wild excesses, drinking bouts, and the pleasures of the chase. But even his powerful frame could not endure such an excessive strain. While he was hunting in Samaria he fell ill, and was obliged there to take to his bed. As his recovery was doubtful, Alexandra began to scheme, so that in the event of his death she might secure the throne to herself. She applied herself to those in command of the two fortified places in Jerusalem, and sought to win them over to her side. But they reported the matter to Herod, and Alexandra, who had long deserved that fate far more than others, was then executed some time in B.C. 28.[40]

Gradually Herod recovered, and soon found occasion for further bloodshed. A distinguished Idumean, Costobar, had been, soon after his accession, appointed by Herod governor of Idumea, and had subsequently been married to Salome, whose first husband, Joseph, had been executed in B.C. 34. Even during this first period he had secretly conspired against Herod with Cleopatra, but had been received into Herod's favour again at the entreaty of Salome.[41] But now Salome herself was tired of her husband, and in order to rid herself of him she had recourse to denunciation. She knew that her husband had preserved the sons of Babas,[42] as it seems, distant relatives of the Asmonean house, whom Herod ever since his conquest of Jerusalem had in vain sought to track out. This information she communicated to her brother. Herod, when he heard this, promptly resolved upon the course he would pursue. Costobar, together with his *protégés*, whose place of concealment Salome had betrayed, was seized and executed in B.C. 25. And now Herod could console himself with the thought that of all the relatives of the aged Hyrcanus there was no longer one surviving who could dispute with him the occupancy of the throne.[43]—Here then the first period closes, the period of conflict with hostile powers.

II.

The period from B.C. 25 to B.C. 13 is the period of glory and enjoyment, although the enjoyment was not altogether unchequered and undisturbed.

Among the glories of the period are to be reckoned the magnificent buildings which he erected. All the provinces

vied with one another in their celebration of the emperor-
cultus, and in the lavishness of display every fourth year at
the festal games in honour of Caesar. For the former purpose
emperor-temples (Καισάρεια) were erected; for the latter,
theatres, amphitheatres, race-courses for men and for horses.
New cities also were founded in honour of Caesar, and called
after his name. "Provinciarum pleraeque super templa et
aras ludos quoque quinquennales paene oppidatim consti-
tuerunt. Reges amici atque socii et singuli in suo quisque
regno Caesareas urbes condiderunt." [44]   All these endeavours
were entered upon by Herod with that energy by which he
was characterized. But he was also unweariedly active in
erecting other buildings for purposes of use and luxury, and
in the reconstruction of entire cities.

In Jerusalem a theatre was reared; in the valley near
Jerusalem, an amphitheatre.[45] Some time later, about B.C. 24,
Herod built for himself a royal palace, upon which marble
and gold were lavished with profusion. It was provided
with strong fortifications, and thus was made to serve also as
a castle for the upper city.[46] Even during the time of Antony
he had had the citadel north of the temple rebuilt and named
Antonia in honour of his patron.[47]—In the non-Jewish cities
of his territory, and farther away in the province of Syria, he
built numerous temples, especially such as he built in honour
of Caesar (Καισάρεια), and adorned them with statuary of
the most beautiful description.[48]

New cities in large number were built under his direction
throughout the land. The old Samaria, which after its destruction had been already rebuilt by Gabinius, was now reconstructed by Herod in a magnificent style, and received from
him the name of Sebaste.[49] Not satisfied with this, he engaged
in the year B.C. 22 on a still more ambitious undertaking, for
he erected on the coast, on the site of the ancient Straton's
Tower, a new city of large and imposing dimensions, to which

he gave the name of Caesarea. As deserving of special mention, Josephus speaks of the commodious haven attached to the city. In order to secure ships while receiving their cargo from the storms, a powerful breakwater was carried far out into the sea, the material for which had to be brought from a considerable distance. On the breakwater were erected dwellings for the seamen, and in front of these paths were made for pleasure walks. In the midst of the city was a hill, on which a temple in honour of the emperor was built, which could be seen far out at sea. Twelve full years were occupied in the building of the city. And when it had been completed, a grand celebration of the event was made with great pomp in the 28th year of Herod, corresponding to B.C. 10–9.[50]

But Herod's love of building had not yet received full satisfaction. In place of the ancient Capharsaba, he founded a city, which he named in honour of his father Antipatris. At Jericho he built a citadel which he named after his mother Cypros. In the Jordan valley, north of Jericho, he founded, in a previously unbuilt but fruitful district, a new city, and named it after his brother Phasaelis.[51] The ancient Anthedon he reconstructed, and, in honour of Agrippa, named it Agrippaeum.[52] In honour of himself, he named two new strongholds Herodium; the one lay in the mountainous region toward Arabia; the other on the spot, three leagues south of Jerusalem, where he had conquered the Jews who pursued him after his flight from Jerusalem. The latter fortress was also supplied with rooms beautifully fitted up for the use of the king.[53] The strongholds of Alexandrium and Hyrcania, built by the Armenians but destroyed by Gabinius, were now restored by Herod, and furnished with new fortifications.[54] He dealt similarly also with the fortresses of Machärus and Masada, both of which he adorned with royal palaces.[55] Military requirements also led to the rebuilding of

Gaba in Galilee and Esbon in Perea, in which places he established military colonies.[56]

Also far beyond the bounds of Palestine architectural works proclaimed the liberality of Herod. For the Rhodians, Herod built at his own cost the Pythian temple. He aided in the construction of most of the public buildings of the city of Nicopolis, which had been founded by Augustus near Actium. In Antioch he caused colonnades to be erected along both sides of the principal street.[57] Happening on one occasion to visit Chios, he spent a large sum on the rebuilding of the piazza, destroyed during the Mithridatic war.[58] In Ascalon he built baths and fountains. Tyre and Sidon, Byblus and Berytus, Tripolis, Ptolemais, and Damascus were also graced with memorials to the glory of Herod's name. And even as far as Athens and Lacedæmonia proofs of his liberality were to be found.[59]

But the most magnificent of all his building operations was the restoration of the temple of Jerusalem. The old temple, built by Zerubbabel, was no longer in keeping with the magnificence of the modern structures. The palaces in its neighbourhood quite eclipsed it in grandeur. But now, as was only proper, it was to be brought into harmony with its beautiful surroundings. The rebuilding was begun in the eighteenth year of Herod, corresponding to B.C. 20—19, or A.U.C. 734-735. After the temple proper was completed it was consecrated; but still the building was carried on for a long period, and only a few years before its destruction, in the time of Albinus (A.D. 62—64), was it actually finished. Its beauty was proverbial. "He who has not seen Herod's building has never seen anything beautiful," was a common proverb of that day.[60]

Besides the buildings, the games, celebrated with great pomp and magnificence, belonged to the glory of the Augustan period. In this department also Herod was quite abreast of the requirements of the age.   Not only in the predominantly pagan Caesarea, but even in Jerusalem, competitive games were celebrated every fourth year.[61]   To the eyes of legalistic Jews these pagan exhibitions, with their slight valuation of the life of men and animals, constituted a serious offence, which could be tolerated only under threat of severe measures.[62] The zeal of the king, however, went so far that he even gave liberal grants in support of the old Olympic games.[63]

How unweariedly and extravagantly he also in other ways promoted culture and learning of every kind we are informed from explicit statements by Josephus.   Very serviceable indeed was the colonizing of the districts west of the lake of Gennesareth hitherto traversed only by robber nomad tribes.[64]   He laid out at great cost the parks and gardens about his palace at Jerusalem.   Walks and water canals were made through the gardens; water fountains decorated with iron works of art were to be seen, through which the water gushed.   In the neighbourhood of these stood dovecots with tamed pigeons.[65] The king seemed to have a special fondness for pigeon-breeding; it is, indeed, only in connection with this that mention is made of Herod in the Mishna.   "Herodian pigeons" is the phrase used for pigeons kept in captivity.[66]   It seems, therefore, that Herod was the first in Judea to keep and rear wild pigeons in an enclosed place.

In order that he might pose before the eyes of the Graeco-Roman world as a man of culture, Herod, who continued to the last a barbarian at heart, surrounded himself with a circle of men accomplished in Greek literature and art.   The highest offices of state were entrusted to Greek rhetoricians.   In all more important matters he availed himself of their counsel and advice.   The most distinguished of these was Nicolas of Damascus, a man of wide and varied scholarship, versed in natural science, familiar with Aristotle, and widely celebrated as a historical writer.   He enjoyed the unconditional con-

fidence of Herod, and was by him entrusted with all serious
and difficult diplomatic missions.   Beside him stood his
brother Ptolemy, also a trusted friend of the king.   Another
Ptolemy was at the head of the finance department, and had
the king's signet ring.[67]   In addition to these, we find in the
circle immediately around the king two Greeks or half-Greeks
—Andromachus and Gemellus.   The latter of these was
also the tutor of Herod's son Alexander.[68]   Finally, in the
proceedings after Herod's death we meet with a Greek
rhetorician, Irenaeus.[69]   Among those Hellenic counsellors of
the king there were indeed some very bad characters, most
conspicuous among them that Lacedæmonian Eurykles, who
contributed not a little in fomenting and intensifying the
trouble between Herod and his sons.[70]

Herod to all appearance had very little real interest in
Judaism.   His ambition led him to foster the liberal arts
and culture.   But any other form of culture than that of
Greece was scarcely recognised by the world of that day.
So he himself submitted to receive instructions, under the
direction of Nicolas of Damascus, in philosophy, rhetoric,
and history, and boasted of being more nearly related
to the Greeks than to the Jews.[71]   But the culture which
he sought to spread throughout his land was essentially
Greek and pagan.   He even erected heathen temples in
the non-Jewish towns of his kingdom.—Under these circumstances it is interesting to observe the place which he gave to
the law and the national aspirations of his people.   The
Pharisaic-national movement had grown up, especially since
the reaction under Alexandra, into a power so strong and so
firmly rooted in the hearts of the people, that Herod could
not possibly think of a violent Hellenizing like that carried
on by Antiochus Epiphanes.   He was sagacious enough to
show respect in many points to the views of the Pharisaic
party.   Hence it is particularly worthy of notice that his

coins bear no human image, but only innocent symbols, like those of the Maccabean coins; at most only one coin, and that belonging probably to Herod's latest period, bears the figure of an eagle. In the building of the temple he was anxiously careful to avoid giving any offence. He allowed only priests to build the temple proper, and even he himself ventured not to go into the precincts of the inner temple, which should be entered only by the priests.[72] Upon none of the many beautiful buildings in Jerusalem were images placed. And when the people once looked with suspicion on the imperial trophies of victory which were set up in the theatre at Jerusalem, because they took them for statues which were covered with the armour, Herod had the trophies taken down in the presence of the most distinguished men, and showed them to their complete satisfaction the bare wooden frames.[73] When the Arabian Sylläus sought to win for himself the hand of Herod's sister Salome, it was required of him that he should adopt the Jewish customs ($\dot{\epsilon}\gamma\gamma\rho\alpha\phi\hat{\eta}\nu\alpha\iota$ $\tau o\hat{\iota}\varsigma$ $\tau\hat{\omega}\nu$ $'Iov\delta\alpha i\omega\nu$ $\ddot{\epsilon}\theta\epsilon\sigma\iota$), and thereupon the proposed marriage was abandoned.[74] Some of the most famous Pharisees, among whom Polio and Sameas may be specially named, were held by Herod in high esteem, and were not punished even when they refused to take the oath of allegiance.[75]

But clearly a thoroughgoing carrying out of Pharisaic views was impossible under his scheme for the furtherance of culture, and he had no intention of promoting them. For a time, what he raised with the one hand he overthrew with the other. After he had carefully studied the Pharisaic requirements in the building of the temple, he at last had an eagle put up over the temple gate as if in insult.[76] Theatre and amphitheatre were already in themselves heathen abominations. The Greek surroundings of the king, the administration of state business by men of Greek culture, the development of heathen splendour within the Holy Land, the provision for heathen worship within the borders of Judea, in the king's own territory, all this completely outweighed those concessions to Pharisaism, and in spite of these lent to Herod's reign more of a heathen than a Jewish character. The Sanhedrim, which according to the opinion of the people was the only court that had any right to exist, under Herod was stripped of all importance, so that doubts have been entertained as to its very existence.[77] The high priests, whom he appointed and removed at his pleasure, were his creatures, and were for the most part Alexandrians, with a veneer therefore of culture, and so offensive to the Pharisees.[92] The treatment of the high-priesthood is quite typical of the home policy of the king. As he had tossed aside with ruthless violence the old Sadducean nobles on the one hand, because of their sympathy with the Asmonean dynasty (see above, p. 131); so, on the other hand, he was just as little satisfied with the Pharisees. Their ideals went far beyond the concessions of the king, and the friendships enjoyed among the Pharisees were only exceptions.[78]

When one considers that in addition to this contempt of the claims and the actual or imagined rights of the people, Herod oppressed them by imposing a heavy taxation, it may be readily supposed that his rule was endured amid much murmuring. All foreign glory could only be distasteful to the people so long as it was secured by the oppression of the citizens and accompanied by the disregarding of the laws of their fathers. Most of the Pharisees regarded the government of the Roman vassal king generally as not existing in right, and refused twice over the oath of allegiance which Herod demanded, first for himself and then for the emperor.[79] The prevailing dissatisfaction sought vent once in the earlier period of his reign, about B.C. 25, in a conspiracy. Ten citizens conspired to murder the king in the theatre. Their plan, indeed, failed, since it was betrayed beforehand. When they were just on the eve of committing the deed, they were seized, dragged before Herod, and immediately condemned to death.[80]

In order to hold the revolting populace in check, Herod had recourse on his part to means of violence; and so his reign the longer it lasted the more despotic it became. The fortresses, which were partly new erections of his own, partly old places made stronger, served not only to protect him from foreign foes, but also for keeping down his own people. The most important were Herodium, Alexandrium, Hyrcania, Machärus, Masada, to which may also be added the military colonies at Gaba in Galilee and Esbon in Perea (compare above, pp. 140–141). Especially to Hyrcania many political offenders were deported in order there to disappear for ever.[81] As props of his government against foreign as well as home foes Herod had dependable mercenary troops, in which there were many Thracians, Germans, and Gauls.[82]—But, finally, he sought by strict police regulations to nip in the bud every attempt at rebellion. All idle loitering about the streets, all common assemblies, yea, even meeting together on the street, was forbidden. And where anything of the kind was nevertheless done, the king had information about it immediately conveyed to him by his secret spies. He is said at times to have in his own person acted the part of the spy.[83]

In order to be just, one must, however, admit that his government had also its good side. Among his buildings many were of a useful description. We need only mention the haven of Caesarea. By his strong hand were conditions created under the protection of which trade and travel became safe. He also for a time at least made attempts to win the hearts of his subjects by proofs of his magnanimity. Once, in the year B.C. 20, he remitted a third of the taxes;[84] at another time, in B.C. 14, he remitted a fourth of them.[85]

Quite amazing was the energy with which he sought to put a
stop to the famine which spread over the land in B.C. 25.
He is said on that occasion to have converted into money even
his own table plate.[86]

But the people in presence of prevailing evils had only a
very feeble and transitory gratitude for such benefits.   And
so, while upon the whole his reign was undoubtedly glorious,
it was by no means happy.

The chief glory of his reign lay in his foreign policy, and
in this department he undeniably achieved great success.   He
had secured the confidence of Augustus to such a degree, that
by imperial favour the extent of his territory was about
doubled.

This is the place to estimate, according to its most essential
and characteristic feature, the position in the eye of the law
of a *rex socius* in the Roman empire of that day.   The
dependence, in which all kings on this side of the Euphrates
stood to the Roman power, was expressed most strikingly in
this, that none could exercise royal authority and use the
title of king without the express approval of the emperor,
with or without confirmation by the senate.[87]   The title was,
as a rule, granted only to such princes as reigned over a
territory of considerable extent; the smaller princes were
obliged to be satisfied with the title of tetrarch or such like.
The permission extended only to the person of the individual
who then received it, and ceased with his death.   Hereditary
monarchies were not generally recognised within the domain
of the Roman authority.   Even the son appointed by his
father as his successor could enter upon his government only
after his nomination had been confirmed by the emperor.
This confirmation was refused if there appeared reasons for so
doing, and then the territorial domain of the father was either
granted to the son with restricted boundaries and with an
inferior title, or given to another, or even taken under direct

Roman administration as a province. All this may indeed
be learned from the history of the Herodian dynasty, but it
is also confirmed by all other records.—The title *socius et
amicus populi Romani* (φίλος καὶ σύμμαχος Ῥωμαίων) seems
as a special designation to have been granted only to individuals, so that not all who actually assumed this position had
really formally received the title.[104]   The possession of Roman
citizenship is indeed expressly witnessed to only on behalf of
a few, but is to be assumed in regard to all as probable.
The family of Herod came into possession of it early through
Antipater, the father of Herod.[88]   From the time of Caligula,
too, honorary senatorial rights (praetorian and consular rank)
were for a time conferred upon confederate kings.[89] —Their
power was restricted especially in the following particulars :
1. They could neither conclude treaties with other States nor
engage in a war on their own account, and so could exercise
sovereign rights only within the boundaries of their own
land. 2. They had the right of coining money only in a
limited degree.   The minting of gold coins seems to have
been almost entirely forbidden ; in many cases also the
minting of silver coins.   To the latter class belonged Herod
and his successors ; at least only copper coins have come
down to us from the whole line of Herodian princes.   This
fact is particularly instructive, since it shows us that Herod
by no means belonged to the most distinguished of those
kings, as by many of his statements Josephus would lead us
to suppose.   3. A special obligation resting on them was
the providing of auxiliary troops in case of a war, as well as
the protection of the frontiers of the empire against foreign
attacks.   Also contributions in money were on special
occasions demanded.   But a regular tribute seems not to
have been raised for the kings during the time of the empire.
Only of Antony is it said that he appointed kings ἐπὶ φόροις
ιεταγμένοις.[89a]—The rights of sovereignty which were left to

dependent kings embraced, under the reservations specified, the whole administration of home affairs and the execution of the laws. They had unlimited power of life and death over their subjects. Their whole territory was generally not regarded as belonging to the province. Within the bounds of their territory they could impose taxes at will, and they administered the revenue independently. Their army also was under their own control, and was organized by themselves.

The position thus described, which afforded such abundant scope to the energy of the individual, was taken advantage of by Herod with all his might. He availed himself, as others ought also to have done, of every opportunity of presenting himself to the emperor and proving his devotion to him.[90] Even in B.C. 30 he had several times visited Augustus.[91] Ten years later, in B.C. 20, Augustus went again to Syria, and Herod did not lose the chance of paying him his respects.[92] In B.C. 18 or 17 Herod fetched home his two sons, Alexander and Aristobulus, who were in Rome for their education, and was on that occasion very graciously received by the emperor.[93] Subsequently he met with Augustus on two occasions, in the years B.C. 12 and 10—9.[94] Herod was also on terms of friendly intercourse with Agrippa, the trusted friend and son-in-law of Augustus. While Agrippa was residing in Mytilene, B.C. 23—21, he there received a visit from Herod.[95] And later still, in B.C. 15, Agrippa himself went to Judea and offered a hecatomb in the temple at Jerusalem. The people were so enthusiastic over the Roman who showed himself so friendly to the Jews, that they accompanied him amid shouts of good-will to his ship, strewing his way with flowers, and expressing admiration at his piety.[96] In the spring of the following year, B.C. 14, Herod returned Agrippa's visit; and as he knew that Agrippa had planned an expedition to the Crimea, he took with him a fleet in order

to afford him assistance.   At Sinope he met his noble friend
and then went with him, after the warlike operations were
finished, over a great part of Asia Minor, dispensing everywhere lavish gifts and granting petitions.[97]—His relations
with Augustus and Agrippa were so intimate that flatterers
affirmed that Herod was dearest to Augustus next to Agrippa,
and to Agrippa next to Augustus.[98]

These Roman friendships also bore their fruits.   Even as
early as B.C. 30, when Herod was with Augustus in Egypt,
he had obtained from him important enlargement of territory
(see above, p. 136).   New gifts were added at a later period.
Herod had in B.C. 25, in the campaign of Aelius Gallus against
Arabia, supplied 500 men of select auxiliary troops.[99]   There
may possibly be some connection between this and the fact
that soon afterwards, in B.C. 23, at the time when Herod sent
his sons Alexander and Aristobulus for their education to
Rome, he received the districts of Trachonitis, Batanea, and
Auranitis, which previously had been occupied by nomad
robber tribes, with whom the neighbouring tetrarch Zenodorus
had made common cause.[100]   When some years later, in B.C.
20, Augustus visited Syria, he bestowed upon Herod the
tetrarchy of Zenodorus, the districts of Ulatha and Panias,
and the surrounding territories north and north-west of the
lake of Gennesareth.[101]   At the same time Herod obtained
permission to appoint his brother Pheroras tetrarch of
Perea.[102]   And the unbounded confidence which Augustus
had in him is shown conspicuously in this, that he, perhaps
only during the period of Agrippa's absence from the East,
gave orders to the procurators of Syria (Coele-Syria ?) to
take counsel with Herod in regard to all important
matters.[103]

It is not left untold how Herod used his influence with the
Roman governors to secure the Jews of the dispersion against
all oppression and infringement of their rights on the part

of their non-Jewish neighbours.[104]   Thus the power of the
Jewish king told in favour even of those Jews who were not
immediately under his rule.

The period from B.C. 20 to B.C. 14 was decidedly the most
brilliant in his reign.   In spite of dependence upon Rome,
his court, so far as outward grandeur was concerned, might
bear comparison with the best times that the nation had seen.
Internal affairs were indeed in a miserable state.   Only by
force could the people be brought to tolerate the semi-pagan
rule of the Idumean; and only his despotic, iron hand prevented an uprising of the fermenting masses.

III.

The last nine years of Herod, B.C. 13-4, constitute the
period of domestic misery.   Especially his unhappy quarrels
with the sons of Mariamme cast a deep, dark shadow over
this period.[105]

Herod had a numerous family.   In all he had ten wives,
which was indeed, as Josephus points out, allowed by the law;
but it affords a striking proof of his sensuality.[106]   His first
wife was Doris, by whom he had one son, Antipater.[107]   Both
were repudiated by Herod, and Antipater was allowed to
appear at Jerusalem only at the great feasts.[108]   In the year
B.C. 37, Herod married Mariamme, the grand-daughter of
Hyrcanus (see above, p. 119), who bore him five children,
three sons and two daughters.   Of the sons, the youngest died
at Rome ;[109] the two elder ones, Alexander and Aristobulus,
are the heroes of the subsequent history.[110]   The third wife,
whom Herod married about B.C. 24, was also called Mariamme.
She was daughter of a famous priest belonging to Alexandria, who was appointed high priest by Herod just at the
time when he married his daughter.[111]   By this wife he had
a son called Herod.[112]   Of the other seven wives, carefully

enumerated by Josephus, *Antiq.* xvii. 1. 3, and *Wars of the Jews*, i. 28. 4, only the Samaritan Malthace, mother of Archelaus and Antipas, and Cleopatra of Jerusalem, the mother of Philip, are of interest to us.

About the year B.C. 23, Herod sent the sons of the first Mariamme, Alexander and Aristobulus, for their education to Rome, where they were hospitably entertained in the house of Asinius Pollio.[113] Some five years later, in B.C. 18 or 17, he himself fetched them home again, and from that time onward kept them at the court in Jerusalem.[114] They would then be young men about seventeen or eighteen years of age. In accordance with the customs of the age and country, they were soon married. Alexander received a daughter of the Cappadocian king Archelaus, whose name was Glaphyra; Aristobulus had given him a daughter of Herod's sister Salome, called Berenice.[115] Although in this way the Asmonean and Idumean line of the Herodian family were connected together by affinity in the closest relationship, they still stood over against one another as two hostile camps. The sons of Mariamme, conscious of their royal blood, might well look down with a certain pride upon the Idumean relationship; and the Idumeans, pre-eminently the estimable Salome, returned the haughtiness of those Asmoneans by common abuse. And so even thus early, after the sons had no more than re-entered their father's house, the knots began to be tied, which afterwards became so twisted that they could not be loosed. For a time, however, Herod did not allow these janglings to interfere with the love he had for his sons.[116]

The evil conscience of the king, however, offered so fruitful a soil for such sowing of slanders, that they could not fail ultimately to take root and to bring forth fruit. He was obliged to admit to himself that the natural heritage of the sons was the desire to avenge the death of their mother. And as now Salome again and again pictured to him the danger which threatened from both, he at last began to believe it, and to look upon his sons with suspicion. [117]

In order to provide what would counterbalance their aspiring projects, and to show them that there was still another in existence who might possibly be heir to the throne, he called back his exiled Antipater, and sent his sons for that reason to Rome, in company with Agrippa, who just then, in B.C. 13, was leaving the East, in order that he might present him to the emperor.[118] But by so doing he put the weapon into the hand of the bitterest foe of his domestic peace. For Antipater from this time forth laboured incessantly, by calumniating his step-brothers, to carve out his way to the throne. The change in their father's attitude was naturally not without effect upon Alexander and Aristobulus. They returned his suspicion with undisguised aversion, and already openly complained of the death of their mother, and of the injurious treatment to which they were subjected.[119] Thus was the rift between father and sons becoming always deeper, until at last Herod, in B.C. 12, came to the conclusion to accuse his sons before the emperor. Along with the two he started on his journey, and appeared before the emperor at Aquileia as complainant against his sons. The mild earnestness of Augustus succeeded for that time in reconciling the opposing parties, and restoring again domestic peace. With thanks to the emperor, father and sons returned home ; and Antipater also himself joined them, and pretended to rejoice in the reconciliation.[120]

Scarcely had they reached home when the old game began afresh. Antipater, who now again was one of those in immediate attendance on the king, continued unweariedly the work of slander, and in this he was faithfully supported by the brother and sister of Herod, Pheroras and Salome. On the other hand, Alexander and Aristobulus assumed a more decidedly hostile attitude.[121] Thus the peace between father and

sons was soon again broken.   The suspicion of the king, which
from day to day received new fuel, became more and more
morbid, and by and by reached a climax in a superstitious
fear of ghosts.[122]   He now caused the adherents of Alexander
to be subjected to the torture, at first unsuccessfully, until at
last one, under the agony of torture, made injurious admis-
sions.   On the ground of these, Alexander was committed to
prison.[123]—When the Cappadocian king, Alexander's father-
in-law, heard of the unfortunate state of matters at the Jewish
court, he began to fear for his daughter and son-in-law, and
made a journey to Jerusalem in order, if at all possible, to
bring about a reconciliation.   He appeared before Herod very
angry over his good-for-nothing son-in-law, threatened to take
his daughter back again to his own house, and expressed
himself so ferociously that Herod himself espoused the side
of his son, and undertook his defence against Archelaus.   By
such a manœuvre the sly Cappadocian succeeded in bringing
about the reconciliation which he desired, and was able to
return home quite satisfied.[124]   Thus once again the wild
storm was broken by a short temporary lull.

In that excited period Herod had also to contend with
foreign enemies, and even with imperial disfavour.   The free-
booting inhabitants of Trachonitis wished to rid themselves of
his strict and severe government, and somewhere about forty
of the worst disturbers of the peace found ready shelter in
the neighbouring parts of Arabia, where a certain Sylleus
carried on the government in the place of the weak King
Obodas.   When Sylleus refused to deliver up these robbers,
Herod undertook, with consent of the governor of Syria,
Saturninus, a warlike expedition against Arabia, and enforced
his rights.[125]   But now Sylleus agitated at Rome, represented
the matter as an unlawful breach of national peace, and was
able thereby to bring Herod seriously into disfavour with the
emperor.[126] — In order to justify himself in regard to his

conduct, Herod sent an embassy to Rome; and when this
was not successful, he sent a second, under the leadership of
Nicolas of Damascus.[127]

Meanwhile the family discord was with rapid strides
approaching its tragical end. The reconciliation, as might
have been expected, was not of long duration. In order to
make the unhappiness complete, there now arrived at the
court a worthless Lacedæmonian, Eurykles, who inflamed the
father against the sons and the sons against the father.[128] At
the same time, all the other mischief-makers continued their
work. At last matters came to such a pass that Herod cast
Alexander and Aristobulus into prison, and laid a complaint
against them before the emperor of being concerned in
treasonable plots.[129]

Nicolas of Damascus had meanwhile accomplished the
task of his mission, and had again won over the emperor to
Herod.[130] When, therefore, the messengers bearing the accusation reached Rome, they found Augustus already in a
favourable mood, and at once spread out before him their
documents. Augustus gave to Herod absolute power to proceed in this matter as he thought best, but advised him to
summon to Berytus a justiciary court consisting of Roman
officials and his own friends, and to have the charges against
his sons investigated by it.[131]

Herod accepted the advice of the emperor. The court
almost unanimously pronounced the sentence of death. Only
the governor of Syria, Saturninus, and his three sons were of
another mind.—Still it was doubtful whether Herod would
carry out the sentence. An old soldier, Teron, therefore
ventured publicly to sue for favour to the condemned. But
the old man and three hundred others, who were denounced
as adherents of Alexander and Aristobulus, were put to death,
and the sentence was now without delay carried into execution.
At Sebaste (Samaria), where thirty years before Mariamme's

marriage had been celebrated, her sons were executed upon the gibbet, probably in B.C. 7.[132]

But such proceedings failed utterly in restoring peace to Herod's household. Antipater was now indeed all-powerful at court, and enjoyed the unconditional confidence of his father. But this did not satisfy him. He wished to have the government wholly in his own hand, and held secret conferences with Herod's brother Pheroras, tetrarch of Perea, at which it was suspected that nothing good was done. Salome, the old serpent, had soon discovered these ongoings, and reported the matter to the king.[133] And so the relations of Antipater and his father soon became strained. Antipater, in order to avoid a conflict, found it convenient to allow himself to be sent to Rome. That Herod did not meanwhile entertain any serious suspicion against him is shown by his will, in which even at that time he nominated Antipater his successor on the throne; only in the event of Antipater dying before himself was Herod, the son of Mariamme the high priest's daughter, named his successor.[134]

While Antipater was in Rome, Pheroras died;[135] and by this also Antipater's fate was sealed. Some freedmen of Pheroras went to Herod and showed him that there was a suspicion that Pheroras had been poisoned, and that Herod should investigate the matter more closely. On examination it came out that poison certainly had been present, that it was sent by Antipater, but that it was intended, not for Pheroras, but was only given to him by Antipater in order that he might administer it to Herod. Herod also now learned from the female slaves of Pheroras' household all the utterances which had escaped Antipater at those secret conclaves, his complaining about the long life of the king, about the uncertainty of his prospects, and other such things.[136] Herod could now no longer entertain any doubt as to the deadly intentions of his favourite son. Under all sorts of false pretences, he recalled him from Rome in order to put him on trial at home. Antipater, who anticipated no trouble, returned, and to his great surprise—for although since the discovery of his plots seven months had passed, he had heard nothing of the matter — he was on his arrival committed to prison in the king's palace.[137] Next day he was brought forth to trial before Varus, the governor of Syria. As in face of the manifest proofs brought against him he could say nothing in defence of himself, Herod had him put in fetters, and made a report of the matter to the emperor.[138]

Herod was now almost seventy years of age. His days were indeed already numbered. He suffered from a disease from which he could not recover. In a new will, which he now executed, he named his youngest son Antipas, the son of the Samaritan Malthace, as his successor.[139]

During his sickness he could not but perceive how anxiously the people longed to be delivered from his yoke, and yearned for the moment when they would be emancipated from his heathenish government. As soon as the news got abroad that his disease was incurable, two rabbis, Judas the son of Sariphäus, and Matthias the son of Margaloth, stirred up the people to tear down the offensive eagle from the temple gate.[140] Only too readily they found an audience, and amid great uproar the work pleasing to God was accomplished. Meanwhile Herod, in spite of his sickness, was still strong enough to pass sentences of death, and to have the principal leaders of the tumult burnt alive.[141]

The days of the old king were now at an end. The disease was always becoming worse, and dissolution rapidly approached. The baths of Callirrhoë, on the other side of the Jordan, to which the king had gone, no longer benefited him.[142] When he had returned to Jericho, he is said to have given orders that upon his death the most distinguished men of the nation, whom he had caused to be shut up in the arena of that place, should be cut down, so that there might be a great lamentation as he passed away.[143] Amid all the pains which his disease caused him, he lived long enough to have the satisfaction of accomplishing the death of his son Antipater, the chief instigator of his domestic misery. Just in the last days of his life the permission of the emperor arrived for the execution of Antipater, which soon afterwards was carried out.[144]

A few days before his death Herod once again altered his will, for he named Archelaus, the older son of Malthace, king, his brother Antipas tetrarch of Galilee and Perea, and Philip, the son of Cleopatra of Jerusalem, tetrarch of Gaulonitis, Trachonitis, Batanea, and Panias.[145]

At last, five days after the execution of Antipater, Herod died at Jericho in B.C. 4, unwept by those of his own house, and hated by all the people.[146]—A pompous funeral procession accompanied the royal corpse from Jericho, a distance of eight furlongs, in the direction of Herodium, where it was laid in its last resting-place.[147]

The end of his reign was bloody as its beginning had been. The brighter portion lay in the middle. But even during his better days he was a despot, and upon the whole, with all the glory of his reign, "he was still only a common man" (Hitzig, ii. 559). The title of "the Great," by which we are accustomed to distinguish him from his more feeble descendants of the same name, is only justified when it is used in this relative sense.[148]

§ 16. DISTURBANCES AFTER HEROD'S DEATH, B.C. 4

By the last will of Herod, Archelaus had been named his successor on the throne. Archelaus therefore made it his first business to secure the emperor's confirmation of his father's arrangement, and with this end in view he resolved to make a journey to Rome. But before he could start on such an expedition, he had to stamp out a rebellion in Jerusalem. The people could not so easily forget the execution of the two rabbis, Judas and Matthias, and violently insisted that Archelaus should bring to punishment the counsellors of Herod. Archelaus endeavoured at first in a conciliatory manner to dissuade the people from their purpose. But when he could not succeed in this way, the only result of his proposals being the increase of the tumult, he resolved to crush the revolt by violence. He accordingly sent forth a detachment of soldiers against the people assembled in the temple, where the people who had flocked into Jerusalem in prospect of the approaching Passover festival were wont to gather at that season in great crowds. But the detachment sent was not strong enough to make way against the excited masses. A portion of the soldiers was stoned by the people; the rest, together with their leader, took to flight. Archelaus was now obliged to call out his whole fighting force; and only by the help of his entire army, amid great bloodshed, was he able to put down the rebellion.[1]

After Archelaus had thus by the exercise of force secured quiet, he hastened to Rome, leaving his brother Philip to act as administrator of the kingdom.   Scarcely had he gone, when Antipas also started for Rome in order to press his own claims there.   He had by the third and last will of Herod received only Galilee and Perea, whereas in the second will he had been appointed successor to the throne.   He therefore now wished to represent to the emperor that to him, and not to Archelaus, did the kingdom properly belong.   Many other members of the Herodian family were also present in Rome at the same time as Archelaus and Antipas, and these now mostly appeared against Archelaus, and expressed a strong desire that Palestine should now be put under immediate Roman government; or if this could not be, then they would rather have Antipas than Archelaus.[2]

Hence the sons of Herod plotted and schemed against one another in Rome.   Augustus, in whose hands the decision lay, meanwhile convoked at his palace a consultative assembly, at which the opposing brothers were called upon to make a statement of their conflicting claims.   A certain Antipater spoke on behalf of Antipas, while Nicolas of Damascus, formerly the minister of Herod, appeared on behalf of Archelaus.   Each party sought to win over the emperor to his side, partly by advancing arguments, partly by insinuating suspicions against his opponent.   When Augustus had heard both parties, he inclined more to the side of Archelaus, and made a statement to the effect that he was most fit to ascend the royal throne.   Yet he did not wish immediately to decide the matter, and so dismissed the assembly without issuing a final and formal judgment.[3]

But before the question about the succession to the throne had been decided in Rome, new troubles had broken out in Judea.   Soon after the departure of Archelaus the Jews had again risen in revolt, but had been restored to quiet by Varus,

the governor of Syria.   Varus had then returned to Antioch,
leaving behind him in Jerusalem a legion to maintain order.
But scarcely had he gone when the storm broke out afresh.
After Herod's death, pending the settlement of the question of
succession to the throne, the emperor had sent to Palestine a
procurator, Sabinus.   But he oppressed the people in every
sort of way, and behaved in all directions in the most reckless
manner.   Hence it was that a revolt broke out again
immediately after the withdrawal of Varus.   It was now the
season of the Passover festival, and therefore crowds of people
were present in Jerusalem.   They were divided into three
great divisions, and attacked the Romans at the three different
points: on the north of the temple, south beside the race-
course, and on the west of the city beside the royal palace.
The keenest struggle took place, first of all, at the temple.   The
Romans pressed forward successfully into the temple court;
but the Jews offered a most stubborn resistance,—mounted upon
the roofs of the buildings which surround the temple court,
and hurled down stones upon the soldiers.   These were
therefore obliged to have recourse to fire, set flames to the
roofs, and in this way succeeded at last in reaching the temple
mount.   When the longed for booty of the treasury of the
temple fell into their hands, Sabinus appropriated to himself
400 talents.[4]

But this first defeat of the rebels was only the signal for
the further spread of the rebellion.   In Jerusalem a portion
of the soldiers of Herod joined the rebels, and consequently
they were able to lay siege to Sabinus and his fighting force
in the palace of Herod.[5]   In the neighbourhood of Sepphoris
in Galilee, Judas, the son of that Hezekiah with whom Herod
had once, to the great indignation of the Sanhedrim, made
so short a process (see above, p. 109), gathered a number
about him, gained possession of the weapons stored up in the
royal arsenal, distributed these among his followers, and was

able then to make all Galilee unsafe. He is even said to have aimed at obtaining the royal crown.[6]   In Perea a certain Simon, formerly a slave of Herod, collected a band, and had himself proclaimed king by his followers ; but was soon afterwards conquered by a Roman detachment, and put to death.[7]   Finally, it is reported of one termed Athronges, formerly a shepherd, that he had assumed the royal crown, and for a long time, along with his four brothers, kept the country in a ferment.[8]—It was a time of general upheaval, when every one sought to secure the greatest possible benefit for himself.   On the part of the people there was agreement only on this one point, that every one wished at any cost to be freed from the power of the Romans.

When Varus was informed of these proceedings, he hastened from Antioch, with the two legions which he still had with him, in order to restore order in Palestine.   On the way he also procured, in addition, Arabian auxiliary troops sent by King Aretas, as well as other auxiliaries.   With this fighting force he first of all reduced Galilee.   Sepphoris, where that Judas had been fermenting disorder, was consigned to the flames, and the inhabitants sold as slaves.   Thence Varus proceeded to Samaria, which, however, he spared because it had not taken part in the revolt.   He then directed his course toward Jerusalem, where the legion stationed there was still being besieged by the Jews in the royal palace.   Varus had there an easy game to play ; for when the besiegers saw the powerful Roman forces approach, they lost their courage and took to flight.   In this way Varus became lord of city and country.   But Sabinus, who in consequence of his robbing the temple and of other misdeeds had no good conscience, made off as quickly as possible.   Varus then led his troops up and down through the country, apprehending the rebels who were now lurking here and there in small parties.   He had two thousand of them crucified, while he granted pardon to the mass of the people. After he had then stamped out the rebellion, he returned to Antioch.[9]

While these things were going on in Judea, Archelaus and Antipas were still in Rome waiting for the decision of the emperor. Before this was issued an embassy from the people of Judea appeared before the emperor, asking that none of the Herodians should be appointed king, but that they should be permitted to live in accordance with their own laws. About the same time Philip also, the last of the three brothers, to whom territories had been bequeathed by Herod, made his appearance in Rome in order to press his claims, and likewise to support those of his brother Archelaus.[10] In regard to these conflicting claims, Augustus was obliged at last to give a decision. In an assembly which he fixed precisely for this purpose in the temple of Apollo, he heard first of all the ambassadors from the Jewish people. These reported a long list of scandalous misdeeds which Herod had allowed and sought them to buttress, their demand that none of the Herodian race should any more govern in Palestine, but that it should be granted them to live according to their own laws under Roman suzerainty. When they had ended, Nicolas of Damascus arose and spoke on behalf of his master Archelaus.[11] When Augustus had thus heard both sides, he issued his decision after a few days. By it the will of Herod was in all essential points sustained. Archelaus obtained the territory assigned to him: Judea, Samaria, Idumea; only the cities of Gaza, Gadara, and Hippos were severed from these domains and attached to the province of Syria; and instead of the title of king, that of ethnarch was given him. Antipas obtained Galilee and Perea, with the title of tetrarch; Philip, also as tetrarch, received the districts of Batanea, Trachonitis, and Auranitis. Archelaus was to derive from his territories an income of 600 talents, Antipas 200 talents, and Philip 100 talents. Also Salome, the sister of Herod the Great, obtained the portion assigned to her, the cities of Jamnia, Azotus, Phasaelis, and 500,000 pieces of silver, in addition to the palace at Ascalon.[12]—Salome lived in the enjoyment of these possessions for some twelve or fourteen years. She died about A.D. 10, in the time of the procurator M. Ambivius, and bequeathed her property to the Empress Livia.[13]

What had been the empire of Herod was therefore now parted into three territories, each of which has for a while its own history.

§ 17. THE SONS OF HEROD

a. PHILIP, B.C. 4–A.D. 34. HIS TERRITORY UNDER THE ROMANS, A.D. 34–37.

THE extent of the territory which Philip received is variously stated in different places by Josephus.[1] Putting altogether, it embraced the districts of Batanea, Trachonitis, Auranitis, Gaulanitis, Panias, and, according to Luke iii. 1, also Iturea.[2] The districts named were not ancient tribal possessions of the Jewish people, but were in great part added to the Jewish territory in later times. The population was a mixed one ; and the non-Jewish, *i.e.* Syrian and Greek, element prevailed.[3] Philip himself was certainly a real exception among the sons and grandsons of Herod. While all the others, copying fathers and grandfathers, were ambitious, imperious, harsh, and tyrannical toward their subjects, nothing but what is honourable is told of Philip. His reign was mild, just, and peaceful. To the traditions of his father he remained faithful only in this, that he also sought renown in the construction of great buildings. The building of two cities by him is expressly reported. The ancient Panias, at the sources of the Jordan, north of the lake of Gennezaret, he rebuilt, with larger dimensions, and gave it, in honour of the emperor, the name of Caesarea. To distinguish it from the well-known Caesarea by the sea, it was called Caesarea Philippi, under which name we are familiar with it in the Gospel history (Matt. xvi. 13 ; Mark viii. 27). The other city which he rebuilt was the Bethsaida situated at the point where the Jordan enters into the lake of Gennezaret, which, in honour of the daughter of Augustus, he named Julias.[4] Josephus tells of him, incidentally, that he first discovered and proved that the supposed sources of the Jordan at Panias obtained their water by a subterranean passage from the so-called Phiala. Philip demonstrated this by throwing in chaff into the Phiala, which came out again at Panias.[5]

We know, however, nothing more about his reign beyond what Josephus tells us in reporting his death:[6] "He had shown himself a person of moderation and quietness in the conduct of his life and government. He constantly lived in that country which was subject to him. He used to make his progress with a few chosen friends; his tribunal, also, on which he sat in judgment, followed him in his progress; and when any one met him who wanted his assistance, he made no delay, but had his tribunal set down immediately, wheresoever he happened to be, and sat down upon it and heard his complaint; he then ordered the guilty, that were convicted, to be punished, and absolved those that were accused unjustly." — Of his private life we know only that he was married to Salome, daughter of Herodias, and that there were no children by this marriage.[7] — According to his political principles, he was a consistent friend of the Romans, and laid great value upon the favour of the emperor. This is shown not only in his giving to his cities the names of Caesarea and Julias, but also in his impressing upon his coins the images of Augustus and Tiberius,—this being the first instance in which any likeness was engraven on the coins of a Jewish prince.[8]

Philip died, after a reign of thirty-seven years, in the 20th year of Tiberius, A.D. 33-34, and was buried in the tomb built by himself.[9] His territory was then added to that of Syria, but retained the right of administering its own revenues;[10] and was again, after a few years, made over to a prince of the Herodian family. The Emperor Caligula, immediately after his succession to the throne, in March A.D. 37, gifted the tetrarchy of Philip to Agrippa, a son of that Aristobolus who had been executed by his father Herod, and so a grandson of Herod and Mariamme.[11]

b. HEROD ANTIPAS, B.C. 4–A.D. 39.

In the partition of their father's possessions, a larger slice than that given to Philip fell to the lot of his half-brother Antipas, or, as he is frequently called by Josephus, on the coins, and in the New Testament, Herod, to whom, as well as to Philip, was given the title of tetrarch.[1] His territory, embracing Galilee and Perea, was indeed broken up into two parts by the so-called Decapolis, which came in like a wedge between Galilee and Perea. But for this he was amply indemnified by the fact that the half of his domains consisted of the beautiful, fertile, and thickly-populated Galilee, with its vigorous and brave, though freedom-loving inhabitants.[2] In point of character, Antipas was a genuine son of old Herod,—sly, ambitious, and luxurious, only not so able as his father.[3] In regard to his slyness we have unmistakable evidence from the life of Jesus, who, on a memorable occasion, attached to him the designation of " that fox." [4] It was always necessary to have recourse to craft in order to keep the Galileans in order, and to guard the frontiers of Perea against the robber raids of the Arabians. For the defence of Galilee he rebuilt Sepphoris, that had been destroyed by fire by the soldiers of Varus(see above,p.161), and surrounded it with strong walls. And for the defence of Perea he fortified Betharamphtha, and named it after the emperor's wife Livias or Julias.[5] He was also undoubtedly induced by political motives to marry the daughter of the Arabian king Aretas.[6]

He thought that in this way he would be better able than by all fortifications to secure the country against the inroads of the Arabians ; and perhaps it was Augustus himself who persuaded him to enter on this marriage.[7]

Like all the Herods, Herod Antipas delighted in magnificent buildings. In this direction he was particularly taken up with the idea of building a splendid capital, which he undertook during the time of Tiberius. He selected, as the site for his city, the most beautiful spot in Galilee, the western bank of the lake of Gennezaret, in the neighbourhood of the warm springs of Emmaus. The choice of this spot was in one respect not a happy one. For just on that spot on which the city was built, as became apparent from the sepulchral monuments, was an ancient burying-ground, and the inhabiting of such a place was impossible to the Jews who strictly observed the law, since every contact with a grave occasioned ceremonial impurity of seven days.[8] Herod was therefore obliged, in order to secure inhabitants for his city, to settle there by force many foreigners, adventurers, and beggars, so that the population was of a very mixed description. But in regard to the beauty of the buildings nothing more perfect could be desired. It had, among other public structures, a στάδιον [9] and a royal palace, which, indeed, by its figures of animals gave offence, and during the war with the Romans was sacrificed to the fanaticism of the Jews.[10] Also there was not wanting a Jewish προσευχή, a μέγιστον οἴκημα.[11] The constitution of the city was wholly modelled upon the Hellenistic pattern. It had a council, βουλή, of 600 members, with an ἄρχων, and a committee of the δέκα πρῶτοι; also Hyparchs and an Agoranomos. In honour of the emperor the new capital was named Tiberias.[12]

During the time of Pilate, A.D. 26–36, Antipas, together with his brother, successfully made complaints against Pilate on account of his having set up an offensive votive shield in the palace at Jerusalem.[13] And as he was in this instance the representation of the Jewish claims, he also did not venture otherwise, notwithstanding his paganish buildings at Tiberias, to break away completely from the traditions of Judaism, and even in this respect showed himself a true son of Herod. From the Gospel we know that he went up to the feast at Jerusalem (Luke xxiii. 7); and his coins, just like those of old Herod, have upon them no image.

The complaint against Pilate was probably not made before A.D. 36.[14] Also what we otherwise known of Herod Antipas belongs to the later period, somewhere in the last ten years of his reign. During that period he was almost wholly under the influence of a woman, who occasioned to him a whole series of misfortunes. When once he made a journey to Rome, we know not for what purpose, nor exactly at what time, he started before the departure of his half-brother Herod, the son of Mariamme the high priest's daughter, who had been designated eventual successor to the throne in the first will of Herod (see above, p. 156). That Herod was married to Herodias, a daughter of Aristobulus, executed in B.C. 7. The issue of this marriage was Salome, the wife of the tetrarch Philip, who was then not the first husband, as the Gospels tell us, but the son-in-law of Herodias.[15] When now Antipas paid a visit to the house of his brother, he was fascinated by Herodias, and made his proposals of marriage, to which the ambitious woman readily assented. It was arranged that Herod on his return from Rome should divorce his wife, the daughter of Aretas, and should be married to Herodias. With this promise he proceeded on his journey to Rome. On his return, his wife, who had meanwhile obtained information about the proposed procedure, entreated him that he would have her sent to Machärus, the strong fortress east of the Dead Sea, which then belonged to Aretas. Since Antipas did not desire that his wife should know about his secret

plans, he granted her wish.   But scarcely had the daughter of
Aretas reached Machärus, when she fled thence to her father,
and let him know what friendly intentions her husband
entertained regarding her.   From that moment the Arabian
king took up an attitude of direct opposition to Herod
Antipas.[16]   Nevertheless Antipas seems to have proceeded
immediately with his marriage with Herodias.

At the time of this marriage, or soon thereafter, John the
Baptist and Jesus Christ made their appearance, both of
them carrying on their labours in the domains of Antipas, the
Baptist in Perea,   Jesus in Galilee.   Of John the Baptist,
Josephus gives the following account:[17] " He was a good man,
and commanded the Jews to exercise virtue, both as to
righteousness towards one another and piety towards God,
and so to come to baptism.   For the washing would be
acceptable to Him, if they made use of it, not in order to the
putting away of some sins only, but for the purification of
the body; supposing still that the soul was thoroughly
purified beforehand by righteousness.   Now, when many
others came to crowd about him, for they were greatly moved
by hearing his words, Herod, who feared lest the great
influence John had over the people might put it into his
power and inclination to raise a rebellion (for they seemed
ready to do anything he should advise), thought it best by
putting him to death to prevent any mischief he might cause,
and not bring himself into difficulties by sparing a man who
might make him repent of it when it should be too late.
Accordingly he was sent a prisoner, out of Herod's suspicious
temper, to Machärus, the castle I before mentioned, and was
there put to death."—This account by Josephus, if it really
belongs originally to him, and the accounts of the New Testament about the Baptist and his relation with the tetrarch
Herod, mutually supplement one another.   What Josephus
says about the contents of the Baptist's preaching of repent-

ance has indeed very much of the style of the cultured
Græco - Roman world. In this respect the short statements
of the synoptic Gospels are truer and more reliable. On the
other hand, it is highly probable that the real occasion of the
imprisonment of the Baptist by Antipas was, just as Josephus
states, fear of political trouble. The powerful popular preacher
did undoubtedly produce a great excitement, which was indeed
first of all of a religious kind, but certainly not without the
mingling of a political element. For the masses of the people
were not then able to keep separate their religious and
political hopes. It is therefore quite credible that Antipas
feared political troubles from the labours of the Baptist, and
so, when he extended his activity to Perea, cast him into
prison. Nevertheless the evangelists may be right (Matt.
xiv. 3 f. ; Mark vi. 17 ; Luke iii. 19 f.) when they say that
he did this because John blamed him for his marriage with
Herodias. The two statements are not inconsistent with one
another. —The place where John was imprisoned is not
named by the evangelists. From Josephus we learn that it
was Machärus, the strong fortress on the east of the Dead
Sea. It must then have been no longer in the possession of
the Arabian king Aretas, as it was at the time of the flight
of the first wife of Antipas, but in the possession of Herod
Antipas himself. We do not indeed know in what way it
had meanwhile come into his hands. —According to Josephus,
it would seem as if the execution of the Baptist followed
immediately upon his arrestment and imprisonment. But
from the Gospel narrative we see that Herod kept the Baptist
a longer time in prison, being undecided as to what he should
do with him.[18] At last the decision was brought about by
Herodias, the chief foe of the rigid preacher of repentance.
When on the occasion of the celebration of Antipas' birthday in the palace of Machärus, for there it was that the
whole business was carried out,[19] a great banquet was given,

the daughter of Herodias, Salome (she was still a κοράσιον, Matt. xiv. 11; Mark vi. 22, 28; therefore not yet married to Philip), by her dancing so delighted the tetrarch, that he promised to fulfil to her any wish she might express. At the instigation of her mother, she demanded the head of the Baptist. Herod was weak enough to gratify the wish immediately, and to give orders that the Baptist should be beheaded in the prison at Machärus.[20]

Even before John had been removed from the scene, the " *Mightier*," to whom he had pointed, had already made His appearance, and had begun to preach the gospel in Galilee. He, too, could not remain unnoticed by the nobles of the land. Yet Antipas first heard of the deeds of Jesus after the Baptist had been put to death. Hence, tormented by his evil conscience, he felt convinced that the Baptist had risen again, and was continuing his dangerous and revolutionary work.[21] In order to make sure whether this was so, he desired to see the miracle-worker who preached in Capernaum, and attracted all the people.[22] He meant in time to get rid of Him, not, however, by violence, but by craft. He won over to him the Pharisees, and got them to undertake the attempt to induce Jesus voluntarily to quit the country by representing to Him that Herod sought His life.[23] The plan was indeed very craftily conceived; but it failed in execution, because Jesus saw through it. Subsequently, indeed, Jesus did quit Galilee in order to take His death journey to Jerusalem. There also Antipas, who was at that time living at Jerusalem that he might keep the Passover, had the satisfaction of meeting with his mysterious subject. Pilate sent the prisoner to him, in order that he, as ruler of the province, might pronounce the death sentence clamoured for by the Jewish hierarchy. Antipas, however, would not lend himself to this scheme, but contented himself with pouring contempt upon Jesus, and sending Him back again to Pilate.[24]

The connection with Herodias brought little good to Antipas. The Arabian king Aretas could not forget that Antipas on her account had repudiated his daughter. The feud arising from this cause was increased through boundary disputes about Galaaditis,—for so we should read the name rather than Gamalitis.[25] Finally, in A.D. 36 the misunderstanding between the two neighbours broke out into the war which ended in the utter destruction of the army of Antipas.[26] The conquered monarch had now no other resource but to complain of his victorious opponent to the Emperor Tiberius.[27]

When Tiberius heard of the bold proceedings of the Arabian prince, he gave Vitellius, governor of Syria, express orders to gain possession of Aretas, dead or alive. Vitellius had indeed little heart to enter on the expedition, for he was not greatly drawn toward Antipas. But he could not oppose the imperial command, and so he prepared himself for the war against Aretas. After he had ordered his army to march round about Judea to Petra, he himself went on a visit to Jerusalem, where a feast was then being celebrated, probably that of the Passover. He waited in that city three days. On the fourth, he received news of the death of Tiberius, which had taken place on 16th March A.D. 37. He considered himself thereby released from his undertaking, and turned back with his army to Antioch.[28] Thus the defeat of Antipas remained unavenged.

About this time we find our Jewish tetrarch present on one occasion at the Euphrates during important negotiations between Vitellius and the king of the Parthians. But it seems that the account of this affair in Josephus is not free from error. We know, for instance, that in the years 35 and 36 the Parthian king Artabanus had to do repeatedly with the Romans. His affairs seemed to be taking a favourable turn when, by the threats of Vitellius and the revolt of his own subjects, he was obliged to betake himself to flight into the remoter provinces. In consequence of this, Vitellius, in the summer of A.D. 36, went to the Euphrates along with the pretender Tiridates, supported by the Romans, and established him as king over the Parthians. Nevertheless, before the end of that same year, Artabanus returned, drove out Tiridates, and secured the government again to himself.[29] Subsequently Vitellius arranged a meeting with Artabanus at the Euphrates, at which Artebanus concluded a peace with the Romans, and in pledge thereof, sent his son Darius to Rome as a hostage.[30] At this meeting, according to Josephus, Herod Antipas was also present. He entertained Vitellius and Artabanus in a magnificent tent erected upon the Euphrates bridge, and hastened, as soon as the negotiations were concluded, to communicate the favourable result to the emperor,—a piece of officiousness which annoyed Vitellius at him exceedingly, since he had thereby completely anticipated his official report.[31] —Thus Josephus places this meeting in the time of Tiberius, and considers that the quarrel arising out of this between Vitellius and Herod Antipas was the reason why Vitellius, after the death of Tiberius, immediately abandoned the campaign against Aretas. But Suetonius and Dio Cassius say expressly, and the silence of Tacitus, in the sixth book of his *Annals*, indirectly proves, that the meeting between Vitellius and Artabanus took place under Caligula. Josephus therefore is certainly in one particular in error. The only question is, in what particular. If it is correct that Herod Antipas took part in the Parthian negotiations on the Euphrates in the time of Tiberius, then these must have been the negotiations between Vitellius and Tiridates in the summer of A.D. 36 (Tacitus, *Annals*, vi. 37). But if it is correct that he took part in the negotiations between Vitellius and Artabanus, it cannot have been before the time of Caligula. The latter supposition is most probably the true account of the matter. For in summer A.D. 36 Herod was engaged in the war against Aretas.

If Antipas had his passion for Herodias to thank as the real occasion of his defeat and damage at the hand of Aretas, the ambition of this wife of his brought about at last the loss of his government and of his freedom. One of the first acts of the new Emperor Caligula on his taking the reins of government into his hands was to assign to Agrippa, the brother of Herodias, what had been the tetrarchy of Philip, together with the title of king. Agrippa at first remained still at Rome. But in the second year of Caligula, March A.D. 38 to March A.D. 39, he went to Palestine, and made his appearance there as king. The success of the adventurer, whose fortunes had once been at so low an ebb, and who had even himself sought aid at the hand of Antipas, excited the envy of Herodias, who therefore insisted upon her husband seeking also from the emperor the royal title. Herod Antipas was not very much disposed to go forth on such an errand. At last, however, he was obliged to yield to the persistent entreaty of his wife, and proceeded to Rome, accompanied by Herodias, to prosecute his suit. But they were immediately followed by a representative of Agrippa, Fortunatus, with a document containing charges against Herod Antipas, in which he was accused of old and recent offences, of having made a compact with Sejanus (who died in A.D. 31), and with the Parthian king Artabanus. In proof of these charges, his accuser pointed to the accumulation of arms made by Antipas. Both parties came at the same time before Caligula at Baiae. When the emperor had heard the petition of Antipas and the accusations against him, he asked Antipas how it was that he had made such a collection of arms. And when Antipas could give no proper account of this, Caligula credited also the other charges, deposed Antipas from his tetrarchy, and banished him to Lyons in Gaul. He wished to allow Herodias, as the sister of Agrippa, to live on her private estate. But the proud woman scorned the imperial favour, and followed her husband into his exile. As a new proof of imperial favour, the

tetrarchy was conferred upon the accuser Agrippa.[32]   Herod
Antipas died in banishment.   A confused statement in Dio
Cassius seems to imply that he was put to death by
Caligula.[33]

c. ARCHELAUS, B.C. 4–A.D. 6.   HIS TERRITORY UNDER ROMAN PROCURATORS, A.D. 6–A.D. 41.

Judea proper with Samaria and Idumea (including the large
cities of Caesarea, Samaria, Joppa, and Jerusalem, but exclud-
ing Gaza, Gadara, and Hippos) was in the partition assigned
to Archelaus, the elder [1] brother of Antipas, not indeed, as
Herod had intended, with the title of king, but only with that
of an ethnarch.[2]   Yet Augustus promised him the kingdom
if he should prove himself to be worthy of it.[3]   Archelaus
also, like Antipas, named himself on the coins and elsewhere
by the family name of Herod.[4]

Among the sons of Herod he procured for himself the
worst reputation.   His rule was violent and tyrannical.[5]   He
set up and removed the high priests at his pleasure.[6]   He
gave special offence by his marriage with Glaphyra, daughter
of the Cappadocian king Archelaus.   She had been married
first to Alexander, the half-brother of Archelaus, executed in
B.C. 7.   See above, p. 152 of this work.   After his death
she was married to Juba, king of Mauritania.[7]   Upon the
dissolution of this marriage,[8] Glaphyra lived in her father's
house.   There Archelaus became acquainted with her, fell in
love with her, and took her to be his wife, for he divorced his
own wife Mariamme.   Seeing that Glaphyra had children by
Alexander, the marriage was unlawful, and therefore gave
great offence.[9]   The marriage was not indeed of long duration,
for Glaphyra died soon after her arrival in Judea,[10] after
having had a remarkable dream, in which her first husband,

Alexander, appeared to her, and made known to her her approaching death.[11]

It will almost go without saying that Archelaus as son of Herod engaged upon great building enterprises. The palace at Jericho was restored in the most magnificent style. An aqueduct was built to lead the water necessary for the palm-groves, which he had laid out anew in the plain north of Jericho, from the village of Neara. He also founded a city, and called it in honour of himself Archelais.[12]

But these beautiful and useful undertakings could not reconcile his subjects to his misgovernment. After tolerating his rule for more than nine years, a deputation of the Jewish and Samaritan aristocracy set out for Rome, in order to lay their complaints against him before Augustus. The points in their accusation must have been very serious; for the emperor felt himself obliged to summon Archelaus to Rome, and, after having heard him, to depose him from his government, and banish him to Vienne in Gaul in A.D. 6. To him also, as to his wife, his fate had been foretold by a remarkable dream.[13]

The territory of Archelaus was taken under immediate Roman rule, for it was attached to the province of Syria, but received a governor of its own from the equestrian order.[14] In consequence of this arrangement the condition of Judea became essentially changed. Herod the Great and his sons had in spite of all their friendship for the Romans considerable respect for and understanding of the national traditions and peculiarities of the Jews, so that they, apart from individual exceptions, did not wantonly wound the most sacred sensibilities of the people. Common prudence demanded in regard to such matters care and consideration. The Romans, on the other hand, had scarcely any appreciation of what was peculiar to the Jewish nationality. As the religious views of the Pharisees and the accumulation of traditions which encompassed the daily life of the people like a net were altogether

unknown to the Romans, they could not at all understand
how a whole people would offer the most persistent resistance
even unto death, and would suffer annihilation on account of
merely ceremonial rites and what seemed matters of indifference.   The Jews again saw in the simplest rules of
administration, such as the proposal of a census made at the
very beginning, an encroachment upon the most sacred rights
of the people, and from day to day the feeling more and more
gained ground that the immediate government of the Romans,
which at the death of Herod they had wished for,[15] was
irreconcilable with the principles of the theocracy.   Thus,
even had there been the best of intentions on both sides, the
relations inevitably became strained and ultimately hostile.
But this good-will was only partially exhibited.   Those at
the head of the government, with the exception of the times
of Caligula, were indeed ready on their part to make concessions and to exercise forbearance in a very large measure.
But their good intentions were always rendered nugatory by
the perversity of the procurators, not infrequently also by
gross miscarriage of justice on the part of these officials.
Those subordinate officers, like all petty governors, were
usually puffed up by a consciousness of their absolute authority, and by their insolent demeanour at last drove the
oppressed and burdened people to such a pitch of excitement
that they rushed headlong with wild fanaticism into a war
that plainly involved annihilation.

———————

Seeing that the political affairs of Judea during the period
A.D. 6–41 were in all essential respects the same as those of
Palestine generally during the period A.D. 44–66, in the
following exposition we take the two periods together, and
make use of materials from the one period as well as from
the other.

Judea, and subsequently all Palestine, was not in the strict sense of the term incorporated with the province of Syria, but had a governor of its own of equestrian rank, who stood only to a certain extent in dependence upon the imperial legate of Syria.[16] It therefore belonged to the third class of imperial provinces, according to Strabo's classification.[17] And this third class is to be regarded as an exception to the rule ; for most of the imperial provinces were, just like the senatorial provinces, administered by men of senatorial rank ; the greater provinces, like that of Syria, by men who had been consuls, the smaller ones, by those who had been praetors. Only a few particular provinces were in an exceptional manner placed under governors of equestrian rank, namely, those in which, on account of special tenacity in adhering to peculiar national customs, or on account of the rudeness and savage state of the country, the government could not be carried on by the usual methods. The best known example is that of Egypt. Elsewhere there were also territories inhabited by a still semi-barbarous people which were administered in this manner.

The usual title for such an equestrian governor was *procurator*, ἐπίτροπος. It seems indeed that Augustus, not only in Egypt, but elsewhere as well, preferred the title *praefactus*, ἔπαρχος. Very soon, however, at farthest in the time of Claudius, except in the case of Egypt, the title *procurator* had become the prevailing one. Josephus, as a rule, designates the governor of Judea ἐπίτροπος, sometimes ἔπαρχος or ἡγεμών.[18] In the New Testament, ἡγεμών = *praeses*, is the term usually employed.[19] That ἐπίτροπος (*procurator*) is the correct title may be also proved by witnesses of another kind.[20] In general this title was used for all imperial finance officers, while *praefactus* was more of a military title. Such finance procurators were found also in all other provinces, in the imperial as well as the senatorial provinces. They were chosen not only from the equestrian order, but even from among the freedmen of the emperor. Those procurators, on the other hand, who had to administer a province, on account of the military command that was necessarily connected with such an appointment, were chosen exclusively from the ranks of the equestrians. It was an unheard of novelty when under Claudius the office of procurator of Judea was given to a freedman, Felix (see below under § 19).

The procurators of Judea seem to have been subordinate to the governor of Syria only to this extent, that it was the right and duty of the governor to interfere in the exercise of his supreme power in cases of necessity. Writers have indeed sometimes expressed themselves as if Judea had been incorporated into the province of Syria. But they do not continue consistent to such a view.[21] The investing the procurator with a military command, and with independent jurisdiction, of itself conferred upon him a position, in virtue of which he was, in regard to ordinary transactions within the limits of his province, as independent as the governors of other provinces. On the other hand, the governor of Syria had the right, according to his own discretion, to interfere if he had reason to fear revolutionary uprisings or the appearance of other serious difficulties. He would then take command in Judea as the superior of the procurator.[22] Whether this superior authority went so far that he might even call the procurator to account seems questionable, since, in the two cases in which this happened, the governor concerned had been probably entrusted with a special commission.[23]

The residence of the procurator of Judea was not at Jerusalem, but at Caesarea.[24] Since the dwelling of the commander-in-chief or governor was called *praetorium*, the πραιτώριον τοῦ Ἡρώδου in Caesarea (Acts xxiii. 35) was nothing else than a palace built by Herod, which served as a residence for the procurator.——On special occasions, especially during the chief Jewish feasts, when, on account of the crowds of people that streamed into Jerusalem, particularly careful oversight was necessary, the procurator went up to Jerusalem, and resided then in what had been the palace of Herod.[25] The praetorium at Jerusalem, in which Pilate was staying at the time of the trial and condemnation of Jesus Christ (Matt. xxvii. 27 ; Mark xv. 16 ; John xviii. 28, 33, xix. 9), is therefore just the well-known palace of Herod, on the west side of the city. It was not only a princely dwelling, but at the same time a strong castle, in which at times (during the rebellion in B.C. 4, and again in A.D. 66) large detachments of troops could maintain their position against the assaults of the whole mass of the people.[26] Hence, also, during the residence there of the procurator, the detachment of troops accompanying him had their quarters within its walls (Mark xv. 16).

With reference to the military arrangements, it deserves specially to be remembered that the Roman army of the days of the empire was divided into two divisions of a thoroughly distinct kind : the legions and the auxiliaries. The legions formed the proper core of the troops, and consisted only of Roman citizens, for those provincials who served in the legions had obtained citizen rights. Each legion formed a compact whole of ten cohorts, or sixty centuries, altogether embracing from 5000 to 6000 men. The auxiliary troops consisted of provincials who, at least in the early days of the empire, did not as a rule possess the right of citizenship. Their arms were lighter and less harmonious than those of the legions ; often in this they were allowed to follow their own national usages. Their infantry was formed into cohorts, whose strength varied from 500 to 1000 men ; the cavalry was formed into *alae*, of similarly varying strength.

Cohorts and *alae* were named after the nation from which they had been recruited.

In regard to the provinces administered by procurators, it may, as a rule, be assumed that in them, and under the command of the procurator, there would be only auxiliary troops. This rule is also confirmed by the history of Judea. There were legions only in Syria; in the time of Augustus three, from the time of Tiberius four.[27] But in Judea, down to the time of Vespasian, there were only auxiliary troops, and, indeed, mostly such as had been raised in the country itself. The honour and burden of this levy lay only on the non-Jewish inhabitants of Palestine. The Jews were exempted from military service. This is abundantly proved to have been the state of matters, at least, from the time of Caesar,[28] and, from all that we positively know about the Palestinian troops down to the days of Vespasian, may also be assumed as certain throughout the imperial period. Remarkable as this unequal treatment of the population may appear to us, it is in thorough correspondence with what is otherwise known regarding the Roman procedure in the conscription. Indeed, in regard to the use made of the inhabitants and the confidence reposed in them, the provinces were treated in very diverse ways and varying measures in the matter of military service.

For the period A.D. 6–41 we are without any direct information about the troops stationed in Judea. But it is highly probable that the *Sebastians*, *i.e.* the soldiers drafted in the region of Sebaste or Samaria, whom we meet with subsequently, constituted even then a considerable portion of the garrison. In the struggles which followed the death of Herod in B.C. 4, the best equipped part of the troops of Herod fought on the side of the Romans, namely, the Σεβασ-τηνοὶ τρισχίλιοι, under the command of Rufus and Gratus, the former of whom commanded the cavalry, the latter the

infantry.[29] The troops thus proved would be undoubtedly
retained by Archelaus, and it is highly probable that, after
his deposition in A.D. 6, they would be taken over by the
Romans, then, from A.D. 41 to A.D. 44, by Agrippa, and after
his death again by the Romans. The following also speaks
in favour of this supposition. At the death of Agrippa in
A.D. 44, the troops of the king stationed in Caesarea, which
were Καισαρεῖς καὶ Σεβαστηνοί, gave expression in a very
unseemly manner to their joy at the death of the ruler that
had shown himself friendly to the Jews. In order to show
respect to the memory of Agrippa, the emperor ordered these
troops, namely, τὴν ἴλην τῶν Καισαρέων καὶ τῶν Σεβαστηνῶν
καὶ τὰς πέντε σπείρας (therefore an *ala* of cavalry and five
cohorts), to be sent by way of punishment to Pontus. On
their presenting a petition, however, it was agreed that they
should remain in Judea, from which they were first removed
by Vespasian.[30] From this it appears that the troops of
Agrippa were certainly taken over by the Romans. From
this it may be inferred that in the same way they were taken
over after the deposition of Archelaus. It is also somewhat
remarkable that the one *ala* of cavalry and five cohorts of
infantry, if we reckon the latter at 500 men, would make
together a force of 3000 men, which is the same number as
is ascribed to the Sebastian troops of B.C. 4.—During the
period A.D. 44–66 these troops are often referred to. The
procurator Cumanus led the *ala Sebastenorum* and four cohorts
of infantry from Caesarea against the Jews.[31] During the
struggles between the Jewish and Gentile inhabitants of
Caesarea, the latter boasted of the fact that the Roman troops
in Caesarea consisted in great part of Caesareans and Sebastians.[32] Finally, in A.D. 67, Vespasian was able to draft into
his army from Caesarea five cohorts and one *ala* of cavalry;[33]
therefore the same detachments as were there in A.D. 44.
Probably also the Sebasteni so often referred to on the

inscriptions are identical with our Sebastian troops.   Also
the σπεῖρα Σεβαστή, which at the time of the imprisonment
of Paul, about A.D. 60, lay in Caesarea (Acts xxvii. 1), is
undoubtedly one of the five cohorts which we hear about
from Josephus.   Many theologians, however, have erroneously
come to the conclusion that the expression σπεῖρα Σεβαστή
is synonymous with σπεῖρα Σεβαστηνῶν.   This is not
possible.   Σεβαστή is rather an exact translation of *Augusta*,
a title of honour very frequently bestowed upon auxiliary
troops.   The cohort in question was therefore probably
called *cohors Augusta Sebastenorum*.   In Caesarea it was
called simply σπεῖρα Σεβαστή, since this sufficed to distinguish it from others. —It is, on the other hand, remarkable,
after other results we have reached, that in Caesarea, about A.D.
40, a σπεῖρα Ἰταλική should have been stationed (Acts x. 1),
by which probably a cohort of Roman citizens of Italy is to
be understood.   Such a band would naturally not have
served in Caesarea during the period A.D. 41–44 under the
Jewish king Agrippa.   But even in reference to a later
period, it is after the above made investigations not probable.
The story of the centurion Cornelius lies, therefore, in this
respect under suspicion, the circumstances of a later period
having been transferred back to an earlier period.   That at
some time or other a *cohors Italica* was in Syria is made
perfectly clear by the evidence of an inscription.

We have hitherto become acquainted only with the state
of the garrison of Caesarea.   In other cities and towns of
Palestine there were also small garrisons.   At the outbreak
of the Jewish war in A.D. 66, we find, for example, a Roman
garrison in the fortified castle of Jericho and in Machärus.[34]
Throughout Samaria such detachments were stationed.[35]   In
the Great Plain there was a *decurio;*[36] in Ascalon (which,
however, did not belong to the domains of the procurator)
there were a cohort and an *ala*.[37]   Vespasian, in the winter

of A.D. 67–68, placed garrisons in all conquered villages and
towns; those in the former under the command of Decurions,
those in the latter under the command of Centurions.[38] This
was indeed an extraordinary proceeding, which we are not to
regard as the rule in time of peace.

In Jerusalem there was stationed only one cohort. For
the χιλίαρχος, so often referred to in the Acts of the
Apostles (more exactly, Acts xxi. 31 : χιλίαρχος τῆς σπείρης,
"One having command of the cohort"), appears throughout as the officer holding the chief command in Jerusalem.[39] With this also Josephus' statement agrees, that
in the fortress of Antonia a τάγμα of the Romans regularly
lay,[40] for the τάγμα there means, not as it often does, a legion,
but, as in the passage quoted in note 48, a cohort. The fort
of Antonia, which Josephus describes as the regular quarters
of the detachment, lay to the north of the temple. At two
points, stairs (καταβάσεις) led down from the fort Antonia
to the court of the temple.[41] This is just the position given
it in the Acts of the Apostles. For when Paul, during the
tumult in the temple, had been taken by the soldiers for his
own safety and was being carried thence into the barracks
(παρεμβολή), he was on account of the pressure of the crowd
borne by the soldiers up the steps (τοὺς ἀναβαθμούς), and
then, with the permission of the chiliarch, he made from these
steps a speech to the people (Acts xxi. 31–40).[42] The officer
in command at fort Antonia, who is certainly identical with
the chiliarch, is also called by Josephus φρούραρχος.[43] The
direct connection between the fort and the court of the temple
was of importance, since the latter required to be under
constant supervision. At the chief feasts, guards were
stationed in the corridors which surrounded the temple.[44]
—From one passage in the Acts of the Apostles (chap. xxiii.
23) we see that there was a detachment of cavalry along with
the Jerusalem cohort, an arrangement that very frequently

existed.   The precise character and position of the δεξιολάβοι
(from λαβή, " the grip," therefore : " those who grasped their
weapons by the right hand "), mentioned in that passage
(xxiii. 23) as accompanying the regular soldiers and cavalry,
are somewhat obscure.   Seeing that the expression occurs
elsewhere in Greek literature only twice, and even then appears
without explanation, we are no longer in a position to explain
it.   This much only is certain, that it designated a special
class of light-armed soldiers (javelin-throwers or slingers).

After the great war of A.D. 66–73 the garrison arrangements of Palestine were essentially changed.   The governor
was then no longer a procurator of the equestrian order, but a
legate of senatorial rank (in the earlier period, one who had
been praetor; in the later period, one who had been consul).
On the site of the destroyed Jerusalem a legion, the *legio X.
Fretensis*, had its headquarters (see under § 20, toward the end).
The native troops, which for decades had formed the garrison
of Caesarea, were drafted by Vespasian to other provinces.[45]
In their place were put auxiliary troops of foreign origin,
drawn in part from the farthest lands of the West.

Besides the troops forming the standing army, the provincial governors sometimes organized a militia, *i.e.* in special
cases of need those of the people capable of bearing arms were
drafted into military service, without being permanently
organized as a part of the army.   An instance of this sort
occurred in the arming of the Samaritans by Cumanus on the
occasion of the war against the Jews.[46]

Like the governors of senatorial rank, the procurators also
had, besides the supreme military command, supreme judicial
authority within their province.   This authority was
exercised by the procurators of Judea only in extraordinary
cases; for the ordinary administration of the law, both in
criminal and in civil matters, was left in the hands of the
native and local courts (see Div. II. vol. i. 184–190). —
The range of the procurator's judicial jurisdiction extended

also to the right of deciding matters of life and death, *jus gladii* or *potestas gladii*. That this also is true of the governors is proved by several inscriptions. With reference to Judea, Josephus says expressly that the procurator had μέχρι τοῦ κτείνειν ἐξουσίαν.[47] This right of the governor over life and death down to the third century after Christ extended even to the case of Roman citizens, with this restriction, however, that such a one had the right of appealing against the sentence of the governor to the emperor. In the earlier days of the empire, it would seem that a Roman citizen accused of an offence constituting a capital charge had the important privilege of appealing to the emperor, even at the beginning of the proceedings and any subsequent stage of the trial, claiming that the investigation be carried on at Rome and the judgment pronounced by the emperor himself.[48] The governor's absolute penal jurisdiction therefore applied only to provincials. It was a gross violation of the law when Florus in Jerusalem, in A.D. 66, had the Jews crucified who were in possession of equestrian rank.[49] But even provincials might be sent by the governor for trial to Rome, if he wished on account of the difficulty of the case to have the decision of the emperor.[50] —The fact known from the Gospels, that the procurator of Judea at the feast of the Passover set free a prisoner, was grounded indeed on a special authorization of the emperor; for the right of remitting a sentence was not otherwise given to the governors.

Although the governor, as sole judge, had to give the decision, he frequently availed himself of the advice of his *comites*. These were partly the higher officials of his court, partly the younger people, who, for the sake of their own training, accompanied the governor. They supported him, not only in administrative matters, but also assisted him in the execution of the law as *consilium*, συμβούλιον (Acts xxv. 12).[51]

The execution of the death sentence was, as a rule, carried

out by soldiers. Le Blant has, indeed, in a learned dissertation, sought to prove that those appointed to this duty were
not soldiers, but belonging to the class of *apparitores*, i.e.
the non-military servants of the governor.[52] But the opposite
opinion, at least with regard to capital sentences pronounced
by the imperial governors, must be considered as absolutely
certain. The imperial governors were military administrators;
their judicial power therefore the outcome of their military
authority.[53] It is, however, unquestionable, and is not disputed
even by Le Blant, that the death sentences on soldiers were
executed by soldiers.[54] According to Le Blant's view, this
inference should be drawn from that fact, namely, that the
governor carried out the death sentences on soldiers by
different parties than those employed upon civilians. This,
in view of the military character of his judicial authority, is
extremely improbable, and it even forms a positive proof for
the opposite theory. The many executions of distinguished
men and women in the times of Claudius and Nero were
carried out by military men, some of them officers of high
rank.[55] Numerous examples of a similar kind might be
cited from the history of the following emperors. Although
these cases might not apply to ordinary courts, yet this much
is clear, that the carrying out of executions by soldiers
was not opposed to Roman sentiment. But further, not
infrequently *speculatores* are spoken of as executing the condemned.[56] These were certainly soldiers; for (1) the *specu-*
latores are frequently described as holding a military office ;
and (2) in several of the passages quoted the *speculatores*
referred to are distinctly characterized as soldiers ;[57] and so
those elsewhere spoken of under the same title, and as
discharging the same functions, will have been also soldiers.
When Le Blant expressly refers to the fact that in many
passages the term *speculator* is interchanged with the expression
lictor, and with other words which designate non - military

offices, this may be said in the first place to result from a certain laxity in the use of language. On the contrary, one would be equally justified in saying that those expressions are now also used for designating military persons. In the New Testament the agents entrusted with the carrying out the sentence, both at the crucifixion of Christ and at the imprisonment of Paul, are named στρατιῶται, and are also plainly described as such.[58]

The third chief function of the procurator - governor, in addition to the command of the troops and judicial authority, was the administration of the finance department. From this, indeed, those equestrian governors got their title; for the imperial finance officials generally were called "procurators." Since everything that is of consequence about the different sorts of revenue and methods of taxation will be considered in the Excursus on the Census of Quirinius (original edition), it is not necessary here to say more than this, that the revenue of Judea as imperial province went, not into the treasury of the Senate, the *aerarium*, but into the imperial treasury, the *fiscus*. Judea therefore, in the strict sense of the word, paid its taxes "to Caesar" (Matt. xxii. 17 ff.; Mark xii. 14 ff.; Luke xx. 22 ff.), which could only in a certain degree be said of the senatorial provinces.—It was probably for the purposes of tax collection that Judea was divided into eleven toparchies (see Div. II. vol. i. pp. 157–161). In the gathering of the revenue the Romans seem to have made use of the Jewish courts, as was their custom in other places (see Div. II. vol. i. p. 162).—That the taxes were oppressive, is seen from the complaints made by the provinces of Syria and Judea in A.D. 17.[59]

From the taxes in the proper sense are to be distinguished the customs, *i.e.* duties upon articles on their being exported from the country. These were imposed in all the provinces of the Roman empire. The great trade emporium which

yielded the largest returns in this direction was Egypt. From
the days of the Ptolemies it had taken advantage of its
geographical position in order to secure the flourishing traffic
between India and Europe. But even in Palestine they
were acquainted with the "custom" as early as the Persian
era (Ezra iv. 13, 20, vii. 24).—The range to which the
"custom" applied, varied certainly according to circumstances.
In general it may be assumed that every province of the
Roman empire formed a customs district by itself. But
also the States and Communes recognised by the Romans as
autonomous, and the number of these was very large, had the
right of independently levying duties within their own
boundaries. To the proofs in regard to these matters
already in earlier times acknowledged, there has now to be
added : a long inscription in Greek and Aramaic, which contains the customs-tariff of the city of Palmyra in the time
of Hadrian. From this inscription it appears that Palmyra,
although it was at that time a Roman city in the same sense
as many other autonomous communes within the Roman
empire, administered independently its own customs, and
enjoyed the revenues thereof. It is therefore perfectly
evident that the kings and tetrarchs "confederate" with
Rome within their own territories could levy their customs
for their own behoof, only with this restriction, that the Roman
citizens (*Romani ac socii nominis Latini*, as it is phrased
by Livy) should be exempted from them. The customs
raised at Capernaum, within the borders of Galilee, in the
times of Christ (Matt. ix. 9 ; Mark ii. 14 ; Luke v. 27) went
therefore, undoubtedly, not into the imperial *fiscus*, but into
the treasury of Herod Antipas. On the other hand, in Judea
at that time, the customs were raised in the interests of the
imperial *fiscus*. We know from the Gospels that in Jericho,
on the eastern borders of Judea, there was an ἀρχιτελώνης
(Luke xix. 1, 2). In the seaport town of Caesarea in A.D.

66, among the influential men of the Jewish community, there John, a τελώνης, is mentioned.[60] It is stated by Pliny that the merchants who exported incense from Central Arabia through Gaza had to pay a high duty, not only to the Arabians on passing through their territory, but also to the Roman customs officers, who, it may be supposed, were stationed at Gaza.[61]—Besides the import and export duties, it would seem as if in Judea, as well as elsewhere, indirect duties of another sort had also to be paid, e.g. a market toll in Jerusalem, introduced by Herod, but abolished in A.D. 36 by Vitellius.[62]

The collecting of the customs was not done by officers of the State, but by lessees, the so-called *publicani*, who leased the customs of a particular district for a fixed annual sum; so that whatever in excess of that sum the revenue yielded was their gain; whereas, if the revenue fell below it, they had to bear the loss.[101] This system was widely prevalent throughout ancient times, and came often to be applied, not only to the customs, but also to the taxes properly so called. Thus, e.g. during the Ptolemaic government of Palestine the taxes of each city were annually leased out to the highest bidder.[63] In the days of the Roman empire the system of leasing was no longer applied to the taxes, i.e. the land-tax and poll-tax. These were now collected by officers of State: in senatorial provinces, by the quaestor; in imperial provinces, by an imperial procurator, assistants to the governor; in provinces like Judea, administered by an equestrian, the governor was himself at the same time procurator. The customs, on the other hand, were, even in the days of the empire, still commonly leased out to *publicani*. So, undoubtedly, it was in Judea. The contrary opinion of Wieseler rests manifestly on a misunderstanding.[64] In the passage cited from Pliny, in note 100, it is expressly said, that for the incense exported from Arabia by way of Gaza a duty had also to be paid to

the Roman *publicani*.   From the universality of the system,
it may be assumed that territorial princes like Herod Antipas
would also make use of it.   Even city communes like Palmyra
did not have their customs collected by municipal officials, but
rented them out to lessees.   —— The lessees again, as may be
readily supposed, had their subordinate officials, who would
usually be chosen from the native population.   But even the
principal lessees were by no means necessarily Romans.   The
tax-gatherers of Jericho (Luke xix. 1, 2) and of Caesarea—
Zaccheus and John—were therefore Jews.   Since they are
described as well-to-do and respectable people, they certainly
cannot have belonged to the lowest class of publicans.[65] ——
The extent to which custom might be charged was indeed
prescribed by the court; but since these tariffs, as we see
from the case of Palmyra, were in early times often very
indefinite, abundant room was left for the arbitrariness and
rapacity of the tax-gatherer.   The advantage taken of such
opportunities, and the not infrequent overcharges that were
made by these officials, made them as a class hated by the
people.   Not only in the New Testament are the terms
" publican and sinner " almost synonymous, but also in
rabbinical literature tax-gatherers (מוֹכְסִין) appear in an even
less favourable light.[66] —— On the other hand, the people
generally then, just as in the present day, were inventive
of contrivances of ways and means for defrauding the
revenue.[67]

Within the limits, which were stated in the very regulations themselves, the Jewish people enjoyed even yet a very
considerable measure of freedom in home affairs and self-
administration.[110] —— The oath of allegiance which the people
had to take to the emperor, presumably on every change of
government, was, if we may judge from analogous cases, more
an oath of confederates than one of subjects, such as had been
given even so early as the times of Herod.[68] ——The constitution

as regards home affairs, during the age of the procurators, is characterized by Josephus, in opposition to the monarchial rule of Herod and Archelaus, in the words : [69] ἀριστοκρατία μὲν ἦν ἡ πολιτεία, τὴν δὲ προστασίαν τοῦ ἔθνους οἱ ἀρχιερεῖς ἐπεπίστευντο. He sees, therefore, in the change which took place after the deposition of Archelaus, a transition from monarchy to aristocracy, because he, and that not incorrectly, considers the Roman procurator only as an overseer, but the aristocratic Sanhedrim as the real governing body. He who held the office of high priest for the time, who also held the presidency of the Sanhedrim, is called by Josephus προστάτης τοῦ ἔθνους. Yet certainly these very high priests were set up and removed at the arbitrary pleasure of the overseer. But even in this matter the Romans restrained themselves within certain limits. Whereas during the period A.D. 6–41 the appointments had been made by the Roman governors, either the legate of Syria or the procurator of Judea, during the the period A.D. 44–66 the right of appointment was transferred to the Jewish princes, Herod of Chalcis and Agrippa II., although these did not reign in Judea. And in both periods the appointments were not made in a purely arbitrary manner, but respect was paid to the claims of certain families (Phabi, Boethos, Ananus, Kamith).

Of greater importance is the fact that the Sanhedrim exercised to a very large extent the right of legislating and of executing the law, to a larger extent indeed than on the average was the case among non-autonomous communities in the Roman empire.[114] The state of the law was in general this, that the communities recognised by Rome as " free " or " autonomous " had expressly guaranteed to them the right of passing and executing their own laws, in fact, even over Roman citizens dwelling within their bounds. In the subject, non-autonomous communities, to which Judea belonged, the practical state of matters was very nearly the same ; but

with this twofold restriction : (1) That this practical state of
matters was not guaranteed them ; and (2) that the Roman
citizens residing within their bounds had their own law and
their own judicatories. The first point was of most importance. The Roman authorities could, in consequence of it,
interfere at pleasure in the legislation and in the administration of the law in non-autonomous communities. In Judea
this right seems to have been taken advantage only to a very
limited extent. It may be assumed that the administration
of the civil law was wholly in the hands of the Sanhedrim
and native or local magistrates : Jewish courts decided according to Jewish law. But even in the criminal law this was
almost invariably the case, only with this exception, that
death sentences required to be confirmed by the Roman
procurator. In such case the procurator decided if he pleased
according to the standard of the Jewish law, as is shown in
the trial of Jesus Christ.[116] Even Roman citizens were not
wholly exempt from the requirements of the Jewish law.
When, indeed, the procurator Festus proposed to judge the
Apostle Paul according to Jewish law, this was frustrated by
the objection of the apostle (see above, p. 187). But the
Jewish law, that no Gentile should be allowed to enter the
inner court of the temple, was recognised by the Roman
authorities, and any one who transgressed it was punished
with death, even if he were a Roman citizen.[70] There was
only one limitation to the far - reaching application of this
right, and that certainly a very important one ; the procurator
and his agents could at any time interfere according to their
own discretion.

The Jewish worship was not only tolerated, but, as the enactment just referred to with regard to the temple shows, stood
under State protection.[71] The cosmopolitan tendency, which
characterized the pagan piety of the time, made it quite
possible for distinguished Romans to present gifts to the

Jewish temple, and even to offer sacrifices there.[72] The oversight of the temple by the State, especially of the administration of its large finances, seems to have been carried out during the period A.D. 6–41 by means of the Roman authorities. During the period A.D. 44–66 it was transferred to the same Jewish princes who had also received the right of appointing the high priests, namely, Herod of Chalcis, and then Agrippa II.[73] A restriction in the freedom of worship, which was in itself quite harmless, but was regarded by the Jews as oppressive, was set aside in A.D. 36. During the period A.D. 6–36 the beautiful robe of the high priest was in the keeping of the Roman commandant in the fort of Antonia, and was only four times in the year, at the three chief feasts and on the Day of Atonement, brought forth for use. At the request of the Jews, in A.D. 36, Vitellius ordered that the robe should be given up. And when the procurator Cuspius Fadus, in A.D. 44, wished again to have the robe put under Roman control, a Jewish embassy went to Rome and procured a rescript from the Emperor Claudius by which the order of Vitellius was confirmed.[74]

Great deference was shown to the religious opinions of the Jews. Whereas in all other provinces the worship of the emperor was zealously insisted upon, and was claimed as a matter of course by the emperor as a proof of respect, no demand of this sort, except in the time of Caligula, was ever made of the Jews. The authorities were satisfied with requiring that twice a day in the temple at Jerusalem a sacrifice was made " for Caesar and the Roman people." The sacrifice for the whole day consisted in two lambs and an ox, and, according to Philo, was provided by Augustus himself, ἐκ τῶν ἰδίων προσόδων, whereas the opinion of Josephus is that it was made at the cost of the Jewish people.[75] Also on extraordinary occasions the Jewish people evidenced their loyal sentiments by a great sacrifice in honour of the emperor. [76] In the Diaspora the emperor was remembered in the prayers of the synagogue, which, however, cannot be proved to have been the case in Palestine. [77] Next to the worship of the emperor, the emperor's images on the coins and the standards of the soldiers were specially offensive to the Jews. But in these matters also they were treated with tolerance. It could not, indeed, be avoided that Roman denaria with the figure of the emperor should circulate in Judea (Matt. xxii. 20; Mark xii. 16; Luke xx. 24), for silver and gold coins were not minted in Judea. But the copper coinage restored to the country bore, even in the time of the direct Roman rule, as well as in the times of the Herodians, no human likeness, but only the name of the emperor and inoffensive emblems. The troops were required in Jerusalem to dispense with standards having on them the likeness of the emperor. The wanton attempt of Pilate to break through this custom was frustrated by the violent opposition of the people. Pilate found himself compelled to withdraw again the imperial likenesses from Jerusalem.[78] When Vitellius, the legate of Syria, took the field against the Arabian king Aretas, at the urgent entreaty of the Jews, he so directed the course of his march that the troops carrying the likeness of the emperor on their standards should not enter Jewish territory. [79]

So far, then, as the civil enactments and the orders of the supreme authorities were concerned, the Jews could not complain of any want of consideration being paid them. It was otherwise, however, with respect to the practical carrying out of details. The average Roman official was always disposed to disregard all such nice, delicate consideration. And the unfortunate thing was, that Judea, especially in the last decades before the war, had had more than one governor who had lost all sense of right and wrong. Besides this, notwithstanding the most painstaking efforts to show indulgence to

Jewish views and feelings, the existing relations were in themselves, according to Jewish ideas, an insult to all the lofty, divine privileges of the chosen people, who, instead of paying tribute to Caesar, were called rather to rule over all nations of the world. [80]

Their first administrative measures which they introduced there show how hard a task the incorporation of Judea into the empire proved to the Romans. Contemporaneously with the appointment of Coponius, the first procurator of Judea, the emperor had sent a new legate, Quirinius, into Syria. It was now the duty of the legate to take a census of the population of the newly-acquired territory, in order that the taxes might be appointed according to the Roman method. But no sooner had Quirinius, in A.D. 6 or A.D. 7, begun to carry out his commission, than he was met with opposition on every hand. Only the quieting representations of the high priest Joazar, who clearly perceived that open rebellion would be of no avail, led to the gradual abandonment of the opposition that had already begun, and then the people with mute resignation submitted to the inevitable, so that, at last, the census was made up. [81] It was, however, no enduring peace, but only a truce of uncertain duration. Judas of Gamala in Gaulanitis, called the Galilean, who is certainly identical with that Judas, son of Hezekiah, of whom we have already learnt on p. 4, in company with a Pharisee of the name of Sadduc, made it his task to rouse the people into opposition, and in the name of religion to preach rebellion and revolutionary war. This movement had not, indeed, any immediate marked success. But the revolutionists got so far as to found now among the Pharisees a more strict fanatical party, that of the patriotic resolutes, or, as they called themselves, the Zealots, who wished not to remain in quiet submission till by God's

decree the Messianic hope of Israel should be fulfilled, but
would rather employ the sword in hastening its realization,
and would rush into conflict with the godless enemy.[82]   It is
to their machinations that we are to ascribe the nursing of
the fires of revolution among the smouldering ashes which
sixty years later burst forth in vehement flames.[83]

Of Coponius and some of his successors little more is known
to us than their names.   Altogether there were seven procurators who administered Judea during the period A.D. 6–41:
(1) Coponius, probably A.D. 6–9 ; (2) Marcus Ambivius,
probably A.D. 9–12 ; (3) Annius Rufus, probably A.D. 12–15 ;
(4) Valerius Gratus, A.D. 15–26 ; (5) Pontius Pilatus, A.D.
26–36 ;   (6) Marcellus, A.D. 36–37 ;   (7) Marullus, A.D.
37–41.[84]   The long period during which Valerius Gratus
and Pontius Pilate held office was owing to the general
principles on which Tiberius proceeded in his appointment of
governors.   In the interest of the provinces he left them as
long as possible at their posts, because he thought that governors acted like flies upon the body of a wounded animal ;
if once they were gorged, they would become more moderate
in their exactions, whereas new men began their rapacious
proceedings afresh.[85]

Among those named, Pontius Pilate is of special interest
to us, not only as the judge of Jesus Christ, but also because
he is the only one of whom we have any detailed account in
Josephus and Philo.   Philo, or rather Agrippa I., in the
letter which Philo communicates as written by him, describes
him as of an "unbending and recklessly hard character"
(τὴν φύσιν ἀκαμπὴς καὶ μετὰ τοῦ αὐθάδους ἀμείλικτος), and
gives a very bad account of his official administration.
"Corruptibility, violence, robberies, ill - treatment of the
people, grievances, continuous executions without even the
form of a trial, endless and intolerable cruelties," are charged
against him.[86]   The very first act by which Pilate introduced

himself into office was characteristic of him who treated with
contempt the Jewish customs and privileges.   Care had
constantly been taken by the earlier procurators that the
troops entering Jerusalem should not carry flags having the
figure of the emperor, in order that the religious feelings of
the Jews should not be offended by the sight of them (see in
regard to these, above, p. 196). Pilate, on the other hand, to
whom such tolerance appeared unworthy weakness, caused
the garrison soldiers of Jerusalem to enter the city by night
with the figure of the emperor on their flags.   When the
news spread among the people, they flocked out in crowds
to Caesarea, and besieged the procurator with entreaties for
five days and nights that the offensive articles might be
removed.   At last, on the sixth day, Pilate admitted the
people into the race-course, into which at the same time he
had ordered a detachment of soldiers.   When the Jews also
here again repeated their complaints, he gave a signal, upon
which the soldiers surrounded the people on all sides with
drawn swords.   But the Jews remained stedfast, bared their
necks, and declared that they would rather die than submit
to a breach of the law.   As further opposition seemed to
Pilate hazardous, he gave orders to remove the offensive
images from Jerusalem. [87]

A new storm burst forth when on one occasion he applied
the rich treasures of the temple to the certainly very useful
purpose of building an aqueduct to Jerusalem.   Such an
appropriation of the sacred treasures was no less offensive
than the introduction of the figures of the emperor.   When,
therefore, he once went to Jerusalem while the building was
being proceeded with, he was again surrounded by a complaining and shrieking crowd.   But he had previously
obtained information of the projected outburst, and had given
orders to the soldiers to mix among the people dressed in
citizen garb armed with clubs.   When the multitude there-

fore began to make complaints and to present petitions, he gave the preconcerted signal, whereupon the soldiers drew forth their clubs which they had concealed under their upper garments, and mercilessly beat down the helpless crowds. Many lost their lives in this melee. The opposition to the useful undertaking was thus indeed crushed; but also the popular hatred against Pilate was stirred up afresh.[88]

The New Testament also contains hints about the popular uprisings in the time of Pilate. " There were present at that season," so runs the narrative in Luke xiii. 1, "some that told Jesus of the Galileans, whose blood Pilate had mingled with their sacrifices." This statement is to be understood as indicating that Pilate had put to the sword a number of Galileans while they were engaged in the act of presenting their offerings at Jerusalem. But nothing more definite as to this incident is known. And just as little do we know about "those who had made insurrection, and had committed murder in the insurrection" (Mark xv. 7; comp. Luke xxiii. 19), to whom among others that Barabbas belonged, whose liberation the Jews demanded of Pilate.

Probably to the later days of Pilate belongs an occurrence about which we are informed in the letter of Agrippa I. to Caligula, which is communicated by Philo. Pilate had learnt from the outburst at Caesarea that the setting up of the figures of the emperor in Jerusalem could not be carried out against the stubborn resistance of the Jews. He thought he now, at least, might attempt the introduction of votive shields without figures, on which the name of the emperor was written. Such shields, richly gilt, did he set up in what had been the palace of Herod, which Pilate himself was now wont to occupy, "less for the honour of Tiberius than for the annoyance of the Jewish people." But the people would not tolerate even this. First of all, in company with the nobles and with the four sons of Herod, who were then present in Jerusalem attending a feast, they applied to Pilate in order to induce him to remove the shields. When their prayer proved unsuccessful, the most distinguished men, among whom certainly were those four sons of Herod, addressed a petition to the emperor, asking that he should order the removal of the offensive shields. Tiberius, who plainly perceived that it was a piece of purely wanton bravado on the part of Pilate, ordered the governor on pain of his severe displeasure to remove at once the shields from Jerusalem, and to have them set up in the temple of Augustus at Caesarea. This accordingly was done. " And thus were preserved both the honour of the emperor and the ancient customs of the city." [89]

At last by his utter recklessness Pilate brought about his own overthrow. It was an old belief among the Samaritans that on the mountain of Gerizim the sacred utensils of the temple had been buried since Moses' times. A Samaritan pseudo - prophet once promised in A.D. 35 to show these sacred things if the people would assemble on Mount Gerizim. The light-minded multitude gave him a hearing, and in great crowds the Samaritans gathered together armed in the village of Tirathana at the foot of Mount Gerizim, so that from thence they might ascend the mountain and behold the sacred spectacle. But before they could carry out their project, they were arrested by Pilate in the village by a strong force, a portion of them was slain, a portion hunted in flight, and again another portion cast into prison. Of those imprisoned also Pilate had the most powerful and the most distinguished put to death.[90] But the Samaritans were convinced that no revolutionary intentions lay to the basis of their pilgrimage to Gerizim, and so they complained of Pilate to Vitellius, the legate in Syria at that time. Their

complaints had actually this result, that Vitellius sent Pilate
to Rome to answer for his conduct, while he made over the
administration of Judea to Marcellus. [91]

Soon thereafter, at the Passover festival of A.D. 36, [92]
Vitellius himself went to Jerusalem, and won for himself on
that occasion the goodwill of the inhabitants of the capital,
for he remitted the taxes on the fruits sold in the city, and
gave up for free use the high priest's robe, which since A.D. 6
had lain in the possession of the Romans. [93]

After he had meanwhile been occupied with the Parthian
expedition (see above, p. 174.), the campaign against Aretas,
which he had been ordered by Tiberius in the spring of
A.D. 37 to undertake, led him again to Jerusalem (see above,
p. 173). On this occasion also he again established a good
understanding by showing consideration for Jewish sentiments.
The way from Antioch to Petra had led him, together with his
army, through Judea proper. But the Roman standards, as is
well known, were offensive to the Jews. They therefore sent
to Vitellius at Ptolemais an embassy, which entreated him
with tears that he should not lead his army through the Holy
Land. Vitellius was so reasonable as to perceive the grounds
of their request, caused the army to march through the Great
Plain, and went himself alone to Jerusalem. On the fourth
day of his stay there he received tidings of Tiberius' death,
whereupon he led his whole army back to Antioch. [94]

The reign of Caligula, A.D. 37—41, was, after the rule of
Tiberius, the enemy of the human race, joyfully greeted
throughout the whole empire, and especially among the Jews.
Since Vitellius was residing in Jerusalem when the news of
the change of government reached him, the Jews were the
first of the nationalities of Syria who professed to the new
emperor the oath of allegiance, and presented sacrifices for
him. [95] Also during the first eighteen months of his reign
the Jews enjoyed peace and quiet. [96] But in the autumn of
A.D. 38 a bloody persecution of the Jews broke out in

Alexandria, which, though apparently at the instance of the Alexandrian mob, was yet indirectly the work of the emperor. In his overweaning self - conceit, joined with a beclouded intellect, he took up the idea of his divine rank with terrible earnestness. With him the worship of the emperor was no mere form of homage which the emperors had taken over as a heritage of the Greek kings ; but he actually believed in his divinity, and regarded the refusal to worship him as a proof of hostility to his person.[97] During the second year of his reign this idea seems to have obtained a complete mastery over him, and to have become known in the provinces. The provincials developed a corresponding zeal. The Jews, who could not follow this course, fell under suspicion of hostility to Caesar. This was to the Jew hating populace of Alexandria a welcome excuse for giving free expression to their hatred of the Jews ; for they might well suppose that by persecuting the Jews they would earn the favour of the emperor. The governor of Egypt at that time, A. Avillius Flaccus, was weak enough for the sake of his own interests to agree to the plans of the enemies of the Jews. He had been governor of Egypt under Tiberius for five years, A.D. 32–37, and, according to the testimony of Philo, had during that time administered his office in a faultless manner.[98] Under Caligula he more and more lost that reputation. As an intimate friend of Tiberius, he stood, as a matter of course, in disfavour with Caligula. With the death of young Tiberius, grandson of the Emperor Tiberius, and of the praetorian prefect Macro, both of whom were compelled by Caligula to commit suicide, he completely lost every support at the court. Thenceforth he set no other end before him than this, namely, to endeavour by all means to secure the favour of the young emperor. This was the one principle that determined his proceedings toward the Jews.[99]

The presence of the Jewish king Agrippa in Alexandria

gave the ostensible occasion for the outbreak of the persecution of the Jews.   He arrived in Alexandria, on his homeward journey from Rome to Palestine, in August A.D. 38.
Although, as Philo has assured us, he avoided everything
calculated to produce a commotion, the mere appearance of a
Jewish king was an offence to the mob of Alexandria.   Agrippa
was first of all treated with indignity and insult in the gymnasium, and then exposed to ridicule in the performances of a
pantomime.   A man called Karabas, suffering from mental
derangement, was decked in uniform similar to the king's
dress, and was mockingly greeted as king, the people addressing him in the Syrian as Μάριν, Lord.[100]   The mob, however,
once roused to riot, was not disposed to be pacified.   They
now insisted upon placing statues of the emperor in the
Jewish synagogues, called by Philo simply προσευχαί.
Flaccus did not venture to oppose them, but rather agreed to
all the demands of the enemies of the Jews.   These again,
the more the governor seemed disposed to yield to them,
became the more extravagant in their demands.   Flaccus
gave permission successively to the setting up of images in
the synagogues, to the pronouncing of the Jews, by an edict,
no longer in the enjoyment of the rights of citizens, and,
finally, he gave his sanction to a general persecution of the
Jews.[101]   Dreadful sufferings were now endured by the Jewish
population of Alexandria.   Their houses and warehouses were
plundered ; the Jews were themselves maltreated, murdered,
the bodies mutilated ; others publicly burned ; others, again,
dragged alive through the streets.   The synagogues were, some
of them destroyed, others profaned by the setting up of the
image of Caligula as a god ; in the largest synagogue the
image of Caligula was set up on a high damaged *Quadriga*,
which they had dragged thither from the gymnasium.[102]   The
governor Flaccus not only let all this go on without interfering, but also himself proceeded with severe measures against

the Jews, for which, according to Philo, he had no other reason than the refusal of the Jews to take part in the worship of the emperor. He caused thirty-eight members of the Jewish *Gerousia* to be carried bound into the theatre, and there to be scourged before the eyes of their enemies, so that some of them died under the infliction of the lash, and others were thrown into long and severe illnesses.[103] A centurion was commanded to search with a select band through the houses of the Jews for arms. Jewish women were compelled before spectators in the theatre to partake of swine's flesh.[104] Flaccus had even before this shown his hostility to the Jews by failing to send to the emperor, as he had promised to do, but retaining in his own possession, a petition from the Jewish community, in which an explanation was given of the attitude of the Jews in reference to the honours demanded by the emperor. This writing was first sent up by Agrippa, with a statement of the reason of the delay.[105]

We are not in possession of any detailed information as to the circumstances of the Alexandrian community after the severe persecution of the autumn of A.D. 38 down to the death of Caligula in January A.D. 41. In autumn of A.D. 38 Flaccus was suddenly, at the command of the emperor, carried as a prisoner to Rome, and banished to the island of Andros in the Aegean Sea, where subsequently he was, together with other distinguished exiles, put to death by the orders of Caligula.[106] Who his successor was is unknown.[107] It may be accepted as highly probable that the Jews did not get back their synagogues during Caligula's lifetime, and that the worship of the emperor continued a burning question, and one involving the Jews in danger. In A.D. 40, probably in spring, in consequence of the still continuing conflicts between the heathen and Jewish population of Alexandria, an embassy from both parties went to the emperor to complain against one another, and seek to win over the emperor to their side. The leader of the Jewish embassy was Philo; the leader of his opponents was the scholar Apion. The result was unfavour-able to the Jews. They were ungraciously received by the emperor, and were obliged to return without having effected their object. So Josephus briefly tells the story.[108] A few incidents connected with this embassy are also told by Philo in his work about Caligula. But it is difficult to obtain any definite information from these fragmentary notices. With-out having referred to the sending of one of the two embassies, Philo first of all states that the ambassadors of the Alex-andrians won over completely to their interests the slave Helicon, a favourite of Caligula. When the Jews perceived this, they made similar endeavours on their part, but in vain.[109] They then concluded to pass on to the emperor a written statement, which contained the main points embraced in the petition shortly before sent in by King Agrippa. Caligula received the Jewish ambassadors first of all in the Campus Martius at Rome, and promised to hear them at a convenient time.[110] The ambassadors then followed the em-peror to Puteoli, where, however, they were not received.[111] Only at a later period—we know not how much later—the promised audience took place at Rome, in the gardens of Maecenas and Lamia, at which the emperor — while he inspected the works that were going on, and gave orders regarding them—caused the Jews to keep moving on always behind him, throwing out to them now and again a contempt-uous remark, amid the applause of the ambassadors of the other party, until at last he dismissed them, declaring that they were to be regarded rather as foolish than as wicked men, since they would not believe in his divinity.[112]

Affairs at Alexandria remained in suspense down to the death of Caligula. One of the first acts of the new emperor, Claudius, was to issue an edict by which all their earlier privileges were confirmed to the Alexandrian Jews, and the unrestricted liberty to practise their own religion was anew granted them.[113]

While the Alexandrian embassy to Rome waited for the imperial decision, a serious storm burst upon the mother country of Palestine. It had its origin in Jamnia, a town on the Philistine coast which was mainly inhabited by Jews. When the heathen inhabitants of that place, in order to show their zeal for Caesar and at the same time to aggravate the Jews, erected a rude altar to the emperor, this was immediately again destroyed by the Jews. The incident was reported by the imperial procurator of the city, Herennius Capito, to the emperor, who, in order to avenge himself upon the refractory Jews, gave orders that his statue should be set up in the temple of Jerusalem.[114] As it was foreseen that such an attempt would call forth violent opposition, the governor of Syria, P. Petronius, received a command to have the one half of the army[115] stationed " on the Euphrates," i.e. in Syria, in readiness to proceed to Palestine, in order by their assistance to carry out the will of the emperor. This moderate and reasonable man obeyed the childish demand with a heavy heart during the winter of A.D. 39–40. While he was getting the statue prepared in Sidon, he gathered about him the heads of the Jewish people, and sought to persuade them to yield with a good grace ; but all in vain.[116]

Soon the news of what was proposed spread over all Palestine, and now the people assembled in great crowds at Ptolemais, where Petronius had his headquarters. " Like a cloud the multitude of the Jews covered all Phoenicia." Well arranged, divided into six groups—old men, able-bodied men, boys, old women, wives and maidens, the mass deputation appeared before Petronius. Their mournful complaints and groans made such an impression upon Petronius that he resolved at all hazards to make the attempt to put off the decision for a time at least.[117] The full truth, that he really wished to have a stop put to the whole business, he dared not indeed write to the emperor. He wrote him rather that he entreated for delay, partly because time was required for the preparing of the statue, partly because the harvest was approaching, which it would be advisable to see gathered in, since otherwise the exasperated Jews might in the end destroy the whole harvest. When Caligula received that letter, he was greatly enraged at the dilatoriness of his governor. But he did not venture to give expression to his wrath, but wrote him a letter of acknowledgment in which he praised his prudence, and only advised him to proceed as quickly as possible with the preparation of the statue, since the harvest would be already about an end.[118]

Petronius, however, did not even yet proceed with any vigour in the matter, but entered anew into negotiations with the Jews. Yea, even late in autumn, down to the season of sowing in November, we find him at Tiberias besieged for forty days by crowds of people to be numbered by thousands, who besought him with tears that he would yet save the country from the threatened horror of temple desecration. When at length Aristobulus also, the brother of King Agrippa and other relatives of his joined their prayers to those of the people, Petronius resolved to take the decisive step of asking the emperor to revoke his order. He led his army back from Ptolemais to Antioch, and set before the emperor, in a letter which he sent for this purpose to Caligula, how upon grounds of equity and prudence it would be advisable to recall the offensive edict.[119]

Meanwhile affairs at Rome affecting matters in question had taken a more favourable turn. King Agrippa I., who in spring of the year 40 had left Palestine, met with Caligula in Rome or at Puteoli in autumn, when the emperor had just returned from his German campaign. He had as yet heard nothing of what was going on in Palestine. But the glance of the emperor's eye assured him that he was nursing secret wrath in his heart. When he sought in vain for the cause of such feelings, the emperor observed his embarrassment, and let him know in a very ungracious tone what the cause of his displeasure was. The king on hearing this was so horror-stricken that he fell into a fainting fit, from which he did not recover till the evening of the following day.[120] On his recovery he made it his first business to address a supplication to the emperor, in which he endeavoured to persuade him to recall his order by showing that none of his predecessors had ever attempted anything of that sort.[121] Contrary to all expectation, the letter of Agrippa had the desired effect. Caligula caused a letter to be written to Petronius, commanding that nothing should be changed in the temple at Jerusalem. The favour was certainly not unmixed; for along with this order there was an injunction that no one who should erect a temple or altar to the emperor outside of Jerusalem should be hindered from doing so. A good part of the concession that had been made was thus again withdrawn; and it was only owing to the circumstance that no one took advantage of the right thus granted, that new disturbances did not arise out of it. The emperor, indeed, soon repented that he had made that concession. And so, as he made no further use of the statue that had been prepared at Sidon, he ordered a new one to be made in Rome which he intended himself, in his journey to Alexandria which he had in prospect, to put ashore on the coast of Palestine as he passed, and have it secretly brought to Jerusalem.[122] Only the death of the emperor that soon followed prevented the carrying out of this enterprise.

For the person of Petronius as well as for the land of Judea the death of the emperor was a favourable occurrence. When, further, Caligula, after he himself had arranged for the stopping of proceedings, received the letter of Petronius

expressing the wish referred to, he fell into a furious passion
about the disobedience of this officer, and caused a command
immediately to be issued, that as a punishment for that he
should take away his own life. Soon thereafter, however,
Caligula was murdered, 24th January A.D. 41 ; and Petronius
received the news thereof twenty - seven days before the
messengers arrived with the order for self-destruction ; for
these, in consequence of unfavourable weather, had been
three full months upon their way. There was now just as
little idea of carrying out the order for self-murder as there
was of setting up the statue in the temple of Jerusalem.[123]

The new emperor, Claudius, who had been raised to the
throne by the soldiers, immediately upon his accession gifted
to Agrippa, besides the dominion which he already had
possession under Caligula, Judea and Samaria, so that now
again all Palestine, to the same extent which it formerly
had under Herod the Great, was united in the hand of a
Herodian.[124]

EXCURSUS.—THE SO-CALLED TESTIMONY OF JOSEPHUS
TO CHRIST, *Antiq.* xviii. 3. 3.

In our manuscripts and editions of Josephus the following
passage concerning Christ is found, *Antiq.* xviii. 3. 3 :—

Γίνεται δὲ κατὰ τοῦτον τὸν χρόνον Ἰησοῦς, σοφὸς ἀνήρ, εἴ
γε ἄνδρα αὐτὸν λέγειν χρή. Ἦν γὰρ παραδόξων ἔργων
ποιητής, διδάσκαλος ἀνθρώπων τῶν ἡδονῇ τἀληθῆ δεχομένων·
καὶ πολλοὺς μὲν Ἰουδαίους πολλοὺς δὲ καὶ τοῦ Ἑλληνικοῦ
ἐπηγάγετο. Ὁ Χριστὸς οὗτος ἦν. Καὶ αὐτὸν ἐνδείξει τῶν
πρώτων ἀνδρῶν παρ᾽ ἡμῖν σταυρῷ ἐπιτετιμηκότος Πιλάτου,
οὐκ ἐπαύσαντο οἱ τὸ πρῶτον αὐτὸν ἀγαπήσαντες· ἐφάνη γὰρ
αὐτοῖς τρίτην ἔχων ἡμέραν πάλιν ζῶν, τῶν θείων προφητῶν
ταῦτά τε καὶ ἄλλα μυρία θαυμάσια περὶ αὐτοῦ εἰρηκότων.

Εἰσέτι τε νῦν τῶν Χριστιανῶν ἀπὸ τοῦδε ὠνομασμένων οὐκ ἐπέλιπε τὸ φῦλον.

"Now there was about this time, Jesus, a wise man, if it be lawful to call him a man, for he was a doer of wonderful works—a teacher of such men as receive the truth with pleasure. He drew over to him both many of the Jews and many of the Gentiles. He was the Christ; and when Pilate, at the suggestion of the principal men amongst us, had con- demned him to the cross, those that loved him at the first did not forsake him, for he appeared to them alive again the third day, as the divine prophets had foretold these and ten thousand other wonderful things concerning him ; and the tribe of Christians so named from him are not extinct at this day."

From the fourth century, when this passage was quoted by Eusebius and others (Eusebius, *Hist. Eccles.* i. 11 ; *Demon- stratio Evangelica*, iii. 3. 105–106, ed. Gaisford ; Pseudo- Hegesippus, *De bello Judaico*, ii. 12), through the whole of the Middle Ages, the genuineness of this paragraph was never disputed. Indeed, it contributed not a little to exalt the reputation of Josephus in the Christian Church. It was eagerly seized upon as a proof of the truth of the evangelical history. It was only in the sixteenth century that criticism first moved in the matter, and since then to the present day the controversy, *pro* and *con*, has gone on uninterruptedly. We may surely be at least unanimous as to this, that the words, as we have them now, were not written by Josephus. Whatever may be advanced in their favour does not amount to much in comparison with the unquestionable indications of spuriousness. Our manuscripts, of which the oldest, the *Ambrosianus F.* 128 *sup.*, do not go further back than the eleventh century(Marcian. 383 - 12th cent.)[1], without exception have this paragraph. But this proves only the great antiquity of the interpolation, which besides is vouched for by Eusebius.

Over against the old citations since Eusebius stands the fact
that it is extremely probable that Origen did not read this
passage in his text of Josephus ; for, just where one would
have expected it, he betrays no knowledge of it.[2]   Even then,
in respect of the external evidences, objections are not
altogether wanting.   But the objections on internal grounds
are more decided.   If reference be made to the genuinely
Josephine style, we may for that only bestow upon the
interpolator the praise of having very skilfully performed
his task.   The similarity of style is not sufficient to outweigh
the non-Josephine character of the contents.   As concerns
the contents then, it is clear that whoever wrote the words
ὁ Χριστὸς οὗτος ἦν was distinctly a Christian ; for that ἦν is
not equivalent to ἐνομίζετο and cannot be rendered : He
was the Christ in the popular belief.   On this point it is not
necessary to say more.   But it is also equally certain that
Josephus was not a Christian.   *Ergo :* the passage, to say
the least of it, has interpolations in it.

The point under discussion is simply this : whether there are
interpolations in the passage or whether it is wholly spurious.
Let us make the attempt to distinguish, and cast out what is
suspicious.   The words εἴ γε ἄνδρα αὐτὸν λέγειν χρή
evidently presuppose belief in the divinity of Christ, and
betray the Christian interpolator.   The following, ἦν παραδόξων ἔργων ποιητής, might in a case of necessity have been
said by Josephus, if it were not that they form the fundamental support of the non-genuine words preceding them.
At any rate, the words διδάσκαλος ἀνθρώπων τῶν ἡδονῇ
τἀληθῆ δεχομένων again must have come from a Christian
pen.   That ὁ Χριστὸς οὗτος ἦν was not written by Josephus
has been already pointed out.   And just as certainly he has
not written : ἐφάνη αὐτοῖς τρίτην ἔχων ἡμέραν πάλιν ζῶν,
τῶν θείων προφητῶν ταῦτά τε καὶ ἄλλα μυρία θαυμάσια περὶ
αὐτοῦ εἰρηκότων.   Finally, also, the concluding words want

the necessary support so soon as the words ὁ Χριστὸς οὗτος ἦν are removed from the text.

If, now, we examine the passage as thus reduced we shall find that as good as nothing remains : a couple of insignificant phrases which, in the form in which they stand after our operation has been performed, could not have been written by Josephus. If one therefore continues to maintain the theory of interpolation, it cannot at any rate be in the sense of a simple insertion of Christian additions, but, with Ewald, Paret, and others, in the sense of a complete working up in a new form of the original text of Josephus.

But if it is once admitted as an established fact, that of the present text scarcely a couple of words are from the hand of Josephus, is it not then more reasonable to recognise the utter spuriousness of the passage, and assume that Josephus has throughout been silent regarding Christ? That this hypothesis is impossible cannot be maintained. It is known that Josephus wished to represent his people in the most favourable light possible. Therefore he speaks as little as he can of the Messianic Hope, since to his cultured readers it could only have appeared as foolishness, and, besides, would have been an unwelcome subject with the favourite of the Caesars ; for in it lay the power of the opposition to Rome. Josephus might casually refer to John the Baptist without making mention of the Messianic Hope ; but this would have been no longer possible had he introduced Christ. He could neither represent Christ as a teacher of virtue, like the Baptist, nor describe the Christian community as a school of philosophy, like those of the Pharisees and Sadducees. Therefore he will be silent throughout about this phenomenon.

If, for proof of the contrary, we should refer to the subsequent mention of James, the brother of Jesus Christ (*Antiq.* xx. 9. 1 : τὸν ἀδελφὸν Ἰησοῦ τοῦ λεγομένου Χριστοῦ, Ἰάκωβος ὄνομα αὐτῷ), in order to draw from it the conclusion that some previous mention of Christ must have been made, it has to be answered, that the genuineness of this passage is also very seriously disputed. Indeed, on the contrary, one must say : the very statements which we have in reference to James prove that Josephus has been interpolated by Christian hands. For Origen, in his text of Josephus, read a passage about James which is to be found in none of our manuscripts, which therefore, without doubt, was a single instance of a Christian interpolation not carried over into the vulgar text of Josephus.

We therefore, although absolute certainty on such questions cannot be attained, are inclined to prefer the theory of the utter spuriousness as simpler than that of the merely partial spuriousness of the passage.

§ 18. HEROD AGRIPPA I., A.D. 37, 40, 41-44

I.

WHEN Agrippa I.[1] ascended the throne of Herod the Great, he had already passed through an eventful and adventurous career. He was born in B.C. 10,[2] as the son of Aristobulus, who was executed in B.C. 7, and Berenice, a daughter of Salome and Costobar.[3] Shortly before the death of his grandfather he was, while a boy of scarcely six years old, sent for his education to Rome. His mother Berenice was there treated in a friendly manner by Antonia, the widow of the elder Drusus, while the young Agrippa himself became attached to the younger Drusus, the son of the Emperor Tiberius. The influence of the Roman society seems not to have been a favourable or healthy one. He was trained up to entertain ambitious projects and in habits of extravagance, which, especially after the death of his mother, knew no measure or bounds. He soon ran through his means. His debts accumulated upon him. And when by the death of Drusus, which took place in A.D. 23, he lost support and favour at court, he found himself obliged to leave Rome and go back again to Palestine.[4] He betook himself to Malatha, a stronghold in Idumea,[5] and meditated committing suicide. When these tidings reached his wife Cypros, she wrote to Agrippa's sister Herodias, who was by this time married to

215

Antipas, and entreated her help.   Herod Antipas was in this
way induced to give to his distressed brother-in-law what
would be at least sufficient for the support of his life, and
gave him, in addition, the appointment of Agoranomos (overseer of markets) in the capital, Tiberias.   This new position
in life did not indeed continue long.   At a banquet in Tyre
the two brothers-in-law once engaged in a dispute, which
ended in Agrippa resigning his situation at Tiberias, and
betaking himself to the Roman governor Flaccus in Antioch.[6]
But here, too, his stay was not of long duration.   In a dispute which broke out on one occasion between the inhabitants
of Sidon and those of Damascus, Agrippa took the side of the
Damascenes, apparently in a thoroughly disinterested manner,
but really in consequence of bribes which he had taken from
them.   When this came to the ears of Flaccus, he broke off
friendly relations with him; and Agrippa found himself once
again deprived of all means of subsistence.   He then resolved
to try his fortune again in Rome.   After he had meanwhile
raised a loan in Ptolemais by the assistance of a freedman of
his mother Berenice, called Peter, and at Anthedon had only
with difficulty escaped the hands of Capito, the procurator of
Jamnia, who wished to apprehend him as a debtor of the
emperor's, and had finally in Alexandria succeeded in raising
large sums on the credit of his wife, he arrived in Italy in
the spring of A.D. 36,[7] and on the island of Capri[8] presented
himself before Tiberius.[9]   The emperor entrusted him with
the oversight of his grandson Tiberius.   He became particularly intimate with Caius Caligula, the grandson of his
patroness Antonia, who afterwards became emperor.   But even
now he could not keep himself out of debt.   Yea, in order
to appease his old creditors he was obliged always to borrow
new and even larger sums.[10]   It was not therefore to be
wondered at that he eagerly desired an improvement in his
circumstances; but there seemed at that time no prospect of

accomplishing it until the aged Tiberius should be succeeded
on the throne by Caligula, whom he had befriended. Un-
thinkingly he once expressed his wish aloud to Caligula in
the presence of his coachman Eutychus. At a later period
he happened to bring a charge of theft against this same
Eutychus, and had him brought before the city prefect Piso.
Eutychus now made a declaration that he had an important
secret to communicate to the emperor. Tiberius at first gave
no heed to the matter.[11] But when, after some time, a
hearing was granted, and Tiberius came to know what
Agrippa had said, he had him immediately put in fetters and
cast into prison. Agrippa now continued in confinement for six
months, until the death of the emperor on 16th March A.D. 37.[12]

With the death of Tiberius and the accession of Caligula
began for Agrippa the period of his good fortune. Caligula
scarcely waited till the solemnities of the funeral of Tiberius
were over before he had delivered his friend from his
imprisonment and conferred upon him what had been the
tetrarchy of Philip, and that also of Lysanias, with the title
of king. To this gift the Senate further added the honorary
rank of a praetor.[13] Instead of the iron chain which he had
worn, Caligula gave him a golden chain of equal weight.[14]
But Agrippa still continued to stay in Rome for a year and a
half. It was not before autumn of A.D. 38 that he went
back by way of Alexandria to Palestine, that he might set in
order the affairs of his kingdom.[15]

Soon afterwards, through imperial favour, he obtained yet
more important territorial additions. It has been already told
(above, p. 175) how Herod Antipas in A.D. 39, by his own
fault, had lost his tetrarchy, and now, probably not before
A.D. 40, Caligula bestowed it also upon Agrippa.

In the autumn of that same year we find Agrippa once
more at Rome or Puteoli, where he contrived by his personal
intercession to prevent Caligula, at least for a long time, from

persisting in his attempt to set up his statue in the temple of
Jerusalem (see above, p. 209).   He then remained in the
company of Caligula, and was still present in Rome when his
patron, on 24th January A.D. 41, was murdered by Chärea,
and contributed not a little to secure the succession to the
throne of the Caesars to the feeble Claudius.[16] It may readily
be supposed that he was not the man to perform such services
without securing some personal advantage.   The new emperor
was obliged, in return, not only to confirm him in the
possessions which he had previously, but also to add to these
Judea and Samaria; so that Agrippa now united under his
sway the whole territory of his grandfather.   Besides this, he
obtained consular rank.   For the confirming of this grant,
according to ancient custom, a solemn covenant was concluded in the Forum, but the documentary deed of gift was
engraved on brazen tablets and placed in the Capitol.[17]

II.

The first act by which Agrippa celebrated his return to
Palestine was significant of the spirit and disposition with
which he was to conduct the government of his kingdom.
It was an act of piety.   The golden chain which Caligula
had bestowed upon him on his liberation from imprisonment
" he hung up within the limits of the temple, over the
treasury, that it might be a memorial of the severe fate he
had lain under, and a testimony of his change for the better;
and that it might be a demonstration how the greatest prosperity may have a fall, and that God sometimes raises what
is fallen down." [18]   At the same time he presented a thank-
offering, " because he would not neglect any precept of the
law;" and bore the expenses of a large number of Nazarites,
in order that they might discharge the obligation of their
vow."[19]

With such acts the quondam adventurer began his new

reign ; and he maintained the same tone throughout the three
years during which he was allowed to live and govern.
There were again golden days for Pharisaism ; a revival of
the age of Alexandra.   Hence Josephus and the Talmud are
unanimous in sounding forth the praises of Agrippa.   "He
loved to live continually at Jerusalem, and was exactly
careful in the observance of the laws of his country.   He
therefore kept himself entirely pure ; nor did any day pass
over his head without its appointed sacrifice."   Thus runs
the eulogistic strain of Josephus ;[20] and the Talmud relates
how he as a simple Israelite with his own hand presented the
first-fruits in the temple.[21]   And not only at home, but also
abroad, he represented the interests and claims of Judaism.
When on one occasion in the Phoenician city of Dora, a mob
of young people erected a statue of the emperor in the Jewish
synagogue, he used his influence with the governor of Syria,
P. Petronius, so that not only for the future was any such
outrage strictly forbidden, but also the guilty parties were
called to account for their proceedings.[22]   And when he
betrothed his daughter Drusilla to Epiphanes, son of King
Antiochus of Commagene, he made him promise that he
would submit to be circumcised.[23]   By such displays of piety
he gave abundant satisfaction to the people who were under
the guidance of the Pharisees.   This was shown in a very
striking manner when, at the Feast of Tabernacles in A.D. 41,
according to the old custom, he read the Book of Deuteronomy,[24] and in the passage, "Thou mayest not set a stranger
over thee that is not thy brother" (Deut. xvii. 15), he burst
forth in tears, because he felt himself referred to in it.   Then
cried out the people to him, "Be not grieved, Agrippa !
Thou art our brother !   Thou art our brother !" [25]

The careful observance of Pharisaic traditions, however,
does not seem to have been the only ground of his popularity.
We must also allow to him a certain natural amiability.

Josephus, at least, ascribes to him an amiable disposition and unbounded benevolence.[26] That he was grateful for service that had been rendered him is proved by his appointment of Silas, a faithful companion who had shared his adventures, to the supreme command of his troops.[27] He must, indeed, have had many unpleasant experiences with this Silas, for he was frequently reminded by him in a rude, rough way of his earlier troubles, and the service which he had rendered him. In order to rid himself of this troublesome prattler, Agrippa was obliged to cast him into prison. But it was a new proof of his goodheartedness that on the next celebration of his birthday he caused the prisoner to be called, so that he might share in the enjoyments of the banquet. This kindly offer, however, had no effect, for Silas would take nothing as a matter of favour, and so was obliged to remain in prison.[28] Agrippa on one occasion exhibited his clemency towards Simon the Pharisee,[29] who in the king's absence had excited a popular tumult in Jerusalem, and had charged the king with transgression of the law. Agrippa obtained information of these proceedings at Caesarea, summoned Simon to his presence, caused him to be seated alongside of himself in the theatre, and said to him in a gentle and kindly tone: " Tell me now, what was done here contrary to the law ? " Overcome with shame the learned scribe could give no answer, and was dismissed by the king with presents.[30]

To a Pharisaic-national policy belonged also emancipation from a position of dependence upon Rome. And even in this direction Agrippa made, at least, two rather shy and timid attempts. In order to strengthen the fortifications of Jerusalem, the capital, he began to build on the north of the city a powerful new wall, which, according to Josephus' account, would, if it had been completed, have made the city impregnable. But, unfortunately, before the work could be carried out, the emperor, at the instigation of Marsus, the governor of

Syria, issued an injunction against the continuance of it.[31]
Of yet greater significance for Rome was the conference of
princes assembled by Agrippa soon after this at Tiberias.
No fewer than five Roman vassal kings: Antiochus of Commagene, Sampsigeram of Emesa, Cotys of Lesser Armenia,
Polemon of Pontus, and Herod of Chalcis, answered the
invitation of Agrippa. But this enterprise also was broken
up by Marsus. The Syrian governor himself put in an
appearance at Tiberias, and ordered the other guests without
delay to return home.[32]

Finally, it was a further consequence of his Jewish policy
that the otherwise good-natured king should become the
persecutor of the young Christian community, especially of
the apostles. James the elder, son of Zebedee, was put by
him to a martyr's death; and Peter escaped his hand only by
the intervention of a miracle.[33]—Moreover, he was an enemy
not of the Christians only. The heathen cities also within
his territories hated him on account of his Jewish policy, as
is proved by the unconcealed jubilation with which the news
of his death was received by the Caesareans and Sebasteans.[34]

That Agrippa's Pharisaic piety was a real conviction of the
heart is, in view of his earlier life, not in the least probable.
He who had spent fifteen years in gaiety and debauchery is
not one of whom it could be expected that in the evening
of his days he should from hearty conviction assume the
Pharisaic yoke. Besides this, we have the most certain
proofs that the king's Jewish piety was maintained only
within the limits of the Holy Land. When he went abroad
he was, like his grandfather, a liberal latitudinarian patron
of Greek culture. Thus, for example, Berytus had much to
tell of the pagan magnificence which he there cultivated. He
had erected there at his own expense a beautiful theatre, an
amphitheatre, baths, and piazzas. At the opening of the
building, games and sports of all sorts were performed, and

among the rest in the amphitheatre there was a gladiatorial
combat, at which 1400 malefactors were made to slaughter
one another.[35]   Also at Caesarea he caused games to be performed.[36]   There also statues of his daughters were erected.[37]
So, too, the coins which were stamped during Agrippa's reign
are in thorough agreement with the description of the state
of matters now given.   Only those stamped in Jerusalem
had on them no image, while of those that were minted in
other cities some had the image of Agrippa, others that of the
emperor.   The official title of Agrippa is the same as that
of the other Roman vassal kings of that time.   From an
inscription we know that his family had been adopted into
the *gens Julia ;* [38] and from another that he bore the title
βασιλεὺς μέγας φιλόκαισαρ εὐσεβὴς καὶ φιλορώμαιος.[39]   From
a survey of all the facts it is evident that his concessions to
Pharisaism were purely matters of policy.   Upon the whole
he was a careful imitator of the old Herod, "only milder
in disposition and somewhat more sly." [40]   Yet even the
grandfather felt himself obliged to make concessions to the
Pharisees.   Agrippa was in this matter only consistently
following out his general lines of policy, for he very well
knew that the peace which he loved could be secured in no
other way.

The country did not long enjoy his rule.   After he had
reigned little more than three years, if we reckon from
A.D. 41, he died at Caesarea very suddenly in A.D. 44.   The
two accounts of his death which we have, in Acts xii. 19–23,
and Josephus, *Antiq.* xix. 8. 2, with many variations, are yet
in thorough and detailed agreement on the principal points.[41]
The Acts of the Apostles relates that in Caesarea, sitting on
the judgment - seat (βῆμα) dressed in his royal robes, he
delivered an oration to the ambassadors representing the
citizens of Tyre and Sidon, with whom, we know not why,
he had been displeased.   While he was speaking the people

called out : It is the voice of a god, and not of a man.   Immediately the angel of the Lord smote him, because he gave not God the glory ; and he was eaten up of worms, and gave up the ghost.   According to Josephus, he was present at Caesarea while games were being celebrated there in honour of the emperor.   On the second day he appeared in the theatre in a robe which was made wholly of silver.   When the robe sparkled in the sun, the flatterers cried out to him declaring that he was a god ($\theta\epsilon\grave{o}\nu$ $\pi\rho o\sigma\alpha\gamma o\rho\epsilon\acute{v}o\nu\tau\epsilon\varsigma$), and entreating that he would have mercy upon them.   The king allowed himself to be carried away by their flattery.   Soon thereafter he saw an owl sitting upon a rope, which at once he accepted as a presage of a speedy death.[42]   He then knew that his hour had come.   Immediately a most severe pain arose in his bowels. He had to be carried into the house, and in five days was a corpse.—It thus appears that the principal points : Caeserea as the scene of the incident, the brilliant robe, the flattering shout, the sudden death—are common to both narratives, although the details have been somewhat diversified in the course of transmission.

Agrippa left, besides his three daughters (Berenice, Mariamme, and Drusilla), only one son, then in his seventeenth year, whose name also was Agrippa.   The Emperor Claudius had been disposed to give over to him the kingdom of his father ; but his advisers restrained him from carrying out his intentions.   And so again the whole of Palestine, as formerly Judea and Samaria had been, was taken possession of as Roman territory, and its administration given over to a procurator under the supervision of the governor of Syria.[43] The younger Agrippa continued meanwhile to live in retirement.

§ 19. THE ROMAN PROCURATORS,

A.D. 44-66

WHEN we glance over the history of the Roman procurators, to whom once more the government of Palestine was entrusted, we might readily suppose that all of them, as if by secret arrangement, so conducted themselves as most certainly to arouse the people to revolt. Even the best among them, to say nothing at all of the others who trampled right and law under foot, had no appreciation of the fact that a people like the Jews required, in a permanent degree, consideration for their prejudices and peculiarities. Instead of exercising mildness and toleration, they had only applied themselves with inexorable strictness to suppress any movement of the popular life.—As compared with those who followed, the words of Josephus are true regarding the first two procurators, that, " making no alterations of the ancient laws and customs, they kept the nation in tranquillity." [1]

1. The first procurator whom Claudius sent to Palestine was Cuspius Fadus (A.D. 44—?). [2] Immediately after he had entered upon his office he had an opportunity for affirming his determination to maintain order. When he arrived in Palestine the inhabitants of Perea were in a state of open war with the city of Philadelphia. The conflict had arisen over disputes about the boundaries of their respective territories. Inasmuch as the Pereans were the parties at fault, Fadus

caused one of the three leaders of the party to be executed and the other two to be banished from the country.—But that Fadus with all his uprightness and love of justice had no appreciation of the peculiar characteristics of the Jewish people, is proved by his demand that the beautiful robe of the high priest, which in earlier times, A.D. 6–36, had laid under Roman keeping, and had been afterwards given up by Vitellius (see above, p. 202), should again be committed to the charge of the Romans.[3]   Thus, without any occasion whatever, by petty annoyances, the feelings of the people, which were most sensitive in matters of this sort, were outraged.   Fortunately, Fadus and the governor of Syria, Cassius Longinus, who on account of this important affair had gone up to Jerusalem, were considerate enough as to at least allow a Jewish embassy to proceed to Rome, which by the mediation of the younger Agrippa obtained an order from Claudius that in the matter of the garments things should continue as they had been.[4]

More serious than this conflict was one which occurred at a later period, and led to open war and shedding of blood.   One who pretended to be a prophet, Theudas by name, gathered a large multitude of followers after him, with whom he marched down to the Jordan, giving them the assurance that he by his mere word would part the stream and lead them across on dry land.   This, indeed, was only to be a proof of his divine mission, and what he had mainly in view, the contest with Rome, would follow.   At any rate this was how the matter was regarded by Fadus.   He sent a detachment of horsemen against Theudas, which completely defeated him and slew a portion of his followers or took them prisoners; and when Theudas himself had been apprehended, they struck off his head and carried it to Jerusalem as a sign of their victory.[5]

2. The successor of Fadus was Tiberius Alexander, down to A.D. 48, descended from one of the most illustrious Jewish

families of Alexandria, a son of the Alabarch Alexander, and
nephew of the philosopher Philo.[6] He had abandoned the
religion of his fathers and taken service under the Romans.
During the period of his government Palestine was visited by
a sore famine.[7] The one fact of any importance that is
recorded about him is that he caused James and Simon, the
sons of Judas of Galilee, to be crucified, ostensibly because
they were entertaining schemes similar to those of their
father.[8]

Although even the days of those first procurators did not
pass without troubles and upheaval, these came to be regarded
as altogether insignificant in comparison with the excitement
and turmoil that followed. Even under the governorship of
the next procurator Cumanus popular tumults, not without
faults on both sides, broke out in far more formidable
proportions.

3. The first rebellion against which Ventidius Cumanus,
A.D. 48–52,[9] had to contend was occasioned by the coarse in-
solence of a Roman soldier. This man had the presumption
at the feast of the Passover, when to maintain order and
preserve the peace a detachment of soldiers was always
situated in the court of the temple,[10] to insult the festive
gathering by assuming an indecent posture. The enraged
multitude demanded satisfaction from the procurator. As
Cumanus, however, attempted first of all to hush up the
matter, he too was assailed with reproachful speeches, until at
length he called for the intervention of the armed forces.
The excited crowds were utterly routed; and their overthrow
was so complete that, according to Josephus' estimate, in the
crush which took place in the streets in consequence of their
flight, 20,000 (!) men lost their lives.[11]

The fault in this case lay with the Romans, but in the
next upheaval the occasion was given by the Jewish people
themselves. An imperial official called Stephanus was

attacked on a public road not far from Jerusalem, and robbed of all his belongings. As a punishment for this the villages which lay in the neighbourhood of the spot where the deed was committed were subjected to a general pillage. It was through a pure mischance that out of this pillage further mischief was very nearly occasioned; for a soldier, before the eyes of all, amid contumelious and reproachful speeches tore up a Thorah roll which he had found. In order to obtain revenge and satisfaction for such profanity, a mass deputation visited Cumanus at Caesarea, demanding the punishment of the offender. This time the procurator saw it to be advisable to give way, and so sentenced the offender to be put to death.[12]

Far more bitter and bloody was a third collision with the people under Cumanus, which though it did not indeed cost him his life, yet led to his loss of office. Certain Galilean Jews, who on their way to the feast at Jerusalem had to pass through Samaria, had been murdered in a Samaritan village. When Cumanus, who had been bribed by the Samaritans, took no steps to secure the punishment of the guilty, the Jewish people took upon themselves the duty of revenge. Under the leadership of two Zealots, Eleasar and Alexander, a great multitude of armed men made an attack upon Samaria, hewed down old men, women, and children, and laid waste the villages. But then Cumanus with a portion of his military force fell upon the Zealots; many were slain, others were taken prisoners. Meanwhile ambassadors from the Samaritans appeared before Ummidius Quadratus, governor of Syria, and lodged a complaint with him about the robber raid of the Jews. At the same time, however, a Jewish embassy also came to Quadratus, and accused the Samaritans and Cumanus, who had accepted bribe from them. Quadratus, therefore, went himself to Samaria and made a strict investigation. All the revolutionists taken prisoners by

Cumanus were crucified ; five Jews, who were proved to have taken a prominent part in the struggle, were beheaded ; but the ringleaders both of the Jews and of the Samaritans were sent along with Cumanus to Rome in order to answer for their conduct there. The Jews were indebted to the intercession of the younger Agrippa, who happened then to be in Rome, for their success in their securing their rights. The decision of Claudius was to this effect, that the ringleaders of the Samaritans, who had been discovered by him to be the guilty parties, should be executed, while Cumanus was to be deprived of his office and sent into banishment.[13]

4. At the request of the high priest Jonathan, one of the Jewish aristocracy whom Quadratus had sent to Rome,[14] the Emperor Claudius transferred the administration of Palestine to one of his favourites, the brother of the influential Pallas, whose name was Felix (A.D. 52–60).[15] This man's term of office constitutes probably the turning-point in the drama which had opened with A.D. 44 and reached its close in the bloody conflicts of A.D. 70. During the days of the first two procurators things had continued relatively quiet ; under Cumanus, indeed, there were more serious uprisings of the people ; yet even then they were only isolated and called forth by particular occurrences ; under Felix rebellion became permanent.

He was, like his brother Pallas, a freedman of the imperial family,[16]—a freedman probably of Antonia the mother of Claudius, and having therefore as his full name, Antonius Felix.[17] The conferring of a procuratorship with military command upon a freedman was something unheard of, and is only to be accounted for by the influence which the freedmen had at the court of Claudius.[18] As procurator of Palestine Felix proved worthy of his descent. "With all manner of cruelty and lust he exercised royal functions in the spirit of a slave ; " in these words Tacitus sums up his estimate of the man.[19]

Felix was three times married. All the three wives, of whom two are known to us, belonged to royal families.[20] The one was a granddaughter of the triumvir Marc Antony and Cleopatra, and by this marriage Felix was brought into relationship with the Emperor Claudius.[21] The other was the Jewish princess Drusilla, the daughter of Agrippa I. and sister of Agrippa II.; and the way in which the marriage with her was brought about serves to confirm the estimate of Tacitus quoted above. Drusilla at the time when Felix entered upon his office was fourteen years of age.[22] Soon after this she was married by her brother Agrippa II. to Azizus, king of Emesa, after the marriage with the son of King Antiochus of Commagene, to whom she had been before betrothed, had been broken off because he refused to submit to circumcision.[23] Soon after her marriage Felix saw the beautiful queen, became inflamed with passion, and determined to possess her. By the help of a magician of Cyprus called Simon, he prevailed on her to marry him. In defiance of the law, which strictly forbade the marriage of a Jewess with a pagan, Drusilla gave her hand to the Roman procurator.[24]

The public career of Felix was no better than his private life. As brother of the powerful and highly favoured Pallas, " he believed that he might commit all sorts of enormities with impunity." [25]—It can be easily understood how under such a government as this the bitter feeling against Rome grew rapidly, and the various stages of its development were plainly carried out to the utmost extent under Felix and by his fault.[26]

First of all, on account of his misgovernment the Zealots, who entertained so fanatical a hatred of the Romans, won more and more sympathy among the ranks of the citizens. How far Josephus had grounds for styling them simply robbers may remain undetermined. In any case, as their following from among the people shows, they were not robbers of the common sort; and their pillaging was con-

fined wholly to the property of their political opponents.
Felix, who was not very scrupulous about the means he used,
contrived to get Eleasar, the head of the party, into his
hands by means of treachery, and sent him, together with
those of his adherents whom he had already in prison, to
Rome. "But the number of the robbers whom he caused to
be crucified was incalculable, as also that of the citizens
whom he arrested and punished as having been in league
with them." [27]

Such preposterous severity and cruelty only gave occasion
to still further troubles. [28] In the place of the robbers of
whom Felix had rid the country, the Sicarii made their
appearance, a still more fanatical faction of the patriots, who
deliberately adopted as their special task the removal of their
political opponents by assassination. Armed with short
daggers (*sicae*), from which they received their name,[29] they
mixed among the crowds especially during the festival seasons,
and unobserved in the press stabbed their opponents (τοὺς
διαφόρους, *i.e.* the friends of the Romans), and feigning deep
sorrow when the deed was done, succeeded in thereby drawing away suspicion from themselves. These political
murders were so frequent that soon no one any longer felt
safe in Jerusalem. Among others who fell victims to the
daggers of the Sicarii was Jonathan the high priest, who, as
a man of moderate sentiments, was hated by the Sicarii as
well as by the procurator Felix, whom he often exhorted to
act more worthily in the administration of his office, lest he
(Jonathan) should be blamed by the people for having
recommended the emperor to appoint him governor. Felix
wished to have the troublesome exhorter put out of the way,
and found that this could be most simply accomplished by
means of assassination, to which the Sicarii, although otherwise the deadly foes of Felix, readily lent themselves.[30]

With these political fanatics there were associated religious

fanatics "not so impure in their deeds, but still more wicked
in their intentions." Advancing the claim of a divine mission,
they roused the people to a wild enthusiasm, and led the
credulous multitude in crowds out into the wilderness, in
order that there they might show them "the tokens fore-
shadowing freedom" (σημεῖα ἐλευθερίας)—that freedom which
consisted in casting off the Roman yoke and setting up the
kingdom of God, or, to use the language of Josephus, in
innovation and revolution. Since religious fanaticism is
always the most powerful and the most persistent, Josephus
is certainly right when he says that those fanatics and
deceivers contributed no less than the "robbers" to the overthrow of the city. Felix also recognised clearly enough the
dangerous tendency of the movement, and invariably broke
in upon all such undertakings with the sword.[31]—The most
celebrated enterprise of this sort was the exploit of that
Egyptian to whom Acts xxi. 38 refers. An Egyptian Jew
who gave himself out for a prophet, gathered around him in
the wilderness a great crowd of people, numbering, according
to Acts, 4000, according to Josephus, 30,000, with whom he
wished to ascend the Mount of Olives, because he promised
that at his word the walls of Jerusalem would fall down and
give them free entrance into the city. Then they would get
the Roman garrison into their power and secure to themselves the government. Felix did not give the prophet time
to perform his miracle, but attacked him with his troops,
slew and scattered his followers or took them prisoners. But
the Egyptian himself escaped from the slaughter and disappeared.[32]

The result of this unfortunate undertaking was temporary
strengthening of the anti-Roman party. The religious and
the political fanatics (οἱ γόητες καὶ λῃστρικοί) united together
for a common enterprise. "They persuaded the Jews to
revolt, and exhorted them to assert their liberty, inflicting

death on those that continued in obedience to the Roman government, and saying that such as willingly chose slavery ought to be forced from such their desired inclinations; for they parted themselves into different bodies, and lay in wait up and down the country, and plundered the houses of the great men, and slew the men themselves, and set the villages on fire; and this till all Judea was filled with their madness." [33]

Thus did the misgovernment of Felix in the end bring about this result, that a large portion of the people from this time forth became thoroughly roused, under the constant strain of this wild reign of terror, to wage war against Rome, and rested not until at last the end was reached.

Besides these wild movements of the popular agitators, internal strifes and rivalries among the priests themselves led to the increase of confusion. The high priests were at feud with the other priests, and in consequence of the illegal arrangements which prevailed in Palestine under Felix' government, they could even go the length of sending their servants to the threshing-floor, and carrying away by force the tithes which belonged to the other priests, so that many of these unfortunate priests actually died for want. [34]

In the last two years of Felix occurred also the imprisonment of the Apostle Paul at Caesarea, of which an account is given in Acts xxiii., xxiv. We are familiar with the story of the personal interview which the apostle had with the Roman procurator and his wife Drusilla, at which the apostle did not fail to speak to both of that which it was specially fit that they should hear: "of righteousness and of temperance, and of judgment to come." [35]

While Paul lay a prisoner at Caesarea, a conflict arose there between the Jewish and Syrian inhabitants of the city over the question of equality in citizen rights ($\iota\sigma o\pi o\lambda\iota\tau\epsilon\iota a$). The Jews laid claim to the possession of certain advantages and privileges, since Herod was the founder of the city. The Syrians were naturally unwilling that any such preference should be given to the Jews. For a long time both parties fought with one another in riots on the public streets. At last on one occasion, when the Jews had obtained an advantage, Felix stepped in, reduced the Jews to order by military force, and gave up some of their houses to be plundered by the soldiers. But when, nevertheless, the disorders still continued, Felix sent the most prominent of both parties to Rome, in order that the question of law might be decided by the emperor.[36] Before, however, the matter had been settled, Felix, probably in A.D. 60, was recalled by Nero.

5. As successor of Felix, Nero sent Porcius Festus, A.D. 60–62,[37] a man who, though disposed to act righteously, found himself utterly unable to undo the mischief wrought by the misdeeds of his predecessor.

Soon after Festus' entrance upon office the dispute between the Jewish and Syrian inhabitants of Caesarea was decided in favour of the Syrians by means of an imperial rescript. The Jewish ambassadors at Rome had not been able to press their charges against Felix, because Pallas took the side of his brother. On the other hand, the two Syrian ambassadors succeeded by bribery in winning over to their interests a certain man called Beryllus, who was Nero's secretary for his Greek correspondence, and by this means obtained an imperial rescript, by which even that equality with the Syrians, with which before they had not been satisfied, was now taken away from the Jews, and the "Hellenes" declared to be the lords of the city. The embittered feelings excited by this decision among the Jews of Caesarea burst forth a few years later, in A.D. 66, in violent revolutionary movements, which Josephus regards as the beginning of the great war.[38]

Festus, after repeated hearings, caused the Apostle Paul,

whom Felix had left in prison (Acts xxiv. 27), at the apostle's own demand as a Roman citizen to be judged before the emperor, to be sent to Rome (Acts xxv., xxvi., xxvii. 1, 2 ; compare also, in addition, pp. 187, 194 of the present work).

The trouble in connection with the *Sicarii* continued under Festus just as great as it had been under Felix. During his government also a *deceiver*, so at least Josephus designates him, led the people into the wilderness, promising redemption and emancipation from all evils to those who should follow him. Festus proceeded against him with the utmost severity, but was unable to secure any lasting success.[39]

Details in regard to a conflict between the priests and King Agrippa II., in which Festus took the side of Agrippa, will be given under the section that treats of the history of that king.

After he had held office for a period of scarcely two years, Festus died while administering his procuratorship, and two men succeeded him, one after the other, who, like genuine successors of Felix, contributed, as far as it lay in their power, to intensify the bitterness of the conflict, and hurry on its final bloody conclusion.

In the interval between the death of Festus and the arrival of his successor, in A.D. 62, utter anarchy prevailed in Jerusalem, which was turned to account by the high priest Ananus, a son of that elder Ananus or Annas who is well known in connection with the history of Christ's death, in order to secure in a tumultuous gathering the condemnation of his enemies, and to have them stoned. His arbitrary government was not indeed of long duration, for King Agrippa, even before the arrival of the new procurator, again deposed him after he had held office only for three months.[40] James, the brother of Jesus Christ (ὁ ἀδελφὸς Ἰησοῦ τοῦ λεγομένου Χριστοῦ), is said to have been among those executed by Ananus. So at least the words run in our present text of Josephus ; and the words had been read even by Eusebius in his copy of Josephus precisely as they occur in our manuscripts.[41] There is considerable ground, however, for suspicion of Christian interpolation, especially as Origen read in Josephus another passage regarding the death of James, in which the destruction of Jerusalem and the temple is described as a divine judgment in consequence of the execution of James. This passage occurs in some of our manuscripts of Josephus, and ought therefore certainly to be regarded as a Christian interpolation which has been excluded from our common text.[42] Also in the account given by Hegesippus of the execution of James it is brought into close connection with the destruction of Jerusalem. The year 62 cannot by any means be accepted as the date of his death.[43]

6. The testimony of Josephus in regard to the new procurator Albinus, A.D. 62–64,[44] is to the effect that there was no sort of wickedness that could be mentioned which he had not a hand in. The leading principle of his procedure seems, however, to have been : To get money from whomsoever he might obtain it. Public as well as private treasures were subjected to his plunderings, and the whole people had to suffer oppression under his exactions.[45] But he also found it to his advantage to seek money as bribes for his favour from both political parties in the country, from the friends of the Romans, as well as from their opponents. From the high priest Ananias, inclined to favour the Romans, as well as from his enemies, the Sicarii, he accepted presents, and then allowed both of them without restraint to do as they liked. He made, indeed, a pretence of opposing the *Sicarii ;* but for money any one who might be taken prisoner could secure his release. " Nobody remained in prison as a malefactor, but he who gave him nothing." [46] The *Sicarii,* indeed, found out another means for securing the liberation of those of their party who had been taken prisoners. They were in the habit

of seizing upon adherents of the opposite party only. Then at the wish of the Roman party, by whom also he was bribed, Albinus would set free as many of the Sicarii as they would of their opponents. Once on a time the Sicarii seized the secretary of the ruler of the temple, Eleasar, a son of Ananias,[47] and in return for the liberation of the secretary they secured the restoration of ten of their own comrades.[48] Under such a government the anti-Roman party gained footing more and more, or, as Josephus puts it, "the boldness of those desirous of change became more and more obtrusive." [49] And seeing that, on the other hand, their opponents also had full scope, utter anarchy soon prevailed in Jerusalem. It was a war of all against all. Ananias, the high priest, behaved in the most outrageous manner. He allowed his servants quite openly to take away from the threshing-floors the tithes of the priests, and those who opposed them were beaten.[50] Two noble relatives of King Agrippa, called Costobar and Saul, also tried their hand at the robber business,[51] and with them was associated the man who had committed to him the maintaining of law and order, even the procurator Albinus himself.[52] In such times it was indeed nothing calculated to excite surprise when on one occasion a high priest, Jesus, son of Damnäos, engaged in pitched battle in the streets with his successor, Jesus, son of Gamaliel, because he had no wish to give up to him the sacred office.[53]

When Albinus was recalled, in order to do a pleasure to the inhabitants of the capital, and also to make the work of his successor as heavy as possible, he left all the prisons empty, having executed the ordinary malefactors, and set at liberty all the other prisoners. "Thus the prisons were left empty of prisoners, but the country full of robbers." [54]

7. The last procurator, Gessius Florus, A.D. 64–66,[55] was at the same time also the worst. He belonged to Clazomenae, and had through the influence of his wife Cleopatra, who was

a friend of the Empress Poppea, obtained the procuratorship of Judea. For the utter baseness which characterized his administration of his office, Josephus can scarcely find words sufficiently strong to express his feelings. In comparison with him, he thinks that even Albinus was extraordinarily law honouring (δικαιότατος). So unbounded was his tyranny, that in view of it the Jews praised Albinus as a benefactor. Whereas Albinus wrought his wickednesses at least in secret, Florus was impudent enough to parade them openly. The robbing of individuals seemed to him quite too small. He plundered whole cities, and ruined whole communities. If only the robbers would share their spoil with him, they would be allowed to carry on their operations unchecked.[56]

By such outrages the measure which the people could endure was at last filled up to the brim. The combustible materials which had been gathering for years had now grown into a vast heap. It needed only a spark, and an explosion would follow of fearful and most destructive force.

SUPPLEMENT. AGRIPPA II., A.D. 50–100.

Agrippa II., son of Agrippa I., whose full name, as given on coins and inscriptions, was Marcus Julius Agrippa, seems like almost all the members of the Herodian family, to have been educated and brought up in Rome. There, at least, we find him at the time of his father's death in A.D. 44, when Claudius wished to appoint him as successor to his father.[1] That the emperor, at the instigation of his counsellors on the plea of Agrippa's youth, did not carry out this purpose has been already narrated above. The youth remained for a while at Rome, and found there abundant opportunities of being useful to his countrymen by making use of his influence and connections with the court. Notable instances of his successful intervention are those of the dispute about the high priest's robe[2] and the conflict waged during the time of Cumanus.[3] To him also it was mainly due that Cumanus did not escape the punishment he deserved. With this last-mentioned incident we are already brought down to A.D. 52. But even before this there had been bestowed upon him by Claudius, in compensation for the loss of his father's territories, another kingdom, though, indeed, a smaller one. After the death of his uncle, Herod of Chalcis, he obtained, though not probably at once, but only in A.D. 50, his kingdom in the Lebanon, and, at the same time, what that prince also had had, the oversight of the temple and the right to appoint the high priests.[4] Of this latter right he frequently available himself by repeated depositions and nominations of high priests down to the outbreak of the war in A.D. 66. Probably after this gift had been bestowed upon him Agrippa continued still to reside for a while in Rome, where we meet with him in A.D. 52, and only after this date actually entered upon the government of his kingdom.

He can only seldom, or perhaps not even once, have revisited Palestine, when, in A.D. 53, in the thirteenth year of Claudius, in return for the relinquishment of the small kingdom of Chalcis, he received a larger territory, namely, the tetrarchy of Philip, including Batanea, Trachonitis, and Gaulanitis, and the tetrarchy of Lysanias, consisting of Abila and the domains of Varus.[5] This territory, after the death of Claudius, was still further enlarged, through Nero's favour for him, by the addition of important parts of Galilee and Perea, namely, the cities of Tiberias and Tarichea, together with the lands around belonging to them, and the city Julias, together with fourteen surrounding villages.[6]

Of Agrippa's private life there is not much that is favourable to report. His sister Berenice, who, from the time of the

death of Herod of Chalcis in A.D. 48, was a widow (Agrippa
I's brother), lived from that date in the house of her brother,
and soon had the weak man completely caught in the meshes
of her net, so that regarding her, the mother of two children,
the vilest stories became current. When the scandal became
public, Berenice, in order to cut away occasion for all evil
reports, resolved to marry Polemon of Cilicia, who, for this
purpose, was obliged to submit to be circumcised. She did
not, however, continue long with him, but came back again to
her brother, and seems to have resumed her old relations with
him. At least this somewhat later came to be the common
talk of Rome.[7]

In the matter of public policy Agrippa was obliged to give
up even the little measure of independence which his father
sought to secure, and had unconditionally to subordinate himself to the Roman government. He provided auxiliary troops
for the Parthian campaign of A.D. 54;[8] and when, in A.D. 60,
the new procurator Festus arrived in Palestine, he hastened,
along with his sister Berenice, surrounded with great pomp
(μετὰ πολλῆς φαντασίας), to offer him a welcome.[9] His
capital Caesarea Philippi was named by him Neronias in
honour of the emperor, and the city of Berytus, which his
father had adorned with magnificent specimens of pagan art,
was still further indebted to his liberality.[10] His coins, almost
without exception, bear the names and images of the reigning
emperor: of Nero, Vespasian, Titus, and Domitian. Like
his father, he also caused himself to be styled βασιλεὺς μέγας
φιλόκαισαρ εὐσεβὴς καὶ φιλορώμαιος.

That upon the whole he was attached to the Roman rather
than to the Jewish side is made very evident from an incident
which, in yet another direction, is characteristic of his indol-
ence and general feebleness. When he paid a visit to
Jerusalem, he was wont to occupy the house that had
formerly been the palace of the Asmoneans.[11] This building,

lofty even in its original form, he caused to be considerably
heightened by the addition of a tower, in order that from it
he might overlook the citadel and the temple, and to observe
in his idle hours the sacred proceedings in the temple. This
lazy onlooker was obnoxious to the priests, and they thwarted
his scheme by building a high wall to shut off his view.
Agrippa then applied for assistance to his friend, the procurator Festus, and he was very willing to give him any help he
could. But a Jewish deputation, which went on its own
authority about the business to Rome, managed by means of
the mediation of the Empress Poppea to obtain permission to
keep up the wall, so that Agrippa was obliged forthwith to
abandon his favourite diversion.[12]

Notwithstanding his unconditional submission to Rome,
Agrippa yet sought also to keep on good terms with the
friends of Judaism. His brothers-in-law, Azizus of Emesa
and Polemon of Cilicia, were required on their marriage with
his sisters to submit to circumcision.[13] The rabbinical tradition tells of questions pertaining to the law which were put
by Agrippa's minister or by the king himself to the famous
scribe Rabbi Elieser.[14] Yea on one occasion we find even
Berenice, a bigot as well as a wanton, a Nazarite in Jerusalem.[15] Judaism was indeed as little a matter of heart
conviction with Agrippa as it had been with his father.
The difference was only this, that as a matter of policy the
father took up decidedly the side of the Pharisees, whereas
the son with less disguise exhibited his utter indifference.
When it is told in the Acts of the Apostles how Agrippa and
Berenice desired out of curiosity to see and hear the Apostle
Paul, while the king could make no other reply to the
apostle's enthusiastic testimony on behalf of Christ than :
" With little wouldest thou win me over to be a Christian,"
and therewith allows the matter to pass away from his mind,
we can see not only that he was free from all fanaticism, but

also that he had no interest whatever in the deeper religious questions of the time.[16]

His interest in Judaism extended only to external matters, and, indeed, only to merely trifling and insignificant points. In order to support the temple when its foundations had begun to sink, and to raise the buildings twenty cubits higher, he caused, at great expense, wood of immense size and fine quality to be imported from the Lebanon. But the wood, owing to the outbreak of the war in the meantime, was never put to that use, and subsequently served for the manufacture of engines of war.[17] He allowed the psalm-singing Levites, when they made the request of him, to wear the linen garments which previously had been a distinctive badge of the priests. For such an offence against the law, the war, as Josephus thinks, was a just punishment.[18] When, in the time of Albinus, the building of the temple of Herod was completed, in order to secure employment for the multitudes of builders, Agrippa had the city paved with white marble.[19] "And thus at least as costume maker, wood-cutter, pavier, and practical inspector of the temple, did he render his services to the sinking Jerusalem." [20]

When, in the spring of A.D. 66, the revolution broke out, Agrippa was in Alexandria, where he had gone to pay his respects to the governor of that place, Tiberius Alexander, while his sister Berenice remained in Jerusalem in consequence of a Nazarite vow.[21] Agrippa then immediately hasted back, and both brother and sister did all in their power to avert the threatening storm. But all in vain. Open hostilities were now begun in Jerusalem between the war and the peace parties, and the king's troops, which he had sent to help, fought on the side of the peace party. When this latter party had been defeated, and among other buildings, the palaces of Agrippa and Berenice had fallen victims to the popular fury,[22] he became the decided choice of that party. Unhesitatingly throughout the whole war he.

stood on the side of the Romans. Even when Cestius Gallus undertook his unfortunate expedition against Jerusalem, King Agrippa was found. in his following with a considerable number of auxiliary troops.[23] As the further course of the revolt proved favourable to the Jews he lost a great part of his territory. The cities Tiberias, Tarichea, and Gamala joined the revolutionary party; but the king remained unflinchingly faithful to the Roman cause.[24] After the conquest of Jotapata, in the summer of A.D. 67, he entertained the commander-in-chief Vespasian in the most magnificent manner in his capital of Caesarea Philippi,[25] and was able soon, after he had been slightly wounded at the siege of Gamala,[26] to take possession again of his kingdom; for at the end of the year 67 the whole of the north of Palestine was again subject to the Romans.

When, after the death of Nero, which occurred on 9th June A.D. 68, Titus went to Rome to pay his respects to the new emperor Galba, he took Agrippa with him also for the same purpose. On the way they received tidings of Galba's murder, which took place on 15th January A.D. 69. While Titus now returned with as great speed as possible to his father, Agrippa continued his journey to Rome, where for a time he continued to reside.[27] But after Vespasian had been, on 30th July A.D. 69, elected emperor by the Egyptian and Syrian legions, Berenice, who had been throughout a hearty supporter of the Flavian party, urged her brother to return without delay to Palestine to take the oath of allegiance to the new emperor.[28] From this time forward Agrippa is to be found in the company of Titus, to whom Vespasian had entrusted the continued prosecution of the war.[29] When Titus, after the conquest of Jerusalem, gave magnificent and costly games at Caesarea Philippi, King Agrippa was undoubtedly present, and as a Roman joined in the rejoicings over the destruction of his people.[30]

After the war had been brought to an end Agrippa, as a faithful partizan of Vespasian, was not only confirmed in the possession of the kingdom which he had previously governed, but had also considerable additions made to his territories, though we have no more detailed account of the precise boundaries of his domains.[31] Josephus mentions only incidentally that Arcaia (Arca, at the north end of the Lebanon, north-east of Tripolis) belonged to the kingdom of Agrippa.[32] We are therefore obliged to conclude that his new possessions stretched very far to the north. The omission on the part of Josephus in *Wars of the Jews*, iii. 3. 5, to refer to these northern possessions, can be accounted for only by the hypothesis that at the time of the composition of that work this extension of territory had not yet taken place. As a matter of fact, Josephus does not refer to them there, because in that passage he does not propose to describe the whole kingdom of Agrippa, but only those districts which were inhabited more or less by Jews (compare Div. II. vol. i. p. 2). Of the southern possessions certain portions seem at a later period to have been taken away from Agrippa. At least, at the time when Josephus wrote his *Antiquities*, i.e. in A.D. 93–94, the Jewish colony of Bathyra in Batanea no longer belonged to the territory of Agrippa.[33]

In A.D. 75 the brother and sister, Agrippa and Berenice, arrived in Rome, and there those intimate relations begun in Palestine between Berenice and Titus were resumed, which soon became a public scandal.[34] The Jewish queen lived with Titus on the Palatine, while her brother was raised to the rank of a praetor. It was generally expected that there would soon be a formal marriage, which it is said that Titus had indeed promised her. But the dissatisfaction over the matter in Rome was so great that Titus found himself under the necessity of sending his beloved one away.[35] After the death of Vespasian, on 23rd June A.D. 79, she returned once more to Rome; but Titus had come to see that love intrigues were not compatible with the dignity of an emperor, and so left her unnoticed.[36]   When she found herself thus deceived she returned again to Palestine.

Of her later life, as well as of that of Agrippa, we know practically nothing. We know indeed only this, that Agrippa corresponded with Josephus about his *History of the Jewish War*, praised it for its accuracy and reliability, and purchased a copy of it.[37]

Numerous coins of Agrippa confirm the idea that his reign continued to the end of that of Domitian. The many inaccuracies which are found on these coins with reference to the imperial title have caused much trouble to numismatists. Yet, in reality, these inaccuracies are in various directions highly instructive.

According to the testimony of Justus of Tiberias,[38] Agrippa died in the third year of Trajan, in A.D. 100; and there is no reason for doubting the correctness of this statement, as Tillemont and many modern writers have done.   Agrippa, it would appear, left no children.[39]   His kingdom was undoubtedly incorporated in the province of Syria.

§ 20. THE GREAT WAR WITH ROME,

A.D. 66-73

1. THE OUTBREAK AND TRIUMPH OF THE REVOLUTION, A.D. 66.

THE ostensible occasion for the outbreak of the long threatened
revolt was given by a deed of Florus which was not in itself
any worse than many others committed by him, but to the
people proved more intolerable because it was at the same
time an outrage upon their religious sensibilities. Whereas
before he had visited only the citizens with his plunderings,
he now ventured to lay his hands upon the treasury of the
temple, and to abstract from it seventeen talents. The
people's patience was thus tried beyond endurance. They
now rose in a great tumult; a couple of sarcastic wits hit
upon a plan for throwing contempt upon the greedy procurator by sending round baskets and collecting gifts for the
poor and unfortunate Florus. When the governor heard of
this he immediately resolved to take bloody vengeance upon
those who had thus insulted him. With a detachment of
soldiers he marched to Jerusalem, and in spite of the weeping
entreaties of the high priests and the principal inhabitants,
he gave over a portion of the city to be plundered by his
soldiers. A large number of citizens, including among them
even Roman knights of Jewish descent, were seized at
random, put in fetters, and then crucified. Even the humble
pleadings of Queen Berenice, who happened to be present in

Jerusalem at that time, had no effect in moderating the fury of the procurator and his soldiers.[1]

This outrage was committed on the 16th Artemisios (Ijjar, May) of the year 66.[2]

On the day following Florus expressed the wish that the citizens should go out to give a formal greeting to the two cohorts which were to enter the city from Caesarea, in order thereby to give a public proof of their submissiveness and of their penitent disposition. Although the people were not by any means inclined to do so, the high priests persuaded them to submit to this indignity lest something worse should befall them. In solemn procession the people went out to meet the two cohorts, and gave them a friendly greeting. But the soldiers, evidently guided by the instructions of Florus, refused to return their greeting. Then began the people to murmur, and to utter reproaches against Florus. The soldiers then seized their swords, and drove the people back amid incessant slaughter into the city. Then in the streets a violent conflict raged, in which the people succeeded in securing possession of the temple mount, and in cutting off the connection between it and the castle of Antonia. Florus could easily see that he was not strong enough to subdue the multitude by violence. He therefore withdrew to Caesarea, leaving behind only one cohort in Jerusalem, and announcing that he would hold the chief men of the city responsible for the quiet and order of the people.[3]

King Agrippa was at this time in Alexandria. When he heard of the disturbances he hastened to Jerusalem, summoned the people to an assembly on the Xystus, an open space in front of the palace of the Asmoneans, in which Agrippa resided, and from his palace addressed the people in a long and impressive speech, in order to urge them to abandon the utterly hopeless, and therefore unreasonable and disastrous

struggle on which they were entering.[4]   The people declared
themselves ready to return to their allegiance to the emperor
They began again to build up the galleries between the
temple mount and the Antonia, which they had torn down,
and they collected the outstanding taxes.   But when Agrippa
insisted that they should again yield obedience to Florus, this
was more than the people could endure.   His proposals were
rejected with contempt and scorn, and he was obliged to withdraw without accomplishing his purpose in his kingdom.[5]

Meanwhile the rebels had succeeded in gaining possession
of the fortress of Masada.   At the instigation of Eleasar, son
of the high priest Ananias, it was now also resolved to dis-
continue the daily offering for the emperor, and no longer to
admit of any offering by those who were not Jews.   The
refusal to offer a sacrifice for the emperor was equivalent to
an open declaration of revolt against the Romans.   All
attempts of the principal men, among the chief priests as
well as among the Pharisees, to induce the people to recall
this foolhardy resolution were in vain.   They firmly adhered
to the decision to which they had come.[6]

When the members of the peace party, to which, as might
be expected, all discerning and judicious men belonged,—the
high priests, the most distinguished of the Pharisees, those
related to the house of Herod,—perceived that they were
incapable of accomplishing any good, they resolved to have
recourse to violent measures.   They accordingly made application for assistance to King Agrippa.   He sent a detachment
of 3000 cavalry under the command of Darius and Philip, by
whose help the peace party gained possession of the upper
city, while the rebels continued to hold the temple mount
and the lower city.   A bitter strife now arose between the
two parties; but the royal troops were not strong enough to
withstand the violent rage of the multitude, and were obliged

to evacuate the upper city. In order to take vengeance upon their opponents, the rebels set fire to the palaces of the high priest Ananias, of King Agrippa, and Berenice.[7]

A few days after this, in the month Loos, that is, Ab or August, they also succeeded in storming the citadel of Antonia, and then they began to lay siege to the upper palace, that of Herod, in which the troops of the peace party had taken refuge. Here, too, it was impossible for the besieged to offer any effectual resistance. Consequently the troops of Agrippa were only too glad to submit on the condition of being allowed to pass out unhurt. The Roman cohorts had betaken themselves to the three strong towers of the palace, known respectively by the names Hippicus, Phasael, and Mariamme, while all the rest of the palace was, on 6th Gorpiaios, that is, Elul or September, set on fire by the rebels.[8] On the following day the high priest Ananias, who had hitherto kept himself concealed, was apprehended in his hiding-place and put to death.[9] The solitary feeble support which still remained to the peace party, was that of the Roman cohorts besieged in the three towers of the palace of Herod. These, too, were obliged at last to yield to the superior power of the people. Upon laying down their arms they were allowed to walk out uninjured. But the rebels, who were now masters of the whole city, celebrated their victory by general slaughter. The Roman soldiers were scarcely gone, leaving their weapons behind them, when they were treacherously fallen upon by the Jews, and were cut down to the last man.[10]

While thus the triumph of the revolution in Jerusalem was decided, bloody conflicts took place also in many other cities, where Jews and Gentiles dwelt together, especially within the borders of Palestine. Wherever the Jews were in the majority, they cut down their Gentile fellow-townsmen; and where the Gentiles predominated, they fell upon the

Jews. The influence of the revolt in the mother country spread even as far as Alexandria.[11]

At last, after long delay and preparation, Cestius Gallus, the governor of Syria, entered upon negotiations for the quieting of the disturbances in Judea. With the twelfth legion, 2000 chosen men from other legions, six cohorts, and four *alae* of cavalry, besides numerous auxiliary troops which the friendly kings, including Agrippa, had been obliged to place at his disposal, he started from Antioch, marched through Ptolemais, Caesarea, Antipatris, Lydda, where he arrived at the time of the Feast of Tabernacles in the month Tizri or October, and finally through Beth-horon to Gabao or Gibeon, 50 stadia from Jerusalem, and there pitched his camp.[12] A sally made by the Jews from Jerusalem put the Roman army into a position of great danger, but was at last driven back.[13] Cestius then advanced nearer to the city, and laid siege to the so-called Scopus, 7 stadia from Jerusalem. Four days later, on the 30th Hyperberetaios, that is, Tizri or October, he took possession unopposed of the northern suburb Bezetha, and set it on fire.[14] But when he ventured upon the bolder task of storming the temple mount his enterprise failed. He thereupon desisted from all further attempts, and began to withdraw without accomplishing his object.[15] Josephus is unable to explain the causes of this procedure. Probably Cestius perceived that his forces were insufficient for making an attack with any hope of success upon the well fortified and courageously defended city. With what determination and with what dauntless resolution the struggle was carried forward on the part of the Jews, was now to be proved to the Roman governor on his retreat. In a ravine near Beth-horon, through which he was pursuing his journey, he found himself surrounded on every side by the Jews, and attacked with such force, that his homeward march was turned into a flight. Only by leaving behind him a great part of his baggage, including much valuable war material, which subsequently proved of great service to the Jews, did he succeed in reaching Antioch with a fragment of his army. Amid great rejoicings the returning conquerors entered Jerusalem on the 8th Dios, that is, Marchesvan or November.[16]

In presence of the excitement caused by victory which now prevailed in Jerusalem all peace counsels were forcibly silenced. After such decisive successes no proposals of compromise would be listened to. Even those inclined to oppose were driven along by the course of events. Those who were inalienably attached to the Romans left the city. All the rest were drawn into their own ranks by the rebels, partly by force, partly by persuasion (τοὺς μὲν βίᾳ τοὺς δὲ πειθοῖ).[17] They now set about organizing the rebellion in a regular methodical fashion, and made preparations for the expected onslaught of the Romans. It is distinctively characteristic of the later period of the war that the men who now had the power in their hands belonged exclusively to the higher ranks. The chief priests, the most distinguished of the Pharisees, were those who directed the organization of the land defences. An assembly of the people, which was held in the temple, made choice of commanders for the provinces. Two men, Joseph, son of Gorion, and the high priest Ananus, were entrusted with the defence of the capital. To Idumea they sent Jesus, son of Sapphias, and Eleasar, son of Ananias, both belonging to the high priestly family. Nearly all the eleven toparchies into which Judea was divided had their own commanders. Finally, to Galilee was sent Josephus, son of Matthias, the future historian.[18]

There is no doubt but that the youthful Josephus had thus one of the most difficult and most responsible positions assigned to him, for it was just in Galilee that the first attack of the Romans might be expected. Great results

could scarcely be looked for in the conducting of warlike
operations from a young man only thirty years of age ; and
he owed his appointment certainly less to his military
capacities than to his friendship with the most distinguished
personages. It was indeed a strange proceeding to send a
young man, who in addition to his natural ability could at
most only point to his rabbinical learning, to enlist an army
with all haste from among the peaceful inhabitants of
Galilee, and with it to hold his ground against the attack of
veteran legions and circumvent the tactics of experienced
generals ! If we are to believe his own account, he set
himself at least with zeal to the solving of the insoluble
problem. For the governing of Galilee he appointed, in
imitation of the Sanhedrim of Jerusalem, a council of seventy
men, which had to decide on difficult points of law ; while for
less important disputes he established in every city a council
of seven men.[19] He intended to prove his zeal for the
law by destroying the palace of Tiberias, which, contrary to
the law, was adorned with animal images ; but in this he
was anticipated by the revolutionary party.[20] The military
part of his task he endeavoured to carry out specially by
strengthening the fortifications of the cities. All the
more important cities of Galilee, Jotapata, Tarichea, Tiberias,
Sepphoris, Gischala, Mount Tabor, also Gamala in Gaulanitis,
and many smaller towns were put more or less in a condition
of defence.[21] But with special pride he boasts of his labours
in organizing the army. He sought to bring together no less
than 100,000 men, and to have them drilled after the
Roman style.[22]

While Josephus thus prepared for war with the Romans, a
violent opposition arose against him in his own province,
which even went the length of openly drawing the sword
upon him. The soul of this hostile movement was John of
Gischala, a bold, reckless party leader, who was filled with

glowing hatred toward the Romans, and had resolved to carry on the struggle against them to the uttermost. But while he had sworn death and destruction to the tyrants, he was himself no less of a tyrant within his own circle. It was intolerable to him to brook the idea of having others over him. Least of all could he yield obedience to Josephus, whose tame method of conducting the war seemed to him no better than friendship for the Romans. Hence he used every endeavour to get the man so hateful to him set aside, and to withdraw the allegiance of the people of Galilee from him.[23] His suspicion of Josephus was indeed not altogether without foundation. Josephus knew the Romans too well to entertain the notion that the rebellion could be really and finally successful. He was therefore necessarily only half-hearted in the business which he had undertaken, and sometimes unwittingly allowed this to appear. On one occasion certain youths from the village of Dabaritta had robbed an official of King Agrippa, and taken rich spoil. Josephus caused them to hand back what they had taken, and intended, if we may believe his own account of the affair, to restore them to the king on the first favourable opportunity. When the people perceived that this was his intention, the suspicion which John of Gischala had insinuated against him was increased, and now broke out into open rebellion. In Tarichea, where Josephus had his residence, a great tumult was made. They threatened the life of the traitor. Only by the most miserable and degrading self-humiliation and the exercise of low cunning could Josephus ward off the threatened danger.[24] Some time later at Tiberias, he escaped the assassins sent against him by John of Gischala only by precipitate flight.[25] At last John carried matters so far that he was able to obtain in Jerusalem a resolution to recall Josephus. Four of the most distinguished men were sent for this purpose to Galilee, accompanied by a detachment of soldiers numbering

2500 men, in order to carry out this decision by force if necessary. But Josephus knew how to frustrate the execution of this decree, and the four ambassadors were again recalled. When they refused compliance with that summons, he had them apprehended and sent them back to Jerusalem. The inhabitants of Tiberias who continued in revolt were subjugated by force, and thus for the time peace was restored.[26] When, a few days later, the inhabitants of Tiberias again rose in revolt,—now, indeed, in favour of Agrippa and the Romans,—they were overcome once more by craft.[27]

Meanwhile in Jerusalem they were by no means inactive. There, too, they were making preparations for meeting the Romans. The walls were strengthened, war material of all sorts was collected, the youth were exercised in the use of arms.[28]

Amid such preparations the spring of A.D. 67 came round, and with it the time when the attack of the Romans was expected, and the young republic would have to pass through its fiery ordeal.

2. THE WAR IN GALILEE, A.D. 67.

The Emperor Nero had received in Achaia the news of the defeat of Cestius.[29] Since the continuance of the war could not have been committed to the defeated general,—he seems indeed soon afterwards to have died,[30]—the difficult task of putting down the Jewish rebellion was made over to the well-proved hands of Vespasian. During winter Vespasian still pushed forward the preparations for the campaign. While he himself went to Antioch and there marshalled his army, he sent his son Titus to Alexandria, in order that he might bring to him from thence the fifteenth legion.[31] So soon as the season of the year allowed, he marched from Antioch and advanced to Ptolemais, where he meant to

await the arrival of Titus.   But before Titus reached that
place, ambassadors from the Galilean city of Sepphoris
appeared before Vespasian and besought him to give them a
Roman garrison.[32] Vespasian hasted to comply with their
request. A detachment of 6000 men under the leadership
of Placidus was sent as a garrison to the city. Thus were
the Romans, without drawing a sword, in possession of one of
the most important and one of the strongest points in
Galilee.[33] Soon after this Titus arrived with his one legion.
The army now at the disposal of Vespasian consisted of 3
distinct legions, the fifth, tenth, and fifteenth, 23 auxiliary
cohorts, 6 *alae* of cavalry, besides the auxiliary troops of
King Agrippa, of King Antiochus of Commagene, of Soemus
of Emesa, and of Malchus of Arabia : in all comprising
somewhere about 60,000 men.[34]

When all arrangements had been made, Vespasian advanced
from Ptolemais and pitched his camp on the borders of
Galilee. Josephus had before this set his camp at the village
of Garis, twenty stadia from Sepphoris (*Life*, lxxi.), in order
that he might there wait the attack of the Romans. The
warlike qualities of his army were soon shown in a very
doubtful light. When it became known that Vespasian
was approaching, the majority of the Jewish troops became
utterly dispirited, even before they had so much as come face
to face with the Romans ; they fled hither and thither ; and
Josephus found himself obliged to hasten with the remnant
to Tiberias.[35] Without drawing a sword, Vespasian had thus
obtained possession of the lowlands of Galilee. Only the
strongholds now remained for him to take.

Josephus soon held communication with Jerusalem, and
insisted that if they wished the war to be carried on they
should send an army able to cope with the Romans, a
petition which now indeed came too late.[36] The most of the
army of Josephus had taken refuge in the strong fortress of

Jotapata.[37]   Even he himself entered that stronghold on the 21st (?) Artemisios, that is, Ijjar or May, so as to conduct the defence in his own person.[38]   On the evening of the immediately following day, Vespasian with his army appeared before the city; and then began the celebrated siege of the certainly not unimportant stronghold, described with a self-glorifying amplitude of details by Josephus.   The first attack led to no result.   It was found necessary to have recourse to a regular siege.   An obstinate struggle made the issue for some time doubtful.   What on the one side was accomplished by art and the experience of war, was accomplished on the other by the courage of despair and the skill of the commander-in-chief.   For although Josephus was indeed no general in the proper sense of the word, he was a past master in little tricks and stratagem.   With profound satisfaction the vain man tells how he deceived the Roman generals as to the scarcity of water in the city by making his soldiers hang their clothes dripping with water over the battlements.   He also tells how he managed to procure supplies of food by sending his men out by night clothed in the skins of beasts, so that they might pass by the Roman sentinels.   He further relates how he broke the force of the battering-ram upon the wall by throwing out bags filled with chaff; how he had boiling oil thrown upon the soldiers, or boiling fenugreek poured on the boards of the scaling ladders, so that those advancing on them slipped and fell back.   But neither by such arts nor by the boldness of the sallies, in one of which Vespasian himself was wounded, could the fate of the city be averted.   After the besieged had endured the utmost extremity of suffering, a deserter betrayed the secret, that in consequence of fatigue the very sentinels could no longer keep themselves awake till the morning. The Romans made use of this information.   With perfect stillness, Titus one morning with a small detachment scaled the wall, cut down the sleeping watch, and pressed into the city. The legions followed in his track, and the outwitted garrison were aware of the entrance of the Romans only when they no longer had power to drive them back. All without exception who fell into the hands of the Romans, armed and unarmed, men and women, were ruthlessly slain or carried off as slaves; the city and its fortifications were levelled with the dust. It was on the 1st of the month Panemos, that is, Thamuz or July, A.D. 67, when this most important fortress of Galilee fell into the hands of the Romans.[39]

Josephus with forty companions had taken refuge in a well which discharged itself into a cave. When he was discovered there, he was willing to surrender to the Romans, but was prevented doing so by his companions. These only offered him the choice of dying along with them, either by their hand or by his own. By some sort of stratagem, having persuaded them that they should fall upon one another in the order determined by the lot, and having by the fortune of the lot been himself reserved to the last, Josephus managed to extricate himself from their hands, and having made his escape, surrendered himself to the Romans.[40] When he was brought before Vespasian, he assumed the role of a prophet, and prophesied to the general his future elevation as emperor. This had for him at least this result, that although kept prisoner, he was dealt with in a generous manner.[41]

On the fourth day of Panemos, Vespasian advanced from Jotapata and marched next past Ptolemais to Caesarea, where he allowed the troops some rest.[42] While the soldiers were refreshing themselves after the exertions of the siege, the general paid a visit to the friendly King Agrippa at Caesarea Philippi, and took part there in extravagant festivities lasting for twenty days. He then sent the legions by Titus from Caesarea by the sea and marched against Tiberias, where, at the sight of the Roman army, the people of their own accord opened their gates, and for Agrippa's sake received honourable treatment.[43] From this point Vespasian pursued his way onward to Tarichea.[44] By a bold stroke of Titus, this city also fell into the hands of the Romans in the beginning of the month Gorpiaios, that is, Elul or September.[45]

In Galilee there now remained in the hands of the rebels only Gischala and Mount Tabor (Itabyrion), and in Gaulanitis the important and strongly fortified Gamala.[46] To the last-named place Vespasian next directed his attention. The siege appeared soon to be successful. The Romans succeeded in storming the walls and forcing an entrance into the city. But there they encountered such bitter resistance that they were forced to retire with very heavy loss. The repulse was so severe that it required all Vespasian's influence and reputation to restore again the courage of the soldiers. At last, on the 23rd Hyperberetaios, that is, Tizri or October, the Romans again forced their way into the city, and were this time successful in making themselves complete masters of the situation.[47] During the siege of Gamala the Mount Tabor (Itabyrion) was also taken by a detachment sent thither.[48]

Vespasian gave over the reducing of Gischala to Titus with a detachment of 1000 cavalry. He himself led the 5th and 15th legions into winter quarters at Caesarea, while he placed the 10th at Scythopolis.[49] Titus made light work of Gischala. On the second day after his appearing before the walls of the city, the citizens of their own accord opened the gates to him, John having secretly, during the previous night, with his Zealot comrades quitted the city and fled to Jerusalem.[50]

Thus by the end of A.D. 67 was the whole of the north of Palestine brought again into subjection to the Romans.

3. From the Subjugation of Galilee to the Siege of Jerusalem, A.D. 68–69.

The unfortunate results of the first year of the war determined the fate of the leaders of the rebellion. On the part of the fanatical section of the people, and not without cause, the unfavourable turn that events had taken was attributed to the lack of energy in the mode of conducting the war hitherto. The men of the people therefore set themselves with all their might to get the reins into their own hands, and to set aside those who had been in command. And since these would not of their own accord withdraw, a fearfully bloody civil war, accompanied by acts of horrid cruelty, broke out during the winter of A.D. 67–68 in Jerusalem, which in its atrocities can only be compared to the first French revolution.

The head of the fanatical popular party, or, as they called themselves, the Zealots, was John of Gischala. After he had escaped the hands of Titus by flight, he went with his followers, in the beginning of November A.D. 67, to Jerusalem, and sought to win over the people to himself and to rekindle in their breasts a determination to continue the war in a bolder and more resolute spirit. He readily succeeded in gaining over the youth to his side. And since now on all hands the war-loving rabble from the country poured into the city, the party of the Zealots was soon in the ascendency.[51] They next proceeded to set aside those who were suspected of friendship for the Romans. Several of the most distinguished men, among them Antipas, who belonged to the family of Herod, were put under arrest, and were murdered in prison.[52] Their next proceeding was to choose a new high priest by lot, for those who had held the office up to this time all belonged to the aristocratic party. The newly-elected high priest, Phannias of Aphtha, was not indeed in the least degree acquainted with the duties of the high priest's office. But he was a man of the people, and that was the main thing.[53]

The men of order, Gorion, son of Joseph,[54] the famous Pharisee Simon, son of Gamaliel,[55] the two high priests, Ananus, son of Ananus, and Jesus, son of Gamaliel, sought on their part to resist the Zealots by force. They exhorted the people to put a stop to the wild schemes of that faction.[56] A discourse which Ananus delivered with this end in view[57] had indeed this result, that a section of the populace declared open hostilities against the Zealots. These enthusiasts were in the minority, and were obliged to retreat before the superior force of their opponents, and to take refuge in the inner court of the temple, where for a time they were carefully guarded, as the people would not violently attack the sacred gates.[58]

In order to obtain support the Zealots secretly sent messengers to the war-loving Idumeans, and besought of them that they would form a confederacy on the pretext that the dominant party in Jerusalem had fallen away to Romans. The Idumeans appeared before the walls of the city, but were not admitted, for no one knew of their alliance with the Zealots.[59] On the night after their arrival a terrible hurricane burst forth. The storm raged, and the rain fell in torrents. Under shelter of this storm the Zealots succeeded in secretly opening the gates to their confederates and letting them in unobserved.[60] Scarcely had the Idumeans obtained a firm footing in the city, when they began the work of murder and robbery, in which the Zealots afforded them ready aid. The party of order was too weak to withstand the attack. The victory of the reign of terror in Jerusalem was complete. The rage of the Zealots and of the Idumeans in league with them was directly mainly against the distinguished, respectable, and well-to-do. All those who had previously been leaders of the revolution were now made away with as suspected friends of the Romans. Conspicuous above all the other victims of their murderous zeal were the high priests Ananus and Jesus.[61] In order to lend to their wild scheme the semblance of legal sanction, the comedy of a formal process at law was on one occasion enacted. But when the court of justice convened for that purpose pronounced the accused, Zacharias, son of Baruch, innocent, he was cut down by a couple of Zealots with the scornful declaration : " Here hast thou also our voices." [62]

When the Idumeans had been satiated with murder, and had, besides, observed that what had been styled threatened treason was only a calumnious charge trumped up against order-loving citizens, they would have no more partnership with the Zealots, and so took their departure.[63] All the more unrestrainedly did the Zealots now pursue their rule of terror. Gorion also now fell under their lash. The party of the well-doing and order-loving had been by this time so sadly thinned that there could no longer be any thought of resistance. John of Gischala was supreme potentate in the city.[64]

At this period, if not even earlier than this, occurred the flight of the Christian community from Jerusalem. The Christians left the city " in consequence of a divine admonition," and migrated to the city of Pella in Perea, which as a heathen city was undisturbed by the war.[65]

Vespasian's generals were of the opinion that they should take advantage of these circumstances, and that now was the time to begin the attack upon the capital. They thought that in consequence of the internal conflicts within the city the task before them would be easily accomplished. Not so Vespasian. He regarded it as more prudent to allow his enemies to waste their strength in the civil strife, and to consume one another.[66] In order that the inhabitants of the capital might have time to carry out their work of self-destruction, he directed his attention meanwhile to Perea. Even before the favourable season had arrived, he marched from Caesarea on the 4th Dystros, that is, Adar or March, of A.D. 68, invested Gadara, in order to guard against the elements in the city hostile to the Romans, left there a garrison, and then turned back again to Caesarea.[67] A detachment of 3000 infantry and 500 cavalry, which he left behind him under the command of Placidus, completed the subjugation of all Perea as far as Machärus.[68] When the more suitable season came round,[69] Vespasian advanced with the greater part of his army from Caesarea and invested Antipatris, took Lydda and Jamnia, drew up the 5th legion before Emmaus, made a successful raid through Idumea, then turned again northward upon Emmaus, pressed through Samaria to Neapolis (Shechem), and thence past Corea, where he arrived on 2 Daisios, that is Sivan or June, to Jericho.[70] At Jericho and Adida he left Roman garrisons, while Gerasa (?) was taken and then destroyed by a detachment sent against it under Lucius Annius.[71]

The country was now so far subdued that it only remained to begin the siege of the capital. Vespasian therefore turned back to Caesarea, and was actually busying himself with preparations for the siege of Jerusalem when the news reached him of the death of Nero, which had taken place on 9th June A.D. 68. By this event the whole situation was suddenly changed. The future of the empire as a whole was uncertain. Vespasian therefore suspended all warlike undertakings, and concluded to wait for the further development of affairs. When the news of Galba's elevation to the throne arrived, which was not till the middle of the winter of A.D. 68–69, he sent his son Titus to Rome in order to convey his greetings to the new emperor, and to receive from him his commands. But Titus had proceeded no farther

than Corinth when he received tidings of the murder of
Galba, which occurred on 15th January A.D. 69, whereupon
he returned to Caesarea to his father. Vespasian was now
inclined to wait without committing himself to see how
things would go.[72]

Circumstances, however, soon obliged him again to take
decisive action. A certain Simon Bar-Giora, that is, son of
the proselyte,[73] a man of like spirit to John of Gischala,
inspired by an equally wild enthusiasm for freedom, and
just as little able to brook the presence of any one over himself, had taken advantage of the cessation of hostilities to
gather around himself a crowd of supporters, with which he
overran the southern parts of Palestine, robbing and plundering wherever he went. Everywhere the course which he
and his horde had taken was marked by devastation. Among
other successes he managed to surprise Hebron, and to carry
off from it abundant spoil.[74]

Vespasian therefore found it necessary to secure possession
of Judea in a more thorough manner than had hitherto been
accomplished. On the 5th Daisios, that is, Sivan or June,
of the year 69, after a whole year had passed without armed
interference, he again advanced from Caesarea, subdued the
districts of Gophna and Acrabata, the cities of Bethel and
Ephraim, and arrived in the neighbourhood of Jerusalem,
while his tribune Cerealis conquered and destroyed the city
of Hebron, which had offered opposition. With the exception
of Jerusalem and the fortresses of Herodium, Masada, and
Machärus, all Palestine was now subject to the Romans.[75]

Even before Simon found himself prevented by this expedition of Vespasian from continuing his robber raids through
Idumea, the gate of the capital had been flung open to receive
him. Up to the spring of A.D. 69, John of Gischala had there
played the part of the omnipotent tyrant. Of the ruinous
confusion and lawlessness that prevailed in Jerusalem under

his rule Josephus has given a thrilling and horrible description.[76]   The inhabitants, who had long desired to be rid of his supremacy, looked with favour upon the arrival of Simon Bar-Giora as a means of freeing them from him who now acted the tyrant over them.   On the suggestion of the high priest Matthias, Simon was invited to come into the city.   He most readily accepted the invitation, and made his public entrance into Jerusalem in the month Xanthicus, that is, Nisan or April, of the year 69.   But, although the hope had been entertained that he would free them from the tyranny of John, it was now found that they rather had two tyrants in the city who fought against one another, both regarding the resident citizens as their common enemies.[77]

Vespasian had scarcely returned back to Caesarea when the news came that Vitellius had been raised to the throne as emperor.   The idea then took possession of the legions in Egypt, Palestine, and Syria that they had as much right to nominate the emperor as had their comrades in the West, and that Vespasian was more worthy of the throne than the glutton Vitellius.   On 1st July A.D. 69, Vespasian was proclaimed emperor in Egypt.   A few days afterwards the Palestinian and Syrian legions made the same proclamation.   Before the middle of July, Vespasian was acknowledged as emperor throughout the whole East.[78]

He had now something else to engage his attention than the prosecution of the war against the rebellious Jews.   After he had received at Berytus the embassies from various Syrian and other cities, he marched on to Antioch, and from thence sent to Rome by road Mucianus with an army.[79]   He then went himself to Alexandria.   During his residence there he obtained the intelligence that his interests had prevailed in Rome, and that Vitellius had been murdered on 20th December A.D. 69.   He himself still remained in Alexandria till the beginning of the summer of A.D. 70;[80] while his son Titus, to whom he had committed the continuing of the Jewish war, marched at the head of the army to Palestine.[81]

In Jerusalem, by this time, the internal feuds had advanced one step further. Instead of the two parties of John and Simon there were now three, for from the party of John a new section had broken off under Eleasar, son of Simon. Simon had in his power the upper city and a great part of the lower city, John held the Temple Mount, and Eleasar the inner Court of the Temple. All three continued incessantly at war with one another, so that the city from day to day presented the aspect of a battlefield. In their mutual hatred of one another they became so foolish that they destroyed by fire the immense store of grain which had been gathered up in the city, lest their rivals should profit by it, without considering that thereby they robbed themselves of the means of sustaining a siege.[82] While thus Jerusalem was tearing its own flesh, Titus was carrying on the preparations for his attack.

4. The Siege and Conquest of Jerusalem, a.d. 70.

The army which Titus had at his disposal consisted of four legions. Besides the three legions of his father, the 5th, 10th, and 15th, he had also the 12th, which had already been in Syria under Cestius, and had so unfortunately begun the war. In addition to these, he had also the numerous auxiliary troops of the confederate kings.[83] The commanders of the legions were—Sextus Cerealis over the 5th legion, Larcius Lepidus over the 10th, Tittius Frugi over the 15th. The commander of the 12th legion is not named. As principal adviser, we would call him Chief of the Staff, Tiberius Alexander, afterwards procurator of Judea, accompanied Titus.[84] While a part of the army received orders to push on to meet him before Jerusalem, Titus himself advanced with the main body of his forces from Caesarea,[85] and a few days before the

Passover, 14th Nisan or April, of A.D. 70, arrived before the walls of the Holy City.[86]

Titus had hurried on in advance of the legions with 600 cavalry in order to obtain information about the country by spies, and had in this got so far ahead of the main body, that he exposed himself most seriously to the danger of being fallen upon by the Jews, and, indeed, owed his safety wholly to his own personal bravery.[87] The Romans, from the moment of their arrival, had painful experience of the daring spirit of their opponents.   While the 10th legion, which had advanced from Jericho to Jerusalem, was still occupied with the strengthening of its camp on the Mount of Olives, it was attacked with such violence that it had well-nigh suffered an utter defeat.   Only by the personal interference of Titus was the yielding legion brought again to a stand, and enabled to ward off the attack.[88]

The conflict of parties within the city, however, was not even yet by any means abated.   Even when the Romans were lying before the gates, during the Passover festival, a carnage of one party by the other was going on within the city.   The faction of Eleasar had opened the gate of the temple court for those who had gone up to attend the feast. John of Gischala took advantage of this in order to smuggle in his people with concealed weapons, and to fall on Eleasar and his followers when least expected.   Those who were thus taken by surprise were not strong enough to sustain the conflict, and were obliged to admit John's adherents into the court.   From this time forward there were again two parties in Jerusalem, that of John and that of Simon.[89]

In order to understand the siege operations that followed, it is necessary to form for oneself at least a general idea of the situation of the city.[90]   Jerusalem lay upon two hills, a higher one to the west and a smaller one to the east, which were separated by a deep ravine running from north to south, the so-called Tyropoeon. On the larger western hill lay the upper city, on the smaller eastern hill the lower city. The latter was also called Acra, because there in former days down to the times of the Maccabees the citadel or castle of Jerusalem had been placed.[91] North of the Acra lay the site of the temple, the area of which had been considerably enlarged by Herod. Attached to the temple site on its northern side was the castle of Antonia. The temple site was surrounded on all its four sides by a strong wall, and thus even by itself alone formed a little fortress. The upper and the lower cities were surrounded by a common wall which was attached to the western wall of the temple site; it then ran on to the west, stretched in a great curve southward over the upper and lower cities, and finally ended at the south-eastmost corner of the temple site. But, further, the upper city must have been separated from the lower city by a wall running from north to south reaching to the Tyropoeon. For Titus was obliged, after he had gained possession of the lower city, to direct an attack against the wall of the upper city.—On the west, south, and east, the walls stood upon the edge of lofty precipices; only on the north did the ground run down tolerably low. Thus was there with a northern curve a second wall which enclosed the older suburb; and then in a still wider curve to the north, a third wall, which had been begun by Agrippa I., but was completed only when found urgently needed during the rebellion. This third wall enclosed the so-called new city or suburb of Bezetha.[92]

As the very situation of the city demanded, Titus directed his attack against the north side, hence first of all against the third wall, or to speak from the standpoint of the besiegers, the first. It was only now, when the battering-ram began their work at three points, the civil war was stilled. Then the two factions, those of John of Gischala and of Simon Bar-Giora, banded together to make a common attack. In

one of these onslaughts they fought with such success that
the preservation of the engines of war were wholly due
to the interference of Titus, who with his own hand cut
down twelve of the enemy.[93]   After fifteen days' work one
of the most powerful of the battering-rams had made a
breach in the wall, the Romans pressed in, and on the 7th
Artemisios, that is, Ijjar or May, were masters of the first
wall.[94]

The attack was now directed against the second wall.
Five days after the taking of the first this one also had to
yield before the blow of the Roman battering-rams.   Titus
pressed in with a chosen band, but was driven back again by
the Jews.   Four days afterwards, however, he once more
secured his position, and this time succeeded in maintaining
it permanently.[95]

He now raised earthworks at one and the same time
against the upper city and against the Antonia, two against
the one, and two against the other ; each of the four legions
had to build one.   Simon Bar-Giora conducted the defence
of the upper city ; John of Gischala that of the Antonia.[96]
While the works were in progress, Josephus, apparently
without success, was made to summon the city to surrender.[97]
The want of the means of support was already beginning to
be felt, and in consequence of this many of the poorer
inhabitants went out of the city in search of victuals.
Whenever any of them fell into the hands of the Romans, he
was crucified in sight of the city, in order to strike terror
into the heart of the besieged, or was sent back with his
members mutilated.[98]

On the 29th Artemisios, that is, Ijjar or May, the four
ramparts were completed.   Simon and John had only wished
their completion, in order that they might direct all their
energies to destroy again the works produced by incredible
exertion and wearisome toil.   Those over against the Antonia

were destroyed by John of Gischala in this way : he dug a subterranean passage under them, supported it with pillars and then set fire to the supports, so that the ramparts fell in and were consumed in the fire. Two days later Simon Bar-Giora destroyed by fire those directed against the upper city.[99]

Before Titus attempted the building of a new rampart, he made use of another device. He caused the whole city to be surrounded with a continuous stone wall ($\tau\epsilon\hat{\iota}\chi o\varsigma$), in order to cut off all escape and to reduce the city by famine. With marvellous smartness this work was finished in three days. Numerous armed watchmen guarded it so that no one could pass it.[100] In consequence of this the famine reached a terrible height in the city ; and if even but the half is true which the inventive imagination of Josephus has recorded, it must certainly have been horrible enough.[101] That under such circumstances John of Gischala should have applied the sacred oil and the sacred wine to profane uses, can be regarded only by a Josephus as a reproach to him.[102]

Meanwhile Titus caused ramparts again to be built, and this time four against the Antonia. The wood used in their construction, owing to the complete devastation of all the district around, had to be carried a distance of 90 stadia (four and a half hours' journey).[103] After twenty-one days' work they were completed. An attempt which John of Gischala made to destroy them on 1st Panemos, that is, Thammuz or July, was unsuccessful, since it was not carried out with the earlier energy, while the Romans had redoubled their vigilance.[104] Scarcely had the Jews retired back again, when the battering-rams began to beat against the walls. At first they had no considerable success. The walls, however, were so shattered by the blows, that soon they sank of themselves at the points where the wall-breakers had been at work. But even yet the storming of the city was a work of difficulty, since John of Gischala had already managed to erect a second behind it. After an encouraging speech of Titus on the 3rd Panemos, that is, Thammuz or July, a Syrian soldier named Sabinus, with eleven comrades, made the attempt to scale the walls, but fell in the struggle with three of his companions. [105] Two days afterwards, on the 5th Panemos, some twenty or thirty others banded together to renew the attempt. They mounted the wall secretly by night and cut down the first sentinels. Titus pressed as quickly as possible after them, and drove the Jews back as far as the temple site. Thence the Romans were indeed beaten back again, but they held the Antonia, which was soon razed to the ground. [106]

In spite of war and famine the daily morning and evening sacrifices had up to this time been regularly offered. On the 17th Panemos, that is, Thammuz or July, these had to be at last discontinued; but even then not so much on account of the famine, but rather "from the want of men." [107] Seeing that a renewed summons to surrender by Josephus proved again unsuccessful, and an attack by night of a select detachment of the army on the temple site proved a failure, [108] Titus now made preparations for a regular siege so as to take the temple by storm. The temple site formed a pretty regular square, which was completely surrounded by strong walls, along which on the inside ran a series of corridors. On the inside of this great space the inner court, surrounded on all sides by strong walls, formed a second position capable of being defended, which afforded to the besieged even after the loss of the outer space a place of safety. Titus was obliged first of all to make himself master of the outer wall. Again four ramparts were erected, for which he was now obliged to carry the material from a distance of 100 stadia (five hours' journey). [109] While they were working at these, a number of Romans met with their death on the 27th Panemos in this way: they allowed themselves to be deceived by the withdrawal of the Jews from the heights of the western corridors into scaling those heights.   But they had been beforehand filled by the Jews with inflammable materials.   So soon then as the Romans had reached the top the Jews set fire to the vaults, and the fire spread with such rapidity that the soldiers could not escape, but were enveloped in the flames.[110]

When the ramparts were completed on the 8th Loos, that is, Ab, or August, the rams were again set to work, and the siege operations began.   But on the immense walls they could make no impression.   In order to obtain his end Titus caused fire to be placed at the gates, and so opened up the entrance to the outer temple space.[111]   On the next day, the 9th Ab, when the gates had been completely burnt down, Titus held a council of war, at which it was resolved that the temple should be spared.[112]   But when on the day following, the 10th Ab, the Jews made two onslaughts rapidly one after the other from the inner court, and on the second occasion were driven back by the soldiers who were occupied with the quenching of the flames in the corridors, a soldier cast a blazing brand into one of the chambers of the temple proper.[113]   When this was reported to Titus he hasted to the spot, followed by the generals and the legions.   Titus gave orders to quench the fire ; but in the wild conflict that now raged around the spot his commands were not heard, and the fire got ever a firmer hold upon the edifice.   Even yet Titus hoped to save at least the inner court of the temple, and renewed his orders to quench the flames ; but the soldiers in their excitement no longer listened to his commands.   Instead of quenching the flames, they threw in new firebrands, and the whole noble work became a prey to the flames beyond redemption.   Titus managed to inspect the inner court before the fire reached it.[114]

While the Romans slaughtered indiscriminately all that fell into their hands, children and old men, priests and people, and intentionally fanned the terrible conflagration, so that nothing escaped the flames, John of Gischala succeeded, along with his Zealot following, to escape into the upper city. Even before the temple had been burnt down, the legions planted their standards in the temple court, and greeted their general as Imperator.[115]

The work of the conqueror, however, was by no means completed with the overthrow of the temple. The upper city, the last refuge of the besieged, had yet to be taken. Titus once again called upon Simon and John to surrender. But the besieged wished to stipulate for liberty to go forth untouched, which would not be granted them.[116] By order of Titus the parts of the city now in the possession of the Romans—the Ophla, the depository of the archives, the council house, the lower city down to Siloah — were set on fire, while at the same time the tyrants in the upper city continued their work of murder and plunder.[117]

Seeing then that there was no hope of securing the voluntary surrender of the besieged, it was necessary once more to resort to the erection of ramparts. They were constructed partly at the north-western corner of the upper city near the palace of Herod, partly at the north-eastern corner, in the neighbourhood of the so-called Xystus. On the 20th Loos (Ab, August) the buildings were begun; on the 7th Gorpiaeus (Elul, September) they were finished. The battering-rams soon made a breach in the walls, through which the soldiers with little difficulty forced their way, because the besieged in their despondent condition could no longer offer a vigorous and determined opposition.[118] One portion of them made the attempt to break away through the besiegers' lines and to force through the cordon which surrounded them at Siloah; but they were driven back, and rushed again into their subterranean hiding-places. Meanwhile the whole of the upper city was taken possession of by the Romans.

The military standards were planted and the song of victory was sung. The soldiers passed through the city murdering, burning, and plundering. After a five months' siege, after having been obliged laboriously to press on step by step, gaining one position after another, the whole city at last, on 8th Gorpiaeus (Elul, September), fell into the hands of the conquerors.[119]

Those of the inhabitants who had not already fallen victims to the famine or the sword were now put to death, or sent to labour in the mines, or reserved for the gladiatorial combats. The handsomest and most powerful of the men were spared to grace the triumph. Among the fugitives who were driven by hunger to go forth out of their subterranean hiding-places was John of Gischala. When he begged for mercy he was granted his life, but was sentenced to life-long confinement in prison. It was not, however, until a considerably later period that Simon Bar Giora was apprehended. He was reserved as a victim for the triumph.[120] The city was then razed to the ground. Only the three gates of the palace of Herod — Hippicus, Phasael, and Mariamme — and a portion of the wall were left standing; the former as monuments of the original strength of the city, the latter as a protection for the garrison that was left in charge. The victory, won by hard fighting, and at the cost of many victims, was celebrated by Titus in an address of thanks to the army, the distribution of rewards to those who had distinguished themselves in battle, the presenting sacrifices of thanksgiving, and a festive banquet.[121]

5. The Conclusion of the War, a.d. 71–73.

Leaving behind him the tenth legion as a garrison in Jerusalem, Titus proceeded with the rest of his army to Caesarea-on-the-Sea, where the spoil was deposited, and the

prisoners consigned to safe keeping.[122]   Thence Titus marched
to Caesarea Philippi, where a portion of the prisoners were
forced to engage in combat with wild animals, and to take
part in the gladiatorial shows.[123]   At Caesarea-on-the-Sea, to
which he returned, he celebrated the birthday of his brother
Domitian, 24th October, with games on a magnificent scale.
At Berytus also he celebrated in a similar manner the birthday of his father Vespasian, on 17th November.   After a
lengthened stay in Berytus,[124] Titus proceeded to Antioch,
giving public entertainments in the cities through which he
passed, at which the Jewish prisoners were set to slay one
another in gladiatorial contests.   After a short stay in
Antioch, he passed on to Zeugma on the Euphrates; and
from thence he returned again to Antioch, and from thence
proceeded to Egypt.   At Alexandria he disbanded the legions.
Of the prisoners there were 700 specially distinguished by
their handsome appearance; and these, together with the
rebel leaders John and Simon, were reserved for the
triumph.[125]   Titus now sailed for Rome,[126] was received by
his father and by the people with joyful demonstrations, and
in common with his father and brother celebrated, in A.D. 71,
one triumph, though the Senate had assigned one separately
to each of them.[127]   During the triumph Simon Bar Giora,
the rebel leader, was in accordance with an old custom carried
away from the festal procession to prison and executed
there.[128]

The conquest of the capital had certainly given to Titus
the right to the celebration of the triumph.   The whole of
Palestine, however, was not yet by any means subdued.   The
strongholds of Herodium, Machärus, and Masada were still in
the hands of the rebels.   The reduction of these fortresses was
the work of the governor of Palestine at that time, Lucilius
Bassus.   In regard to the Herodium, this seems to have
been accomplished by him without difficulty.[129]   The siege of

Machärus occupied a longer time.[130] Yet even this stronghold, before it was taken by storm, yielded by a voluntary
surrender. The decision to surrender was finally taken in
consequence of the apprehension of a youth called Eleasar, who
had particularly distinguished himself in the defence. Bassus
threatened to crucify him in view of the city, and in order to
prevent this the Jews gave over the fortress.[131] In the meantime
Lucilius Bassus died. To his successor, Flavius Silva, fell the
task of taking Masada.[132] In that fortress the Sicarii, under
the leadership of Eleasar, the son of Jairi, and a descendant
of Judas of Galilee,[133] had established themselves at the com-
mencement of the war, and had continued to maintain their
position. The siege proved a very difficult business, since
the rock upon which the fortress was built rose on all sides
so high and steep that it was almost impossible to bring the
engines of destruction near. Only at one point, and even
there only by means of difficult and ingenious preparatory
operations, was it possible to secure a place for a battering-
ram. But by the time that this machine had made a breach
in the wall, the besieged had already erected behind that
wall another bulwark of wood and earth, which, owing to its
elasticity, could not be destroyed by the battering-ram. The
enemy, however, by the use of fire succeeded in setting this
obstacle also aside. When Eleasar saw that there was no
longer any hope of resisting the attack, he held a council
with the garrison, in which he urged that they should first
of all slay the members of their own families, and then put
one another to death. This, therefore, was done. When the
Romans entered, they beheld with horror that no more work
was left for them to do. Thus was the very last stronghold
of the rebellion conquered in April A.D. 73.[134]

After the fall of Masada disturbances were made by the
Jews in Alexandria and in Cyrene, which in the former place
resulted in the closing of the temple of Onias at Leontopolis.[135]

But these after-vibrations of the great revolution in the mother country are scarcely worthy of being mentioned alongside of the original movement, The fate of Palestine was sealed by the overthrow of Masada. Vespasian retained the country as a private possession, and the taxes levied went into his own purse.[136]   Only to 800 veterans did he distribute grants of land at Emmaus near Jerusalem.[137]   The former temple-tax of two drachmas was henceforth exacted of all Jews for the temple of Jupiter Capitolinus.[138] The inhabitants of Palestine became impoverished, and by the seven years' war their numbers had been terribly reduced. A Jewish magistracy, of the kind formerly possessed, no longer existed. The one gathering point which still remained for the people was the law. Around this they gathered now with anxious and scrupulous faithfulness, and with the indomitable hope that some day, under an established civil government, and even among the nations of the world, it would come again to have a recognised place and practical authority.

§ 21. FROM THE DESTRUCTION OF
JERUSALEM TO THE OVERTHROW
OF BAR-COCHBA

1. THE STATE OF AFFAIRS IN PALESTINE FROM VESPASIAN TO HADRIAN.

THE separation of Judea from the province of Syria, which had been resolved upon at the time when Vespasian was sent thither (Judea as a distinct province!), continued also after the conclusion of the war. Judea—and indeed under that very name—formed from this time forth an independent province.[1] Since it had as a garrison only one legion, the *legio X. Fretensis* (see above, p. 272), alongside of which were only auxiliary troops (see above, p.186), the commander of that legion was at the same time governor of the province. It appears that, as a rule, the position was held by men of praetorian rank. It was only at a later period that the province came to be administered by men of consular rank, probably after the time of Hadrian, since even then the *legio VI. Ferrata* was stationed in Judea, and the governor was not of an order superior to the commander of a legion.[2]

From the series of governors only certain names are now known to us. The first of these who exercised their functions during the war of A.D. 70–73 have already been briefly referred to:—

1. Sex. Vettulenus Cerialis, who at the siege of Jerusalem

commanded the fifth legion (see above, p. 264). He remained
after the departure of Titus as commander of the garrison
troops, that is, of the tenth legion and of the detachments
joined with it, and gave them over to Lucilius Bassus (*Wars
of the Jews*, vii. 6. 1).

2. Lucilius Bassus, who took the strongholds of Herodium
and Machärus (Josephus, *Wars of the Jews*, vii. 6. 1–6). He
died as governor (*Wars of the Jews*, vii. 8. 1). The procurator
serving under him, L. Laberius (not Διβέροις) Maximus
(*Wars of the Jews*, vii. 6. 6), is also mentioned in the Acts of
the Arval priesthood : *Corpus Inscriptionum Latinorum*, t. vi.
n. 2059, and in the military diploma of A.D. 83 (*Ephemeris
epigraphica*, v. p. 612 sq.). According to the latter authority,
he was the governor of Egypt.

3. L. Flavius Silva, the conqueror of Masada (Josephus,
Wars of the Jews, vii. 8–9). He was consul in A.D. 81. His
full name is given as L. Flavius Silva Nonius Bassus in the
Acta Arvalium, *Corpus Inscriptionum Latinorum*, t. vi. n. 2059.

4. M. Salvidenus, about A.D. 80, is witnessed to by a
Palestinian coin of Titus, with the superscription ΕΠΙ Μ.
ΣΑΛΟΤΙΔΗΝ(ΟΤ), Madden, *Coins of the Jews*, p. 218.

5. Cn. Pompeius Longinus, A.D. 86.

6. Atticus, about A.D. 107.

7. Pompeius Falco, about A.D. 107 and onwards.

8. Tiberianus, about A.D. 114.

9. Lusius Quietus, about A.D. 117.—This distinguished
general, after he had put down the outbreak of the Jews in
Mesopotamia, was appointed governor of Judea (Eusebius,
Hist. eccl. iv. 2. 5 : Ἰουδαίας ἡγεμὼν ὑπὸ τοῦ αὐτοκράτορος
ἀνεδείχθη. Eusebius, *Chronicon*, ed. Schoene, ii. 164; in Greek,
in Syncellus, ed. Dindorf, i. 657, at the 18th year of Trajan
[2131 Abr.] : ἡγεμὼν τῆς Ἰουδαίας διὰ τοῦτο καθίσταται).
Dio Cassius merely says that he administered the government
of Palestine after his consulship of A.D. 115 (Dio Cassius,

lxviii. 32 : ὑπατεῦσαι τῆς τε Παλαιστίνης ἄρξαι). That
Trajan sent to Palestine a consular legate, not merely one of
praetorian rank, was occasioned by the peculiarly difficult
condition of affairs at that time.—By Hadrian, Lusius Quietus
was recalled (*Spartian. vita Hadriana*, c. 5 : " Lusium Quietum
. . . exarmavit "), and soon thereafter put to death (*ibid.* c. 7 ;
Dio Cassius, lxix. 2).

10. Tineius Rufus, A.D. 132.—When the revolution of
Barcochba broke out, one Rufus was governor of Judea
(Eusebius, *Hist. eccl.* iv. 6. 1 : ῾Ροῦφος ἐπάρχων τῆς Ἰουδαίας).
In the Chronicle of Eusebius he is called Tineius Rufus
(Eusebius, *Chronicon*, ed. Schoene, ii. 166 sq. *ad. ann. Abr.*
2148; in Greek, in Syncellus, ed. Dindorf, i. 660 : ἡγεῖτο δὲ
τῆς Ἰουδαίας Τίννιος ῾Ροῦφος; in Latin, in Jerome : " tenente
provinciam Tinnio Rufo "). In Jerome on Daniel c. 9, *s. fin.*
ed. Vallarsi, v. 695 : Timo Rufo; on Zechariah viii. 16 sqq.
ed. Vallarsi, vi. 852 : T. Annio Rufo (so the earlier editions;
the reading *Turannio Rufo* is only a conjecture of Vallarsi).
Undoubtedly the correct form is Tineius Rufus, as is proved
by Borghesi. For one Q. Tineius Rufus, who was consul
under Commodus, is referred to on several inscriptions. He
may have been son or grandson of one Rufus. See Borghesi,
Oeuvres, iii. 62–64, viii. 189 sq.; Renan, *L'église chrétienne*,
p. 192 sq.; and also *Corpus Inscriptionum Latinorum*, t. vi.
n. 1978.

In order to suppress the rebellion, Publicius Marcellus,
who up to that time had been governor of Syria, was also
sent into Judea (*Corpus Inscriptionum Graecorum*, n. 4033 =
Archäolog.-epigr. Mittheilungen aus Oesterreich-Ungarn Jahrg.
ix. 1885, p. 118 : ἡνίκα Πουβλικιος Μάρκελλος διὰ τὴν
κίνησιν τὴν Ἰουδαϊκὴν μεταβεβήκει ἀπὸ Συρίας; the same
statement also is found in *Corpus Inscript. Graec.* n. 4034).
This strengthening of the fighting forces in Judea is also
referred to by Eusebius (*Hist. eccl.* iv. 6. 1 : στρατιωτικῆς

αὐτῷ συμμαχίας ὑπὸ βασιλέως πεμφθείσης. Compare *Chronicon ad. ann. Abr.* 2148).

11. Julius Severus, A.D. 135.—The suppression of the Jewish revolution was thoroughly completed only by Julius Severus, who was sent to Judea from Britain, where he had been up to that time governor (Dio Cassius, lxix. 13). The *cursus honorum* of this man is given in the inscription, *Corpus Inscriptionum Latinorum*, t. iii. n. 2830, where the higher offices are enumerated in the following order : " leg(ato) pr(o) pr(aetore) imp(eratoris) Traiani Hadriani Aug(usti) provinciae Daciae, cos. leg. pr. pr. provinciae Moesiae inferioris, leg. pr. pr. provinciae Brittaniae, leg. pr. pr. provinciae Judeae, leg. pr. pr. provinciae Suriae." This therefore confirms the statement of Dio Cassius that he came from Britain to Judea. On the other hand, the statement of Dio Cassius, or rather that of his unskilful epitomizer Xiphilinus, that after the conclusion of the Jewish revolt he was made governor of Bithynia (Dio Cassius, lxix. 14), is the result of a confusion between him and another Severus. Our Julius Severus, who was consul in A.D. 127, was called Sextus Julius Severus (*Corpus Inscript. Lat.* iii. p. 874, Dipl. xxxi.), but the governor of Bithynia was *Τι. Σεουῆρος* (*Corpus Inscript. Graec.* n. 4033 and 4034), or, according to a more recent copy of one of these inscriptions, *Π. Σεουῆρος* (*Archäolog.-epigr. Mittheilungen aus Oesterreich-Ungarn*, ix. 118 = *Corpus Inscript. Graec.* n. 4033).

The residence of the imperial governor, as in earlier times that of the procurators had also been, was not Jerusalem, but Caesarea, the important coast town built by Herod the Great.[3] It was formed by Vespasian into a Roman colony, and bore the official name *col(onia) prima Fl(avia) Aug(usta) Caesarensis* or *Caesarea*. Jerusalem had been so completely razed to the ground " that there was left nothing to make those that came thither believe it had ever been inhabited." [4] It was first of all only a Roman camp, in which, if not the whole of the tenth legion, yet at least the chief portion of it, had its head-quarters, together with its baggage and followers.

In regard to the other changes made upon the organization of the Palestinian city communities we have only scattered notices. To what extent Vespasian held the country as a private possession cannot be very clearly understood from the indefinite statements of Josephus (see above, p. 275). His private possessions seem to have extended not merely to the town domains of Jerusalem, but to all Judea — that term being understood in its proper and more restricted sense (πᾶσαν γῆν τῶν Ἰουδαίων). The only new town which Vespasian here founded was the military colony of Emmaus (see above, p. 275). In Samaria, Flavia Neapolis, which rapidly grew and flourished, was then founded. For that its founding belongs to the time of Vespasian is proved not only by its name and by the reference in Pliny, but also by the era of the city, the starting-point of which is to be reckoned about A.D. 72.[5] It lay upon the site of a place which was previously called Mabortha or Mamortha, in the immediate vicinity of Shechem, so that it soon came to be identified with Shechem.[6] In the later days of the empire it was one of the most important cities of Palestine.[7] The inhabitants were wholly or predominantly pagan, as their modes of worship witnessed to by coins prove. Upon not a few of these coins, later than the time of Hadrian, Gerizim is represented, and on its top a temple which was dedicated, according to Damascius, to Ζεὺς ὕψιστος.[8] The festive games of Neapolis during the second century, and certainly even at a later date, were regarded as amongst the most important in Palestine.[9] —The founding of Capitolias in Decapolis belongs to the time of Nerva or Trajan; its era begins in A.D. 97 or 98. Hadrian founded Aelia on the site of Jerusalem, the history of which is given below in the

account of the war.   Other new foundings of Palestinian
cities belong to a period later than that of which we treat,
such as that of Diocaesarea = Sepphoris (known under its
new name from the time of Antoninus Pius, see Div. II. vol.
i. p. 136), Diospolis = Lydda, Eleutheropolis (both under
Septimius Severus),   Nicopolis = Emmaus (under Helio-
gabulus).

The destruction of Jerusalem brought about a violent
revolution in the inner life of the Jewish people.   No longer
a Sanhedrim and no longer a sacrificial service,—the loss of
those two great institutions was of itself sufficient to produce
a profound change in the conditions of Jewish life.   But it
has first of all to be established that the sacrificial service
actually did cease.[10]   Not only the Epistle to the Hebrews,
the date of the composition of which is uncertain, but also
Clement of Rome and the author of the Epistle to
Diognetus, who undoubtedly wrote after the destruction of
Jerusalem, speak as if in their time the Jewish sacrificial
worship was still maintained.[11]   And Josephus also expresses
himself quite to the same effect.   Not only where he describes
the Jewish sacrificial worship in accordance with the Old
Testament,[12] but also where he apparently speaks of the
customs and practices of his own time, he employs the present
tense.[13]   It is indeed the fact that when speaking of the
sacrifices for the Roman people and for the Roman emperor
he makes use of this mode of expression, although this was
purely a later custom, and was not a prescription of the Old
Testament.[14]   Besides this, we have also scattered allusions
in the rabbinical literature, which seem to indicate the
continuance of the sacrificial service after A.D. 70.[15]   It is
not to be wondered at that many on the basis of such material
should have maintained the continuance of the sacrificial
worship.   In itself this was quite a possible thing.   In an
interesting passage in the Mishna,[16] R. Joshua testifies : " I

have heard that one ought to present sacrifice even if there
be no temple; that one should eat that which is sanctified
[on this see Division II. vol. i. p. 236], even though there
be no wall around the court; that one may eat what is holy
in a lower degree [see on this Division II. vol. i. p. 240]
and the second tithe, even if there should be no wall around
Jerusalem; for the first consecration has sanctified, not only
for its own time, but for all future time." It was not therefore in utter opposition to the views of the Rabbis that men
should continue after the destruction of the temple to offer
sacrifices in holy places. But as a matter of fact this was
not done. In the enumeration of the unfortunate days of
Israel it is distinctly said that on 17th Thammuz the daily
sacrifice was abolished (בָּטַל הַתָּמִיד),[17] while there is nowhere
any reference made to its restoration. In the description of
the Passover in the Mishna, the enumeration of the dishes that
had to be set upon the table is concluded with the remark:
" During the time that the temple was standing the Passover
offering also was served.[18] This implies that after the
destruction of the temple it was no longer offered. In speaking of the legal enactments for determining the new moon it
is said: " So long as the temple remained standing those who
had seen the new moon were allowed to violate the Sabbath
by going to Jerusalem, in order to testify thereto, for the sake
of the observance of the sacrifice on the festival of the new
moon."[19] The harmonious testimony of those passages of the
Mishna is confirmed by others in the Babylonian Talmud of a
character yet more direct, if that were possible, which assume
even in regard to the times of Rabban Jochanan ben Saccai,
Rabban Gamaliel II. and R. Ishmael, i.e. the first decade after
the destruction of the temple, that the whole sacrificial
worship had ceased.[20] Finally, Justin also appears as a
witness on behalf of this view. He says to his opponent
Trypho: " God never appointed the Passover to be offered

except in the place where His name was to be called upon, knowing that after the passion of Christ the days would come, when even Jerusalem would be given over to our enemies, and all sacrifices should cease." [21]   And in another passage Trypho himself says in answer to Justin's question as to whether it was not then still possible to observe all the commands of Moses : " By no means, for we know well that it is not allowable to slay the paschal lamb nor the goats for the Day of Atonement, nor generally to present any of the other offerings in any other place." [22]—If, then, Christian writers and Josephus, even long after the destruction of the temple, still speak of the presenting of sacrifices in the present tense, they only describe thereby what is still allowable, but a right that was no longer actually exercised.   Precisely the same view is presented in the Mishna from the first page to the last, for all institutions that are legally correct are described as existing customs, even although their observance owing to the circumstances of the time was impossible. [23]

Two facts, therefore, of the highest importance and most widely influential are well established : the abolition of the Sanhedrim and the cessation of the sacrificial worship. [24] In the Sanhedrim there had been embodied the last remnant of the political independence of Judaism, and consequently also the last remnant of the power of the Sadducean nobles. The influence of the Sadducean nobility even since the times of Alexandra had been waning before the advancing strength of the Pharisees.   They still managed, however, to exert a very considerable influence so long as the Sanhedrim continued to exist.   For the jurisdiction of that aristocratic senate of Judea was down to the time of the procurators pretty extensive, and at its head stood the Sadducean high priest.   With the destruction of Jerusalem this Jewish council was immediately brought to an end; the Roman provincial constitution was enforced in a stricter form.   With the disappearance of the Sanhedrim, Sadduceanism also disappears from history.——The overthrow of the city, however, led also to the suppression of the sacrificial worship, and therewith the gradual recession of the priesthood from public life. This was only carried out by degrees. It could not for a long time be believed that the disastrous circumstances in which the people were placed were to continue. It seemed to be only a question of the time when the priests should be able again to resume their services. Naturally, all dues were exacted after as well as before the catastrophe. Only the taxes which had been contributed directly for the maintenance of the temple and of the public sacrifices were declared by the Rabbins to be suspended. The contribution devoted to the personal support of the priests continued after as well as before a duty according to the law, and where there were priests, were given over directly to them.[25] But notwithstanding all this, the priesthood, now that it could no longer perform its service, lost its importance. It was a memorial of a past age, which indeed, as time went on, sank more and more into obscurity and decay.

The Pharisees and the Rabbis now entered into the heritage of the Sadducees and priests. They had an admirable preparation for entering upon this heritage. During two centuries they had been making steady progress toward dominant power. And now for a time they entered upon the enjoyment of absolute sovereignty. The overthrow of Jerusalem means nothing more or less than the passing over of the people to Pharisaism and the Rabbis; for the factors which had hitherto stood in opposition to these had now sunk into utter insignificance.

After the overthrow of Jerusalem, Jamnia (Jabne) seems in a special way to have become a centre of literary activity. There, during the first decade after the destruction of the temple, wrought Rabban Jochanan ben Saccai, and, at the

end of the first and beginning of the second century, Rabban
Gamaliel II., gathering around them a whole band of scholars.
The most celebrated of the contemporaries of Gamaliel were
R. Josua ben Chananja and R. Elieser ben Hyrcanus, the
latter of whom had his residence at Lydda. Younger con-
temporaries and pupils of these men were R. Ishmael,
R. Akiba, and R. Tarphon.

By these men and by their numerous colleagues and
scholars, the interpretation of the law was carried on with
greater zeal than ever. It was as though, after the political
overthrow, the whole strength of the nation had concentrated
itself upon the care of the law as its own highest and proper
task. Everything pertaining to it, the criminal and the civil
law, and the manifold religious statutes and ordinances, were
dealt with by these scholars with painful particularity, and
drilled into the memories of the scholars by their teachers.
It did not matter in the least whether the circumstances of
the time allowed these ordinances to be put in practice or not.
All the minutiae of the temple service, the entire ritual of the
sacrificial worship, were discussed as diligently and as earnestly
as the laws of purifying, the Sabbath commandment, and
other religious duties, the observance of which was still
possible. There is nothing so fitted to produce before us a
lively picture of the faith of the people in their future as the
conscientiousness with which the prescriptions about the
temple service and the sacrificial worship were treated by the
guardians of the law. The time of desolation might continue
for a longer or shorter period, but once again the day of
restoration would surely dawn. And hence, in the cataloguing
by the scribes in the second century of the Jewish law in the
corpus juris or Mishna, there are included a topography of the
temple in the tract *Middoth* and a description of the distribution of the priests in the daily service in the tract *Tamid*.
Their descendants, to whom was to be granted the privilege

of a restored worship, were to be told how it had previously been conducted in the days of the fathers.

The scholars who after this fashion cared for the highest interests of Israel formed now even more exclusively and unrestrictedly than before the rank of the highest authorities among the people. The priests, who had previously been the most influential in the direction and practice of religious duties, were now relegated to a condition of inactivity. All the energies of the pious had now to be restricted to the doing of that which the Rabbins prescribed to them. There was no need of any external compulsion. Whatever the most distinguished teachers had laid down was regarded by the pious without any further question as obligatory. Indeed, they were not only recognised as lawgivers in spiritual and temporal things, but in all matters of dispute they were appealed to as judges, even in questions of *meum* and *tuum*. During this period it was indeed no uncommon occurrence to see, *e.g.*, R. Akiba, purely by means of his spiritual authority, condemning a man to pay 400 denarii compensation, because he had on the street uncovered his head to a woman.[26]

The court of law at Jamnia enjoyed the highest reputation toward the end of the first and in the beginning of the second century after Christ, a college of learned men, which can scarcely have had any formal recognition from the Roman authorities, but yet actually stepped into the place of the old Sanhedrim of Jerusalem, as the supreme court of law for Israel. The enactments passed by Rabban Jochanan ben Saccai in Jamnia after the destruction of the temple, in order to adapt certain legal requirements to the altered circumstance of the times, were regarded as binding.[27] Rabban Gamaliel II. and his court of justice watched over the correct reckoning of the contents of the calendar. To its decisions the elder R. Josua submitted, even if he considered them to be erroneous.[28] As a rule the decisions on points of law issuing from Jamnia were treated as constituting the authoritative standard.[29] Indeed, the succession of Jamnia to the privileges of Jerusalem was so generally acquiesced in, that where this was not the case, it was pointed to as an exception to the rule.[30] Even in regard to the number of members, they seem to have copied the pattern of the Sanhedrim of Jerusalem. At least there occurs in one place a statement to the effect that " the seventy-two elders " appointed as president R. Eleasar ben Asariah.[31]—We may assume that this court of justice at Jamnia was voluntarily accepted by the Jewish people as authoritative, not only in the domain of the ceremonial law, but also in the domain of the civil and criminal law. In reference to the civil law it may indeed have received actual authorization, in accordance with the general procedure in legislation. For the Roman legislation, so far as we can understand it, recognised the authority of the Jewish communities in the Dispersion to administer the law in civil suits among their countrymen, wherever the contending parties chose to bring their disputes before their own communal court.[32] But in criminal matters this jurisdiction bore the character of a usurped authority, rather than of one conferred by the emperor. Origen very vividly, and at the same time authentically, describes to us the state of matters which then prevailed. In vindicating the story of Susanna and Daniel, he endeavours to prove that the Jews might quite well have had their own judicatories during the Babylonian exile. In proof of this he refers to the state of matters in Palestine in his own days, of which he knew from his own observation. The power of the Jewish Ethnarch (so Origen designates him) is so great, that he is in no respect different from a king ($\dot{\omega}_S$ $\mu\eta\delta\grave{\epsilon}\nu$ $\delta\iota\alpha\phi\acute{\epsilon}\rho\epsilon\iota\nu$ $\beta\alpha\sigma\iota\lambda\epsilon\acute{\upsilon}o\nu\tau o_S$ $\tau o\hat{\upsilon}$ $\check{\epsilon}\theta\nu o\upsilon_S$). " There are also secret legal proceedings in accordance with the law, and many are condemned to death without any general authority having been obtained for the exercise of such functions, and without any attempt to conceal such doings from the governor."[33] This was the state of matters during the third century. In the first decades after the destruction of Jerusalem, they would not have ventured to go so far. Yet this was the direction in which things were tending.—To this Jewish central court in Palestine, whose president subsequently received the title of Patriarch, were also paid the contributions of the Jews of the Dispersion, so far as these continued to be collected after the destruction of the temple. At least for the period of the later days of the empire this can be proved to demonstration. In this matter also the Rabbis take the place of the priests. For previously the contributions were cast into the central treasury of the priests at Jerusalem. It was now a rabbinical board which made the collection by means of their *apostoli*, and superintended its proper distribution.

All zeal for the law of their fathers in this later time, at least among the great majority of the pious, had its motive power in the belief in a glorious future for the nation. Such was the case even before the great catastrophe; and so it continued in a yet more exaggerated degree after that terrible event. If now, more zealously than ever, the people occupied themselves with the scrupulous fulfilment of the commandments of God, certainly the most powerful motive working in this direction was the wish to render themselves thereby worthy of the future glory in which they so confidently believed. In regard to this religious movement during the first decades after the overthrow of the holy city, the Apocalypses of Baruch and Ezra, which had their origin in that very period, afford us a lively as well as an authentic picture. The immediate consequence of the terrible slaughter was indeed a profound and paralyzing shock to the feelings. How could God permit this disaster to befall His own chosen people? But this grand mystery was only a particular

instance of the universal mystery : How is the misfortune of
the righteous generally and the good fortune of the unrighteous possible ?   Through the darkness of this latter
problem the pious consciousness of Israel had long ago successfully struggled.   So now also a satisfactory answer was
soon found.   It is a chastisement which God has inflicted
upon His people because of their sin.   It has its own
appointed time.   When the people by means of it shall have
learned righteousness, the promised day of redemption will
soon dawn for them.   This is the fundamental idea of both of
these apocalypses, and their purpose is to comfort the people
in their distress, to inspire them with courage and with holy
zeal by visions of the redemption that will come to them
surely and soon.   The confident belief in this future was
therefore only intensified, confirmed, and inflamed by the sore
sufferings and sad disasters of the time.   Out of the grief for
the overthrow of the sanctuary, the Messianic hope drew new
nourishment, new strength.   This was also, from a political
point of view, important, and productive of serious consequences.   For this Messianic hope was a wonderful blending
of religious and political ideals.   The political aspirations of
the nation had never been abandoned, and the element of danger
just lay in the combination of them with religious motives.
The political freedom of the nation, which the people longed
for, was now represented as the end of the ways of God.
The more firmly this was believed, the more readily did the
people set out of view the cool calculations of what is humanly
possible, the bolder became their resolve to dare even the impossible.   It was this feeling which even in the time of Nero
had broken out in rebellion.   In it there also still lay hidden
elements that yet would lead to new and frightful catastrophes.

Under the emperors of the Flavian dynasty (Vespasian,
Titus, Domitian, down to A.D. 96) there does not seem to
have been any more serious development of these tendencies.

Sufficient occasion, however, was presented for giving expression to those already present. For the command to contribute what had been the temple-tax to the Capitoline Jupiter at Rome (see above, p. 275), was an outrage upon the religious sensibilities of the Jews, which every year, on the levying of the tax, must afresh have roused the feeling of resentment. Under Domitian this tax was levied with great strictness, as generally this emperor posed as a decided enemy of the Jews, and conversion to Judaism was punished by the imposition of severe penalties.[34]

Eusebius speaks of an actual persecution of the Jews after the destruction of Jerusalem, even during Vespasian's reign, referring to Hegesippus as his authority. Vespasian, as well as Domitian and Trajan, is said by Hegesippus to have hunted for and executed all Jews of the house of David with great rigour, in order that the royal family, on which the Jews rested their hopes, should be rooted out.[35] This order led to a great persecution of the Jews under Vespasian.[36] We have no longer any means of determining how far this story is historical. It can scarcely be altogether without foundation, for that a Messiah descending from the house of David was expected is beyond dispute. The existence, therefore, of descendants of David might actually be looked upon as a source of political danger. This " persecution," however, cannot have been of great dimensions and importance, since it is not taken notice of by any other writer.——Whether political uprisings occurred in Judea under Domitian is certainly very questionable. From certain hints in a military diploma of A.D. 86, some have supposed that such disturbances must have taken place. Meanwhile, these conclusions have not by any means been satisfactorily proved.——On the other hand, the outbursts which occurred, first outside of Judea and afterwards in Judea itself, under Trajan and Hadrian, spread widely, and led to scenes of terrible violence.

2. The War under Trajan, a.d. 115–117.

Trajan, during the last years of his life, A.D. 114–117, was incessantly occupied in bold expeditions of conquest in the farthest eastern parts of the empire.   While he was, in A.D. 115, engaged in the conquest of Mesopotamia, the Jews in Egypt and Cyrene, taking advantage of the emperor's absence, "as if driven along by the wild spirit of revolution, began to make riots against the non-Jewish inhabitants of the land." [37]   The rebellion reached such dimensions in the following year, A.D. 116, that it assumed the character of a formal war.   The Roman governor of Egypt, M.. Rutilius Lupus, seems not to have been aware of the strength of the Jews.   In an engagement the rebel Jews conquered the "Greeks," and compelled them to fly to Alexandria.   There, in the capital, the Greeks had decidedly the upper hand, and the Jews residing there were seized and slain. [38]

Still more furiously did the Jews in Cyrene conduct themselves.   Of the cruelties which the Jews there perpetrated upon their non-Jewish fellow-inhabitants a dreadful picture is presented by Dio Cassius.   They ate their flesh, besmeared themselves with their blood, sawed them through from above downward, or gave them for food to the wild beasts.   The number of the murdered is said to have been as many as 220,000. [39]   Though here, certainly, the pen has been directed by the most extravagant fancy, the extent and importance of the revolt are beyond all dispute.   The leader of the Jewish population of Cyrene, whom they proclaimed as their king, is called by Eusebius, Lukuas, by Dio Cassius, Andrew. [40]

To suppress this revolt Trajan sent one of his best generals, Marcius Turbo.   By means of long-continued and persistent fighting (πολλαῖς μάχαις ἐν οὐκ ὀλίγῳ τε χρόνῳ) he brought the war to an end, and slew many thousands of the Jews, not only of Cyrene, but also those of Egypt, who had attached themselves to their "king" Lukuas.[41]

The outbreak had also spread to the island of Cyprus. Under the leadership of a certain Artemio, the Jews there imitated the example of their co-religionists of Cyrene, and murdered 24,000 non-Jewish inhabitants of the island.[42] The very capital, Salamis, was laid waste by them.[43] In regard to the suppression of the revolt we have no information. The consequence of it was that henceforth no Jew was allowed to appear upon the island; and if through stress of weather any Jew should happen to be cast upon its coasts, he was put to death.[44]

Finally, when Trajan had pressed on as far as Ctesiphon, the capital of the Parthian empire, the Jews of Mesopotamia in his rear had become disturbed. Such a disturbance there upon the very frontier of the empire was a most serious affair. Trajan gave orders to the Moorish prince Lusius Quietus, who was at the same time a Roman general, to sweep the rebels out of the province (ἐκκαθᾶραι τῆς ἐπαρχίας αὐτούς). With barbarous cruelty Quietus executed his commission. Thousands of Jews were put to death. Thus was order restored, and Quietus, in recognition of his services, was appointed governor of Palestine.[45]

The Jewish revolt was not, it would seem, finally suppressed until the beginning of Hadrian's reign in A.D. 117. At least Eusebius speaks of disturbances in Alexandria which Hadrian had to quell;[46] and the biographer of Hadrian states that Palestine also had taken its share in the rebellion.[47] In any case, however, perfect quiet seems to have been restored in the first year of Hadrian.

It is very doubtful indeed whether Palestine generally had any share in the rebellion. This is maintained by Volkmar and Grätz in the interest of their conception of the Book of Judith, which they place in this period; but it has been rightly contested by Lipsius and others.[48] Rabbinical tradition makes mention distinctly of a "war of Quietus," פּוּלְמוֹס שֶׁל קִיטוֹם;[49] but there is nothing to oblige us to understand by this any other than the well-known war of Quietus in Mesopotamia. In *Megillath Taanith* § 29, the 12th Adar is designated the "day of Trajan," יוֹם טוריינוס,[50] and the commentary upon this passage remarks that this day was celebrated in commemoration of the following incident:[51] Two brothers, Julianus and Pappus, were arrested by Trajan at Laodicea, when the emperor called out to them in mockery: Let your God now save you as he saved Hananiah, Mishael, and Azariah. The two brothers replied that neither he nor they were worthy of having such a miracle wrought, but that God would indeed require their blood of him if he slew them. But before Trajan left that place, an order came from Rome, in consequence of which he was put to death. This fable, which deserves no attention whatever, as it proceeds on the assumption that Trajan was only a subordinate officer, is now forsooth offered as the principal evidence regarding the war of Trajan in Palestine! But it should be observed that even in it there is no mention either of a war or of Judea, but expressly of Laodicea.[52]—The one thing that seems to favour Volkmar's view is the statement of Spartian above referred to, according to which, in the beginning of Hadrian's reign, Palestine *rebelles animos efferebat*. From this statement, indeed, it would seem to have been not altogether in a quiet condition. But it can hardly have gone the length of an actual war. Otherwise our original authorities would have given a more circumstantial account of it.

3. THE GREAT REBELLION UNDER HADRIAN, A.D. 132–135.

A late Jewish legend tells how in the days of Joshua ben Chananiah, that is, in the time of Hadrian, the pagan govern-

ment had granted authority to proceed with the building of
the temple. But the Samaritans had made representations
against the enterprise. And in consequence of these the
emperor had not indeed withdrawn the permission, but issued
a decree that the new building should not be erected precisely
on the site of the old temple, which came to the same thing
as an actual prohibition. Then the Jews gathered together
in factions in the valley of Beth-Rimmon. But R. Joshua,
in order to quiet them, told them the story of the lion and
the stork: as the stork ought to be glad to have got its
head uninjured out of the jaws of the lion, so also ought they
to be glad if they were allowed to live in peace under a heathen
government.[53] The historical value of this legend is simply
nil, and yet it forms the chief ground for the view insisted
upon by many modern scholars, that Hadrian had given permission for the rebuilding of the temple, and that the withdrawal of this permission was the real cause of the great
Jewish rebellion.[54] In confirmation of this view reference is
made to statements by Christian writers. But even these
are little calculated to support such a theory. Chrysostom,
Cedrenus, and Nicephorus Callistus only say that the Jews
in the time of Hadrian had rebelled and made an attempt to
rebuild the temple, and that Hadrian put a stop to that undertaking. The *Chronicon Paschale* speaks of a destruction by
Hadrian of the temple that had actually been built.[55] Of a
permission to build the temple that had first been given by
Hadrian and afterwards withdrawn, there is no mention whatever. The attempt to rebuild the temple was really itself
one of the acts of the rebellion. An apparent support for this
theory is to be found only in one passage in the Epistle of
Barnabas, of which, however, the explanation is uncertain.
Barnabas seeks to show that it is not according to God's will
that the Jews should continue to observe the law. Their
Sabbath is not the true one. " And almost like the heathens

have they honoured God in a temple." In order to prove the
heathenish character of the Jewish temple, Barnabas, in chap.
xvi., quotes the prophecy of Isa. xlix. 17 (LXX.): "Behold,
they who have cast down this temple, even they shall build
it up again;" and then proceeds, in chap. xvi. 4: "It has so
happened. For through their going to war it was destroyed
by their enemies; and now they [together with] the servants
of their enemies shall rebuild it" (γίνεται· διὰ γὰρ τὸ πολεμεῖν
αὐτοὺς καθηρέθη ὑπὸ τῶν ἐχθρῶν· νῦν καὶ αὐτοὶ [καὶ] οἱ τῶν
ἐχθρῶν ὑπηρέται ἀνοικοδομήσουσιν αὐτόν). Only if the
bracketed καί be retained, is the expectation there set forth
that now the Jews and the heathens together were to build
in common the Jewish temple. By striking out the καί the
meaning of the sentence becomes this: the heathens themselves build the temple, that is, for heathenish purposes.
But on external grounds also the latter reading deserves the
preference. Barnabas seems therefore to allude to Hadrian's
intention to erect a building for heathen worship.[56]——Of the
alleged permission given by Hadrian for the rebuilding of
the Jewish temple, therefore, we do not meet with any trace
when we investigate the causes of the rebellion. Such permission, at least in the form of active encouragement, is also
improbable on internal grounds. For while Hadrian zealously
patronized the Greek-Roman religious rites, he looked with
contempt upon all foreign superstitions.[57]

Only two accounts of the causes of the great rebellion are
worthy of consideration. Spartian says.[58] "moverunt ea
tempestate et Judaei bellum, quod vetabantur mutilare geni-
talia." Dio Cassius, on the contrary, gives his account thus:[59]
"When Hadrian had founded at Jerusalem a city of his
own in place of the one destroyed, which he called Aelia
Capitolina, and on the site of the temple of their God erected
another temple to Jupiter, the great and long-continued war
broke out. For the Jews regarded it as a horrible outrage

that foreigners should settle in their city, and that temples for strange gods should be built in it." Since Spartian mentions only the one and Dio Cassius only the other, it is doubtful whether without more ado we are entitled to combine the two. Gregorovius rejects the statement of Spartian, and regards that of Dio Cassius as alone worthy of credence. In fact, a prohibition of circumcision, without any special occasion, seems little in accordance with the mild character of Hadrian, although it might quite conceivably be used for the purpose of securing the extinction of the Jews after the suppression of the revolt.[60] Nevertheless, the statement of Spartian is to be defended. For, according to all that we know, the prohibition of circumcision was not limited to the Jews, and was not immediately directed against them. When, under Antoninus Pius, the Jews were again allowed to circumcise their children, the prohibition still stood good against the non-Jewish peoples. It was therefore originally a general order.[61] The special feature of this legislation was not that it aimed at the rooting out of Judaism, but that it placed circumcision on the same level with castration, and punished its practice accordingly.[62] The prohibition was not, therefore, first of all directed against Judaism, but it is at the same time quite evident that Judaism would receive from it a deadly wound. In addition to this it was now made known that Hadrian designed the erection of a new heathen city upon the ruins of Jerusalem. In this also the ruling motive was not hostility to Judaism. The rearing of magnificent buildings and the founding of cities was the work to which Hadrian devoted the energies of his life. But this proposal must also have been regarded as a blow in the face to Judaism. So long as Jerusalem lay in ruins, the Jews could cherish the hope of its restoration. The founding of a heathen city, the erection of a heathen temple on the holy place, put an end to these hopes in terrible manner. It was an outrage as great as that which Antiochus Epiphanes had formerly committed, and was answered, as that had been, by a general uprising of the excited people.—Both reasons, therefore, are not in themselves improbable. A combination of the two is a suggestion which has much to commend it, if the two enactments of Hadrian were not too far separated in time from one another.

In regard to the date at which the building of the Aelia Capitolina was begun, various statements are given in the original authorities. Epiphanius had been informed that Hadrian, forty-seven years after the destruction of Jerusalem, when he arrived there on his second journey, gave orders to rebuild the city (not the temple), and commissioned Aquila to see the work done.[63] This indication of date gives us A.D. 117, immediately after Hadrian's accession to the throne. He was then certainly in the East, but Epiphanius expressly refers to his later journey taken from Rome, and thus his statement regarding the time is deprived of all its value. The *Chronicon Paschale* places the founding of Aelia Capitolina in A.D. 119 ; but it does so only because it has also placed the great Jewish rebellion in that year, after the quelling of which Aelia was founded.[64] With the date fixed for the Jewish rebellion, which is demonstrably false, falls also that fixed for the founding of Aelia. Eusebius also regards the founding of the city as a consequence of the rebellion.[65] This is correct, inasmuch as only thereafter was the plan carried out. But, according to Dio Cassius, it is not to be doubted that the building had already been begun before the outbreak of the rebellion, and indeed not very long before, for he says that the Jews, who were irritated about the building, remained quiet so long as Hadrian stayed in Egypt and Syria, but that they broke out so soon as he had left those regions.[66]

In accordance with this, it must be assumed that the founding
of the city took place during the period of Hadrian's visit to
Syria, which occurred in A.D. 130.

Hadrian at that time—it was during his last great journey
in the East—arrived in Syria from Greece, and thence went
to Egypt, and then back again to Syria.[67]   It is made certain
from inscriptions and coins that he was in Syria in A.D. 130,
in Egypt in November A.D. 130, and so again in Syria in
A.D. 131.   Generally, wherever he went he furthered the
interests of culture: artistic and useful buildings were erected:
games were celebrated: he was a *restitutor* in all the provinces.[68]   In the cities of Palestine also we come upon traces
of his presence.   Tiberias had obtained an Ἀδριάνειον; Gaza,
a πανήγυρις Ἀδριανή; Petra, in grateful remembrance of the
benefactions of the emperor, took the name of Ἀδριανὴ
Πέτρα.[69] His residence in Judea was commemorated by coins
bearing the inscription, *adventui Aug(usti) Judaeae.*[70]

The founding of Aelia also, without doubt, belongs to the
period of the emperor's activity.   Pliny calls Jerusalem
longe clarissima urbium orientis, non Judaeae modo.[71]   This
celebrated city now lay in ruins, or was still merely a Roman
camp.   What then could be more attractive to the emperor
than the restoring of such a city to its former magnificence ?
It was, however, manifestly intended that this new magnificence
should be of a heathen character.   A temple of the Capitoline
Jupiter was to be erected on the spot where formerly the
temple of the God of the Jews had stood.   This was the fatal
proposal.   The Jews had been roused to a most violent
degree by means of the order, issued probably not long before,
against the practice of circumcision.   And now to that was
added a new outrage.   By means of this proposed profanation
of their city matters were brought to a crisis.   The people
remained quiet so long as the emperor remained in Egypt,
and during his second visit to Syria.   But when he was no

longer in the neighbourhood, that is, in A.D. 132, they broke out into revolt: an uprising that, in its extent and violence, and its unhappy consequences, was at least as serious as that of the time of Vespasian. If it does not bulk so largely in our records, it is only because of the meagreness of the original sources of information that have come down to us.[72]

The leader of the revolt is called in the works of Christian writers Cochba or Bar-Cochba, and by the rabbinical authorities Barcosiba or Bencosiba.[73] The one as well as the other is only a designation; the former distinguishes him as the star, or the son of the star, with reference to Num. xxiv. 18, which passage R. Akiba applied to him;[74] the latter is a name derived either from his father (the son of Cosiba) or from his home (the man of Cosiba), and not until a comparatively late period, and only by a few individual writers, in view of his miserable collapse, was it taken to mean liar or deceiver.[75] The designation Cochba or Bar-Cochba was apparently chosen on account of its similarity in sound to Barcosiba, but seems to have become pretty generally current, since the Christian authorities are acquainted with it alone. The coins have preserved for us the proper name of two men. For it is a fact scarcely admitting of question that the Simon-coins, some of which certainly, and others most probably, were stamped during the period of this outbreak, were issued by the leader of this outbreak, who was certainly Bar-Cochba. Those minted in the first year have the inscription, "Simon, Prince of Israel," שמעון נשיא ישראל; those minted in the second year have only the name "Simon" שמעון. On some the figure of a star appears over that of a temple. Besides the Simon-coins there are also coins of the first year with the inscription, "Eleasar the Priest," אלעזר הכהן. There thus seem to have been two men at the head of the rebellion, besides the Prince Simon, the Priest Eleasar. After the second year there are no more Eleasar-coins. Since in late rabbinical documents the R. Eleasar of Modein, who is also known from other sources, is described as the uncle of Barcosiba,[76] some have ventured to conjecture that this man is the same as the one named " Eleasar the Priest" on the coins.[77] But there is nothing anywhere to indicate that Eleasar of Modein was a priest.

The application of the designation of the " Star," which should come out of Jacob, to Barcosiba, shows that he was regarded as the Messiah. R. Akiba, the most celebrated doctor of the law in his time, is said to have distinctly announced him as such.[78] And though, indeed, all the colleagues of Akiba did not recognise him, he had the mass of the people on his side. As in the days of Vespasian, so also at this time there was a widespread idea that the day had come when the old prophecy of the prophets would be fulfilled, and Israel would cast off the yoke of the Gentiles. The Christian legends also declare that Barcosiba bewitched the people by deceitful miracles.[79]—Just by reason of the Messianic character of the movement it was quite impossible for Christians to take part in it. They could not deny their own Messiah by recognising the leader of the political revolution as such. Hence they were persecuted with peculiar violence by the new Messiah, as Justin Martyr and Eusebius testify.[80]

The rebellion spread rapidly over all Palestine. Wherever strongholds, castles, caverns, subterranean passages afforded hiding - places, there were those who struggled for native customs and freedom gathered together. An open conflict they avoided; but from their dens in the mountains they made devastating raids upon the country, and fought with all who did not attach themselves to their party.[81] Jerusalem also was certainly beset by the rebels. The doubt which many, on the other hand, have raised is mainly supported by this, that in the more trustworthy sources (Dio Cassius and Eusebius' *Church History*) there is no mention of a war at Jerusalem. But how unspeakably meagre are these sources generally! Even upon internal grounds it is probable that the rebels, who were at the beginning victorious, should have made themselves masters of Jerusalem, which was not then a strongly fortified city, but only a Roman camp. But this conjecture is confirmed by twofold testimony. In the first place by the coins. The coins that with the greatest confidence can be set down to this period, bear on the one side the name of Simon, שמעון, and on the other side the superscription, לחרות ירושלם, *lechêruth Jeruschalem*, "the freedom of Jerusalem." Therefore, the freeing of Jerusalem was commemorated by Simon on the coins. But there are among the coins belonging to this period also examples which, besides the date "First Year of the freeing of Israel" or "Second Year of the freedom of Israel," bear only the name Jerusalem, ירושלם. These, therefore, have been minted by the city itself in its own name, and hence we see that this city in the first year as well as in the second was in the hands of the rebels. In addition to this witness from the coins, we have the contemporary Appian, by whom, as will be told farther on, the fact of the reconquest of Jerusalem by the Romans is declared as a fact. —Whether during these troubled years of war the rebuilding of the Jewish temple may actually have been begun must be left undecided. Late Christians declare that this was so, and the intention to carry on this work was certainly entertained.[82]

In regard to the progress of the war we know almost nothing. When it broke out Tineius Rufus was governor of Judea. When he was unable with his troops to crush the rebels, the revolt not only increased in dimension and importance throughout all Palestine, but also spread itself far out beyond the limits of that country. Unstable and restless

elements indeed of another sort attached themselves to the
Jewish rebellion, so that at last " the whole world, so to speak,
was in commotion." [83]   The severest measures were necessary
in order to put an end to the uproar.   Large bodies of troops
from other provinces were called in to strengthen the resident
garrison.   The best generals were commissioned for Palestine.[84]
Even the governor of Syria, Publicius Marcellus, hasted to
the aid of his endangered colleague.[85]   But it seems that
Rufus for the most of the time retained the supreme command;
for Eusebius names no other Roman commander, and speaks
as if the suppression of the revolt was accomplished by Rufus.[86]
In rabbinical authorities also, " Rufus the Tyrant," טורנס רופוס,
appears the chief enemy of the Jews at that time.[87]   But
from Dio Cassius, whose statements on this point are
corroborated by the testimony of inscriptions, we know that
during the last period of the war Julius Severus, one of the
most distinguished of Hadrian's generals, had the supreme
command, and that it was he who succeeded in bringing the
rebellion to an end.   He was summoned from Britain to
conduct this war, and took a considerable time in crushing
the revolt.   In an open engagement no decisive result was
gained.   The rebels had to be hunted out of their hiding-
places one by one; and, where they kept concealed in mountain
caverns, they were exhausted by having their supplies cut off.
Only after long continued conflicts with individuals, in which
there was great expenditure of life, did he at last succeed in
harrying, exterminating, and rooting them out of the whole
country (κατατρῖψαι καὶ ἐκτρυχῶσαι καὶ ἐκκόψαι).[88]

Where Hadrian was residing during the war cannot be
determined with certainty.   Probably during the critical year
he was himself personally present at the seat of war.   He
had left Syria before the rebellion broke out.   The evil
tidings seem to have led him to return to Judea; for his
presence at the seat of war is not only presupposed in the

rabbinical legends,[89] but is also made probable by some particulars derived from inscriptions.[90]   There is no reference to
his presence in Rome again till May of A.D. 134.[91]   He would
return so soon as he had been assured of a successful issue to
the war, without waiting for the completion of the operations.

Dio Cassius as well as Eusebius is silent regarding the fate
of Jerusalem.   It certainly did not form the middle point of
the conflict, as it had done in the Vespasian war.   Its fortifications were quite unimportant.   Even although the rebels
had succeeded in driving out the Roman garrison, the recapture of the city would have been no very serious undertaking
for a sufficiently strong Roman military force.   But that it
had been actually taken after a violent assault is plainly
stated by Appian, a contemporary witness.[92]   When Appian
speaks of a destruction (κατασκάπτειν), he is undoubtedly
right, inasmuch as violent seizure is not conceivable without
destruction to a certain extent.   But after all, as following
the thoroughgoing work of Titus, the object arrived at was
comparatively limited.   And, on the other hand, the Romans
after once they had made themselves masters of the city,
would not go further in the work of destruction.   This was
necessary in view of their purposed new building of Aelia.   A
siege of the city is assumed by Eusebius in his *Demonstratio
evangelica*.[93]   Many Church Fathers (Chrysostom, Jerome, and
others) maintain that Hadrian completely destroyed the
remnants of the old city which were still left standing after
the destruction by Titus.   By this they really only mean
that Hadrian made an utter end of the old Jewish city, and
erected a new heathen city in its place.[94]   In the Mishna it
is related that Jerusalem was run over on the 9th Ab by the
plough.   By this, as the context shows, the time of Hadrian
is meant.   In the Babylonian Talmud and by Jerome this
deed is ascribed to Rufus ; only they both speak, not of a
ploughing of the city, but of the site of the temple.[95]   The

short statement in the Mishna is specially deserving of notice.
What this ceremony would signify, however, would be, not
the destruction, but the new founding; and the incident must
therefore be placed before the outbreak of the revolt.[96]   The
story of the conquest of Jerusalem by Hadrian as told in the
Samaritan chronicle is wholly fabulous.[97]

The last hiding-place of Bar-Cochba and his followers was
the strong mountain fastness of Beth-ther,[98] according to
Eusebius not very far from Jerusalem, probably on the site
of the modern Bettir, three hours south-west of Jerusalem.[99]
After a long and stubborn defence this stronghold was also
conquered in the eighteenth year of Hadrian = A.D. 134–135,[100]
according to rabbinical calculation on the 9th Ab.[101]   In the
sack of the city they found Bar-Cochba, "the originator of all
the mad fanaticism which had called down the punishment.' [102]
We have absolutely no information about the siege and
conquest.   The rabbinical legends tell all manner of stories
about this struggle ; but these productions of the wildest
fancy do not deserve even once to be mentioned.   This one
point alone may perhaps deserve to be repeated, that before the
fall of the city R. Eleasar, the uncle of Bar-Cochba, is said to
have been slain by his nephew because he falsely suspected
him of having come to an understanding with the Romans.[103]

With the fall of Beth-ther the war was brought to a close,
after having continued for somewhere about three years and
a half, A.D. 132–135.[104]   During the course of it also many
Rabbis died a martyr's death.   The later legends have
glorified by poetic amplification and exaggeration especially
the death of ten such martyrs, among them that of R. Akiba.[105]

In honour of the victory Hadrian was greeted for the
second time as *Imperator*.[106]   Julius Severus received the
ornamenta triumphalia ; to officers and men were given the
customary rewards.[107]   The victory was won indeed at a very
heavy cost.   So great were the losses that Hadrian in his

letter to the Senate omitted the usual introductory formula,
that "he and the army were well." [108]   Still more grievous
than this direct loss of men was the desolation of the fruitful
and populous province.   "All Judea was well-nigh a desert."
Fifty fortresses, 985 villages were destroyed, 580,000 Jews
(?) fell in battle, while the number of those who succumbed
to their wounds and to famine was never reckoned. [109]
Innumerable was the multitude of those who were sold
away as slaves.   At the annual market at the Terebinth of
Hebron they were offered for sale in such numbers that a
Jewish slave was of no more value than a horse.   What
could not be disposed of there was brought to Gaza and there
sold or sent to Egypt, on the way to which many died of
hunger or by shipwreck. [110]

With respect to the capital Jerusalem, that was now proceeded with which had been projected before the war: it
was converted into a Roman colony with the name Aelia
Capitolina.   In order to make permanent the purely
heathen character of the city, the Jews still residing there
were driven out, and heathen colonists settled in their
stead. [111]   No Jew was allowed thereafter to enter the
territory of the city; if any one should be discovered there
he was put to death. [112]   The official name of the newly-
founded city is given on the coins as *Col(onia) Ael(ia)
Cap(itolina)*; writers designate it in their works, as a rule,
only Aelia. [113]   Its constitution was that of a Roman colony,
but it had not the *jus Italicum*. [114]   It may readily be
supposed that it did not want beautiful and useful buildings.
The *Chronicon Paschale* mentions: τὰ δύο δημόσια καὶ τὸ
θέατρον καὶ τὸ τρικάμαρον καὶ τὸ τετράνυμφον καὶ τὸ
δωδεκάπυλον τὸ πρὶν ὀνομαζόμενον ἀναβαθμοὶ καὶ τὴν
κόδραν. [115]   At the south gate of the city toward Bethlehem
the figure of a swine is said to have been engraved. [116]   The
chief religious worship in the city was that of the Capitoline

Jupiter, to whom a temple was erected on the site of the former Jewish temple.[117] It would also seem that in it there was the statue of Hadrian of which Christian writers speak.[118] On the coins, as deities of the city, besides Jupiter are mentioned : Bacchus, Serapis, Astarte, the Dioscuri. A sanctuary of Aphrodite (Astarte) stood on the place where, according to the Christian tradition, the sepulchre of Christ had been ;[119] or, according to another version, a sanctuary of Jupiter on the site of the sepulchre, and a sanctuary of Venus on the site of the cross of Christ.[120]

The complete ethnicizing of Jerusalem was the actual accomplishment of a scheme which previously Antiochus Epiphanes had in vain attempted. In another respect also the enactments of Hadrian were similar to those of the former attempt. The prohibition of circumcision, which had been issued probably even before the war, and was directed not specially against the Jews (see above, p. 296), was now without doubt continued in force. It was only under Antoninus Pius that the Jews were again allowed to circumcise their children (see above, p. 296). The Jewish tradition, which certainly refers to this prohibition, affirms that even the observance of the Sabbath and the study of the law had been forbidden.[121] Whether this statement be reliable or not, the prohibition of circumcision was, according to Jewish notions, equivalent to a prohibition of the Jewish religion generally. So long as this prohibition was maintained and acted on, there was no use speaking of a pacification of the Jewish people. In fact we hear again, even in the time of Antoninus Pius, of an attempted rebellion which had to be put down by strong measures.[122] To the Roman authorities there was here only the choice : either to tolerate the religious ceremonies, or to completely exterminate the people. We may indeed assume that the knowledge which the emperor Antoninus had of this alternative, led him to allow again and grant toleration to the practice of circumcision.

Under Hadrian's successor, therefore, essentially the same state of matters is seen still to exist as had existed since the time of Vespasian.   He did not by any means answer the political ideals of the Jews.   But in regard to religious matters they could be satisfied with him.   The extinction of their political existence just led to this, that those tendencies obtained the supremacy which represented undiluted Judaism : Pharisaism and Rabbinism.

The development now proceeded forth upon those lines which became prominent in consequence of the great revolution of sentiment that followed the destruction of Jerusalem. Without a political home, grouped together into a unity only by the ideal power of the common law, the Jews continued all the more persistently to hold by and cherish this birth-right in which they all shared.   In this way the separation between them and the rest of the world was more and more sharply defined.   While, during the period in which Hellenistic Judaism flourished, the boundaries between the Jewish and Graeco-Roman view of the world threatened to melt away, the Jews and their opponents now gave attention with all their combined strength to deepen the cleft even more and more.   Jewish Hellenism, which proclaimed the common brotherhood of man, disappeared, and Pharisaic Judaism, which sharply repudiated all communion with the Gentile world, won universal acceptance.   But paganism also had become more intolerant : the rush of the masses to the worship of the Jewish God had ceased, partly because of other powerful spiritual forces, pre-eminently that of Christianity, which exercised a more potent influence, but partly also because of the civil legislation which, without abrogating the guaranteed toleration of the Jewish religion, imposed legal limitations to the further expansion of Judaism.

And thus the Jews became more and more what they properly and essentially were: strangers in the pagan world. The restoration of a Jewish commonwealth in the Holy Land was, and continued even to be, a subject of religious hope, which they held by with unconquerable tenacity.

NOTES

§ 4. RELIGIOUS DESTITUTION AND REVIVAL (B.C. 175-165).

[1] See the list of high priests from Joshua, the contemporary of Zerub-babel, down to Jaddua, in Neh. xii. 10, 11. Jaddua was a contemporary of Alexander the Great. (Josephus, *Antiq.* xi. 7. 2, 8. 7). The successors of Jaddua, according to Josephus, were :—

Onias I., son of Jaddua (*Antiq.* xi. 8. 7), or, according to 1 Macc. xii. 7, viii. 20, a contemporary of King Areus of Sparta, B.C. 309-265.

Simon I. the Just, son of the preceding (*Antiq.* xii. 2. 4. Compare Div. ii. vol. i. 355).

Eleasar, brother of the preceding (*Antiq.* xii. 2. 4), according to the book of Aristeas, a contemporary of Ptolemy II. Philadelphus, B.C. 283-247.

Manasseh, uncle of the preceding (*Antiq.* xii. 4. 1).

Onias II., son of Simon the Just (*Antiq.* xii. 4. 1-2), of the age of Ptolemy III. Euergetes, B.C. 247-222.

Simon II., son of the preceding (*Antiq.* xii. 4. 10). Compare Sirach l. 1 ff. ; 3 Macc. ii. 1.

Onias III., son of the preceding (*Antiq.* xii. 4. 10), of the time of Seleucus IV. and Antiochus Epiphanes, B.C. 175, and hence referred to in the early history of the Maccabean struggle; 2 Macc. iii.-iv. ; Josephus, *Antiq.* xii. 5. 1.

The high priest Hezekiah, spoken of by the Pseudo-Hecataeus (quoted in Josephus, *contra Apion.* i. 22) as the contemporary of Ptolemy Lagus, is not reckoned by Josephus in the list given in his history.

[2] One such who may be cited as an example was that Timothy, ἡγούμενος of the Ammonites, against whom Judas Maccabees fought (1 Macc. v. 6, 11, 34, 37, 40). For it is extremely improbable, from what we are told in 1 Macc. ix. 35-42 of the independence of the tribes living there, that he was a general set over the Ammorites by the King of Syria.—Also Aretas, the τύραννος of the Nabateans (2 Macc. v. 8), belonged to that same class.

[3] This is made quite evident from the two thoroughly harmonizing accounts given in Josephus, *Antiq.* xii. 4. 1 and xii. 4. 4.

[4] Pseudo-Hecataeus in Josephus, *contra Apionem*, ii. 4 .

[5] 1 Macc. xi. 34 :Compare xi. 28. This present was promised before, but not bestowed (1 Macc. x. 30, 38); it was confirmed by Antiochus VI. (1 Macc. xi. 57).

[6] "Judea" when mentioned alongside of "Samaria" can only mean Judea in the narrower sense, that is, the southern province. This also is in accordance with the linguistic usage of the First Book of Maccabees, in which, so far as I see, always Judea proper is meant by γῆ 'Ιούδα or 'Ιουδαία (so *e.g.* 1 Macc. xii. 46-52). The linguistic usage prevailing in Josephus, in the New Testament, and in the Mishna, which distinguishes "Judea," "Samaria," and "Galilee" as three separate districts (see § 22. 1),

was thus already firmly maintained in the Maccabean age. But if we admit that in the quoted passages (1 Macc. x. 30, 38, xi. 28, 34) Judea in the narrower sense is meant, then this result follows, that not only before the beginning of the Maccabean rising, but also even under the Maccabean high priests Jonathan and Simon, the province of Galilee did not belong to the territory of the Jewish high priest. For it is always only Judea that is spoken of in the three νομοί of Samaria attached thereto. It is only in 1 Macc. x. 30 that three νομοί of "Samaria and Galilee" are said to have been united with Judea. But, on the one hand, that scheme was never fully carried out; and so even here, in accordance with the exact parallels in other passages, only the three νομοί in the south of Samaria can be meant. There has therefore been either an interpretation of Γαλιλαίας, or "Samaria and Galilee" are taken together to mean the province of Samaria. Most probably it was first through the conquests of John Hyrcanus and his successors that Samaria and Scythopolis, as also Galilee, were united politically with the Jewish domain.

[7] Observe how in 1 Macc. xi. 34, "doing sacrifice at Jerusalem" is brought forward as a characteristic of the position of those who are free from tribute.

[8] See the proofs given in § 22. 2 and § 23. 1.

[9] Josephus, *Wars of the Jews*, ii. 6. 3.

[10] The proof for this and many of the following statements is given in § 23. 1.

[11] On the Philotera of Upper Egypt (that name is so written), see Strabo, p. 769. Our Philoteria in Palestine had this name conferred upon it at a later date, and is identical with some town known formerly under another designation. A trace of its existence is still to be found in the days of Alexander Jannäus. See § 10 towards the conclusion.

[12] Josephus, *Wars of the Jews*, ii. 6. 3.

[13] On the spread of Greek culture in Palestine in the times of the Maccabees, and that even among men well disposed towards Judaism, compare: Freudenthal, *Alexander Polyhistor* (1875), pp. 127–129. Freudenthal calls attention particularly to the following points. 1. The Book of Aristeas takes for granted that the Palestinian scholars, who had been summoned to Alexandria for the translation of the Pentateuch, were skilled in Greek. 2. The grandson of Jesus Sirach, who translated his proverbs into Greek, was a native of Palestine. The Greek translator of the book of Esther was also a Palestinian, according to the representation of the book in the Septuagint.

[14] Polyb. xxvi. 10.

[15] Compare generally, Polybius, xxviii. 18. 3, xxix. 9. 13, xxxi. 3 f.— Diodorus, xxix. 32, xxxi. 16 (ed. Müller).—Livy, xli. 30.—Ptolemy VII. in Müller, *Fragm. hist. graec.* iii. 186.—Heliodorus in Müller, *Fragm. hist. graec.* iv. 425.

[16] Athenaeus, lib. x. p. 439 (in the editions of Polybius, xxvi. 10):

[17] Tacitus, *Historia*, v. 8.

¹⁸ That Jason was originally called Jesus. is mentioned by Josephus, *Antiq.* xii. 5. 1.

¹⁹ 2 Macc. iv. 7–10.—Josephus tells the story differently. For while, according to 2 Maccabees, Onias had been deposed and subsequently, even after Jason had himself lost the high-priesthood, murdered (2 Macc. iv. 33, 34), Josephus simply says that after the death of Onias his brother Jesus obtained the rank of high priest (*Antiq.* xii. 5. 1 : ἀποθανόντος Ὀνίου τοῦ ἀρχιερέως τῷ ἀδελφῷ αὐτοῦ Ἰησοῦ τὴν ἀρχιερωσύνην Ἀντίοχος δίδωσιν). But the narrative of Josephus is evidently given in a summary manner and inexactly ; and the representation of 2 Maccabees is confirmed by Dan. ix. 26, xi. 22, since these passages probably refer to Onias III.

²⁰ See generally, 2 Macc. iv. 11–17 ; 1 Macc. i. 11–15 ; Josephus, *Antiq.* xii. 5. 1. Removing the traces of circumcision (1 Macc. i. 15, ἐποίησαν ἑαυτοῖς ἀκροβυστίας) was done with a view to escape the reproach of the heathen in the baths and in the exercise grounds. It seems, according to various reports, to have become still more common in later times.

²¹ 2 Macc. iv. 18–20.

²² 2 Macc. iv. 23–27. According to Josephus, *Antiq.* xii. 5. 1, consult also xv. 3. 1, xix. 6. 2, Menelaus was Jason's brother. But this is in contradiction to the Second Book of Maccabees, which seems generally at this point to be pretty accurately informed.

²³ See generally, 2 Macc. iv. 27–50.

²⁴ 2 Macc. v. 1–11.

²⁵ According to 1 Macc. i. 20, supported by Josephus, *Antiq.* xii. 5. 3, this expedition was made in the Seleucid year 143, or B.C. 170–169.

²⁶ 1 Macc. i. 20–24 ; Josephus, *Antiq.* xii. 5. 3 ; 2 Macc. v. 11–21.—For the fact of the plundering of the temple, Josephus in *Contra Apionem*, ii. 7, refers to the statements of Polybius, Strabo, Nicolaus Damascenus, Timagenes, Castor, Apollodorus.

²⁷ Polybius, xxix. 11. Diodorus, xxxi. 2 (ed. Müller). Livy, xlv. 12 Appian, *Syriaca*, c. 66. Justin, xxxiv. 3. Compare Dan. xi. 29 f.

²⁸ This connection between the failure of the Egyptian campaign and the persecutions in Palestine is pointed out in Dan. xi. 30 f.

²⁹ The sending of this Apollonius, if we compare 1 Macc. i. 20 and i. 54 with 1 Macc. i. 29, occurred in the Seleucid year 145, or B.C. 168–167.

³⁰ 1 Macc. i. 29–40 ; 2 Macc. v. 23–26 ; Josephus, *Antiq.* xii. 5. 4.—It is evident from 1 Macc. i. 38 compared with 1 Macc. i. 30–32 and 2 Macc. v. 24, that what was chiefly aimed at was the exterminating of the Jewish population and the repeopling of the city with Greek or Grecianized inhabitants. It was therefore quite the same procedure which the Jews themselves carried out at a later period in Joppa and Gazara (1 Macc. xiii. 11 and 43–48). On the consequences of these measures, see 1 Macc. ii. 18, iii. 35, 45.

³¹ The ἀκρόπολις of Jerusalem had been already frequently referred to during the previous years (2 Macc. iv. 12, 27, v. 5). But it was now

newly strengthened, 1 Macc. i. 33–36 ; Josephus, *Antiq.* xii. 5. 4, while the walls of the city were thrown down, 1 Macc. i. 31. On the taking of this citadel by Simon, see 1 Macc. xiii. 49–52 ; during the period intervening it is often referred to (1 Macc. ii. 31, iii. 45, iv. 2, 41, vi. 18–21, 26, 32, ix. 52, 53, x. 6–9, 32, xi. 20 f., 41, xii. 36, xiii. 21).

[32] See generally : 1 Macc. i. 41–64 ; 2 Macc. vi. 1–11. Josephus, *Antiq.* xii. 5. 4 ; Dan. vii. 25, viii. 11 f., ix. 27, xi. 31 ff., xii. 11.—The month Chisleu of the Seleucid year 145 (1 Macc. i. 54) is not, as has been usually assumed, December B.C. 167, but December B.C. 168.

[33] 2 Macc. vi. 18–vii. 42. This story forms the theme of the Fourth Book of Maccabees,

[34] 1 Macc. ii. 1–5. Josephus, *Antiq.* xii. 6. 1.

[35] 1 Macc. ii. 15–26. Josephus, *Antiq.* xii. 6. 2.

[36] 1 Macc. ii. 27–38. Josephus, *Antiq.* xii. 6. 2.

[37] The reading συναγωγὴ ʼΑϛιδαίων, 1 Macc. ii. 42, has been rightly received by Fritzsche into the text. That the Asidaeans were not identical with the circle of Mattathias has been specially emphasized by Wellhausen in his *Pharisäer und Sadducäer*, pp. 78–86. They did indeed make common cause with the Maccabees, but afterwards they again separated from them (1 Macc. vii. 13). Compare also Lucius, *Der Essenismus*, 1881, p. 91 f.; and Div. ii. of this work, vol. ii. p. 26 ff. The correct view of Wellhausen is adopted by Montet in his *Essai sur les origines des partis saducéen et pharisien*, 1883, pp. 139–142, 161 ff., especially 177–188. — The word חֲסִידִים frequently occurs in the Old Testament (*e.g.* Ps. xxx. 5, xxxi. 24, xxxvii. 28), and means simply the "pious ;" but it is used to designate specially those who are peculiarly distinguished for their piety or rigid observance of the law. So also in the Mishna, *Berachoth* v. 1 ; *Sukka* v. 4 ; *Chagiga* ii. 7 ; *Sota* iii. 4, ix. 15. It is therefore essentially the same circle which subsequently received the party name of Pharisees.

[38] 1 Macc. ii. 39–48. Josephus, *Antiq.* xii. 6. 2.

[39] 1 Macc. ii. 49–70. Josephus, *Antiq.* xii. 6. 3–4.

[40] Compare generally the characteristics given in 1 Macc. iii. 1–9.

[41] 1 Macc. iii. 10–12. Josephus, *Antiq.* xii. 7. 1.

[42] 1 Macc. iii. 13–26. Josephus, *l.c.*—Βαιθωρῶν, in the Old Testament בֵּית חֹרֹן ; according to Eusebius, *Onomasticon*, ed. Lagarde, p. 233, sixteen miles west-north-west of Jerusalem, and so identical with the present Beit-ur.

[43] 1 Macc. iii. 31. Tacitus, *Historia*, v. 8.

[44] 1 Macc. iii. 27–37. Josephus, *Antiq.* xii. 7. 2.

[45] 1 Macc. iii. 38–41. Josephus, *Antiq.* xii. 7. 3. 2 Macc. viii. 8–11. According to the Second Book of Maccabees, Ptolemy was the governor of Coele-Syria and Phoenicia, who transferred the military operations to Nicanor and Gorgias.

[46] Μασσηφά, 1 Macc. iii. 46, is the ancient מִצְפָּה, which in the times of the Judges was the religious and political capital of Israel (Judg. xx. xxi.;

1 Sam. vii. 5 ff., x. 17 ff.). According ω 1 Macc. iii. 46, it lay κατέναντι Ιερουσαλήμ, therefore not far from Jerusalem. Its situation cannot with any certainty be more exactly determined.

⁴⁷ 1 Macc. iii. 42-60. Josephus, *Antiq.* xii. 7. 3.—'Εμμαούμ (1 Macc. iii. 40, 57), in the Roman times the capital of a toparchy, exists down to the present day under the name of Amwâs. The New Testament Emmaus is probably a different place lying near Jerusalem.

⁴⁸ 1 Macc. iv. 1-25. Josephus, *Antiq.* xii. 7. 4 ; 2 Macc. viii. 12 ff.— The chronology is made out by means of a combination of 1 Macc. iii. 37, which gives the Seleucid year 147, with 1 Macc. iv. 28, ἐν τῷ ἐχομένῳ ἐνιαυτῷ, or, what is the same, ἐν τῷ ἐρχομένῳ ἐνιαυτῷ, meaning "in the following year," and chap. iv. 52, which gives the Seleucid year 148. The incidents in question therefore occurred in the year of the Seleucid era 147, or B.C. 166-165 ; but whether in B.C. 166 or in B.C. 165 cannot be determined.—As the enemy's general, the First Book of Maccabees names only Gorgias, the Second Book of Maccabees names only Nicanor. Both are probably correct, inasmuch as the former led the army in the field, and the latter was commander-in-chief of the whole army.

⁵⁴⁹ 1 Macc. iv. 26-35. Josephus, *Antiq.* xii. 7. 5. 2 Macc. xi. 1-15.

⁵⁰ The stones of the heathen altar of sacrifice, or rather of several such altars, were carried out to "an unclean place," therefore completely outside of the temple precincts (1 Macc. iv. 43). The stones of the earlier Jewish altar of burnt-offerings, on the other hand, were laid on the temple mount, on a suitable place, "until there should come a prophet to show what should be done with them" (1 Macc. iv. 46). According to Mishna, *Middoth* i. 6, the stones of the Jewish altar were laid down in a chamber within the bounds of the inner court, but no longer on "holy" ground.

⁵¹ The date 25th Chisleu as the day of the consecration of the temple is obtained from *Megillath Taanith*, § 23.

⁵² Compare generally : 1 Macc. iv. 36-59. Josephus, *Antiq.* xii. 7. 6-7. 2 Macc. x. 1-8.—To this date belongs the Feast of the Dedication of the Temple, τὰ ἐγκαίνια of John x. 22. Compare Josephus, *Antiq.* xii. 7. 7 : καὶ ἐξ ἐκείνου μέχρι δεῦρο τὴν ἑορτὴν ἄγομεν καλοῦντες αὐτὴν Φῶτα, because during this festival it was the custom to burn lights (compare *Baba kamma* vi. 6, and Maimonides). According to 2 Macc. x. 6, it was celebrated after the manner of the Feast of Tabernacles, and is therefore actually called in 2 Macc. i. 9, "The Feast of Tabernacles of the month Chisleu." The Egyptian Jews were invited to take part in its celebration by two letters preserved in the beginning of the Second Book of Maccabees. For the literature with reference to this see Div. ii. vol. iii. p. 215. It was called in Hebrew חֲנֻכָּה, *Megillath Taanith*, § 23, and was observed for a period of eight days ; *Bikkurim* i. 6 ; *Rosh Hashana* i. 3 ; *Taanith* ii. 10 ; *Megilla* iii. 4, 6 ; *Moed katan* iii. 9 ; *Baba kamma* vi. 6. A complete description of the festival in post-Talmudic times is given by Maimonides, *Hilchoth Megilla wa-Chanukka*, c.

iii.-iv., in the third volume of his great work, *Jad-ha-chasaka* or *Mishne Tora*, St. Petersburg 1850–1852, Bd. ii. pp. 532–542 ; also in Shulchan-Arukh, § 670–685.

§ 5. THE TIMES OF JUDAS MACCABAEUS, B.C. 165-161.

[1] 1 Macc. iv. 60, 61. Josephus, *Antiq.* xii. 7. 7.

[2] 1 Macc. v. 1–8. Josephus, *Antiq.* xii. 8. 1.

[3] 1 Macc. v. 9–20. Josephus, *Antiq.* xii. 8. 1–2.

[4] 1 Macc. v. 21-23. Josephus, *Antiq.* xii. 8. 2.

[5] 1 Macc. v. 24–54. Josephus, *Antiq.* xii. 8. 3–5. Compare 2 Macc. xii. 10–31.

[6] 1 Macc. v. 18, 19, 55–62. Josephus, *Antiq.* xii. 8. 6.

[7] 1 Macc. v. 63–68. Instead of Σαμάρειαν, 1 Macc. v. 66, we have in Josephus, *Antiq.* xii. 8. 6, Μάρισσαν, as also in the Latin text of the *codex Sangermanensis*. Compare also 2 Macc. xii. 35. Marissa, in the Old Testament מָרֵשָׁה, is a very well known town in the south of Judea, then under Edomite rule (*Antiq.* xiii. 9. 1), and lying, according to Eusebius, *Onomasticon*, ed. Lagarde, p. 279, in the neighbourhood of Eleutheropolis, that is, just between Hebron and Ashdod.

[8] 1 Macc. vi. 1–16. Josephus, *Antiq.* xii. 9. 1. Polybius, xxxi. 11. Porphyry in Jerome on Dan. xi. 44, 45 (Hieronym. *Opp.* ed. Vallarsi, v. 722).—Instead of Artemis, as given by Polybius, Appian. *Syriaca*, c. 66, names Aphrodite.

[9] 1 Macc. vi. 14–17. Josephus, *Antiq.* xii. 9. 2.

[10] 1 Macc. vi. 18–27. Josephus, *Antiq.* xii. 9. 3.

[11] Βαιθζαχαρία (1 Macc. vi. 32), according to Josephus, *Antiq.* xii. 9. 4, seventy stadia north of Beth-zur, is in the present day called Beit-Sakaria.

[12] 1 Macc. vi. 28–48. Josephus, *Antiq.* xii. 9. 3–5 ; *Wars of the Jews*, i. 1. 5. 2 Macc. xiii. 1–17. The defeat is only very shyly hinted at in the First Book of Maccabees vi. 47 ; while in the Second Book of Maccabees it is actually transformed into a victory !

[13] 1 Macc. vi. 49–54. Josephus, *Antiq.* xii. 9. 5. 2 Macc. xiii. 18–22. The mentioning of the Sabbatical year (1 Macc. vi. 49 : ὅτι σάββατον ἦν τῇ γῇ ; vi. 53 : οιὰ τὸ ἔβδομον ἔτος εἶναι) shows us that the events occurred in B.C. 163. For the Seleucid year 150 (in which they are placed by 1 Macc. vi. 20 compared with vii. 1) runs, according to the mode of reckoning followed in the First Book of Maccabees, from spring of B.C. 163 to spring of B.C. 162. The Sabbatical year, however, always begins in autumn (Mishna, *Rosh hashana* i. 1). Since, then, they were already in want of victuals, they must have been in the second half of the Sabbatical year, after the fields during winter and spring had been left

unsown. This, therefore, brings us to the summer of B.C. 163.

[14] 1 Macc. vi. 55–62. Josephus, *Antiq.* xii. 9. 6–7. 2 Macc. xiii. 23–26.

[15] Compare Wellhausen, *Pharisäer und Sadducäer*, p. 84 : " The year 162 marks the proper end of the religious war of the Jews. Thereafter the occasion of the conflict was not religion, but government."

[16] We get no information from the First Book of Maccabees as to the person who administered the office of the high priest after the restoration of the Jewish worship. Nominally Menelaus was still high priest. He is said to have been put to death by Antiochus V. Eupator when he made definite concessions to the Jews, and the reason assigned for that was that Menelaus by his evil counsels was indirectly responsible for the rebellion of the Jews (Josephus, *Antiq.* xii. 9. 7 ; compare 2 Macc. xiii. 3–8). But Menelaus was naturally unable in presence of Judas, who was in possession of the actual power, to exercise the functions of the high priest's office. Perhaps, indeed, Onias IV., son of Onias III., may have officiated. But, according to Josephus, *Antiq.* xii. 5. 1, he was not of age at the time of his father's death, and went immediately down into Egypt, and so after the execution of Menelaus the office was given, not to him, but to Alcimus (*Antiq.* xii. 9. 7).

[17] 1 Macc. vi. 63. Josephus, *Antiq.* xii. 9. 7.

[18] Eusebius, *Chronicon*, ed. Schoene, i. 254 (=Syncell. ed. Dindorf, i. 550 sq.). 2 Macc. xiv. 1.

[19] Justin, xxxiv. 3 : *Delatus in Syriam secundo favore omnium excipitur.*

[20] 1 Macc. vii. 1–4. Josephus, *Antiq.* xii. 10. 1. 2 Macc. xiv. 1–2, Livy, *Epit.* xlvi. Appian, *Syriaca*, c. 47.

[21] Polybius, xxxi. 23, xxxii. 4.

[22] Josephus, *Antiq.* xii. 9. 7 : Ἄλκιμος ὁ καὶ Ἰάκειμος κληθείς. In the sketch given by Josephus in *Antiq.* xx. 10, he names him simply Ἰάκιμος. Also in the text of the First Book of Maccabees, vii. 5, 12, 20, 21, 23, 25, and ix. 54–57, as well as 2 Macc. xiv. 3, various manuscripts have the addition ὁ καὶ Ἰάκιμος.

[23] 1 Macc. vii. 5–9. Josephus, *Antiq.* xii. 10. 1–2. 2 Macc. xiv. 3–10.— According to Josephus, *Antiq.* xii. 9. 7, Alcimus had been already nominated as high priest by Antiochus V. Eupator. According to 2 Macc. xiv. 3 ff., he had once even earlier than this filled the office of high priest.

[24] 1 Macc. vii. 10–15. Josephus, *Antiq.* xii. 10. 2. The Second Book of Maccabees, xiv. 6, falsely identifies the Asidaeans with the party of Judas.

[25] 1 Macc. vii. 16–25. Josephus, *Antiq.* xii. 10. 2–3.

[26] The position of this place is unknown.

[27] 1 Macc. vii. 26–38. Josephus, *Antiq.* xii. 10. 4–5.

[28] Ἀδασά, 1 Macc. vii. 40, 45, according to Josephus, *Antiq.* xii. 10. 5, thirty stades from Beth-Horon, is identical with the Ἀδασά in the neighbourhood of Gophna which was known to Eusebius (*Onomasticon*, ed.

Lagarde, p. 220 : καὶ ἔστι νῦν κώμη ἐγγὺς Γουφνῶν). It lay therefore north-east of Beth-Horon.

²⁹ 1 Macc. vii. 39–50. Josephus, *Antiq.* xii. 10. 5. 2 Macc. xv. 1–36. *Megillath Taanith,* § 30 (in Derenbourg, p. 63). — The year in which Nicanor's defeat occurred is not directly stated in the First Book of Maccabees, but by a comparison of 1 Macc. vii. 1 with ix. 3, it must be set down as the Seleucid year 151, or B.C. 162–161. But the month Adar of the Seleucid year 151 is equivalent to March B.C. 161. The considera-tion which in the first edition of this work was regarded as telling against this date, that it made the time since the accession of Demetrius too short for the occurrence of such events, I can no longer regard as offering any serious difficulty.

³⁰ On the death of Alcimus, see 1 Macc. ix. 54-56. On the high-priest-hood of Judas, Josephus, *Antiq.* xii. 10. 6, 11. 2. In itself it would not be inconceivable that Judas should also have usurped the functions of the high priest. But the First Book of Maccabees says nothing about such a pro-ceeding. There was also a legitimate claimant present in the person of Onias IV., who would certainly be respected as such by Judas. Josephus himself in another place expressly says that after the death of Alcimus the office of the high priest remained unoccupied for seven years (*Antiq.* xx. 10 : διεδέξατο δὲ οὐδεὶς αὐτόν, ἀλλὰ διετέλεσεν ἡ πόλις ἐνιαυτοὺς ἑπτὰ χωρὶς ἀρχιερέως οὖσα).

³¹ Thus Antiochus Epiphanes was obliged to abandon Egypt by Popilius Laenas. After the death of Antiochus Epiphanes, the Roman senate forced from Antiochus Eupator and his regent-guardian Lysias a considerable reduction of the standing army of Syria (Polybius, xxxi. 12 ; Appian. *Syriaca,* c. 46).

³² 1 Macc. viii. Josephus, *Antiq.* xii. 10. 6.

³³ 1 Macc. viii. 31, 32.

³⁴ From the general drift of the First Book of Maccabees, it may be assumed that Judas had first arranged the embassy after the victory over Nicanor. On this supposition he cannot have lived to see the return of his ambassadors, for his death occurred only two months after Nicanor's defeat.

³⁵ Both places are unknown.

³⁶ 1 Macc. ix. 1-21. Josephus, *Antiq.* xii. 11. 1-2.

§ 6. THE TIMES OF JONATHAN, B.C. 161-143.

¹ 1 Macc. ix. 23-27. Josephus, *Antiq.* xiii. 1. 1.

² 1 Macc. ix. 28-31. Josephus, *l.c.*

³ 1 Macc. ix. 32-49. Josephus, *Antiq.* xiii. 1. 2-4.—The fight with Bacchides took place on the eastern bank of the Jordan. For the account

in 1 Macc. ix. 43–49 goes back again, after the intercalated story of 1 Macc. ix. 35–42, upon the statement of 1 Macc. ix. 34 (Βακχίδης . . . ἦλθεν . . . πέραν τοῦ Ἰορδάνου). If, then, Jonathan and his adherents saved themselves by swimming over the river, they must have reached the western bank, and so remained in the wilderness of Judea (compare ix. 33).

⁴ 1 Macc. ix. 50–53. Josephus, *Antiq.* xiii. 1. 3.—The most of the towns here named are otherwise unknown. On Emmaus, see Div. ii. vol. i. p. 159 ; on Beth-Horon, see above, page 31. —Bethel is the well-known ancient centre of Israelitish worship, according to Eusebius, *Onomasticon,* ed. Lagarde, p. 209, twelve Roman miles north of Jerusalem.—Thamnatha is in Hebrew תִּמְנָתָה or תִּמְנָה, the name of these places in Southern Palestine, see Div. ii. vol. i. p. 158.   The best known is תִּמְנַת־סֶרַח, where the tomb of Joshua was. According to the received text of 1 Macc. ix. 50, Thamnatha-Pharathon is to be taken as the name of one place. But probably Josephus, the Syriac, and the *Vet. Lat.* are right when they read καί between the two words.   Pharathon is in Hebrew פִּרְעָתוֹן, a town in the tribe of Ephraim, Judg. xii. 13, 15, perhaps the modern Ferata, south-west of Nablous (Robinson, *Later Bibl. Researches,* p. 65 sq.; Guérin, *Samaria,* ii. 179 f.). But this Pharathon, as well as Thimnath-Serach, belonged to Samaria, according to 1 Macc. xi. 34. It is therefore questionable whether other similarly named towns in Judea may not be meant.—Τεφών or Τεφώ is usually identified with the Hebrew תַּפּוּחַ. If this were only more certain than it is, it would still be doubtful which of the different Old Testament towns of the name were meant (see Mühlau in Riehm's *Handwörterbuch,* p. 1612, art. " Tappuah ; " and p. 185, art. " Beth-Tappuah ").—On Beth-zur, see above, p. 32 ; on Gazara, see § 7 on the history of Simon.

⁵ 1 Macc. ix. 54–56. Josephus, *Antiq.* xii. 10. 6 (Josephus places the death of Alcimus before the death of Judas, see above, p. 41). The levelling of the walls, according to 1 Macc. ix. 54, was only partially carried out.

⁶ Josephus assumes this in *Antiq.* xiii. 1. 5.

⁷ 1 Macc. ix. 57. Josephus, *Antiq.* xiii. 1. 5.

⁸ 1 Macc. ix. 57–72. Josephus, *Antiq.* xiii. 1. 5–6.

⁹ 1 Macc. ix. 73. Josephus, *Antiq.* xiii. 1. 6. — Μαχμάς is the Old Testament מִכְמָס, according to Eusebius, *Onomasticon,* ed. Lagarde, p. 280, nine Roman miles north of Jerusalem, in the neighbourhood of Rama, the modern *Mukhmas.*

¹⁰ 1 Macc. x. 1–14. Josephus, *Antiq.* xiii. 2. 1.

¹¹ 1 Macc. x. 15–21. Josephus, *Antiq.* xiii. 2. 2–3.

¹² 1 Macc. x. 22–45. Josephus, *Antiq.* xiii. 2. 3.

¹³ 1 Macc. x. 45–60. Josephus, *Antiq.* xiii. 2. 4. Polybius, iii. 5. Justin. xxxv. 1 ; Appian. *Syr.* c. 67.—The account of the death of Demetrius is

given in fullest detail by Josephus, whose story is confirmed by Justin: *invicto animo inter confertissimos fortissime dimicans cecidit.*

¹⁴ⁱ 1 Macc. x. 46–50. Josephus, *Antiq.* xiii. 4. 1–2.—Στρατηγός and μεριδάρχης may be taken as equivalent to military and civil governor.

¹⁵·1 Macc. x. 67–87. Josephus, *Antiq.* xiii. 4. 3–4. Josephus describes the affair so erroneously as to make Apollonius take the side of Alexander Balas.

¹⁶1 Macc. x. 88–89. Josephus, *Antiq.* xiii. 4. 4. Josephus assigns as motive for the donation, that Alexander Balas wished to make it appear that Apollonius, as his general, had attacked Jonathan against the king's will. —Ἀκκαρών is the old Philistine עֶקְרוֹן, according to Eusebius, *Onomasticon*, ed. Lagarde, p. 218, between Ashdod and Jamnia, toward the east, therefore probably identical with the modern Akir, east of Jamnia.

¹⁷ Justin. xxxv. 2.

¹¹⁸ 1 Macc. xi. 1–13. Josephus, *Antiq.* xiii. 4. 5–7. Diodorus in Müller, *Fragm. Hist. Graec.* ii. p. xvi. n. 19. Livy, *Epit.* 52.

¹⁹ 1 Macc. xi. 14–19. Josephus, *Antiq.* xiii. 4. 8. Diodorus in Müller, *Fragm. Hist. Graec.* ii. p. xvi. n. 20. Livy, *Epit.* 52.—The locality of the battle is given by Strabo, xvi. 2. 8, p. 751.

²⁰ 1 Macc. xi. 20–37. Josephus, *Antiq.* xiii. 4. 9.—Confirmation of former dignities, 1 Macc. xi. 27. The three provinces, xi. 34 (compare x. 30, 38, xi. 28, 57); freedom from tribute, xi. 34, 35.—Ἀφαίρεμα is in all probability that Ephraim to which Christ withdrew shortly before the Passover (John xi. 54), according to Josephus, *Wars of the Jews*, iv. 9. 9, in the neighbourhood of Bethel; according to Eusebius, *Onomasticon*, ed. Lagarde, p. 254, twenty Roman miles north of Jerusalem (καὶ ἔστι νῦν κώμη Ἐφραεὶμ μεγίστη περὶ τὰ βόρεια Αἰλίας ὡς ἀπὸ σημείων κ'), and five Roman miles east of Bethel (Jerome, *Onomasticon*, ed. Lagarde, p. 94, *et est hodie vicus Efrem in quinto miliario Bethelis ad orientem respiciens*; the parallel Greek text of Eusebius, p. 222, is defective). Also אֶפְרַיִם of 2 Sam. xiii. 23, and עֶפְרוֹן of 2 Chron. xiii. 19, designate probably the same place. For conjectures about its situation, see Robinson, *Researches in Palestine*, vol. iii. 67–72. Guérin, *Judée*, iii. 45–51. — On Lydda, the modern Ludd, see Div. ii. vol. i. p. 159.—Ῥαμαθέμ is certainly the well-known city of Samuel, 1 Sam. i. 1, רָמָתַיִם צוֹפִים, elsewhere more shortly named הָרָמָה; but its position still continues very doubtful. According to 1 Sam. i. 1, it lay on Mount Ephraim. Eusebius places it in the neighbourhood of Diospolis - Lydda (*Onomasticon*, ed. Lagarde, p. 225 sq.: Ἀρμαθὲμ Σειφά· πόλις Ἑλκανὰ καὶ Σαμουήλ· κεῖται δὲ αὕτη πλησίον Διοσπόλεως, ὅθεν ἦν Ἰωσήφ, ἐν εὐαγγελίοις ἀπὸ Ἀριμαθίας. In Jerome, *Onomasticon*, ed. Lagarde, p. 96, the passage runs: *Armathem Sophim civitas Helcanae et Samuhelis in regione Thamnitica juxta Diospolim, unde fuit Joseph, qui in evangeliis, de Arimathia scribitur*). One passage, 1 Macc. xi. 34, vouches for the correctness of this statement, for it says

that down to the time of Jonathan the city belonged to Samaria. It is probably to be identified with the modern Beit Rima, north-east of Lydda, in the neighbourhood of Thamna (see Furrer in Schenkel's *Bibellexicon*, art. "Rama"). Distinct from this one is another Ramah, in the tribe of Benjamin, which lay much nearer Jerusalem.

²¹ Josephus, *Antiq.* xiii. 5. 1 : 'Απαμεύς τό γένος. More exactly, Strabo, xvi. 2. 10, p. 752 .—The fortress of Apamea, famous on account of its strength, lay on the Orontes, south of Antioch.

²² 1 Macc. xi. 39, 40, 54. Josephus, *Antiq.* xiii. 5. 1 and 2. Diodorus in Müller, *Fragm. Hist. Graec.* t. ii. p. xvii. n. 21. Livy, *Epit.* 52.—Appian. *Syr.* c. 68, erroneously calls the young king Alexander. The name of the Arab, Εἰμαλκουαί or 'Ιμαλκουέ (1 Macc. xi. 39), in Hebrew יִמְלְכוּ, which is met with on Palmyrian inscriptions ; see Nöldeke in Euting, *Nabataïsche Inschriften* (1885), p. 74. Josephus, the Syriac, and the Latin text of the *cod. Sagerm.* read here Malchus ; Diodorus gives Jamblichus, which also is nothing else than יִמְלְכוּ, Latin Jamblichus, *Corp. Inscr. Rhenan.*, ed. Brambach, n. 1233.

²³ 1 Macc. xi. 33, 41–52. Josephus, *Antiq.* xiii. 5. 2–3.

²⁴ 1 Macc. xi. 53–59. Josephus, *Antiq.* xiii. 5. 3–4.—The κλίμαξ Τύρου or Τυρίων is, according to Josephus, *Wars of the Jews*, ii. 10. 2, a high hill, a hundred stades north of Ptolemais. By the appointment as στρατηγός over the district named, Simon became an officer of the king of the highest rank, and that also outside of Judea. The position must first have been given him in opposition to the στρατηγός of Demetrius.

²⁵ 1 Macc. xi. 60–62. Josephus, *Antiq.* xiii. 5. 5.—On Askalon and Gaza, see Div. ii. vol. i. pp. 74 ff., 68 ff. It is deserving of notice that Jonathan is here regarded as a partisan of Trypho and Antiochus. It was not therefore intended to unite these cities with the Jewish territory, but only to compel them to attach themselves to the party to which Jonathan belonged.

²⁶ 1 Macc. xi. 63–74. Josephus, *Antiq.* xiii. 5. 6–7. —'Ασώρ, 1 Macc. xi. 67, is the חָצוֹר of Josh. xi. 1, 10–13, xii. 19, xix. 36 ; Judg. iv. 2, 17 ; 1 Sam. xii. 9 ; 1 Kings ix. 15 ; 2 Kings xv. 29. According to Josephus, *Antiq.* v. 5. 1 (compare Josh. xi. 5), it lay in the neighbourhood of the Lake Semechonitis or Merom (ὑπέρκειται τῆς Σεμεχωνίτιδος λίμνης), therefore in the extreme north of Palestine. The name is probably still retained in the modern Merj Hadîreh (valley of Hadîreh), and Jebel Hadîreh (Mount Hadireh), west of the Merom lake, in the great wady running down to the Merom lake.

²⁷ 1 Macc. xi. 65, 66. Josephus, *Antiq.* xiii. 5. 6.

²⁸ 1 Macc. xii. 1–4 ; the names of the ambassadors, xii. 16. Josephus, *Antiq.* xiii. 5. 8.

²⁹ 1 Macc. xii. 2 : πρὸς Σπαρτιάτας καὶ τόπους ἑτέρους. The letter to the Spartans in particular, 1 Macc. xii. 5–23 ; Josephus, *Antiq.* xiii. 5. 8. The answer of the Spartans, 1 Macc. xiv. 16–23.

[30] 1 Macc. xii. 7, 8, 19–22. Josephus, *Antiq.* xii. 4. 10, xiii. 5. 8.—The fiction of a relationship between the Jews and the Spartans, which constituted the motive for the Spartans to write their letter (1 Macc. xii. 6, 7, 21 ; compare 2 Macc. v. 9), was not unheard of during the era of Hellenism. Freudenthal, *Alexander Polyhistor*, p. 29, Anm., refers in illustration and for proof to Stephen of Byzantium under the word Ἰουδαία. . . . ὡς Κλαύδιος Ἰούλιος ἀπὸ, Οὐδαίου Σπάρτων ἑνὸς ἐκ Θήβης μετὰ Διονύσου ἐστρατευκότος. In a decree of the Pergamenes (Josephus, *Antiq.* xiv. 18. 22) there is also mention of a relation between the Jews and the Pergamenes.

[31] 1 Macc. xii. 24–30. Josephus, *Antiq.* xiii. 5. 10.—On the fact recorded here and in what follows, Derenbourg in his *Histoire de la Palestine*, pp. 99, 100, would refer to the statement in *Megillath Taanith*, § 33 : " On the 17th Adar, when the Gentiles had risen against the little group of the scribes in the districts of Chalcis and Zabdea, there came salvation to the house of Israel." This combination seems to me exceedingly venturous, although even Wellhausen in his *Pharisäer und Sadducäer*, p. 58, is inclined to agree to it.

[32] 1 Macc. xii. 31–37. Josephus, *Antiq.* xiii. 5. 10–11.

[33] 1 Macc. xii. 33, 34, 38. Josephus, *Antiq.* xiii. 5. 10.—Σεφήλα is the Hebrew שְׁפֵלָה, the lowland west of the mountainous region of Judea.

In the Mishna, *Shebiith* ix. 2, a distinction is made between שפלת לוד (lowlands near Lydda) and שפלת הדרום (lowlands of the south). So, too, Jerome in his commentary on Obadiah ver. 19 (*Opp.* ed. Vallarsi, vi. 381) : *qui autem habitabant in Sephela id est in campestribus, Liddam et Emmaus, Diospolim scilicet Nicopolimque, significans.* . . . *Alii vero putant eam Sephelam id est campestrem regionem, quae circa Eleutheropolim est, repromitti etc.* Less definite is the statement in Eusebius, *Onomasticon*, ed. Lagarde, p. 296 : Σεφηλά. . . . καὶ εἰς ἔτι νῦν Σεφηλὰ καλεῖται. αὕτη ἐστὶν πᾶσα ἡ περὶ τὴν Ἐλευθερόπολιν πεδινὴ χώρα πρὸς βορρᾶν καὶ δυσμάς. In our passage the district of Lydda is meant.—Ἀδιδά, 1 Macc. xii. 38, xiii. 13, to the חָדִיד of Ezra ii. 33 ; Neh. vii. 37, xi. 34. In the Mishna, *Arachin* ix. 6, חדיד is referred to as one of the old cities which were surrounded with walls as early as the days of Joshua. A Rabbi Jakim of Chadid is met with in *Edujoth* vii. 5. The common printed text has been indeed הדד or הדר, but all the better copies have חדיד. The Greek forms Ἀδδιδα or Ἀδιδα are given in Josephus, *Antiq.* xiii. 6. 4, 15. 2 ; *Wars of the Jews*, iv. 9. 1. According to the latter passage, it commanded the main road which led from the west, therefore from Joppa to Jerusalem. The fact that in Ezra ii. 34 and Neh. vii. 37 it is named together with Lydda and Ono, is in agreement with this. The *Aditha juxta Diospolim quasi ad orientalem plagam respiciens*, referred to by Eusebius and Jerome, *Onomasticon*, ed. Lagarde, p. 93, is therefore probably to be identified with the modern Haditheh, east of Lydda.

[34] 1 Macc. xii. 39, 40. Josephus, *Antiq.* xiii. 6. 1.

[35] 1 Macc. xii. 41–53. Josephus, *Antiq.* xiii. 6. 1–3.

[36] 1 Macc. xiii. 1–11. Josephus, *Antiq.* xiii. 6. 3.

[37] 1 Macc. xiii. 12–24. Josephus, *Antiq.* xiii. 6. 4–5. Adora is an Idumean city, which was afterwards conquered by John Hyrcanus (*Antiq.* xiii. 9. 1 ; see below, § 8).—Bascama is otherwise unknown. According to the connection of the story, it is to be looked for in the country east of the Jordan.

[38] 1 Macc. xiii. 25–30. Josephus, *Antiq.* xiii. 6. 5.—The sepulchral monument at Modein was still existing in the time of Eusebius.

§ 7. SIMON, B.C. 142–135.[1]

[1] The date of Jonathan's death is not given in the First Book of Maccabees, which between xi. 19 and xiii. 41 makes no mention of any particular year. But since, according to xiii. 41 and xiv. 27, the year of Simon's rule is to be connected from Seleucid year 170, or B.C. 143–142, Jonathan's death must be placed at the end of B.C. 143 or the beginning of B.C. 142. It is given in 1 Macc. xiii. 22 as occurring in winter. With this also agrees the statement of Josephus, that Simon reigned for eight years (*Antiq.* xii. 7. 4), from B.C. 142 to B.C. 135 ; while the statement in *Antiq.* xiii. 6. 5, that Jonathan had been high priest for four years, is erroneous.

[2] 1 Macc. xiii. 31, 32. Josephus, *Antiq.* xiii. 7. 1. Diodorus in Müller, *Fragm. Hist. Graec.* t. ii. p. xix. n. 25. Livy, *Epit.* 55. Appian, *Syr.* c. 68 ; Justin, xxxvi. 1.

[3] Grätz, *Geschichte der Juden,* Bd. iii., 4 Aufl. p. 566, and Derenbourg, p. 69, refer to *Megillath Taanith,* § 6. According to this authority, the 27th Ijjar, or May, was the day when the tribute was remitted.

[4] 1 Macc. xiii. 33–42 ; compare xiv. 27. Josephus, *Antiq.* xiii. 6. 6.

[5] Merzbacher in Sallet's *Zeitschrift für Numismatik,* Bd. v. 1878, pp. 292–319. He is followed by Madden, *Coins of the Jews,* 1881, pp. 65–67.

[6] According to 1 Macc. xv. 6, it was Antiochus VII. Sidetes, in the Seleucid year 174, or B.C. 139–138, who first gave Simon the right of issuing coins. On this point, however, no special weight should be laid, since it may quite fairly be regarded as simply the confirmation of a privilege that had been previously usurped. Of more importance is the fact that the coins of Simon's immediate successor, John Hyrcanus, are of quite a different style. Hence a very thorough change in the art of minting must have taken place.

[7] Besides the shekel, copper coins with the inscription on the obverse לגאלת ציון, and on the reverse שנת ארבע : the deliverance of Zion, year 4, are assigned by many numismatists to the age of Simon. The support for this supposition is even less certain than that for the shekel coining. Decidedly false, and now generally abandoned, is the conjecture of the

earlier numismatists, that the coins which bore the name of Simon belong to Simon the Maccabee.

[8] 1 Macc. xiii. 43-48 ; compare xiv. 34. Josephus, *Antiq.* xiii. 6. 6. Strabo, p. 759 : ἐν δὲ τῷ μεταξὺ καὶ ἡ Γαδαρὶς ἔστιν, ἥν καὶ αὐτὴν ἐξιδιά-σαντο οἱ Ἰουδαῖοι. The Gadaris here referred to by Strabo is identical with our Gazara. — The manuscripts of the First Book of Maccabees have in our passage (1 Macc. xiii. 43) Γάζαν. That instead of this Γάζαρα should be read, is proved, not only by the parallel text of Josephus, but also by the text of the First Book of Maccabees, in another passage referring to our incident (1 Macc. xiii. 53, xiv. 7, 34, xv. 28, 35, xvi. 1, xix. 21). It is the Old Testament גֶּזֶר, an important Canaanitish town.

[9] 1 Macc. xiii. 53, xvi. 1, 19, 21.

[10] 1 Macc. xiii. 49-52 ; compare xiv. 7, 36, 37. Josephus, *Antiq.* xiii. 6. 6. The date 23rd Ijjar, that is, the second month, is given not only in 1 Macc. xiii. 51, but also in *Megillath Taanith*, § 5. Compare Grätz, *Geschichte der Juden*, Bd. iii., 4 Aufl. p. 565. Derenbourg, p. 67. If the conjecture is correct that the Seleucid era of the First Book of Maccabees begins in spring, in Nisan, then Ijjar of the Seleucid year 171 corresponds to May B.C. 142.—With the story of the conquest of the citadel Josephus connects, in *Antiq.* xiii. 6. 6 and *Wars of the Jews*, v. 4. 1, the remarkable statement that not only was the citadel destroyed, but also the whole hill on which it was built was levelled by the uninterrupted labour of the people during three years, so that the site of the temple should be higher than that of the citadel. Since the First Book of Maccabees says nothing about this, but, on the contrary, says that Simon strengthened the citadel and placed in it a Jewish garrison (1 Macc. xiv. 36, 37, compare also xv. 28), the historical reliability of the statement is very questionable. It seems to me that the thing is not in itself improbable, since the place where the citadel stood is now in fact almost level, whereas it must previously have had another form more suitable as a position for a citadel. The Jews had, indeed, a strong inducement to level it in the fact that from that point, so soon as it fell into the hands of a hostile power, the temple mount would immediately be placed in extremest peril. This only in the narrative is unhistorical, that Josephus makes the levelling to have taken place in the time of Simon. This, according to 1 Macc. xiv. 36, 37 and xv. 28, is quite impossible.

[11] 1 Macc. xiv. 4-7. Compare also the motive for the popular decree in 1 Macc. xiv. 33-37. In these two passages are gathered together what had already previously been told in connection with the story of the First Book of Maccabees. Compare on Beth-zur, 1 Macc. xi. 65 ff. ; on Joppa, xii. 33 f., xiii. 11 ; on Gazara and the citadel, xiii. 43-52.

[12] 1 Macc. xiv. 8-15.—On the severe proceedings of Simon against the apostates, Grätz, Bd. iii., 4 Aufl. p. 565, and Derenbourg, *Histoire*, p. 68 sq., refer to the statement in *Megillath Taanith*, § 15.

[13] See generally, 1 Macc. xiv. 25-49.

[14] Compare on the significance of the popular decree, Lucius, *Essenismus* (1881), pp. 86–88.—The family name of the dynasty is οἱ 'Ασαμωναίου παῖδες (Josephus, *Life*, i. ; *Antiq.* xx. 8. 11, xx. 10), τὸ 'Ασαμωναίων γένος (*Antiq.* xv. 11. 4), οἱ 'Ασαμωναῖοι (*Wars of the Jews*, ii. 16. 3, v. 4. 1), after the ancestor of the race 'Ασαμωναῖος (*Antiq.* xii. 6. 1, xiv. 16. 4, xvi. 7. 1), not mentioned in the First Book of Maccabees. In the Mishna, *Middoth* i. 6, they are called בני חשמונאי or בני חשמוני, the latter form in the Cambridge manuscript edited by Lowe. In the Targum of Jonathan on 1 Sam. ii. 4 they are בית חשמונאי. For other rabbinical passages, see Levy, *Chald. Wörterbuch und Neuhebr. Wörterbuch*, under the word חשמונאי.—Wellhausen, *Pharisäer und Sadducäer*, p. 94, Anm., had ventured the guess that Hasmon may have been the grandfather of Mattathias, and that in 1 Macc. ii. 1 *ben chashmon* may have stood in place of τοῦ Συμεών.

[15] 1 Macc. xiv. 27, 48, 49.

[16] Compare generally, 1 Macc. xiv. 24, xv. 15–24.—The First Book of Maccabees speaks as if the Romans had even previously, of their own accord, addressed a letter to the Jews about the renewal of the covenant (1 Macc. xiv. 16 ff.). This is scarcely historical.—According to 1 Macc. xiv. 24 compared with xiv. 25 ff., it must be assumed that the embassy had already gone away before the popular decree of 18th Elul of the Seleucid year 172, or September B.C. 141. This is hardly conceivable, since it did not return before the Seleucid year 174, or B.C. 139–138 (1 Macc. xv. 10. 15). Perhaps the author had by anticipation inserted the account of the starting of the embassy before that of the popular decree, because in consequence of the incorrect version of the popular decree (1 Macc. xiv. 40) he was led to regard it as the result of that embassy.—It is also to be observed that the list of states to which the Roman circular letter was addressed (1 Macc. xv. 16, 22, 23) corresponds exactly to the state of matters at that time. For all the little separate states and communes which are named alongside of the kings of Egypt, Syria, Pergamum, Cappadocia, and Parthia, were at that time, in fact, subject neither to the Romans nor to any of these kings.

[17] Valerius Maximus, i. 3. 2 : " Idem (viz. the praetor Hispalus) Judaeos, qui Sabazi Jovis cultu Romanos inficere mores conati erant, repetere domos suas coegit."

[18] 1 Macc. xiv. 1–3. Josephus, *Antiq.* xiii. 5. 11. Appian, *Syr.* c. 67. Justin, xxxvi. 1, xxxviii. 9. Eusebius, *Chronicon*, ed. Schoene, i. 255 sq. Syncellus, ed. Dindorf, i. 554.

[19] 1 Macc. xv. 1–9.

[20] 1 Macc. xv. 10–14. Josephus, *Antiq.* xiii. 7. 1–2.

[21] 1 Macc. xv. 37.

[22] Josephus, *Antiq.* xiii. 7. 2.—Compare also Appian, *Syr.* 68, and Strabo, xiv. 5. 2, p. 668.

[23] 1 Macc. xv. 25–36. Josephus, *Antiq.* xiii. 7. 2–3.

[24] 1 Macc. xv. 38–41. Josephus, *Antiq.* xiii. 7. 3.

[25] 1 Macc. xvi. 1–10. Josephus, *l.c.*

[26] 1 Macc. xvi. 11–17 ; Josephus, *Antiq.* xiii. 7. 4.—Δώκ, 1 Macc. xvi. 15, is in any case identical with the Δαγών of Josephus, *Antiq.* xiii. 8. 1 ; *Wars of the Jews*, i. 2. 3. The name is still retained in that of the fountain *Ain ed-Duk*, north of Jericho, on the border of the mountain land, in a position very suitable as the site of a fortress.

§ 8. JOHN HYRCANUS I., B.C. 135–105.[1]

1 On the chronology of the Asmoneans the following statement may be made once for all. Josephus gives as the period of the reigns of the princes from John Hyrcanus I. to Alexandra inclusive the following dates :—

John Hyrcanus,	.	.	.	31 years (*Antiq.* xiii. 10. 7).
Aristobulus,	.	.	.	1 „ (*Antiq.* xiii. 11. 3).
Alexander Jannäus,	.	.	27 „	(*Antiq.* xiii. 15. 5).
Alexandra,	.	.	.	9 „ (*Antiq.* xiii. 16. 6).

These dates are also given by Josephus in two other places : *Antiq.* xx. 10, and *Wars of the Jews*, i. 2–5. Only in regard to Hyrcanus do these accounts vary. In *Antiq.* xx. 10 he is assigned thirty years, and in *Wars of the Jews*, i. 2. 8, it is given as thirty-three. The latter is probably erroneous, and like much else in the *Wars of the Jews* is corrected in the later production of the *Antiquities*. The discrepancy in the *Antiquities* itself, however, is only apparent, for Hyrcanus reigned between thirty and thirty-one years.

The following points are well established : 1. The death of Simon in the month Shebat of the Seleucid year 177, or in February B.C. 135 (1 Macc. xvi. 14) ; and 2. The beginning of the war between the brothers Aristobulus II. and Hyrcanus II., immediately after the death of Alexandra, according to Josephus, *Antiq.* xiv. 1. 2, in the third year of the 177th Olympiad, that is, in the summer B.C. 70–69, and during the consulate of Q. Hortensius and Q. Metellus Creticus. These were consuls in B.C. 69. The beginning of that war of the brothers, and consequently also the death of Alexandra, occurred therefore in the first half of B.C. 69. This is confirmed by *Antiq.* xiii. 16. 4, *Wars of the Jews* i. 5. 3, according to which Alexandra survived the attack of Lucullus on the Armenian empire, which took place in B.C. 69.—From the death of Simon to the death of Alexandra, B.C. 135–B.C. 69, is thus a period of sixty-six years, while by adding the numbers given by Josephus we obtain sixty-eight. Josephus has therefore also reckoned the current year as if it were complete. If we take this into consideration, the two statements will be found thoroughly to agree, and we obtain the following dates :—

John Hyrcanus,	.	.	.	.	.	B.C. 135–105.
Aristobulus,	.	.	.	.	.	„ 105–104.
Alexander Jannäus,	.	.	.	.	„ 104–78.
Alexandra,	.	.	.	.	.	„ 78–69.

[1] It is an error on the part of Josephus, *Antiq.* xiii. 8. 2, to fix the first year of John Hyrcanus in the 162nd Olympiad, that is, in a summer during the period B.C. 132–128.

[2] Eusebius and others explain the surname Hyrcanus by saying that John had conquered the Hyrcanians (Eusebius, *Chron.*, ed. Schoene, ii. 130 sq.; in Greek, in Syncellus, i. 548 : Ὑρκανοὺς νικήσας Ὑρκανὸς ὠνομάσθη ; in Latin, in Jerome : *adversum Hyrcanos bellum gerens Hyrcani nomen accepit;* and also Sulpicius Severus, ii. 26 : *qui cum adversum Hyrcanos, gentem validissimam, egregie pugnasset, Hyrcani cognomen accepit*). In favour of his explanation the fact may be adduced that John actually did take part in the campaign of Antiochus VII. Sidetes against the Parthians. But it falls to pieces over the fact that the name Hyrcanus had been in use in Jewish circles long before the time of John Hyrcanus (Josephus, *Antiq.* xii. 4. 6–11 ; 2 Macc. iii. 11). It may conceivably be explained according to the analogy of יַדּוּעַ הַבַּבְלִי, *Baba mezia* vii. 7 ; נָחוּם הַמָּדִי, *Schabbath* ii. 1 ; *Nasir* v. 4 ; *Baba bathra* v. 2. The Jews were transported by Artaxerxes Ochus to Hyrcania (see Div. ii. vol. ii. p. 223). A Jew belonging to a family settled there, who had gone back again to Palestine, would at first be distinguished by the personal designation ὁ Ὑρκανός. And thus the name would come to be a distinctive designation of the family.

[3] 1 Macc. xvi. 19–22. Josephus, *Antiq.* xiii. 7. 4.

[4] Josephus, *Antiq.* xiii. 8. 1 ; *Wars of the Jews,* i. 2. 3–4.

[5] Josephus, *Antiq.* xiii. 8. 2–3. Diodorus, xxxiv. 1, ed. Müller. Porphyry in Eusebius, *Chronicon,* ed. Schoene, i. 255. Justin, xxxvi. 1. Hyrcanus obtained the demanded sum by extracting three thousand talents from the sepulchre of David. So says Josephus, *Antiq.* vii. 15. 3, whereas in *Antiq.* xiii. 8. 4 he merely says that Hyrcanus applied the money thus taken to the payment of his soldiers. Compare on the sepulchre of David, Neh. iii. 16 ; Josephus, *Antiq.* xvi. 7. 1 ; Acts ii. 29. According to Neh. iii. 15, 16, it lay in the south of the city, not far from Siloah.

[6] Josephus, *Antiq.* xiii. 8. 4, with reference to Nicolaus Damascenus.

[7] On the campaign and death of Antiochus, compare Justin, xxxviii. 10, xxxix. 1 ; Diodorus, xxxiv. 15–17, ed. Müller ; Livy, *Epit.* 59 ; Appian, *Syr.* 68 ; Josephus, *Antiq.* xiii. 8. 4 ; Porphyry in Eusebius, *Chronicon,* ed. Schoene, i. 255.

[8] Medaba is a well-known town on the east side of the Jordan, south of Heshbon, and its name and ruins are preserved to this day. It is the Old Testament מֵידְבָא, Num. xxi. 30 ; Josh. xiii. 9, 16 ; Isa. xv. 2 ; 1 Chron. xix. 7. Compare 1 Macc. ix. 36 ; Josephus, *Antiq.* xiii. 1. 2, xiii. 15. 4, xiv. 1. 4 ; Ptolemy, v. 17. 6, viii. 20. 20 ; Stephen of Byzantium on the name ; Mishna, *Mikwaoth* vii. 1 ; Eusebius, *Onomasticon,* ed. Lagarde, p. 279.

[9] Josephus, *Antiq.* xiii. 9. 1 ; *Wars of the Jews,* i. 2. 6 ; compare *Antiq.* xv. 7. 9.—Adora is the modern Dura, west of Hebron.

On Marissa, see above, page 35 (on 1 Macc. v. 66).—In consequence of
the Judaizing by John Hyrcanus, the Idumeans came by and by to regard
themselves as Jews (*Wars of the Jews*, iv. 4. 4). The Jewish aristocracy
would only have them treated as ἡμιιουδαῖοι, and so considered even the
Idumean Herod as not equal to them in birth (*Antiq.* xiv. 15. 2 : 'Ηρώδη
. . . ἰδιώτῃ τε ὄντι καὶ 'Ιδουμαίῳ τουτέστιν ἡμιιουδαίῳ).

[10] Josephus, *Antiq.* xiii. 8. 4.

[11] The former according to Justin, xxxix. 1 ; the latter according to
Porphyry in Eusebius, *Chronicon*, ed. Schoene, i. 257 sq.

[12] Josephus, *Antiq.* xiii. 9. 3 ; Justin, xxxix. 1 ; Porphyry in Eusebius,
Chronicon, ed. Schoene, i. 257 sq.

[13] Josephus, *Antiq.* xxxiii. 9 3.

[14] Justin, xxxix. 2. 9 :

[15] Porphyry in Eusebius, *Chronicon*, ed. Schoene, i. 260; Josephus,
Antiq. xiii. 10. 1 ; Justin, xxxix. 2–3 ; Appian, *Syr.* 69.

[16] Diodorus, xxxiv. 34, ed. Müller .

[17] Josephus, *Antiq.* xiii. 10. 1 :

[18] Josephus, *Antiq.* xiii. 10. 2–3 ; *Wars of the Jews*, i. 2. 7. According
to the statement of the *Wars of the Jews*, Scythopolis was not surrendered
to the Jews by treachery, but was conquered by them. Compare on this
important city, Div. ii. vol. i. p. 110.—The day of the conquest of Samaria
was, according to *Megillath Taanith*, the 25th Marcheschwan, or November.
See Grätz, iii., 4 Aufl. p. 566 ; Derenbourg, *Histoire*, p. 72 sq. The year
may be approximately fixed from this, that, on the one hand, Antiochus
Cyzicenos was already in undisturbed possession of Coele-Syria, which
began with B.C. 111; and, on the other hand, Ptolemy Lathurus was still
co-regent with his mother Cleopatra, which lasted till B.C. 107. The
conquest of Samaria therefore falls between B.C. 111 and B.C. 107, probably
not long before B.C. 107, for Cleopatra was so enraged at Ptolemy for
affording assistance to Antiochus, that she had "almost already" driven
him out of the government. So Josephus, *Antiq.* xiii. 10. 2 .

[19] Josephus, *Antiq.* xiii. 10. 3. The rabbinical passages in Derenbourg,
p. 74.

[20] Josephus tells the story first of all in connection with the times
of Jonathan, *Antiq.* xiii. 5. 9.

[21] Josephus says in regard thereto, *Antiq.* xiii. 10. 5 : μαθητὴς δ' αὐτῶν
καὶ 'Υρκανὸς ἐγεγόνει καὶ σφόδρα ὑπ' αὐτῶν ἠγαπᾶτο.

[22] Josephus, *Antiq.* xiii. 10. 5–6. The rabbinical tradition is given in
Grätz. iii., 4 Aufl. 684 ff. (note 11) ; Derenbourg, pp. 79, 80 .

[23] Josephus, *Antiq.* xiii. 16. 2.

[24] *Maaser sheni* v. 15 = *Sota* ix. 10 : "Jochanan the high priest
abolished the confession for the time of tithing. He also abolished the
singing of the verse 'Awake' (Ps. xliv. 23), and the inflicting a wound on
the sacrificial victim. Also down to his time on the days between the
festival seasons was the hammer in use in Jerusalem. Finally, in his

days men were not wont to ask about Demai, *i.e.* not to ask whether
tithes had been paid on bought corn."
—For the confession at the tithing, see Deut. xxvi. 12–15 ; Josephus,
Antiq. iv. 8. 22 ; Mishna, *Maaser sheni* v. 6–15 ; Hottinger, *De decimis
Judaeorum* (1713), pp. 204–227. It may also be mentioned that in *Para*
iii. 5, Jochanan is named as one of those high priests in whose time a red
heifer was burnt, according to the law of Num. xix.

    25 Josephus, *Antiq.* xiii. 10. 7.
    26 Josephus, *Wars of the Jews,* v. 6. 2, 7. 3, 9. 2, 11. 4 ; vi. 2. 10.

§ 9. ARISTOBULUS I., B.C. 105–104.

    1 Josephus, *Antiq.* xiii. 10. 7.
    2 Josephus, *Antiq.* xiii. 11. 1 : ἐκείνην γὰρ Ὑρκανὸς τῶν ὅλων κυρίαν
καταλελοίπει. So, too, *Wars of the Jews,* i. 3. 1.
    3 Josephus, *Antiq.* xiii. 11. 1 ; *Wars of the Jews,* i. 3. 1. On the chrono-
logy, see above, page 326[1].
    4 Josephus, *Antiq.* xiii. 11. 1–3 ; *Wars of the Jews,* i. 3. 1–6.
    5 Josephus, *Antiq.* xiii. 11. 1 ; *Wars of the Jews,* i. 3. 1.—Strabo, xvi.
2. 40, p. 762, tells this of Alexander Jannäus, because he overlooked the
short reign of Aristobulus.
    6 Josephus, *Antiq.* xiii. 11. 3.
    7 Josephus, *Antiq.* xx. 10 : Ἰούδᾳ τῷ καὶ Ἀριστοβούλῳ κληθέντι. On the
coins which de Saulcy originally ascribed to Judas Maccabaeus, see de
Saulcy, *Recherches,* p. 84. Cavedoni, *Bibl. Numismatik,* ii. 18 f. Levy,
Gesch. der jüd. Münzen, pp. 53 – 55. Madden, *History,* pp. 61 – 63.
    8 Josephus, *Antiq.* xiii. 11. 3.
    9 The fact that the districts north and east of Galilee were predomi-
nantly Gentile down to the time of the Herodians is in favour of this view.
They could not therefore have been previously judaized by Aristobulus.
But then the portion judaized by Aristobulus could scarcely have been
any other than Galilee itself. That Josephus does not give it the usual
territorial designation of Galilee, is explained by his making use of non-
Jewish documents.—A more serious difficulty is presented by the fact that
John Hyrcanus had his son, Alexander Jannäus, brought up in Galilee
(*Antiq.* xiii. 12. 1). But perhaps it should be said in this case that
Hyrcanus had his son, whom he wished to prevent from succeeding to the
throne, brought up outside of the country. It is also possible that
Hyrcanus had already taken possession of the southern parts of Galilee.
Then what is told above would refer only to the northern division. The
statement about Alexander's education in Galilee is, owing to the connec-
tion in which it occurs, open to considerable suspicion.
    10 Josephus, *Antiq.* xiii. 11. 3 ; *Wars of the Jews,* i. 3. 6.
    11 Strabo in the name of Timagenes, according to Josephus, *Antiq.* xiii.
11. 3 : ἐπιεικής τε ἐγένετο οὗτος ὁ ἀνὴρ καὶ πολλὰ τοῖς Ἰουδαίοις χρήσιμος.

§ 10. ALEXANDER JANNÄUS, B.C. 104–78.

[1] Josephus, *Antiq.* xiii. 12. 1 ; *Wars of the Jews*, i. 4. 1.

[2] This last statement is nowhere expressly made. But when Josephus names Salome Alexandra as the wife of Aristobulus (*Antiq.* xiii. 12. 1), both which names are borne by the wife of Alexander Jannäus, the identity is placed almost beyond doubt.

[3] On the chronology, see above, p. 326 [1]

[4] Josephus, *Antiq.* xiii. 12. 2–4.

[5] Asochis is often referred to by Josephus in his *Life*, 41, 45, 68. It lay near Sepphoris (*Antiq.* xiii. 12. 5 : μιxρὸν ἄπωθεν ; *Life*, 45 : παρὰ δὲ Σεπφωριτῶν εἰς ’Ασωχὶν xαταβάντες), and on the plain (*Life*, 41, 45), and so undoubtedly in the modern valley *el-Battôf*.

[6] ’Ασωφών, not otherwise known. Perhaps the same as עֲפֹן of Josh. xiii. 27.

[7] Josephus, *Antiq.* xiii. 12. 4–5.

[8] Josephus, *Antiq.* xiii. 13. 1–3.

[9] Gadara, which is well known from the Gospel history, lies south-east of the lake of Gennesareth, then an important Hellenistic city.

[10] Josephus, *Antiq.* xiii. 13. 3.

[11] Josephus, *Antiq.* xiii. 13. 3 ; *Wars of the Jews*, 1. 4. 2.

[12] Josephus, *Antiq.* xiii. 13. 4.

[13] See Derenbourg, pp. 96–98, especially upon *Bereshith rabba*, c. 91. Compare also Grätz, iii., 4 Aufl. pp. 127, 703 f. (note 13).

[14] Josephus, *Antiq.* xiii. 13. 5 ; *Wars of the Jews*, i. 4. 3.—In the Talmud (*Sukka* 48b) it is related that once a Sadducee poured out the usual libation of water, not on the altar, but on the earth, on account of which the people pelted him with citrons. Alexander's name is not mentioned. Possibly he is intended. But "the narrative of Josephus is not improved by inserting its Talmudic re-echo as giving the motive for the action of the people" (Wellhausen, *Pharisäer und Sadducäer*, p. 96). So Grätz, iii., 4 Aufl. pp. 128 f., 704 f. (note 13). Derenbourg, p. 98 sq. note.

[15] So Josephus, *Antiq.* xiii. 13. 5. According to the *Wars of the Jews*, i. 4. 4, it was at Gaulana, the ancient גּוֹלָן, east of the lake of Gennesareth.

[16] Josephus, *Antiq.* xiii. 13. 5 ; *Wars of the Jews*, i. 4. 3–4.

[17] Josephus, *Antiq.* xiii. 14. 1–2 ; *Wars of the Jews*, i. 4. 4–5.

[18] The former according to *Antiq.* xiii. 14. 2 ; the latter according to *Wars of the Jews*, i. 4. 6. Neither of the two is capable of demonstration.

[19] Josephus, *Antiq.* xiii. 14. 2 ; *Wars of the Jews*, i. 4. 5–6.

[20] Josephus, *Antiq.* xiii. 15. 1 ; *Wars of the Jews*, i. 4. 7.—Capharsaba (כפר סבא), now called *Kefr Saba*, north-east of Joppa, was afterwards called Antipatris.

[21] Josephus, *Antiq.* xiii. 15. 2 ; *Wars of the Jews*, i. 4. 8.—On Adida, see

above, p. 322,[33] and 1 Macc. xii. 38. It lay east of Lydda, and commanded the road from Joppa to Jerusalem.

[22] Josephus, *Antiq.* xiii. 15. 3 ; *Wars of the Jews*, i. 4. 8.—The places named all lie east of the Jordan. On Pella, Dium, and Gerasa, see Div. ii. vol. i. pp. 113–119 ; Josephus in the *Wars of the Jews* names only Pella and Gerasa, in the *Antiquities* only Dium and Essa, the latter certainly a corruption of the text for Gerasa, since the facts given in reference to both places are clearly identical. — Gaulana is the ancient גּוֹלָן, east of the Lake of Gennesareth, from which the province of Gaulanitis takes its name (Deut. iv. 43 ; Josh. xx. 8, xxi. 27 ; 1 Chron. vi. 56). It was even in the days of Eusebius a large village (*Onomasticon*, ed. Lagarde, p. 242 : καὶ νῦν Γαυλὼν καλεῖται κώμη μηγίστη ἐν τῇ Βαταναίᾳ). But its situation is nc longer discoverable.—Seleucia is also often referred to by Josephus in the history of the Jewish war (*Wars of the Jews*, ii. 20. 6, iv. i. 1 ; *Life*, 37). According to the *Wars of the Jews*, iv. 1. 1, it lay on the Lake Seme-chonitis, or Lake Merom, therefore in the extreme north of Palestine.— On Gamala, the conquest of which by Vespasian is related in detail by Josephus in *Wars of the Jews*, iv. 1, see § 20.

[23] Josephus, *Antiq.* xiii. 15. 5 ; *Wars of the Jews*, i. 4. 8.—Ragaba lay, according to Josephus, in the district of Gerasa, ἐν τοῖς Γεραϲηνῶν ὅροις, therefore east of the Jordan. It can be identified with רְגַב in Perea, mentioned in the Mishna, *Menachoth* viii. 3, which produced valuable oil.

[24] Josephus, *Antiq.* xiii. 16. 1. The monument to Alexander is referred to by Josephus in *Wars of the Jews*, v. 7. 3.

[25] Josephus, *Antiq.* xiii. 15. 4, expressly mentions as then in the posession of the Jews : Rhinocorura, south of Raphia on the Egyptian coast, Raphia, Gaza, Anthedon, Azotus, Jamnia, Joppa, Apollonia, Straton's Tower ; see Div. ii. vol. i. pp. 66–87. But Dora also must have belonged to the domain of Alexander ; for Straton's Tower and Dora had previously belonged to a tyrant Zoilus, who had been subdued by Alexander (*Antiq.* xiii. 12. 2 and 4). On the other hand, it is not by accident that Ascalon is wanting. It was from B.C. 104 an independent city, as the era used by it and the acknowledgment of its freedom by the Romans prove ; see Div. ii. vol. i. p. 74.

[26] Josephus, in *Antiq.* xiii. 15. 4, gives a summary sketch of the extent of the Jewish territory at the death of Alexander. Compare in addition, Tuch, *Quaestiones de Flavii Josephi libris historicis*, Lips. 1859, pp. 12–19. See also for further particulars the list of places taken by the Arabs in *Antiq.* xiv. 1. 4, *fin.*

[27] This is expressly stated in regard at least to Pella, *Antiq.* xiii. 15. 4 : ταύτην δὲ κατέσκαψαν, οὐχ ὑποσχομένων τῶν ἐνοικούντων εἰς τὰ πάτρια τῶν Ἰουδαίων ἔθη μεταβαλέσθαι.—The fact that such destruction was executed is told in regard to many other cities, or it may be deduced from this, that Pompey and Gabinius had them built again (*Antiq.* xiv. 4. 4, v. 3 ;

Wars of the Jews, i. 7. 7, 8. 4.   See especially, *Antiq.* xiv. 5. 3 : τὰς πόλεις πολὺν χρόνον ἐρήμους γενομένας).

§ 11. ALEXANDRA, B.C. 78-69.

[1] Josephus, *Antiq.* xvi. 1–2 ; *Wars of the Jews*, i. 5. 1.—Only a couple of coins of Alexandra's are known, bearing the inscription ΒΑΣΙΛΙΣ. ΑΛΕΞΑΝΔ.

[2] On the chronology, see above, p. 326,[1]—On the Hebrew name, see especially Derenbourg, p. 102, for the rabbinical tradition. In Eusebius, *Chronicon ad annum Abr.* 1941, she is called *Alexandra quae et Salina.* In accordance with this see the Armenian translation and Jerome ; see Eusebius, *Chronicon,* ed. Schoene, ii. 134, 135. So, too, the imitators and continuators of Eusebius, *Chronicon paschale,* ed. Dindorf, i. 351 ('Αλεξ-άνδρας τῆς Σαλίνας). Syncellus, ed. Dindorf, i. 559 (Σαλίνα ἡ καὶ 'Αλεξάνδρα). Accordingly, in Eusebius, *Chronicon,* ed. Schoene, i. 130, instead of the Σααλίνα of the common text, we should read, not Σαλλίνα, with Gutschmid, but Σαλίνα. Compare also Jerome, comment. on Daniel ix. 24 sqq. (*Opp.* ed. Vallarsi, v. 687) : *Alexandra quae et Salina vocabatur.* Jerome there translates Eusebius, *Demonstr. evangel.* viii. 2 ; but just where these words occur our Greek text is defective.—Josephus calls her only Alexandra.   See further, above, p. 82 .

[3] Josephus, *Antiq.* xiii. 15. 5.—According to the Talmud, *Sota* 22*b*, in Derenbourg, p. 101, he is said to have given this advice : " Fear neither the Pharisees nor their opponents, but fear the hypocrites who pretend to be Pharisees, whose deeds are those of Zimri, and who claim a reward like that of Phinehas."

[4] Josephus, *Antiq.* xiii. 16. 2 :   Compare also *Wars of the Jews*, i. 5. 2.

[5] Passages in *Megillath Taanith* are § 1, 2, 10, 19, 24.   In addition, see Grätz, *Geschichte der Juden,* Bd. iii., 4 Aufl. pp. 567–572 (note 1). Derenbourg, p. 102 sq.   For criticism, consult Wellhausen, *Die Pharisäer und die Sadducäer,* pp. 56–63.

[6] *M. Sanhedrin* vi. 4.—Derenbourg, at p. 69, refers this to Simon the Maccabee ; but there is opposition thereto.   On p. 106 he attributes it to Simon ben Shetach.   Compare also Jost, *Geschichte des Judenthums,* i. 242. Grätz, *Geschichte der Juden,* iii. 146 f.—Ascalon did not indeed belong to the Jewish territory.   See above, p. 90.

[7] Josephus, *Antiq.* xiii. 16. 2–3 ; *Wars of the Jews*, i. 5. 3.

[8] Josephus, *Antiq.* xiii. 16. 2 and 6 ; *Wars of the Jews*, i. 5. 2.

[9] Josephus, *Antiq.* xiii. 16. 3 ; *Wars of the Jews*, i. 5. 3.

[10] Josephus, *Antiq.* xiii. 16. 4 ; *Wars of the Jews*, i. 5. 3.

[11] *Taanith* 23*a*, in Derenbourg, p. 111.

[12] Josephus, *Antiq.* xiii. 16. 5–6 ; *Wars of the Jews*, i. 5. 4.—The death of Alexandra occurred in the first half of the year B.C. 69.

§ 12. ARISTOBULUS II., B.C. 69-63.

[1] Josephus, *Antiq.* xiii. 16. 2, xiv. 1. 3, 3. 2.

[2] Josephus, *Antiq.* xiv. 1. 2 ; *Wars of the Jews,* i. 6. 1.—According to *Antiq.* xv. 6. 4, the reign of Hyrcanus lasted for three months

[3] In regard to the descent of the family, the most contradictory reports have come down to us. According to Nicolas of Damascus in Josephus, *Antiq.* xiv. 1. 3, Antipater is said to be a descendant of the first Jews who returned from Babylon. Since this statement is in contradiction to all other early documents, Josephus is certainly right in treating it as a piece of flattery to Herod on the part of Nicolas of Damascus (*l.c. : ταῦτα.δὲ λέγει χαριζόμενος Ἡρώδῃ*). According to Josephus, Antipater was an Idumean of an honourable family (*Wars of the Jews,* i. 6. 2 : *γένος δ᾽ ἦν Ἰδουμαῖος, προγόνων τε ἕνεκα καὶ πλούτου καὶ τῆς ἄλλης ἰσχύος πρωτεύων τοῦ ἔθνους*). Justin Martyr gives it as a report current among the Jews that he was an Ascalonite (*Dialogue with Trypho,* c. 52 : *Ἡρώδην Ἀσκαλωνίτην γεγονέναι*). And that statement also occurs in Julius Africanus in the more definite shape, that Antipater's father, Herod, had been a temple attendant of Apollo at Ascalon, and that Antipater, as a boy, had been carried off by the Idumeans when they robbed the temple of Apollo, and thus grew up among the Idumean robbers as one of themselves (Julius Africanus, *Epist. ad Aristidem,* in Eusebius' *Hist. Eccles.* i. 7. 11 ; compare i. 6. 2-3 ; also in the *Chronicle* of Julius Africanus, cited by Syncellus, ed. Dindorf, i. 561). The following copy these stories from Julius Africanus : Eusebius, *Chronicon,* ed. Schoene, i. 130, ii. 134, 138 ; *Chronicon paschale,* ed. Dindorf, i. 351, 358 ; Sulpicius Severus, ii. 26 ; Epiphanius, *Haer.* xx. 1, and other Christian writers. Josephus and Julius Africanus are fundamentally agreed as to his Idumean extraction ; only that it was according to Josephus a distinguished one, according to Julius Africanus a mean one,—he distinctly emphasizes his poverty. Josephus calls Antipater's father also Antipater ; Julius Africanus calls him Herod. In favour of his Ascalon descent are certain allusions of Herod to that city ; see Div. ii. vol. i. p. 76. It is further well deserving remark that the names of Antipater and Herod were once to be met with in Ascalon. An Antipatros of Ascalon figures on a tombstone at Athens, *Corpus Inscript. Semit.* t. i. n. 115 ; a Herod of Ascalon on a tombstone at Puteoli, *Corpus Inscript. Lat.* t. x. n. 1746. But for the rest, the story told by Julius Africanus reveals such bitter hatred, that we can scarcely get rid of the suspicion of Jewish or Christian prejudice. As Julius Africanus refers in support of the story to the *συγγενεῖς* of Jesus Christ (Eusebius, *Hist. Eccles.* i. 7. 11 : *τοῦ γοῦν σωτῆρος οἱ κατὰ σάρκα συγγενεῖς . . . παρέδοσαν καὶ ταῦτα* ; compare i. 7. 14 : *οἱ προειρημένοι δεσπόσυνοι καλούμενοι διὰ τὴν πρὸς τὸ σωτήριον γένος συνάφειαν*), it would seem to be derived from a Christian source.

[4] Josephus, *Antiq.* xiv. 1. 3–4 ; *Wars of the Jews*, i. 6. 2.

[5] Josephus, *Antiq.* xiv. 2. 1.   The story of the hearing of the prayer of Onias when he once prayed for rain is very vividly depicted in the Mishna, *Taanith* iii. 8.   He is there called חוֹנִי הַמְעַגֵּל (מעגל meaning properly the "circle diviner," because he prayed standing in a circle). Compare also Derenbourg, p. 112 sq.

[6] It must have been the Passover of the year B.C. 65, for immediately afterwards Scaurus arrived in Judea.

[7] Josephus, *Antiq.* xiv. 2. 2. — Compare the rabbinical traditions in Derenbourg, p. 113 sq.

[8] Josephus, *Antiq.* xiv. 2. 3 ; *Wars of the Jews.* i. 6. 2–3.

[9] Josephus, *Antiq.* xiv. 3. 1.

[10] According to Dio Cassius, xxxvii. 7, Pompey passed the winter in the town of Aspis, the situation of which is not known.

[11] *E.g.*,Silas, a Jew;   *Antiq.* xiv. 3. 2.   See Reinach, *Actes et conférences de la société des études juives*, 1887, p. cxcvi. sq. ; *Les Monnaies juives*, p. 28 sq. For the coins, see also Babelon, *Monnaies de la république romaine*, t. ii. 1886, p. 324 sq. The theory of the Duc de Luynes, that Bacchius is the Hebrew name of Aristobulus II. (*Revue numismatique*, 1858, p. 384), is absolutely impossible. Reinach thinks he might rather be identified with that Dionysius of Tripoli mentioned by Josephus in *Antiq.* xiv. 3. 2.

[12] Josephus, *Antiq.* xiv. 3. 2.   The order of march here given is an absurdity.   Pella is either an interpolation, as Hitzig, p. 496, thinks, or a textual error for Abila.   Still it is to be noted that the golden vine of Aristobulus was first brought to Pompey in Damascus (*Antiq.* xiv. 3. 1). Josephus indeed tells about it before he relates the previous march of Pompey by Heliopolis and Chalcis to Damascus, which would naturally make it seem as if Pompey had gone twice to Damascus, in B.C. 64 and B.C. 63.   But evidently the affair is to explained thus : that Josephus derived the story of the golden vine from another source, and did not place it in quite the right setting in relation to the main narrative.

[13] Josephus, *Antiq.* xiv. 3. 2.   Diodorus, xl. 2nd ed., Müller.

[14] Josephus, *Antiq.* xiv. 3. 3.

[15] On the situation of Corea, see Gildemeister, *Zeitschrift des deutschen Palästina-Vereins*, iv. 1881, p. 245 f. Also Grätz's criticism of this in *Monatschrift für Geschichte und Wissenschaft des Judenthums*, 1882, pp. 14–17. Gildemeister rightly identifies it with the Karawa of to-day in Wadi Faria in the valley of the Jordan, scarcely two hours' journey north from Mount Sartaba. The neighbouring fortress of Alexandrium must therefore just have been Mount Sartaba. Pompey thus marched from Scythopolis, in the Jordan valley, directly south to Jericho. In this way the marking of the route of march in Menke's *Bibelatlas*, resting on the older hypothesis, is to be vindicated as quite correct.

[16] Josephus, *Antiq.* xiv. 3. 3–4 ; *Wars of the Jews*, i. 6. 4–5.

17 Josephus, *Antiq.* xiv. 4. 1 ; *Wars of the Jews*, i. 6. 6–7. 1. Pompey's camp is also referred to in *Wars of the Jews*, v. 12. 2.

18 Josephus, *Antiq.* xiv. 4. 2 ; *Wars of the Jews*, i. 7. 2.

19 Josephus, *Antiq.* xiv. 4. 2–4 ; *Wars of the Jews*, i. 7. 3–5. Dio Cassius, xxxvii. 16. In general matters, also Strabo, xvi. 2. 40, p. 762 sq Livy, *Epitome*, 102. Tacitus, *Hist.* v. 9. Appian, *Syr.* 50 ; *Mithridates*, 106. The day of atonement : τῇ τῆς νηστείας ἡμέρᾳ, *Antiq.* xiv. 4. 3. The Sabbath : ἐν τῇ τοῦ Κρόνου ἡμέρᾳ, Dio Cassius, xxxvii. 16. Compare Strabo, *l.c.* The day of atonement falls upon the 10th Tishri, or October. That Josephus means this by the term "Fast day," is rendered quite certain when we consider the use of the word among the Jews. See Acts of Apostles, xxvii. 9. Josephus, *Antiq.* xvii. 6. 4. Philo, *Vita Mosis*, lib. ii. § 4 ; *de victimis*, § 3 ; *de septenario*, § 23 [the principal passage] ; *legat. ad Cajum*, § 39 (ed. Mangey, ii. 138, 239, 296, 591). Mishna, *Menachoth* xi. *fin.*—The third month, περὶ τρίτον μῆνα, *Antiq.* xiv. 4. 3, is not the third month of the year, either Jewish or Greek, but the third month of the siege, as Josephus expressly says, *Wars of the Jews*, i. 7. 4 : τρίτῳ γὰρ μηνὶ τῆς πολιορκίας ; *Wars of the Jews*, v. 9. 4 : τρισὶ γοῦν μησὶ πολιορκηθέντες.

20 Josephus, *Antiq.* xiv. 4. 4 ; *Wars of the Jews*, i. 7. 6.—Compare Cicero, *Pro Flacco*, 67 : *Cn. Pompeius captis Hierosolymis victor ex illo fano nihil attigit.*

21 Compare on these cities and their condition under the Romans, § 23, I. Div. ii. vol. i. pp. 57–149. The list in Josephus, *Antiq.* xiv. 4. 4 ; *Wars of the Jews*, i. 7. 7, is not complete. He mentions only the most important. Undoubtedly not only did all the coast towns lose their freedom, but also all those towns on the east of the Jordan which afterwards formed the so-called Decapolis. For in almost all the towns of Decapolis coins have been found upon which the Pompeian era is used.

22 Josephus, *Antiq.* xiv. 4. 4 ; *Wars of the Jews*, i. 7. 6–7. Compare *Antiq.* xx. 10 .

23 Josephus, *Antiq.* xiv. 4. 5 ; *Wars of the Jews*, i. 7. 7.

24 Compare the description of the triumph in Plutarch, *Pompeius*, 45 ; Appian, *Mithridates*, 117. Appian conjectures wrongly that Aristobulus had been put to death after the triumph, for this did not take place until B.C. 49. See the following section.

25 Compare Philo, *De legatione ad Cajum*, § 23 .

§ 13. HYRCANUS II., B.C. 63–40. REBELLION OF ANTIPATER AND HIS SONS PHASAEL AND HEROD.

1 Josephus, *Antiq.* xiv. 5. 1 ; *Wars of the Jews*, i. 8. 1. Appian, *Syr.* 51.
2 On the Alexandrium, see p. 98. The position of Hyrcania is unknown. Machaerus, now called *Mkaur*, lay to the east of the Dead Sea.

[3] Josephus, *Antiq.* xiv. 5. 2–4 ; *Wars of the Jews*, i. 8. 2–5.

[4] Josephus, *Antiq.* xiv. 5. 4 ; *Wars of the Jews*, i. 8. 5.—About Amathus, in the country east of the Jordan, see above, p. 84. On Sepphoris in Galilee, see Div. ii. vol. i. pp. 136–141. The other three towns were situated in Judea proper. On Gazara, see above, p. 60. Josephus, *Antiq.* xiv. 5. 4 ; *Wars of the Jews*, i. 8. 5, has also the form Gadara. But by this it is quite evident he does not mean the Hellenistic Gadara in Peraea, which had a population mainly pagan, and had been separated from the Jewish territory by Pompey. We are to understand by it the Gazara Judaized by Simon the Maccabee, for which also elsewhere the form Gadara is found. So Josephus, *Antiq.* xii. 7. 4 and 1 Macc. iv. 15. Also in Strabo, xvi. 2. 29, p. 759, by Γαδαρὶς, ἣν καὶ αὐτὴν ἐξιδιάσαντο οἱ Ἰουδαῖοι, we are to understand the region of Gazara, which indeed he confounds with Gadara in Peraea ; for from this latter place were sprung the celebrated men who are referred to by him.

[5] On the erection of a province, the Romans were wont to divide the country into customs or taxation districts, each of which was grouped round one of the larger towns. The communal court of such a town was utilized by the Romans as a fiscal or customs court, for it had to make arrangements for collecting the taxes in its district. More extensive, as a rule, than these customs districts, were the juristic circuits (*conventus juridici*). For the purpose of deciding civil matters (only about these had it jurisdiction), a diet was held from time to time at a certain place, to which the depute judges of the circuit went, in order, under the presidency of the governor, to decide cases that had arisen since last session.

[6] Josephus, *Antiq.* xiv. 6. 1 ; *Wars of the Jews*, i. 8. 6. Dio Cassius, xxxix. 56. Plutarch, *Antony*, 3.

[7] Josephus, *Antiq.* xiv. 6. 2–3 ; *Wars of the Jews*, i. 8. 7.

[8] Josephus, *Antiq.* xiv. 7. 1 ; *Wars of the Jews*, i. 8. 8.

[9] Josephus, *Antiq.* xiv. 7. 3 ; *Wars of the Jews*, i. 8. 9.

[10] Josephus, *Antiq.* xiv. 7. 4 ; *Wars of the Jews*, i. 9. 1–2. That Caesar sent Aristobulus into Palestine is also reported by Dio Cassius, xli. 18.

[11] Antipater, even before Caesar's interference in the affairs of Palestine, is described as procurator of Judea. He is so described, not only by Josephus (*Antiq.* xiv. 8. 1 : ὁ τῶν Ἰουδαίων ἐπιμελητής), but also by Strabo, who refers again to Hypsicrates (Josephus, *Antiq.* xiv. 8. 3: τὸν τῆς Ἰουδαίας ἐπιμελητήν). Possibly he obtained this position through Gabinius, who, on account of Antipater's many services in the interest of Rome, "settled the affairs which belonged to the city Jerusalem in accordance with Antipater's inclinations" (*Antiq.* xiv. 6. 4 : καταστησάμενος δὲ Γαβίνιος τὰ κατὰ τὴν Ἱεροσολυμιτῶν πόλιν ὡς ἦν Ἀντιπάτρῳ θέλοντι. *Wars of the Jews*, i. 8. 7 : Γαβίνιος ἐλθὼν εἰς Ἱεροσόλυμα πρὸς τὸ Ἀντιπάτρου βούλημα κατεστήσατο τὴν πολιτείαν). Since this must have been an institution not in contradiction to the other ordinances of Gabinius, it may perhaps be assumed that to Antipater was made over the chief administration of the taxes in the

Jewish territory. For ἐπιμελητής is an administrative officer ; in its primary application, an officer of finance. Certainly Antipater cannot have been a political official in the service of Hyrcanus ; for Hyrcanus, since the passing of the measures of Gabinius, had no longer any political functions. If, then, he acted ἐξ ἐντολῆς Ὑρκανοῦ (*Antiq*. xiv. 8. 1), this is to be explained of the spiritual authority which Hyrcanus had as high priest (*Antiq*. xiv. 5. 1 : κατ᾽ ἐντολὴν Ὑρκανοῦ, belongs to a period when Hyrcanus had no longer any political power). On Antipater's services to the cause of Rome in the period B.C. 63-48, see Josephus, *Antiq*. xiv. 5. 1, 2, 6. 2, 3, 7. 3 ; *Wars of the Jews*, i. 8. 1, 3, 7, 9.

¹² *Bellum Alexandr.* c. 26.

¹³ Josephus, *Antiq*. xiv. 8. 1–3 ; *Wars of the Jews*, i. 9. 3-5.—In the decree of Caesar, *Antiq*. xiv. 10. 2, the number of the Jewish auxiliary troops is given only as 1500.

¹⁴ *Bellum Alexandrinum,* 65.

¹⁵ Josephus, *Antiq*. xiv. 8. 4 ; *Wars of the Jews*, i. 10. 1–2.

¹⁶ Josephus, *Antiq*. xiv. 8. 3 : Ὑοκανῷ μὲν τὴν ἀρχιερωσύνην βεβαιώσας, Ἀντιπάτρῳ δὲ πολιτείαν ἐν Ῥώμη δοὺς καὶ ἀτέλειαν πανταχοῦ. So, too, *Wars of the Jews*, i. 9. 5.

¹⁷ Josephus, *Antiq*. xiv. 8. 5 : Ὑρκανὸν μὲν ἀποδείκνυσιν ἀρχιερέα . . . [Ἀντίπατρον] ἐπίτροπον ἀποδείκνυσι τῆς Ἰουδαίας. Ἐπιτρέπει δὲ καὶ Ὑρκανῷ τὰ τῆς πατρίδος ἀναστῆσαι τείχη. Similarly, *Wars of the Jews*, i. 10. 3.—These enactments seem to be different from those referred to in the preceding note ; the concessions referred to in the one case having been granted before, and those in the other after the intervention of Antigonus.

¹⁸ In this document Caesar designates himself αὐτοκράτωρ καὶ ἀρχιερεύς, δικτάτωρ τὸ δεύτερον (*imperator et pontifex maximus dictator II.*). Caesar's second dictatorship extended from October 48 to the end of the year 46 (see Mommsen, *Corp. Inscr. Lat.* t. i. pp. 451-453). But since the title of consul is not in the formula, whereas Caesar held the consulship in the years 48, 46, 45, and 44, the document must be assigned to the year 47.

¹⁹ Josephus, *Antiq*. xiv. 10. 2 :

²⁰ The documents in Josephus, *Antiq*. xiv. 10. 3-4, contain scarcely anything else beyond the decree of Caesar of the year B.C. 47, as already given in *Antiq*. xiv. 10. 2. Since they belong to a year during which Caesar was consul, though the number of the consulship is wanting, the date must have been 46, 45, or 44.

²¹ Josephus, *Antiq*. xiv. 10. 6.—If it is correct that the beginning of *Antiq*. xiv. 10. 6 belongs to a decree of the year B.C. 47, a portion of the tribute of Joppa would have been assigned, even so early as that, to the Jews. It is uncertain who is intended by "the kings of Syria and Phoenicia confederate with the Romans" that had formerly possessed some of the territories now given over to the Jews. Probably they were princes to whom Pompey had gifted Jewish lands.

²² See Div. ii. vol. ii. p. 244.

[23] Josephus, *Antiq.* xiv. 10. 8 and 20–24.—The decrees there gathered together were not, indeed, directly issued by Caesar, but are, with a high degree of probability, to be attributed to his initiative. See also Div. ii. vol. ii. p. 225 f.

[24] Suetonius, *Caesar*, 84 : " In summo publico luctu exterarum gentium multitudo circulatim suo quaeque more lamentata est, *praecipueque Judaei*, qui etiam noctibus continuis bustum frequentarunt."

[25] Josephus, *Antiq.* xiv. 9. 2 ; *Wars of the Jews*, i. 10. 4.

[26] The traditional text of Josephus in *Antiq.* xiv. 9. 2 reads fifteen. The number twenty-five, which Dindorf and Bekker have put into the text, is purely conjectural. But this change is necessary : 1. Because a boy fifteen years old could not possibly have played the role which Herod had already played ; and 2. Because Herod at his death is represented to have been about seventy years of age ; *Antiq.* xvii. 6. 1 : καὶ γὰρ περὶ ἔτος ἑβδομηκοστὸν ἦν ; *Wars of the Jews*, i. 33. 1 : ἦν μὲν γὰρ ἤδη σχεδὸν ἐτῶν ἑβδομήκοντα.

[27] Josephus, *Antio.* xiv. 9. 2 ; *Wars of the Jews*, i. 10. 5.

[28] Josephus, *Antiq.* xiv. 9. 3–5 ; *Wars of the Jews*, i. 10. 6–9. The rabbinical tradition preserves the remembrance of the scene before the Sanhedrim. The names there given, however, are altogether different. Instead of Hyrcanus, Jannäus ; instead of Herod, a slave of Jannäus ; instead of Shemaiah, Simon ben Shetach. See Derenbourg, *Histoire de la Palestine*, pp. 146–148.

[29] Josephus, *Antiq.* xiv. 11. 1 ; *Wars of the Jews*, i. 10. 10.

[30] Josephus, *Antiq.* xiv. 11. 2 ; *Wars of the Jews*, i. 11. 1–2.

[31] Josephus, *Antiq.* xiv. 11. 4 ; *Wars of the Jews*, i. 11. 4.

[32] Josephus, *Antiq.* xiv. 11. 4 ; *Wars of the Jews*, i. 11. 4.

[33] Josephus, *Antiq.* xiv. 11. 6 ; *Wars of the Jews*, i. 11. 8.

[34] Josephus, *Antiq.* xiv. 12. 1 ; *Wars of the Jews*, i. 12. 2–3.—In the narrative of Josephus, which is based upon the statements of Nicolaus Damascenus, a veil is thrown over the circumstance that Herod could not prevent the conquests of the Tyrians. But he makes this clear from the subsequent letter of Antony, which ordered the Tyrians to restore the places that they had conquered .

[35] Josephus, *Antiq.* xiv. 12. 2 ; *Wars of the Jews*, i. 12. 4.

[36] Josephus, *Antiq.* xiv. 12. 2. The original documents, a letter of Antony to Hyrcanus and two letters to the Tyrians, *Antiq.* xiv. 12. 3–5. One of the letters to the Tyrians (*Antiq.* xiv. 12. 4) refers expressly to the restoring of the conquered places ; the other (*Antiq.* xiv. 12. 5) refers to the liberating of Jewish slaves. Similar letters were also sent to the cities of Sidon, Antioch, and Aradus (*Antiq.* xiv. 12. 6).

[37] Josephus, *Antiq.* xiv. 13. 1 ; *Wars of the Jews*, i. 12. 5.

[38] Appian, *Civ.* v. 7 .

[39] Josephus, *Antiq.* xiv. 13. 3 ; *Wars of the Jews*, i. 13. 1–2.

[40] Josephus, *Antiq.* xiv. 13. 4–5 ; *Wars of the Jews*, i. 13. 3.

[41] Josephus, *Antiq.* xiv. 13. 5–6 ; *Wars of the Jews*, i. 13. 4–5.

[42] Masada was built on a steep rock on the western bank of the Dead Sea. In the war of Vespasian it was the last place of refuge for the rebels, who yielded only after the Romans had carried on long and fatiguing siege operations, in A.D. 73.

[43] Josephus, *Antiq.* xiv. 13. 6–9 ; *Wars of the Jews*, i. 13. 6–8.

[44] Josephus, *Antiq.* xiv. 13. 9–10 ; *Wars of the Jews*, i. 13. 9–11.—Dio Cassius, xlviii. 26, erroneously names him Aristobulus instead of Antigonus.

§ 14. ANTIGONUS, B.C. 40–37.

[1] Josephus, *Antiq.* xiv. 14. 1–3.   *Wars of the Jews*, i. 14. 1–3.

[2] Josephus, *Antiq.* xiv. 14. 4–5.   *Wars of the Jews*, i. 14. 4.

[3] Josephus, *Antiq.* xiv. 14. 6 ; *Wars of the Jews*, i. 15. 2.   Dio Cassius, xlviii. 41.

[4] Josephus, *Antiq.* xiv. 15. 1–3 ; *Wars of the Jews*, i. 15. 3–6.

[5] Josephus, *Antiq.* xiv. 15. 5 ; *Wars of the Jews*, i. 16. 4.—According to *Antiq.* xiv. 15. 4, and *Wars of the Jews*, i. 16. 2, these caverns were situated in the neighbourhood of Arbela. The caves there referred to are often elsewhere spoken of by Josephus (*Antiq.* xii. 11. 1 ; *Life*, 37). The description which he gives in *Antiq.* xiv. 15. 5, and in *Wars of the Jews*, i. 16. 4, corresponds exactly with the actual character of the caves which are to be seen at the present day in the neighbourhood of Jrbid (Arbed), not far from the lake of Gennesareth, north-west of Tiberias. There can therefore be no doubt that Jrbid is identical with Arbela, and the caverns there with those mentioned by Josephus.

[6] Josephus, *Antiq.* xiv. 15. 7–9 ; *Wars of the Jews*, i. 16. 6–7.

[7] Josephus, *Antiq.* xiv. 15. 10 ; *Wars of the Jews*, i. 17. 1–2.

[8] Josephus, *Antiq.* xiv. 15. 11–13 ; *Wars of the Jews*, i. 17. 3–8.— Instead of ΙΣΑΝΑ (*Antiq.* xiv. 15. 12), we have in *Wars of the Jews*, i. 17. 5, KANA, which evidently is simply a corruption of the text. By a combination of the narratives it appears that the place lay either in the south of Samaria or in the north of Judea ; for Pappus had been sent to Samaria, but Herod met him going against him from Jericho. Our Isana is therefore undoubtedly to be identified with יְשָׁנָה, which in 2 Chron. xiii. 19 is mentioned along with Bethel (in Josephus, *Antiq.* viii. 11. 3, 'Ισανά).

[9] Josephus, *Antiq.* xiv. 15. 14 ; *Wars of the Jews*, i. 17. 8.—Mariamme (Μαριάμμη is not to be written Μαριάμνη) was a daughter of Alexander, the son of Aristobulus II. and of Alexandra, a daughter of Hyrcanus II. (*Antiq.* xv. 2. 5).—She was the second wife of Herod. His first wife was called Doris, by whom he had one son called Antipater (*Antiq.* xiv. 12. 1).

[10] Josephus, *Antiq.* xiv. 16. 1–3 ; *Wars of the Jews*, i. 17. 9, 18. 1–3. Dio Cassius, xlix. 22.—The date of the conquest of Jerusalem is variously given by the two sources which we have at our disposal. Dio Cassius, xlix. 22, places it in the consulship of Claudius and Norbanus in B.C. 38. He is followed by Clinton, *Fasti Hellenici*, iii. pp. 222 sq. (*ad ann.* 38), 299 sq., and Fischer, *Römische Zeittafeln*, p. 350, who adopt December B.C. 38 as the date of the conquest. Josephus, on the other hand, says that it occurred under the consulship of M. Agrippa and Caninius Gallus in B.C. 37 (*Antiq.* xiv. 16. 4). He is followed by almost all the moderns. It is, in fact, quite clear that the short and summary report of Dio Cassius cannot come into competition with the detailed and circumstantial narrative of Josephus, which rests on thoroughly good and reliable sources. But from the statement of Josephus it must certainly be concluded that the fall of the city did not occur before B.C. 37. We know that Pacorus was conquered by Ventidius on the 9th of June B.C. 38. Ventidius thereupon directed his energies against Antiochus of Commagene, and besieged him in Samosata. It was only after the siege had begun (compare especially Plutarch, *Antony*, 34), therefore at the earliest in July B.C. 38, that Antony arrived at Samosata. He there received the visit from Herod ; and when Samosata after a long siege (Plutarch, *Antony*, 34 : τῆς δὲ πολιορκίας μῆκος λαμβανούσης) had capitulated, and he himself had again returned to Athens, he sent back Sosius with orders to give assistance to Herod (*Antiq.* xiv. 15. 8–9). It must therefore have been autumn of B.C. 38 before Herod received this support ; and the statement of Josephus puts it beyond question that a winter was past before the conquest of Jerusalem was accomplished (*Antiq.* xiv. 15. 11 : πολλοῦ χειμῶνος καταρραγέντος ; *Antiq.* xiv. 15. 12 : χειμὼν ἐπέσχε βαθύς ; then again, 15. 14 : λήξαντος δὲ τοῦ χειμῶνος ; and finally, 16. 2 : θέρος τε γὰρ ἦν). Accordingly the conquest of Jerusalem cannot be assigned to an earlier date than the summer of B.C. 37.

[11] Josephus, *Antiq.* xiv. 16. 4, xv. 1. 2, where Josephus also quotes a passage from the now lost historical work of Strabo. *Wars of the Jews*, i. 18. 3. Dio Cassius, xlix. 22. Plutarch, *Antony*, 36.

§ 15. HEROD THE GREAT, B.C. 37–4.

[1] We prefix this chronological summary, because in what follows the chronological order is not always adhered to.

[2] The appointment was made some time after Alexandra had sent the portraits of Aristobulus and Mariamme to Antony in Egypt (*Antiq.* xv. 2. 6 ; *Wars of the Jews*, i. 22. 3 : εἰς Αἴγυπτον).

[3] Since Aristobulus, according to the above statement, died in the end of the year B.C. 35, this summons to Laodicea would fall in the spring of B.C. 34, when Antony undertook the expedition against Armenia (Dio

Cassius, xlix. 39); not, as we may assume, in B.C. 36, when Antony went forth against the Parthians. The correct view is taken by van der Chijs. —When Josephus says that then Antony went against the Parthians (*Antiq.* xv. 3. 9), his statement is loose and inexact, but not altogether incorrect. For Antony had, indeed, the design of going against the Parthians, see Dio Cassius, xlix. 39. But Josephus is clearly in error when he names in *Wars of the Jews*, i. 18. 5, "Parthians" instead of "Armenians."—The campaign ἐπὶ Πάρθους, referred to in *Antiq.* xv. 3. 9, is therefore identical with the campaign ἐπ' 'Αρμενίαν of *Antiq.* xv. 4. 2. The impression given by Josephus, that two different occurrences are there reported, probably results from his having used two different sources.

⁴ These presents are referred to by Plutarch, *Antony*, 36 (Φοινίκην, κοίλην Συρίαν, Κύπρον, Κιλικίας πολλήν, ἔτι δὲ τῆς τε 'Ιουδαίων τὴν τὸ βάλσαμον Φέρουσαν καὶ τῆς Ναβαταίων 'Αραβίας ὅση πρὸς τὴν ἐντὸς ἀποκλίνει θάλασσαν), and Dio Cassius, xlix. 32 (πολλὰ μὲν τῆς 'Αραβίας τῆς τε Μάλχου καὶ τῆς τῶν 'Ιτυραίων, τὸν γὰρ Λυσανίαν . . . ἀπέκτεινεν . . . πολλὰ δὲ καὶ τῆς Φοινίκης τῆς τε Παλαιστίνης, Κρήτης τέ τινα καὶ Κυρήνην τὴν τε Κύπρον). Both writers assign these proceedings to the year B.C. 36. Plutarch indeed places the transaction before the Parthian campaign; Dio Cassius, after the return from it. According to Josephus, on the other hand, the presentation of portions of Arabia, Judea, and Phoenicia took place in B.C. 34, when Antony was entertaining the idea of going against Armenia. For that this campaign is intended in *Antiq.* xv. 4. 1–3; *Wars of the Jews*, i. 18. 5, cannot be doubted when we compare these passages with Dio Cassius, xlix. 39–40. The date given by Plutarch and Dio Cassius obtains an apparent confirmation from the statement of Porphyry, that Cleopatra had reckoned the sixteenth year of her reign the first, because Antony in that year, after the death of Lysimachus (it ought to be Lysanias), had gifted to her the kingdom of Chalcis (Porphyry in Eusebius, *Chronicon*, ed. Schoene, i. 170 : τὸ δ' ἑκκαιδέκατον ὠνομάσθη τὸ καὶ πρῶτον, ἐπειδὴ τελευτήσαντος Λυσιμάχου [1. Λυσανίου] τῆς ἐν Συρίᾳ Χαλκίδος βασιλέως, Μάρκος 'Αντώνιος ὁ αὐτοκράτωρ τήν τε Χαλκίδα καὶ τοὺς περὶ αὐτὴν τόπους παρέδωκε τῇ Κλεοπάτρᾳ).

⁵ The seventh year of Herod corresponds to B.C. 31–30, and is to be reckoned from 1st Nisan to 1st Nisan. See the note at the close of the section.—The earthquake, therefore, took place in the Nisan of the year B C. 31. Nisan is also elsewhere described as the beginning of spring. See *Wars of the Jews*, iv. 8. 1 (ὑπὸ τὴν ἀρχὴν τοῦ ἔαρος); compare this with iv. 7. 3 (τετράδι Δύστρου). According to Mishna, *Taanith* i. 2, *Nedarim* viii. 5, *Baba Mezia* viii. 6, the rainy season is reckoned from the Feast of Tabernacles to the Passover, therefore down to the middle or even to the end of Nisan.

⁶ Zonaras, *Annales*, v. 14, *fin.*: ἐν ἐτῶν ὀγδοήκοντα πρὸς ἑνί. Also some of the manuscripts of Josephus have eighty-one.

⁷ The most detailed description of the campaign is given by Strabo, xvi. 4. 22–24, pp. 780–782 ; while it is reported more briefly by Dio

Cassius, liii. 29 ; Pliny, *Historia Naturalis*, vi. 28. 160 sq. ; *Monumentum Ancyranum*, v. 18 sq. (in Mommsen, *Res gestae divi Augusti*, ed. 2, p. 105). —Dio Cassius places the whole campaign within the tenth consulship of Augustus, B.C. 24, or A.U.C. 730. But, according to Strabo, the campaign proper did not begin until the year after Aelius Gallus had pushed on to Leuke Kome with great loss, and had there, in consequence of the numerous invalids in his army, been obliged to spend the winter (Strabo, xvi. 4. 24, p. 781 : ἠναγκάσθη γοῦν τό τε θέρος καὶ τὸν χειμῶνα διατελέσαι αὐτόθι τοὺς ἀσθενοῦντας ἀνακτώμενος). The whole campaign, therefore, embraced the years B.C. 25-24. This may be accepted as certain. It is on the other hand, questionable whether Aelius Gallus conducted the expedition as governor of Egypt, and was followed in that office by Petronius, or whether, on the contrary, Petronius was at the time of the Arabian campaign governor of Egypt, and was followed in that office by Gallus. We know definitely that both held the office of *praefectus Aegypti* (see on Aelius Gallus, Strabo, pp. 118 and 806 ; Dio Cassius, liii. 29 ; on Petronius, Strabo, pp. 788 and 819 ; Dio Cassius, liv. 5 ; Pliny, vi. 29. 181). We know further that Petronius undertook several expeditions against the Ethiopians which happened to occur just at the same time as the expedition of Gallus against Arabia (*Monumentum Ancyranum*, v. 18 sq. : " Meo jussu et auspicio ducti sunt duo exercitus eodem fere tempore in Aethiopiam et in Arabiam quae appellatur eudaemon ;" Strabo, xvii. 1. 54, p. 820 sq. ; Dio Cassius, liv. 5 ; Pliny, *Historia Naturalis*, vi. 29. 181 sq.; according to Strabo, the Ethiopians had made an attack upon the Thebaid, when the garrison of Egypt was weakened by the withdrawal of the troops of Aelius Gallus ; and thus the expedition of Petronius became necessary. Dio Cassius places this occurrence in B.C. 22).

[8] The games at Actium were celebrated on 2nd September for the first time in B.C. 28, then in the years B.C. 24, 20, 16, etc. That enlargement of territory therefore took place " after the course of the first Actiad had run," *i.e.* in the end of B.C. 24 or beginning of B.C. 23.

[9] Josephus only says, Herod visited Agrippa περὶ Μυτιλήνην χειμάζοντα. Since Agrippa was in Mytilene from spring B.C. 23 till spring B.C. 21, this may have been the winter of B.C. 23-22 or of B.C. 22-21.

[10] According to *Wars of the Jews*, i. 21. 1, the building was begun in the fifteenth year, which either is wrong, or refers to the earlier preparations for the building. That the building of the temple began in the year B.C. 20-19 is quite certain, from the fact that it was begun in the same year in the beginning of which the emperor went to Syria, which, according to Dio Cassius, liv. 7, was in the spring or summer of B.C. 20.—The building of the court of the temple occupied eight years, the building of the temple proper a year and a half (*Antiq.* xv. 11. 5-6 ; it is not clear whether these $8 + 1\frac{1}{2}$ years are to be added, or whether the latter period is to be regarded as identical with the first year and a half of the whole building period). After the completion of the temple

a great festival was celebrated. Seeing that it synchronized with the day of Herod's ascending the throne (*Antiq.* xv. 11. 6), the temple building, if we are right in setting down the date of Herod's accession at July, must have been begun in winter, therefore in the end of the year B.C. 20, A.U.C. 734, or in the beginning of B.C. 19, A.U.C. 735.

[11] That is to say, from the time of his ascending the throne, and so without taking into consideration his journey in the year B.C. 40–39.

[12] Compare generally the description given in *Wars of the Jews*, i. 21. 13.

[13] Josephus, *Antiq.* xvi. 9. 2.

[14] Compare the sketch of Herod's character given by Josephus, *Antiq.* xvi. 5. 4.

[15] Herod is called Ἡμιιουδαῖος in *Antiq.* xiv. 15. 2. The Idumeans had been converted only by John Hyrcanus. See above, p. 71. On the ancestry of Herod, see above, p. 95.

[16] Josephus, *Antiq.* xv. 1. 1 ; compare xiv. 9. 4, *fin.*

[17] Josephus, *Antiq.* xv. 1. 2 ; compare xiv. 9. 4, *fin.* ; *Wars of the Jews*, i. 18. 4.

[18] Josephus, *Antiq.* xv. 2. 1–4.

[19] Josephus, *Antiq.* xv. 2. 4.—Herod could not himself assume the position, since he was not even a full-born Jew, let alone a member of the sacerdotal family.

[20] Josephus, *Antiq.* xv. 2. 5–7, 3. 1.—In respect to the chronology, I refer once for all to the previous summary.

[21] Josephus, *Antiq.* xv. 3. 2.

[22] Josephus, *Antiq.* xv. 3. 3–4 ; *Wars of the Jews*, i. 22. 2.

[23] Josephus, *Antiq.* xv. 3. 5, 8–9.

[24] Josephus, *Antiq.* xv. 3. 5–6, 9. On the parallel passage, *Wars of the Jews*, i. 22. 4–5, see under, note 50.

[25] The district of Jericho was at that time the most fruitful part and the most profitable for revenue in all Palestine. This is stated most decidedly in Strabo, xvi. 2. 41, p. 763, and in Josephus, *Wars of the Jews*, iv. 8. 3. Near Jericho there was, according to Strabo, the palm forest (ὁ Φοινικών), extending to a hundred stadia, and the balsam garden (ὁ τοῦ βαλσάμου παράδεισος), which produced the precious balsam resin used as a means of healing. Josephus also represents the date palm and the balsam shrub as the two principal plants grown in the district. This region, peculiarly rich in revenue in consequence of its being so well watered and possessing so hot a climate, is reckoned by Josephus as extending to twenty stadia in breadth and seventy stadia in length. Since both of these products were greatly in request (compare Strabo, xvii. 1. 15, p. 800), Josephus rightly designates this region a θεῖον χωρίον, ἐν ᾧ δαψιλῆ τὰ σπανιώτατα καὶ κάλλιστα γεννᾶται (*Wars of the Jews*, iv. 8. 3). Elsewhere, too, he takes every opportunity of expatiating upon the fruitfulness of the district of Jericho, with its palm trees and balsam

shrubs (*Antiq.* iv. 6. 1, xiv. 4. 1 ; *Wars of the Jews*, i. 6. 6 ; *Antiq.* xv. 4. 2 ; *Wars of the Jews*, i. 18. 5). In one passage he expressly declares that it was the most fruitful part of Judea (*Wars of the Jews*, i. 6. 6 : τὸ τῆς ᾿Ιουδαίας πιότατον). Subsequently Herod extended the palm plantations as far as Phasaelis (see Div. ii. vol. i. p. 131). Archelaus built near Jericho a new aqueduct for watering the palm groves there (*Antiq.* xvii. 13. 1).

[26] Josephus, *Antiq.* xv. 4. 1–2 ; *Wars of the Jews*, i. 18. 5.—Plutarch, *Antony*, 36, and Dio Cassius, xlix. 32, assign this gift of territory to an earlier period. Compare above, p. 121f.

[27] Josephus, *Antiq.* xx. 4. 2 ; *Wars of the Jews*, i. 18. 5.

[28] Josephus, *Antiq.* xv. 5. 1 ; *Wars of the Jews*, i. 19. 1–3.

[29] Josephus, *Antiq.* xv. 5. 2–5 ; *Wars of the Jews*, i. 19. 3–6.

[30] Josephus, *Antiq.* xv. 6. 7 ; *Wars of the Jews*, i. 20. 2. Dio Cassius, li. 7.

[31] Josephus, *Antiq.* xv. 6. 1–4 ; *Wars of the Jews*, i. 22. 1.

[32] Suetonius, *Augustus*, c. 17.

[33] Josephus, *Antiq.* xv. 6. 5–7 ; *Wars of the Jews*, i. 20. 1–3.

[34] Josephus, *Antiq.* xv. 6. 7 ; *Wars of the Jews*, i. 20. 3.

[35] Josephus, *Antiq.* xv. 7. 3 ; *Wars of the Jews*, i. 20. 3.

[36] Josephus, *Antiq.* xv. 7. 4.

[37] *Ibid.* xv. 6. 5.

[38] *Ibid.* xv. 7. 1–2.

[39] Josephus, *Antiq.* xv. 7. 3–6.—A fabulous Talmudic story about the death of Mariamme is given by Derenbourg, p. 151.—In criticism of the account repeated by us from Josephus Destinon (*Die Quellen des Flavius Josephus*, 1882, p. 113) : "It is remarkable how precisely in order of time the succession of events correspond in the two journeys of the king to Antony and Augustus (*Antiq.* xv. 3. 5–6 and 9, xv. 6. 5, 7. 1–6). On both occasions he put his wife under the guardianship of a trusted individual, with instructions, if anything should happen to prevent his return, that she should be slain ; both times her guardians, meaning no harm, communicated the secret to her ; the king returning home learns this, becomes suspicious of gross infidelity, and has the innocent executed. . . . Moreover, it is remarkable that the second story is wholly omitted in the *Wars of the Jews*, i. 22. 4–5 ; according to the story given there, Herod kills not only Joseph, but also Mariamme, on his return from Antony. It might be supposed that the two narratives in the *Antiquities* refer to one and the same occurrence, that Josephus found the second story perhaps in some secondary document, and regarding it, in consequence of the introduction of the name Soemus, as different from the story given in his principal document, incorporated it in his narrative of the journey of Herod to Augustus, so that no particular might be omitted." — This explanation might without more ado be accepted, were it not, on the other hand, firmly established that the *Wars of the Jews* frequently reproduces in a greatly

abbreviated form the same original document as is used in the *Antiquities*, and that the first story is expressly presupposed in the second tale of the *Antiquities* (xv. 7. 1 : τὰς Ἰωσήπῳ δοθείσας ἐντολὰς ἀνεμνημόνευεν). That the same story would have been repeated in an almost identical form, is scarcely probable. But it does seem to me probable that both stories had already had a place in the principal source used by Josephus, and that specially for this reason, that in both passages the narrative of domestic circumstances is so clearly bound up with the exposition of the political history. In both passages the political history is introduced between the beginning and end of the domestic affairs.

[40] Josephus, *Antiq.* xv. 7. 7–8.

[41] *Ibid.* xv. 7. 9.

[42] The name Βαβας is found on an inscription given by Euting, *Sitzungsberichte der Berliner Akademie*, 1885, p. 685, Tafel xi. n. 80.—A בבא בוטי בן appears in *Keritoth* vi. 3 ; a בבא בן יהודה in *Erubin* ii. 4–5 ; *Jebamoth* xvi. 3, 5, 7 ; *Edujoth* vi. 1, viii. 2 (the Cambridge Manuscript has בבא בן four times, and אבא בן three times).

[43] Josephus, *Antiq.* xv. 7. 10. At the close of the narrative Josephus says expressly : ὥστε εἶναι μηδὲν ὑπόλοιπον ἐκ τῆς Ὑρκανοῦ συγγενείας. It is indeed only the male relatives that are here intended. For, according to *Antiq.* xvii. 5. 2, *fin.*, the daughter of Antigonus, the last of the Asmonean kings, continued alive for about twenty years after this, and she had been married to Herod's eldest son Antipater.

[44] Suetonius, *Augustus*, 59–60.

[45] Josephus, *Antiq.* xv. 8. 1 : καὶ θέατρον ἐν Ἱεροσολύμοις ᾠκοδόμησεν, αὖθις τ' ἐν τῷ πεδίῳ μέλιστον ἀμφιθέατρον. Also the hippodrome in Jerusalem, which is casually referred to (*Antiq.* xvii. 10. 2 ; *Wars of the Jews*, ii. 3. 1), was certainly built by Herod ; so, too, were the theatre, amphitheatre, and hippodrome in Jericho.

[46] Josephus, *Antiq.* xv. 9. 3 ; *Wars of the Jews*, i. 21. 1. Compare the description given in *Wars of the Jews*, v. 4. 3–4.—A tower of the palace of Herod is in a state of partial preservation to this day, the so-called Tower of David.

[47] Josephus, *Antiq.* xv. 8. 5, 11. 4, xviii. 4. 3 ; *Wars of the Jews*, i. 21. 1. Compare the description given in *Wars of the Jews*, v. 5. 8 ; Tacitus, *History*, v. 11, *fin.*

[48] Josephus, *Antiq.* xv. 9. 5 ; *Wars of the Jews*, i. 21. 4. Compare *Antiq.* xv. 10. 3 ; *Wars of the Jews*, i. 23. 3 (temple at Paneion). Also the reconstructed cities of Sebaste and Caesarea contained each a temple of Augustus.

[49] Josephus, *Antiq.* xv. 8. 5 ; *Wars of the Jews*, i. 21. 2 ; Strabo, xvi. p. 760.

[50] Josephus, *Antiq.* xv. 9. 6, xvi. 5. 1 ; *Wars of the Jews*, i. 21. 5–8. Compare also, *Antiq.* xv. 8. 5 ; Pliny, *Historia Naturalis*, v. 13. 69.

[51] Josephus, *Antiq.* xvi. 5. 2 ; *Wars of the Jews*, i. 21. 9.

[52] Josephus, *Wars of the Jews*, i. 21. 8. Compare *Antiq.* xiii. 13. 3 ; *Wars of the Jews*, i. 4. 2. In the two latter passages the name is given in the form of Agrippias.

[53] *Wars of the Jews*, i. 21. 10. On the second-named and more important of these fortresses, see also *Antiq.* xv. 9. 4 ; comp. *Antiq.* xiv. 13. 9 ; *Wars of the Jews*, i. 13. 8. During the Roman period it was the chief town of a toparchy (*Wars of the Jews*, iii. 3. 5 ; Pliny, *Historia Naturalis*, v. 14. 70 : *Herodium cum oppido inlustri ejusdem nominis*). During the war of Vespasian it formed one of the last refuges for the rebels (*Wars of the Jews*, vii. 6. 1). According to *Wars of the Jews*, iv. 9. 5, Herodium lay in the neighbourhood of Tekoa (στρατοπεδευσάμενος δὲ κατά τινα κώμην ἢ Θεκωὲ καγεῖται, πρὸς τοὺς ἐν Ἡρωδείῳ Φρουρούς, ὅπερ ἦν πλεσίον). According to *Antiq.* xiv. 13. 9, xv. 9. 4 ; *Wars of the Jews*, i. 13. 8, 21. 10, it was 60 furlongs south of Jerusalem.

[54] Both fortresses are mentioned first in the time of Alexandra (*Antiq.* xiii. 16. 3). In Alexandrium, Aristobulus waited the arrival of Pompey, but was forced to surrender the fortress to him (*Antiq.* xiv. 3. 4 ; *Wars of the Jews*, i. 6. 5). Both the fortresses were razed by Gabinius, because they had been strongholds to Alexander in his revolt (*Antiq.* xiv. 5. 2–4 ; *Wars of the Jews*, i. 8. 2–5). Alexandrium was fortified again by Pheroras (*Antiq.* xiv. 15. 4 ; *Wars of the Jews*, i. 16. 3). Hyrcania for a long time served as a place of refuge for the sister of Antigonus, and it was only shortly before the battle of Actium that Herod secured possession of it (*Wars of the Jews*). The new fortifications which Herod erected in both places were so important that he showed them to Agrippa on his visit as worthy of attention (*Antiq.* xvi. 2. 1). The situation of Hyrcania is not known. Alexandrium is probably identical with Mount Sartaba on the border of the Jordan valley north of Jericho (see above, p. 98).

[55] Machärus had been first fortified by Alexander Jannäus (*Wars of the Jews*, vii. 6. 2). Its restoration by Herod is fully described by Josephus, *Wars of the Jews*, vii. 6. 2.—Masada had been fortified by the high priest Jonathan (*Wars of the Jews*, vii. 8. 3). On its restoration by Herod, see *Wars of the Jews*, vii. 8. 3.—Both fortresses played an important part in the war of Vespasian. On their situation and history, see further details in § 20 at the end.

[56] Josephus, *Antiq.* xv. 8. 5. Compare *Wars of the Jews*, iii. 3. 1.

[57] Josephus, *Antiq.* xvi. 5. 3.

[58] *Ibid.* xvi. 2. 2.

[59] Josephus, *Wars of the Jews*, i. 21. 11.—In an inscription at Athens (*Corpus Inscript. Graec.* n. 361 = *Corpus Inscript. Attic.* iii. 1, n. 556), Berenice, the daughter of Agrippa I., is named : μεγάλων βασιλέων εὐεργετῶν τῆς πόλεως ἔκγονος.—Perhaps also the inscription at Athens (*Corpus Inscript. Attic.* iii. 1, n. 550) refers to Herod the Great : Ὁ δῆμος βασιλέα Ἡρώδην Φιλορώμαιον εὐεργεσίας ἕνεκεν καὶ εὐνοίας τῆς εἰς ἑαυτόν. Another similar one (*CIA.* iii. 1, n. 551) is, on account of its divergent title, referred to another Herod, Herod of Chalcis.

[60] On the history of the building, see Josephus, *Antiq.* xv. 11 ; *Wars of the Jews*, i. 21. 1. In the former passage Josephus gives a detailed description of the whole extent of the temple buildings, with their beautiful porticoes. The inner court and the temple proper are described with the most minute accuracy (*Wars of the Jews*, v. 5). With this description of Josephus the account given in the Mishna, in the tract *Middoth*, agrees in all essential particulars. A brief and merely summary description is given by Philo, *De monarchia*, lib. ii. § 2 (ed. Mangey, ii. 223 sq.).—The Jewish proverb and other Rabbinical traditions are given in Derenbourg, pp. 152-154.—With all its grandeur, however, the temple was still inferior to the palace of Herod (*Wars of the Jews*, i. 21. 1).—On the date of the building, see above, p. 125. On its completion in the time of Albinus, see *Antiq.* xx. 9. 7.—On the measures taken in order to maintain the ordinances of worship while the building was proceeding, see *Edujoth* viii. 6. "Rabbi Elieser said : I have heard that when the temple (היכל) was being built, they made curtains (קלעים) for the temple and curtains for the court ; and then they built the walls of the temple outside of the curtains, but those of the court inside of the curtains." While the temple was building, it is said that rain fell only by night (Josephus, *Antiq.* xv. 11. 7 ; Derenbourg, p. 152 sq.)

[61] In Caesarea, *Antiq.* xvi. 5. 1 ; *Wars of the Jews*, i. 21. 8. In Jerusalem, *Antiq.* xv. 8. 1.

[62] On the view taken of the games by the strict loyalists among the Jews, see Div. ii. vol. i. p. 32, and the literature there referred to.

[63] Josephus, *Antiq.* xvi. 5. 3 ; *Wars of the Jews*, i. 21. 12.

[64] Josephus, *Antiq.* xvi. 9. 2 (colonizing by 3000 Idumeans). *Antiq.* xvii. 2. 1–3 (settlement of a colony of Babylonian Jews).

[65] Josephus, *Wars of the Jews*, v. 4. 4 .

[66] In the Mishna the name of Herod occurs only in the two following passages : *Schabbath* xxiv. 3, " On the Sabbath one should not, indeed, place water for the hens and pigeons in the dovecot, but for the geese, and hens, and the pigeons of Herod (יוני הרדסיות)."—*Chullin* xii. 1, the law, Deut. xxii. 6. 7 (that from a bird's nest only the young may be taken, but the mother must be allowed to escape), applies only to such birds as build in the open, *e.g.* geese and hens, but not to such as build in houses, *e.g.* the pigeons of Herod (יוני הרדסיות).—In both passages the pigeons of Herod are distinguished as pigeons kept in captivity from those that fly about in freedom. The passage in Josephus, *Wars of the Jews*, v. 4. 4, shows us that they are wild pigeons (πελειάδες), not tame house pigeons (περιστεραί), that are referred to. The reading הדרסיות (*hadoresijoth*) is given even in the Babylonian Talmud on *Chullin* xii. 1, along with the other, but is certainly false.—The *Aruch* (the rabbinical lexicon of Nathan ben Jechiel) gives, *s.v.* יון, the following explanation : "King Herod had pigeons brought from the wilderness, and bred them in breeding-houses."

[67] That at the court of Herod two men of the name of Ptolemy are to be distinguished, is put beyond doubt from what took place immediately after

his death. At that time Ptolemy, brother of Nicolas of Damascus, was on the side of Antipas (*Antiq.* xvii. 9. 4 ; *Wars of the Jews*, ii. 2. 3) ; while at that same period another Ptolemy represented the interests of Archelaus (*Antiq.* xvii. 8. 2 ; *Wars of the Jews*, i. 33. 8 ; *Antiq.* xvii. 9. 3 and 5 ; *Wars of the Jews*, ii. 2. 1 and 4). By the latter Archelaus had Herod's accounts and signet-ring carried to Rome to the emperor.

[68] Josephus, *Antiq.* xvi. 8. 3.

[69] Josephus, *Antiq.* xvii. 9. 4 ; *Wars of the Jews*, ii. 2. 3.

[70] Josephus, *Antiq.* xvi. 10. 1 ; *Wars of the Jews*, i. 26. 1–4.

[71] Josephus, *Antiq.* xix. 7. 3 : Ἕλλησι πλέον ἤ Ἰουδαίοις οἰκείως ἔχειν.— On the humanistic studies of Herod under the direction of Nicolas of Damascus, see *Nicolaus Damascenus* in Müller, *Fragm. Hist. Graec.* iii. 350 sq.

[72] Josephus, *Antiq.* xv. 11. 5–6.

[73] *Ibid.* xv. 8. 1–2.

[74] *Ibid.* xvi. 7. 6.

[75] *Ibid.* xv. 1. 1, 10. 4.

[76] Josephus, *Antiq.* xvii. 6. 2 ; *Wars of the Jews*, i 33. 2.

[77] Indeed, this may be accepted as certain.

[78] Wellhausen, *Die Pharisäer und die Sadducäer*, pp. 105–109, has indeed rightly stated that the Pharisees could be contented with Herod sooner than the Sadducees. But he has too strongly accentuated this correct idea.

[79] The two cases of refusal to take the oath, which are reported in *Antiq.* xv. 10. 4 and in xvii. 2. 4, seem to be quite distinct. In the former passage it is said that Herod persecuted his enemies in all manner of ways ; "but for the rest of the multitude he required that they should be obliged to take the oath of fidelity to him, and at the same time compelled them to swear that they would bear him goodwill and continue so to ·do in the management of his government" (*Antiq.* xv. 10. 4 : τὸ δ' ἄλλο πλῆθος ὅρκοις ἠξίου πρὸς τὴν πίστιν ὑπάγεσθαι, καὶ συνηνάγκαζεν αὐτῷ ἐνόμιτον τὴν εὔνοιαν ἦ μὴν διαφυλάξειν ἐπὶ τῆς ἀρχῆς ὁμολογεῖν). It is an oath of fidelity to the king that is here referred to. The Pharisees who refused were, out of respect to Polio and Sameas, left unpunished. So, too, the Essenes. But all the others were punished. In the other passage it is told that when the whole Jewish people promised an oath of submission to the emperor and the king, more than 3000 Pharisees refused to swear (*Antiq.* xvii. 2. 4 : παντὸς γοῦν τοῦ Ἰουδαϊκοῦ βεβαιώσαντος δι' ὅρκων ἦ μὴν εὐνοῆσαι Καίσαρι καὶ τοῖς βασιλέως πράγμασι, οἵδε οἱ ἄνδρες οὐκ ὤμοσαν, ὄντες ὑπὲρ ἑξακισχίλιοι). Here the oath to the emperor seems to have been the chief thing. The Pharisees who refused were sentenced to pay a money fine, which was paid by the wife of Pheroras.—The latter passage is the earliest instance that I know of showing that in the days of the empire not only soldiers and officers, but also the people in Italy and in the provinces, had to take the oath of fidelity to the emperor. Later evidence of the practice we have from the time of Tiberius, Caligula, and Trajan.

[80] Josephus, *Antiq.* xv. 8. 3–4.

[81] *Ibid.* xv. 10. 4.

[82] Josephus, *Antiq.* xvii. 8. 3 ; *Wars of the Jews*, i. 33. 9.

[83] Josephus, *Antiq.* xv. 10. 4.

[84] *Ibid.* xv. 10. 4.

[85] *Ibid.* xvi. 2. 5.

[86] *Ibid.* xv. 9. 1–2.

[87] Herod had his kingdom δόσει Καίσαρος καὶ δόγματι Ῥωμαίων, Josephus, *Antiq.* xv. 6. 7.

[88] Josephus, *Antiq.* xiv. 8. 3 ; *Wars of the Jews*, i. 9. 5.

[89] Agrippa I. obtained in the first place praetorian rank (Philo *in Flacc.* § 6, Mangey, ii. 523), subsequently consular rank (Dio Cassius, lx. 8). Herod of Chalcis obtained praetorian rank (Dio Cassius, *ibid.*), as also Agrippa II. (Dio Cassius, lxvi. 15).—The conferring of honorary senatorial rights (*ornamenta*, τιμαί) on those not senators, first came into vogue under Tiberius (Mommsen, *Röm. Staatsrecht*, 1 Aufl. i. 375 f.). The interest of the question entirely centres on the point as to their right of taking their place on public occasions among the senators, and of wearing the insignia of their respective offices.

[89a] **Appian,** *Civ.* **v.** 75.

[90] Compare Suetonius, *Augustus*, 60 .

[91] See above, p. 135 ff.

[92] Josephus, *Antiq.* xv. 10. 3.—Augustus does not seem ever to have visited Judea.

[93] Josephus, *Antiq.* xvi. 1. 2.

[94] Josephus, *Antiq.* xvi. 4. 1–5, and 9. 1.

[95] Josephus, *Antiq.* xv. 10. 2.

[96] Josephus, *Antiq.* xvi. 2. 1 ; Philo, *Legat. ad Cajum*, § 37 (ed. Mangey, ii. 589) .

[97] Josephus, *Antiq.* xvi. 2. 2–5.   Compare Nicolas of Damascus in Müller, *Fragmenta Hist. Graec.* iii. 350.

[98] Josephus, *Antiq.* xv. 10. 3 ; *Wars of the Jews*, i. 20. 4.

[99] Josephus, *Antiq.* xv. 9. 3 ; Strabo, xvi. 4. 23, p. 780.

[100] Josephus, *Antiq.* xv. 10. 1 ; *Wars of the Jews*, i. 20. 4.—The districts named all lie west of the lake of Gennesareth.

[101] Josephus, *Antiq.* xv. 10. 3 ; *Wars of the Jews*, i. 20. 4 ; Dio Cassius, liv. 9.

[102] Josephus, *Antiq.* xv. 10. 3 ; *Wars of the Jews*, i. 24. 5.

[103] Josephus, *Antiq.* xv. 10. 3 ; *Wars of the Jews*, i. 20. 4.

[104] Josephus, *Antiq.* xvi. 2. 3–5.   Compare also, *Antiq.* xvi. 6. 1–8 ; xii. 3. 2.

[105] Many things belong to this period that were treated of in the preceding section, for the boundaries of the periods cannot be always strictly observed.   It is in general undoubtedly correct to say that the domestic quarrels reached their height between B.C. 13 and B.C. 4.

[106] Josephus, *Wars of the Jews*, i. 24. 2, *fin.* ; *Antiq.* xvii. 1. 2 : πάτριον γὰρ ἐν ταὐτῷ πλείοσιν ἡμῖν συνοικεῖν. According to the Mishna, *Sanhedrin*

ii. 4, eighteen wives were allowed to the king. How many a private man should have is not expressly stated in the Mishna, but it is assumed that he may have four or five (four : *Jebamoth* iv. 11 ; *Kethuboth* x. 1–6 ; five : *Kerithoth* iii. 7. Compare in general also : *Kiddushin* ii. 7 ; *Bechoroth* viii. 4).

[107] Josephus, *Antiq.* xiv. 12. 1.—According to *Antiq.* xvii. 5. 2, Antipater was married to a daughter of the last Asmonean Antigonus.

[108] Josephus, *Antiq.* xvi. 3. 3 ; *Wars of the Jews*, i. 22. 1.

[109] Josephus, *Wars of the Jews*, i. 22. 2.

[110] The two daughters were called Salampso and Cypros. Their descendants are enumerated by Josephus, *Antiq.* xviii. 5. 4.

[111] Josephus, *Antiq.* xv. 9. 3. The name Mariamme : *Wars of the Jews*, i. 28. 4, and elsewhere. Josephus, in *Antiq.* xv. 9. 3, names her father Simon, her grandfather Boethos. In other places Boethos himself is called her father.

[112] Josephus, *Antiq.* xvii. 1. 2.

[113] Josephus, *Antiq.* xv. 10. 1.

[114] *Ibid.* xvi. 1. 2.

[115] Josephus, *Antiq.* xvi. 1. 2. Berenice was a daughter of Salome and Costobar (*Antiq.* xviii. 5. 4). She is also spoken of by Strabo, xvi. 2. 46, p. 765.

[116] Josephus, *Antiq.* xvi. 1. 2.

[117] Josephus, *Antiq.* xvi. 3. 1–2.

[118] Josephus, *Antiq.* xvi. 3. 3 ; *Wars of the Jews*, i. 23. 1–2.

[119] Josephus, *Antiq.* xvi. 3. 3.

[120] Josephus, *Antiq.* xvi. 4. 1–6 ; *Wars of the Jews*, i. 23. 3–5.

[121] Josephus, *Antiq.* xvi. 7. 2 ff. ; *Wars of the Jews*, i. 24. 1 ff.

[122] Compare especially : Josephus, *Antiq.* xvi. 8. 2, 5 ; *Wars of the Jews*, 24. 8.

[123] Josephus, *Antiq.* xvi. 8. 4 ; *Wars of the Jews*, i. 24. 8.

[124] Josephus, *Antiq.* xvi. 8. 6 ; *Wars of the Jews*, i. 25. 1–6.

[125] Josephus, *Antiq.* xvi. 9. 1–2.

[126] Josephus, *Antiq.* xvi. 9. 3. Compare Nicolas of Damascus in Müller, *Fragm. Hist. Graec.* iii. 351 ; Feder, *Excerpta Escurialensia*, p. 64.

[127] Josephus, *Antiq.* xvi. 9. 4.

[128] Josephus, *Antiq.* xvi. 10. 1 ; *Wars of the Jews*, i. 26. 1–4.

[129] Josephus, *Antiq.* xvi. 10. 5–7 ; *Wars of the Jews*, i. 27. 1.

[130] Josephus, *Antiq.* xvi. 10. 8–9. Nicolas of Damascus in Müller.

[131] Josephus, *Antiq.* xvi. 11. 1 ; *Wars of the Jews*, i. 27. 1.—Berytus was probably fixed upon by Augustus because it was a Roman colony, and so a centre of Roman activity and officialdom in the neighbourhood of Palestine. According to Strabo, xvi. 2. 19, p. 755 sq., Agrippa placed two legions in Berytus, *i.e.* the veterans of those legions. This would be in B.C. 15, on the occasion of Agrippa's visit to that quarter (see above, p. 125).

[132] Josephus, *Antiq.* xvi. 11. 2–7 ; *Wars of the Jews*, i. 27. 2–6. Nicolas

of Damascus in Müller, *Fragmenta Hist. Graec.* iii. 351 sq. Feder, *Excerpta Escurialensia*, p. 65.

[133] Josephus, *Antiq.* xvii. 1. 1, 2. 4; *Wars of the Jews*, i. 28. 1, 29. 1.

[134] Josephus, *Antiq.* xvii. 3. 2; *Wars of the Jews*, i. 29. 2.

[135] Josephus, *Antiq.* xvii. 3. 3; *Wars of the Jews*, i. 29. 4.

[136] Josephus, *Antiq.* xvii. 4. 1–2; *Wars of the Jews*, i. 30. 1–7.

[137] Josephus, *Antiq.* xvii. 4. 3, 5. 1–2; *Wars of the Jews*, i. 31. 2–5.

[138] Josephus, *Antiq.* xvii. 5. 3–7; *Wars of the Jews*, i. 32. 1–5. Compare generally also, Nicolas of Damascus in Müller, *Fragmenta Hist. Graec.* iii. 352 sq.; Feder, *Excerpta Escurialensia*, p. 66 sq.

[139] Josephus, *Antiq.* xvii. 6. 1; *Wars of the Jews*, i. 33. 1–4.

[140] The names of the rabbins in *Antiq.* xvii. 6. 2: 'Ιούδας ὁ Σαριφαίου καὶ Ματθίας ὁ Μαργαλώθου; in *Wars of the Jews*, i. 33. 2: 'Ιούδας τε υἱὸς Σεπφωραίου καὶ Ματθίας ἕτερος Μαργάλου.

[141] Josephus, *Antiq.* xvii. 6. 2–4; *Wars of the Jews*, i. 33. 1–4.

[142] Josephus, *Antiq.* xvii. 6. 5; *Wars of the Jews*, i. 33. 5.—Callirrhoë is also mentioned by Pliny, *Historia Naturalis*, v. 16. 72, and by Ptolemy, v. 16. 9. The Jewish tradition identifies Callirrhoë and the biblical לָשַׁע, Gen. x. 19 (*Targum Jerus.* on Gen. x. 19; *Bereshith rabba*, c. 37).

[143] Josephus, *Antiq.* xvii. 6. 5; *Wars of the Jews*, i. 33. 6. The order was not carried out (*Antiq.* xvii. 8. 2; *Wars of the Jews*, i. 33. 8). Compare the similar rabbinical tradition in Derenbourg, p. 164 sq.

[144] Josephus, *Antiq.* xvii. 7; *Wars of the Jews*, i. 33. 7; Nicolas of Damascus in Müller.

[145] Josephus, *Antiq.* xvii. 8. 1; *Wars of the Jews*, i. 33. 7–8.

[146] Josephus, *Antiq.* xvii. 8. 1; *Wars of the Jews*, i. 33. 8.

Herod died shortly before a Passover (*Antiq.* xvii. 9. 3; *Wars of the Jews*, ii. 1. 3), therefore in March or April. Since Josephus says that he reigned thirty-seven years from the date of his appointment, thirty-four years from his conquest of Jerusalem (*Antiq.* xvii. 8. 1; *Wars of the Jews*, i. 33. 8), it would seem as if, counting thirty-seven years from the year B.C. 40, he must have died in B.C. 3. But we know that Josephus elsewhere counts a year too much, according to our reckoning. Thus he counts from the conquest of Jerusalem by Pompey to that by Herod twenty-seven years (*Antiq.* xiv. 16. 4), whereas the true number is twenty-six (B.C. 63–B.C. 37). Again, from the conquest of Herod down to that by Titus he counts 107 years (*Antiq.* xx. 10), whereas there were only 106 (A.U.C. 717–A.U.C. 823). He reckons the spring of B.C. 31 the seventh year of Herod (*Antiq.* xv. 5. 2; *Wars of the Jews*, i. 19. 3), whereas it was only the sixth year (his reign beginning with July B.C. 37). The reason of this is that he counts portions of a year as a year; and, indeed, he probably, according to the example of the Mishna (comp. *Rosh hashana*, i. 1: בְּאֶחָד בְּנִיסָן רֹאשׁ הַשָּׁנָה לַמְּלָכִים), reckons the years of the king's reign from Nisan to Nisan. If this be so, the thirty-fourth year of Herod would begin on the 1st Nisan of the year B.C. 4, and Herod must in that case have died between 1st and 14th Nisan, since his death occurred before the Passover. That this is indeed the correct reckoning is confirmed by astronomical date, and by the chronology of the successors of Herod.

1. Shortly before Herod's death an eclipse of the moon occurred (*Antiq.* xvii. 6. 4). This only corresponds to the year B.C. 4, in which on the night of March 12–13 an eclipse of the moon took place; whereas in the years 3 and 2 B.C. in Palestine generally there was no such phenomenon

2. The chronology of two successors of Herod, Archelaus and Antipas, requires B.C. 4 = A.U.C. 750, as the year of Herod's death.

(*a*) Archelaus. He was, according to Dio Cassius, lv. 27, deposed by Augustus in the year A.U.C. 759, during the consulship of Aemilius Lepidus and L. Arruntius, in the tenth year of his reign. So also says Josephus in *Antiq.* xvii. 13. 2, and in *Life,* 1, where the earlier statement of the *Wars of the Jews,* ii. 7. 3, that this occurred "in the ninth year of his reign," is corrected. Hence his reign began in A.U.C. 750.

(*b*) Antipas. He was deposed by Caligula in the summer of A.D. 39 = A.U.C. 792 (see under § 17*b*). Since we still have coins of his bearing date the forty-third year of his reign, the year of the beginning of his reign must at latest have been A.U.C. 750.

All these facts therefore yield this result, that Herod died in the year B.C. 4 = A.U.C. 750, shortly before the Passover.

[147] Josephus, *Antiq.* xvii. 8. 3, *fin.*: ἦσαν δὲ ἐπὶ Ἡρωδείου στάδια ὀκτώ; *Wars of the Jews,* i. 33. 9, *fin.*: σταδίους δὲ ἐκομίσθη τὸ σῶμα διακοσίους εἰς Ἡρώδειον.—The former passage states how far upon the way the funeral procession went; the latter passage gives the distance from Jericho to Herodium. It is undoubtedly the more important of the two fortresses that is intended (see above, p. 140), and its distance from Jericho is somewhere about 200 stadia or furlongs. Since Herod was buried there, the μνημεῖον of Herod at Jerusalem (*Wars of the Jews,* v. 3. 2, 12. 2) was only a memorial, not an erection over his tomb.

[148] In this sense is the title intended even in Josephus in the single passage in which he uses it (*Antiq.* xviii. 5. 4).

§ 16. DISTURBANCES AFTER HEROD'S DEATH, B.C. 4.

[1] Josephus, *Antiq.* xvii. 9. 1–3 ; *Wars of the Jews,* ii. 1. 1–3.

[2] Josephus, *Antiq.* xvii. 9. 3–4; *Wars of the Jews,* ii. 2. 1–3.

[3] Josephus, *Antiq.* xvii. 9. 5–7 ; *Wars of the Jews,* ii. 2. 4–7.

[4] Josephus, *Antiq.* xvii. 10. 1–2 ; *Wars of the Jews,* ii. 3. 1–3.

[5] Josephus, *Antiq.* xvii. 10. 3 ; *Wars of the Jews,* ii. 3. 4.

[6] Josephus, *Antiq.* xvii. 10. 5 ; *Wars of the Jews,* ii. 4. 1.

[7] Josephus, *Antiq.* xvii. 10. 6 ; *Wars of the Jews,* ii. 4. 2.

[8] Josephus, *Antiq.* xvii. 10. 7 ; *Wars of the Jews,* ii. 4. 3.

[9] Josephus, *Antiq.* xvii. 10. 9–10, 11. 1 ; *Wars of the Jews*, ii. 5. 1–3.—This war of Varus is also referred to in *contra Apionem*, i. 7, as one of the most important between that of Pompey and that of Vespasian. The name Varus is therefore probably to be restored in a corrupt passage in *Seder olam, s. fin.*, in which it is said that " from the war of Asveros down to the war of Vespasian there were eighty years," מפולמוס של אסוירוס ועד פולמוס של אספסיינוס שמנים שנה. Although the number eighty is somewhat too high, and although the best text exemplars give אסוירוס, it is yet highly probable that ורום should be read, *i.e.* Varos (so Grätz, *Geschichte der Juden*, 4 Aufl. iii. pp. 249, 714 ff. ; Derenbourg, *Histoire*, p. 194 ; Brann, *De Herodis qui dicitur Magni filiis*, p. 24 sq.).

[10] Josephus, *Antiq.* xvii. 11. 1 ; *Wars of the Jews*, ii. 6. 1.—The facts here related have unquestionably afforded the outward framework for the parable of the Pounds, Luke xix. 12 ff. Compare especially ver. 12 : " A certain nobleman (Archelaus) went into a far country (Rome) to receive for himself a kingdom (Judea), and to return." Ver. 14 : " But his citizens hated him, and sent a message after him, saying : We will not have this man to reign over us."

[11] Josephus, *Antiq.* xvii. 11. 2–3 *Wars of the Jews*, ii. 6. 2.

[12] Josephus, *Antiq.* xvii. 11. 4–5 ; *Wars of the Jews*, ii. 6. 3 ; generally also, Nicolas of Damascus in Müller, *Fragmenta*, iii. 354 ; Strabo, xvi. 2. 46, p. 765.

—The title ἐθνάρχης evidently signifies a rank somewhat higher than that of τετράρχης. The former had been conferred, *e.g.*, by Caesar upon Hyrcanus II. (see above, p. 107), but is otherwise rare. On the other hand, the title τετράρχης is very common. Herod the Great and his brother Phasael had it conferred upon them by Antony (*Antiq.* xiv. 13. 1 ; *Wars of the Jews*, i. 12. 5). In B.C. 20, Pheroras was made tetrarch of Perea (*Antiq.* xv. 10. 3 ; *Wars of the Jews*, i. 24. 5).

[13] Josephus, *Antiq.* xviii. 2. 2.

§ 17. THE SONS OF HEROD.

(a) Philip, B.C. 4–A.D. 34.

[1] Josephus, *Antiq.* xvii. 8. 1, 11. 4, xviii. 4. 6 ; *Wars of the Jews*, ii. 6. 3. In the latter passage, undoubtedly, instead of 'Ιάμνειαν should be read Πανειάδα, in accordance with *Antiq.* xvii. 8. 1, 11. 4.

[2] Batanea corresponds to the Old Testament Bashan (בָּשָׁן) ; Eusebius, *Onomasticon*, ed. Lagarde, p. 232 : Βασάν . . . αὕτη Βασανῖτις ἡ νῦν καλουμένη Βαταναία. Yet the ancient Bashan was of larger extent than the modern Batanea. By Bashan was understood the whole region on the other side of Jordan between Hermon on the north and the district of Gilead on the south, extending eastward as far as Salcha, on the southern slope of the Hauran. See Deut. iii. 10, 13 ; Josh. xii. 4, xiii. 11, 30, xvii. 1, 5 ; 1 Chron. v. 23. But within this district lay the later provinces of Trachonitis, Auranitis, and Gaulanitis ; so that thus Batanea is only a part

of the ancient Bashan. The expression, however, is sometimes used even by later writers in the wider sense ; *e.g.* Josephus, *Life*, 11 *med.*: μετὰ τῶν ἐν Βαταναίᾳ Τραχωνιτῶν. Since the cities of Ashtaroth and Edrei are named as the chief cities of Bashan (Josh. xii. 4, xiii. 11, 30), it may be assumed that these also formed the centre of the modern Batanea. Edrei, later Adraa, the modern Derʻa, lies almost exactly in the middle between the southern point of the lake of Gennezaret and the southern end of the mountains of Hauran.

Trachonitis or ὁ Τράχων (so Josephus, *Antiq.* xiii. 16. 5, xv. 10. 1 ; *Wars of the Jews*, ii. 6. 3 ; and the inscription of Mismie) is the rugged plateau south of Damascus, stretching on to Bostra, which is now called the Lejâh. It lies, therefore, north-east of Batanea proper.

Auranitis is the חַוְרָן mentioned by Ezekiel, xlvii. 16, 18 ; which also in the Mishna, *Rosh hashana* ii. 4, is spoken of as one of the stations for the five signals from Judea to Babylon. Some manuscripts of the Mishna have חַוְרָן, others חברה. Since the Hauran, according to the context of the Mishna, must be a mountain, Auranitis is undoubtedly the country round about the mountain peak, which now is called Jebel Hauran.

Gaulanitis has its name from the town Golan, which in the Bible is reckoned in Bashan (Deut. iv. 43 ; Josh. xx. 8, xxi. 27 ; 1 Chron. vi. 56 ; Eusebius, *Onomasticon*, ed. Lagarde, p. 242). Josephus distinguishes Upper and Lower Gaulanitis, and remarks that in the latter lies the city Gamala (*Wars of the Jews*, iv. 1. 1 ; according to the same passage, Gamala lay on the eastern bank of the lake of Gennezaret). According to *Wars of the Jews*, iii. 3. 1, Gaulanitis formed the eastern boundary of Galilee. Hence Gaulanitis is practically within the same lines as what is now called Djaulan, embracing the lowlands east of the Jordan from its source down to the southern point of the lake of Gennezaret.

The district of Panias, at the sources of the Jordan (see on the town Panias, Div. II. vol. i. pp. 132–135), had in earlier times belonged to Zenodorus, and before that to the kingdom of the Itureans

[3] In Batanea, Herod the Great, in the last years of his reign, had settled a Jewish colony from Babylon, under the leadership of a certain Zamaris, and conferred on them the privilege of complete freedom from taxation, which was also, in all essential points, respected by Philip. See *Antiq.* xvii. 2. 1–3. For the history of this colony, compare also Josephus, *Life*, 11 ;

[4] Josephus, *Antiq.* xviii. 2. 1 ; *Wars of the Jews*, ii. 9. 1.

[5] Josephus, *Wars of the Jews*, iii. 10. 7. According to the description of Josephus, the " Phiala " can scarcely be anything else than the present Birket Ram. But then the story told by him is not possible, owing to the relative levels.

[6] Josephus, *Antiq.* xviii. 4. 6 :

[7] Josephus, *Antiq.* xviii. 5. 4.

[8] In explanation of this, it should be remembered that Philip's domain was predominantly pagan.

9 Josephus, *Antiq.* xviii. 4. 6.

10 Josephus, *Antiq.* xviii. 4. 6.

11 Josephus, *Antiq.* xviii. 6. 10 ; *Wars of the Jews,* ii. 9. 6.

(*b*) Herod Antipas, B.C. 4–A.D. 39.

1 Thus is he correctly named in Matt. xiv. 1 ; Luke iii. 19 ; on the other hand, he is incorrectly called βασιλεύς in Mark vi. 14.

2 Compare the description of Galilee in Josephus, *Wars of the Jews,* iii. 3. 2–3, 10. 8.

3 Josephus in *Antiq.* xviii. 7. 2, characterizes him as ἀγαπῶν τὴν ἡσυχίαν.

4 Luke xiii. 32.

5 Josephus, *Antiq.* xviii. 2. 1 ; *Wars of the Jews,* ii. 9. 1.

6 Josephus, *Antiq.* xviii. 5. 1.

7 Compare Suetonius, *Augustus,* c. 48 : " Reges socios etiam inter semet ipsos necessitudinibus mutuis junxit, promptissimus affinitatis cujusque atque amicitiae conciliator et fautor."

8 Num. xix. 16 ; Josephus, *Antiq.* xviii. 2. 3. More detailed particulars about impurity caused by graves are given in *Mishna Ohaloth* xvii., xviii.

9 Josephus, *Wars of the Jews,* ii. 21. 6, iii. 10. 10 ; *Life,* 17, 64.

10 Josephus, *Life,* 12.

11 Josephus, *Life,* 54.

12 Compare on the building of Tiberias generally : Josephus, *Antiq.* xviii. 2. 3 ; *Wars of the Jews,* ii. 9. 1 ; *Life,* 9.

13 Philo, *Legat. ad Cajum,* sec. 30 (ed. Mangey, ii. 589 sq.).

14 This conclusion may be drawn from Philo, *Legat. ad Cajum,* § 24 (ed. Mangey, ii. 569), according to which Tiberius, during the lifetime of Sejanus (who died A.D. 31), was unfavourably disposed toward the Jews, whereas after his death he became decidedly favourable to their religious peculiarities.

15 Josephus, *Antiq.* xviii. 5. 4.—Philip is named as first husband of Herodias in Mark vi. 17. The parallel passage, Matt. xiv. 3, omits the name in cod. D, and is put in brackets by Tischendorf (ed. 8), but is inclined, owing to the unanimous testimony of all the other manuscripts, to hold it as genuine. In Luke iii. 19, on the other hand, where it is inserted in the *textus receptus,* it ought certainly to be struck out.—Since, according to Josephus, not the tetrarch Philip, but the above-named Herod, was the first husband of Herodias, the statement of Mark and Matthew is evidently a mistake.

16 Josephus, *Antiq.* xviii. 5. 1.—On Machärus, see above, p. 140 and § 20 toward the end. Machärus at all other periods, before and after, formed part of the Jewish territory. Alexander Jannaeus fortified it, as did also Herod the Great (*Wars of the Jews,* vii. 6. 2). Herod Antipas put John the Baptist in prison there. In the Vespasian war it was one

of the best places of refuge for the rebels (*Wars of the Jews*, ii. 18. 6, vii. 6). It is therefore very remarkable that it should then have belonged to the Arabian king. The words of Josephus are as follows : εἰς τὸν Μαχαιροῦντα τότε [*al.* τῷ τε, Bekker, *conj.* τὸν τῷ] πατρὶ αὐτῆς ὑποτελῇ. It is equally remarkable that Antipas should have guilelessly allowed his wife to go to this fortress belonging to the Arabian king. Or did he consciously agree to it in order to smooth the way for her flight, wishing thus to be rid of her? Josephus did not so conceive of the matter, for according to his representation Herod Antipas knew nothing of the meditated flight.

[17] Josephus, *Antiq.* xviii. 5. 2.

[18] Matt. xiv. 5 ; Mark vi. 20 ; Matt. xi. 2-6.

[19] The Gospels of Matthew and Mark evidently assume that the banquet was given in the same place where the Baptist lay a prisoner. See Meyer on Matt. xiv. 10 ff. But that was Machärus. And there the banquet may, in fact, have been given. For Machärus had a beautiful palace, which had been built by Herod the Great (*Wars of the Jews*, vii. 6. 2).

[20] Matt. xiv. 6-11 ; Mark vi. 21-28 ; Luke ix. 9.—In Mark vi. 22 some very important and authoritative texts, accepted by Westcott and Hort and Volkmar, read: τῆς θυγατρὸς αὐτοῦ Ἡρωδιάδος. According to this reading the maiden herself was called Herodias, and may have been a daughter of Herod Antipas, and not merely the daughter of Herodias. But a child of the marriage of Antipas with Herodias could not then have been more than two years old ; whereas, on the other hand, we know from Josephus that Herodias by her first marriage had a daughter called Salome (*Antiq.* xviii. 5. 4). Also in the Gospel narrative itself the maiden appears only as a daughter of Herodias. The statement, therefore, that would result from that reading of Mark, cannot in any case be regarded as historically correct, be that reading ever so old.

[21] Matt. xiv. 1 f. ; Mark vi. 14-16 ; Luke ix. 7-9.

[22] Luke ix. 9.—Among the female followers of Christ there is mentioned the wife of an officer of Antipas (Luke viii. 3 : Ἰωάννα γυνὴ Χουζᾶ ἐπιτρόπου Ἡρώδου).

[23] So at least is Luke xiii. 31, 32 understood by many expositors.

[24] Luke xxiii. 7-12.

[25] The district of Gamala belonged to what had been the tetrarchy of Philip, and cannot therefore have been a subject of contention between Antipas and Aretas. On the other hand, the province of Galaaditis (Gilead) lay on the borders of their territories. But from ΓΑΛΑΑΔΙΤΙΣ the other word ΓΑΜΑΛΙΤΙΣ might easily be made. Undoubtedly the text of the passage in question (*Antiq.* xviii. 5. 1) is defective.

[26] The date is derived from this, that the defeat of Antipas, as what follows shows, took place not long—somewhere about half a year—before the death of Tiberius in March A.D. 37.

[27] Josephus, *Antiq.* xviii. 5. 1.

[28] Josephus, *Antiq.* xviii. 5. 1–3. Since the imperial legates had their office only at the personal will of the emperor, so, strictly taken, every command ceased with the death of the emperor.

[29] Tacitus, *Annals,* vi. 31–37, 41–44. With respect to the date, compare also : *Annals,* vi. 38 ; Dio Cassius, lviii. 26 ; Josephus, *Antiq.* xviii. 4. 4. —The fixing of the date results from the statement of Tacitus.

[30] Suetonius, *Caligula,* 14, *Vitellius,* 2 ; Dio Cassius, lix. 27 ; Josephus, *Antiq.* xviii. 4. 5. Besides Josephus, Dio Cassius, lix. 17, and Suetonius, *Caligula,* 19, speak of Darius as present in Rome in A.D. 39.

[31] Josephus, *Antiq.* xviii. 4. 5.

[32] Josephus, *Antiq.* xviii. 7. 1–2 ; *Wars of the Jews,* ii. 9. 6. The latter passage contains some inaccuracies, which are corrected in the *Antiquities,* namely : (1) According to the *Wars of the Jews,* Agrippa himself immediately followed Antipas to Rome, where, according to the *Antiquities,* he sent Fortunatus ; (2) According to the *Wars of the Jews,* Antipas was banished to Spain ; but, according to the *Antiquities,* to Lugdunum in Gaul.

[33] Dio Cassius, lix. 8 (*Caligula*): Ἀγρίππαν τὸν τοῦ Ἡρώδου ἔγγονον λύσας τε . . . καὶ τῇ τοῦ πάππου ἀρχῇ προστάξας, τὸν ἀδελφὸν ἢ καὶ τὸν υἱὸν οὐχ ὅτι τῶν πατρῴων ἀπεστέρησεν, ἀλλὰ καὶ κατέσφαξε. Although the relationship is not very clearly expressed, the reference can only be to Herod Antipas. To execute those whom he banished was a common custom with Caligula, Suetonius, *Caligula,* 28 ; Dio Cassius, lix. 18 ; Philo, *In Flaccum,* sec. 21, ed. Mangey, ii. 543 ; Lewin, *Fasti sacri,* n. 1562.— According to Josephus, *Wars of the Jews,* ii. 9. 6, Antipas died in banishment in Spain. Instead of Spain we are to read, according to *Antiq.* xviii. 7. 2, Lugdunum in Gaul. For one has no right so to combine contradictory statements of Josephus that a later removal of the banished one from Lyons to Spain may be assumed.

(c) Archelaus, B.C. 4–A.D. 6.

[1] Josephus, *Wars of the Jews,* i. 32. 7, 33. 7.

[2] He is inaccurately styled βασιλεύς in Matt. ii. 22, and in Josephus, *Antiq.* xviii. 4. 3.

[3] Josephus, *Antiq.* xvii. 11. 4 ; *Wars of the Jews,* ii. 6. 3.

[4] By Josephus he is never indeed called Herod, but he is so called by Dio Cassius, lv. 27. That the coins with the inscription ΗΡΩΔΟΥ ΕΘΝΑΡΧΟΥ belong to him cannot be doubted, for no other Herodian besides him bore the title of ethnarch.

[5] Ὠμότης καὶ τυραννίς are charged against him in *Antiq.* xvii. 13. 2. Compare also *Wars of the Jews,* ii. 7. 3.

[6] Josephus, *Antiq.* xvii. 13. 1.

[7] It is this same one who made himself known as a writer. Reports about him and the fragments of his writings are collected by Müller, *Fragmenta Histor. Graec.* iii. 465–484.

[8] Josephus says "after the death of Juba," which, however, is wrong.

[9] Compare generally *Antiq.* xvii. 13. 1 and 4 ; *Wars of the Jews,* ii. 7. 4.

[10] Μετ᾽ ὀλίγον τοῦ ἀφίξεως χρόνον, *Wars of the Jews,* ii. 7. 4.

[11] Josephus, *Antiq.* xvii. 13. 4 ; *Wars of the Jews,* ii. 7. 4.

[12] Josephus, *Antiq.* xvii. 13. 1.

[13] Josephus, *Antiq.* xvii. 13. 2-3 ; *Wars of the Jews,* ii. 7. 3 ; Dio Cassius, lv. 27. Without mentioning the name of Archelaus, Strabo, xvi. 2. 46, p. 765, says that a son of Herod ἐν φυγῇ διετέλει παρὰ τοῖς᾽Αλλόβριξι Γαλάταις λαβὼν οἴκησιν. Vienne, south of Lyons, was the capital of the Allobrogi.—As regards the chronology, Dio Cassius, lv. 27, places the banishment of Archelaus in the consulship of Aemilius Lepidus and Lucius Arruntius, A.D. 6. With this agree the statements of Josephus, *Antiq.* xvii. 13. 2, that it occurred in the tenth year, or, according to the *Wars of the Jews,* ii. 7. 3, in the ninth year of Archelaus.—According to a statement of Jerome, the grave of Archelaus was pointed out near Bethlehem (*Onomasticon,* ed. Lagarde, p. 101 : " sed et propter eandem Bethleem regis quondam Judaeae Archelai tumulus ostenditur "). If this be correct, he must have died in Palestine.

[14] Josephus, *Antiq.* xvii. 13. 5, xviii. 1. 1 ; *Wars of the Jews,* ii. 8. 1.

[15] Josephus, *Antiq.* xvii. 11. 2 ; *Wars of the Jews,* ii. 6. 2.

[16] Josephus, *Wars of the Jews,* ii. 8. 1.

[17] Strabo, xvii. 3. 25, p. 840 .

[18] ᾽Επίτροπος in the following passages : *Wars of the Jews,* ii. 8. 1, 9. 2, 11. 6 (in the parallel passage, *Antiq.* xix. 9. 2 : ἔπαρχος) ; *Antiq.* xx. 6. 2 ; *Wars of the Jews,* ii. 12. 8. ἐπιτροπεύων, *Antiq.* xx. 5. 1. ἐπιτροπή, *Antiq.* xx. 5. 1 *fin.*, 11. 1 ; *Wars of the Jews,* ii. 12. 1, 14. 1.—ἔπαρχος, *Antiq.* xviii. 2. 2, xix. 9. 2 (in parallel passage, *Wars of the Jews,* ii. 11. 6 : ἐπίτροπος).—ἡγησόμενος, *Antiq.* xviii. 1. 1. ἡγεμών, *Antiq.* xviii. 3. 1. προστησόμενος, *Antiq.* xx. 7. 1.—ἐπιμελητής, *Antiq.* xviii. 4. 2.—ἱππάρχης, *Antiq.* xviii. 6. 10 *fin.*

[19] Matt. xxvii. 2, 11, 14, 15, 21, 27, xxviii. 14 ; Luke iii. 1, xx. 20 ; Acts xxiii. 24, 26, 33, xxiv. 1, 10, xxvi. 30.

[20] The decree of the Emperor Claudius in Josephus, *Antiq.* xx. 1. 2 : Κουσπίῳ Φάδῳ τῷ ἐμῷ ἐπιτρόπῳ.—Tacit. *Annal.* xv. 44 : " Christus Tiberio imperitante per procuratorem Pontium Pilatum supplicio adfectus erat." *Ibid.* xii. 54 : " praedas ad procuratores referre . . . jus statuendi etiam de procuratoribus." Cumanus and Felix are intended.

[21] Josephus says, *Antiq.* xvii. *fin.*: τῆς δὲ ᾽Αρχελάου χώρας ὑποτελοῦς προσνεμηθείσης τῇ Σύρων. But when he also, in *Antiq.* xviii. 1. 1, calls Judea a προσθήκη τῆς Συρίας, he evidently does not mean to describe it as a properly integral part, but only as an appendix or annex to the province of Syria. According to the *Wars of the Jews,* ii. 8. 1, the territory of Archelaus had been made into a province, therefore with the privilege of independence, τῆς δὲ ᾽Αρχελάου χώρας εἰς ἐπαρχίαν περιγραφείσης. In reference also to the state of matters after Agrippa's death, Josephus affirms distinctly that the governor of Syria was not set over the kingdom

of Agrippa (*Antiq.* xix. 9. 2), while he immediately afterwards states that this governor had interfered in the affairs of that country (*Antiq.* xx. 1. 1).
—Tacitus refers, in A.D. 17, to Syria and Judea as two provinces alongside of one another (*Annals*, ii. 42 : "provinciae Suria atque Judaea), and says of the arrangements after the death of King Agrippa, *History*, v. 9 : "Claudius ... Judaeam provinciam equitibus Romanis aut libertis permisit." When, therefore, he reports this same fact in another place (*Annals*, xii. 23) in these words : "Ituraeique et Judaei defunctis regibus, Sohaemo atque Agrippa, provinciae Suriae *additi;*" that word *additi* is to be understood in the same way as the προσθήκη of Josephus.

²² Examples : Petronius (*Antiq.* xviii. 8. 2–9 ; *Wars of the Jews*, ii. 10. 1–5), Cassius Longinus (*Antiq.* xx. 1. 1), Cestius Gallus (*Wars of the Jews*, ii. 14. 3, 16. 1, 18. 9 ff.).

²³ Of Vitellius, who deposed Pilate (*Antiq.* xviii. 4. 2), Tacitus (*Annals*, vi. 32) says : "Cunctis quae apud orientem parabantur L. Vitellium praefecit." Of Ummidius Quadratus, who sent Cumanus to Rome (*Antiq.* xx. 6. 2 ; *Wars of the Jews*, ii. 12. 6), it is expressly said in Tacitus (*Annals*, xii. 54) ; "Claudius ... jus statuendi etiam de procuratoribus dederat."

²⁴ Josephus, *Antiq.* xviii. 3. 1 ; *Wars of the Jews*, ii. 9. 2 (Pilate); *Antiq.* xx. 5. 4 ; *Wars of the Jews*, ii. 12. 2 (Cumanus); Acts xxiii. 23–33 (Felix) ; Acts xxv. 1–13 (Festus) ; Josephus, *Wars of the Jews*, ii. 14. 4 *fin.*, 15. 6 *fin.*, 17. 1 (Florus). Tacitus, *History*, ii. 78 : "Caesaream ... Judaeae caput."

²⁵ Josephus, *Wars of the Jews*, ii. 14. 8, 15. 5 ; Philo, *Legat. ad Cajum*, sec. 38 (ed. Mangey, ii. 589 sq.).

²⁶ Josephus, *Antiq.* xvii. 10. 2–3 ; *Wars of the Jews*, ii. 3. 1–4, 17. 7–8. Compare the description, *Wars of the Jews*, v. 4. 3–4.

²⁷ Three legions under Augustus (Josephus, *Antiq.* xviii. 10. 9 ; *Wars of the Jews*, ii. 3. 1, 5. 1) ; four under Tiberius (Tacitus, *Annals*, iv. 5). Seeing that in Egypt under Augustus there were three legions, and under Tiberius only two, see Strabo, xvii. 1. 12, p. 797 , Tacitus, *Annals*, iv. 5, there was meanwhile one of the Egyptian legions transferred to Syria.

²⁸ Josephus, *Antiq.* xiv. 10. 6 .

²⁹ Josephus, *Wars of the Jews*, ii. 3. 4, 4. 2–3. Compare *Antiq.* **xvii. 10. 3 ff.**

³⁰ Josephus, *Antiq.* xix. 9. 1–2.

³¹ Josephus, *Antiq.* xx. 6. 1 : τὴν τῶν Σεβαστηνῶν ἴλην καὶ πεζῶν τέσσαρα τάγματα ; *Wars of the Jews*, ii. 12. 5 : μίαν ἴλην ἱππέων καλουμένην Σεβαστηνῶν.

³² Josephus, *Antiq.* xx. 8. 7 : μέγα φρονοῦντες ἐπὶ τῷ τοὺς πλείστους τῶν ὑπὸ Ῥωμαίους ἐκεῖσε στρατευομένων Καισαρεῖς εἶναι καὶ Σεβαστηνούς. In the parallel passage, *Wars of the Jews*, ii. 13. 7, "Syrians" is the word in the received text.

³³ Josephus, *Wars of the Jews*, iii. 4. 2.

³⁴ Josephus, *Wars of the Jews*, ii. 18. 6.

³⁵ Josephus, *Wars of the Jews*, iii. 7. 32 .

[36] Josephus, *Life*, 24 .

[37] Josephus, *Wars of the Jews*, iii. 2. 1.

[38] *Ibid.* iv. 8. 1.

[39] Acts xxi. 31–37 ; chaps. xxii. 24–29, xxiii. 10, 15–22, xxiv. 7. 22.

[40] Josephus, *Wars of the Jews*, v. 5. 8 .

[41] Josephus, *Wars of the Jews*, v. 5. 8.

[42] The παρεμβολή, barracks or "castle," as in the English version, is referred to in Acts xxi. 34, 37, xxii. 24, xxiii. 10, 16, 32.

[43] Josephus, *Antiq.* xv. 11. 4, xviii. 4. 3.

[44] Josephus, *Wars of the Jews*, v. 5. 8 ; *Antiq.* xx. 5. 3 ; *Wars of the Jews*, ii. 12. 1 ; *Antiq.* xx. 8. 11.

[45] Josephus, *Antiq.* xix. 9. 2.

[46] Josephus, *Antiq.* xx. 6. 1 .

[47] Josephus, *Wars of the Jews*, ii. 8. 1.

[48] Acts xxv. 10 ff., 21, xxvi. 32. Pliny, *Epist.* x. 96 (*al.* 97): "Fuerunt alii similis amentiae, quos quia cives Romani erant adnotavi in urbem remittendos." Mommsen, *Staatsrecht*, ii. 1. 244–246.—Notwithstanding the small number of examples, the above statement (which, in Div. II. vol. ii. pp. 278, 279, I characterized as not quite certain) ought to admit of no doubt. The most important case is that of the Apostle Paul. From it we may conclude that the governor was not obliged in all circumstances to send accused Roman citizens to Rome for judgment ; for the procurator by his own authority takes up the case of Paul though he was aware of his Roman citizenship (according to Acts xxii. 25 ff., xxiii. 27) ; and Paul allows matters to proceed without protesting against this. Only after two years Paul speaks the word that determines his future course : Καίσαρα ἐπικαλοῦμαι (Acts xxv. 11). We must therefore suppose that the procurator could judge even a Roman citizen, unless his prisoner lodged a protest. Only if the accused himself made the claim to be judged in Rome, was the governor obliged to give effect to his claim. But that the governor could himself do that is perfectly conceivable. For he was in every respect the representative of the emperor ; even his tribunal was called " Caesar's judgment-seat" (Acts xxv. 10 : ἑστὼς ἐπὶ τοῦ βήματος Καίσαρός εἰμι). It is therefore quite conceivable that an accused Roman citizen might voluntarily submit himself to such a tribunal as Paul at first did ; for the imperial tribunal of the governor afforded in ordinary circumstances the same protection as the imperial tribunal at Rome, and there could be no pleasure in merely lengthening out the proceedings by a jouruey to Rome. Only if the accused did not trust the impartiality of the governor, had he any interest in claiming the transference of the trial to Rome. Paul makes use of this privilege, when he sees that the procurator is going to judge him in accordance with Jewish ideas.—That this privilege extended only to Roman citizens and not to all provincials may be held as certain, although Paul in his appeal does not make mention of his citizenship (Acts xxv. 10 ff.). Provincials

were judged by the procurator without any right of appeal (Josephus, *Antiq.* xx. 1. 1, 5. 2 ; *Wars of the Jews,* ii. 13. 2). This appears also in the crucifixion of Jesus Christ by Pilate.

⁴⁹ Josephus, *Wars of the Jews,* ii. 14. 9.

⁵⁰ Examples : Josephus, *Antiq.* xx. 6. 2 ; *Wars of the Jews,* ii. 12. 6 (Ummidius Quadratus sent the most distinguished of the Jews and the Samaritans to Rome); *Antiq.* xx. 8. 5 ; *Wars of the Jews,* ii. 13. 2 (Felix sent Eleasar and other Zealots) ; Josephus, *Life,* 3 (Felix sent some of the Jewish priests).

⁵¹ Caesar's decree nominating Hyrcanus begins (Josephus, *Antiq.* xiv. 10. 2): Ἰούλιος Καῖσαρ . . . μετὰ συμβουλίου γνώμης ἐπέκρινα.—Sueton. *Tiber.* 33 : "magistratibus pro tribunali cognoscentibus plerumque se offerebat consiliarium."—The details of a consultation which Petronius, as governor of Syria, held with his *assessores* are described by Philo, *Legat. ad Cajum,* sec. 33, ed. Mangey, ii. 582 sq.

⁵² Le Blant, "Recherches sur les bourreaux du Christ et sur les agents chargés des exécutions capitales chez les Romains " (*Mémoires de l'Académie des inscr. et belles-lettres,* xxvi. 2, 1870, pp. 137–150).

⁵³ Dio Cassius, liii. 13 .

⁵⁴ See, *e.g.,* Suetonius, *Caligula,* 32 : "Saepe in conspectu prandentis vel comissantis . . . miles decollandi artifex quibuscumque e custodia capita amputabat." — Tertullian asks in his treatise, *De corona militis,* c. 11, in order to show the incompatibility of military service with the faith of a Christian : "et vincula et carcerem et tormenta et supplicia administrabit, nec suarum ultor injuriarum ? " The passage proves at least that soldiers were employed at the carrying out of death sentences, even if we should here with Le Blant refuse to believe that this implies more than their employment at soldiers' executions.

⁵⁵ Tacitus, *Annals,* xi. 37 f., xii. 22, xiv. 8, 59, xv. 59 ff., 64, 67, 69.

⁵⁶ Mark vi. 27 : ἀποστείλας ὁ βασιλεὺς σπεκουλάτορα ἐπέταξεν ἐνέγκαι τὴν κεφαλὴν αὐτοῦ.—Seneca, *De Ira,* i. 18. 4 : " Tunc centurio supplicio praepositus condere gladium speculatorem jubet."—Idem, *De beneficiis,* iii. 25 : "speculatoribus occurrit nihilque se deprecari, quominus imperata peragerent, dixit et deinde cervicem porrexit." — *Firmicus Maternus Mathes.* viii. 26 (ed. Basil. 1533, p. 234) : "spiculatores faciet, qui nudato gladio hominum amputent cervices."—*Digest.* xlviii. 20. 6 (aus Ulpian): "neque speculatores ultro sibi vindicent neque optiones [optio in military language = the servant of a Centurio oder Decurio] ea desiderent, quibus spoliatur, quo momento quis punitus est." The soldiers engaged at the executions were therefore in later times no longer allowed, as in the times of Christ, to part the garments of the executed person among them.

⁵⁷ So not only Seneca, *De ira,* i. 18. 4 (where reference is made to the execution of a soldier), but also *Acta Rogatiani et Donatiani,* c. 6 (*lancea militari*), and Linus, *De passione Petri et Pauli, s. fin.* (*vestimenta militis*).

58 στρατιῶται : Matt. xxvii. 27 ; Mark xv. 16 ; Luke xxiii. 36 ; John xix. 2, 23 sq., 32, 34 ; Acts xxi. 35, xxiii. 23, xxvii. 31, 42, xxviii. 16.— Jesus was pierced with a spear (John xix. 34).—A centurion was present at the crucifixion of Jesus (Mark xv. 39, 44 f.; Matt. xxvii. 54 ; Luke xxiii. 47); also at the scourging of Paul (Acts xx. 25). Everything connected with the imprisonment of Paul was of a military character. Hence centurions had immediate charge of him (Acts xxiii. 17, xxiv. 23, xxvii. 1 f.).

59 Tacitus, *Annals*, ii. 42.

60 Josephus, *Wars of the Jews*, ii. 14. 4.

61 Pliny, *Historia Naturalis*, xii. 63–65.

62 Josephus, *Antiq.* xvii. 8. 4 *fin.*, xviii. 4. 3.

63 Josephus, *Antiq.* xii. 4. 3 : ἔτυχε δὲ κατ' ἐκεῖνον τὸν καιρὸν πάντας ἀναβαίνειν τοὺς ἐκ τῶν πόλεων τῶν τῆς Συρίας καὶ Φοινίκης πρώτους καὶ ἄρχοντας ἐπὶ τὴν τῶν τελῶν ὠνήν· κατ' ἔτος δὲ ταῦτα τοῖς δυνατοῖς τῶν ἐν ἑκάστῃ πόλει ἐπίπρασκεν ὁ βασιλεύς. — *Ibid.* xii. 4. 4 : ἐνστάσης δὲ τῆς ἡμέρας καθ' ἣν ἔμελλε τὰ τέλη πιπράσκεσθαι τῶν πόλεων. — Compare also xii. 4. 5. From the latter passage it seems plain that we have here to do, not with customs, but with taxes (Φόροι). The most important of these was the poll-tax (*Antiq.* xii. 4. 1 : τὰς ἰδίας ἕκαστοι τῶν ἐπισήμων ὠνοῦντο πατρίδας Φορολογεῖν, καὶ συναθροίζοντες τὸ προστεταγμένον κεφάλαιον τοῖς βασιλεῦσιν ἐτέλουν). But there was also yet another class of taxes ; for the Jerusalem priesthood had been freed by Antiochus the Great (Josephus, *Antiq.* xii. 3. 3) : ὧν ὑπὲρ τῆς κεφαλῆς τελοῦσι καὶ τοῦ στεφανίτου Φόρου καὶ τοῦ ὑπὲρ τῶν ἄλλων.

64 Wieseler, *Beiträge zur richtigen Würdigung der Evangelien*, 1869, p. 78 f., seeks support for his theory from Josephus, *Antiq.* xiv. 10. 5 : μήτε ἐργολαβῶσί τινες. But here the matters referred to are not the customs, but the revenue derived from the land-tax. Besides, these enactments of Caesar had long been antiquated in the days of the empire by the convulsions that had meanwhile occurred.

65 The assertion of Tertullian, that all tax-gatherers were heathens (*de pudicitia*, c. 9), was rightly contested as early as by Jerome (*Epist.* 21 *ad Damasum*, c. 3, *Opera*, ed. Valarsi, i. 72).

66 According to *Baba kamma* x. 1, one should not take payment in money from the cash-box of the tax-gatherers—should not even receive alms from them (because their money has been gained by robbery). If, however, tax-gatherers have taken away one ass and given another in exchange for it, or robbers have robbed him of his garment and given him another for it, he ought to keep what is given, because it has already ceased to be his property (*Baba kamma*, x. 2). — According to *Nedarim* iii. 4, should one promise, in consequence of a vow, to robbers and tax-gatherers, he may declare the thing the property of the priests or of the king, though it be not so! — Throughout, therefore, tax-gatherers (מוכסין) are placed in the same category as robbers.

67 *Kelim* xvii. 16, speaks of "a walking-stick with a secret place for

pearls," *i.e.* for the purpose of defrauding the revenue. — In treating of the prohibition against wearing garments made of a mixture of linen and wool (Lev. xix. 19 ; Deut. xxii. 11), *Kilajim* ix. 2, remarks, that this is allowed under no circumstances, "not even in order to defraud the revenue" (לִגְנוֹב הַמֶּכֶם). — In this connection, also, may be quoted the passage *Shabbath* viii. 2, where, as an example of a small piece of paper which, on the Sabbath, ought not to be carried from one place to another, a קֶשֶׁר of the tax-gatherer's is mentioned. The expositors understand by the word, a receipt which has been given at one customs office so that the party might pass free at the next, say on the other side of the river. The philological explanation is certainly beset with difficulty, since קֶשֶׁר elsewhere means "binding" (*e.g.* a knot on a string, or a joint in a human body). May it not mean a piece of paper, by which a "connection" between two customs offices is established ?

[68] Compare generally, p. 145. — We have clear evidence of the taking of an oath on the accession of Caligula ; Josephus, *Antiq.* xviii. 5. 3.

[69] Josephus, *Antiq.* xx. 10 *fin.*

[70] Josephus, *Wars of the Jews*, vi. 2. 4 .

[71] This protection extended also to the synagogue services and the Holy Scriptures. When the pagan inhabitants of Dora had placed a statue of the emperor in the Jewish synagogue there, the council of the city was ordered by the legate Petronius to deliver up the guilty parties, and to take care that such outrages should not occur in future (Josephus, *Antiq.* xix. 6. 3). A soldier, who had wantonly torn up a Thorah roll, was put to death by the procurator Cumanus (Josephus, *Antiq.* xx. 5. 4 ; *Wars of the Jews*, ii. 12. 2).

[72] Even the Emperor Augustus and his wife sent brazen wine vessels to the temple at Jerusalem, ἀκρατοφόροι (*Wars of the Jews*, v. 13. 6) and other costly presents (Philo, *Legat. ad Cajum*, sec. 23 and sec. 40, ed. Mangey, ii. 569 *init.*, 592 *fin.*). Marcus Agrippa, on the occasion of his visit to Jerusalem, gave presents (Philo, *Legat. ad Cajum*, sec. 37, ed. Mangey, ii. 589), and offered as a sacrifice a hundred oxen (Josephus, *Antiq.* xvi. 2. 1). Also Vitellius sacrificed there (Josephus, *Antiq.* xviii. 5. 3).

[73] Herod of Chalcis, Josephus, *Antiq.* xx. 1. 3 : τὴν ἐξουσίαν τοῦ νεὼ καὶ τῶν ἱερῶν χρημάτων.—Agrippa II. : *Antiq.* xx. 9. 7 .

[74] Josephus, *Antiq.* xviii. 4. 3, xx. 1. 1–2, xv. 11. 4. Compare, on this beautiful robe of the high priest, Div. II. vol. i. p. 256. On the conquest of Jerusalem by Titus it fell into the hands of the Romans (Josephus, *Wars of the Jews*, vi. 8. 3).

[75] Philo, *Legat. ad Cajum*, sec. 23 and sec. 40, Mangey, ii. 569, 592) ; Josephus, *Wars of the Jews*, ii. 10. 4, 17. 2–4 ; *Against Apion*, ii. 6 *fin.*

[76] This was done thrice over in the time of Caligula, Philo, *Legat. ad Cajum*, sec. 45 (Mangey, ii. 598) ; compare also sec. 32 (Mangey, ii. 580 . the offering presented on the occasion of his accession).

[77] Philo, *In Flaccum*, sec. 7 (ed. Mangey, ii. 524) .

78 Josephus, *Antiq.* xviii. 3. 1 ; *Wars of the Jews,* ii. 9. 2–3. In reference to the military flags and standards, as Domaszewski has shown (Domaszewski, *Die Fahnen im römischen Heere, Abhandlungen des archäolog.-epigraph. Seminares der Universität Wien,* 5 Heft 1885), two different classes are to be distinguished : (1) Those which were used for tactical purposes, and (2) those which had only a symbolical significance. The former were by far the most numerous : to the latter belonged the eagles of the legions and the *signa* which bore the figure of the emperor. Mommsen indeed believes, however, that even to them should be assigned a certain tactical significance ; see *Archäologisch-epigraphische Mittheilungen aus Oesterreich-Ungarn Jahrgang,* x. 1886, p. 1 ff. The figures of the emperor were in the form of a medallion, and were usually attached to the *signa.* Among the legionaries, as well as among the auxiliary cohorts we hear of *imaginiferi* (see list in Cauer, *Ephemeris epigr.* iv. pp. 372–374). —The earlier procurators, therefore, had taken with them to Jerusalem only the *signa* which did not bear the figure of the emperor, that is, the common ones used for tactical purposes ; but Pilate took also those bearing the figure of the emperor.

79 Josephus, *Antiq.* xviii. 5. 3.

80 This was, at least, the popular sentiment. From these religious premises in themselves one might, indeed, arrive at the very opposite result, namely, that even the pagan government was of God, and that it must be submitted to so long as God wills. But this way of considering the subject was not in favour during the period A.D. 6–66, and, as the years went on, those who held it were in an ever-decreasing minority.

81 According to Josephus, *Antiq.* xviii. 2. 1, in the 37th year of the *aera Actiaca, i.e.* autumn, 759–760 A.U.C., or A.D. 6–7. The Actian era begins on 2nd Sept. 723 A.U.C. or B.C. 31.

82 Ζηλωταί, compare Luke vi. 15 ; Acts i. 13 ; *Wars of the Jews,* iv. 3. 9, 5. 1, 6. 3, vii. 8. 1.—For the Biblico-Hebraic קַנָּא we find in later Hebrew also קַנָּאִי and קַנְאָן (see Buxtorf, *Lexicon Chaldaicum;* Levy, *Chaldaisches Wörterbuch;* Levy, *Neuhebräisches Wörterbuch*). The Greek Καναναῖος is constructed out of the later form of the word through the modification of the plural, קַנְאָנַיָּא, as ought to be used in Matt. x. 4, Mark iii. 18, instead of the received Κανανίτης.—In the Mishna, *Sanhedrin* ix. 6, and *Aboth derabbi Nathan* c. 6, we have קַנְאִין or קַנָּאִים. In the former passage, however, are meant, not political, but religious zealots.

83 Compare generally : Josephus, *Antiq.* xviii. 1. 1 and 6 ; *Wars of the Jews,* ii. 8. 1 ; Acts v. 37. Art. "Judas" in the Biblical Dictionaries. Chr. Alfr. Körner, "Judas von Gamala" (*Jahresbericht der Lausitzer Prediger-Gesellschaft zu Leipzig,* 1883–1884, pp. 5–12).—Also the descendants of Judas distinguished themselves as Zealots. His sons James and Simon were executed by Tiberius Alexander (*Antiq.* xx. 5. 2) ; his son Menachem (Manaim) was one of the principal leaders at the beginning of the rebellion in A.D. 66 (*Wars of the Jews,* ii. 17. 8–9). A descendant of Judas and

relative of Menahem of the name of Eleasar conducted the defence of
Masada in A.D. 73 (*Wars of the Jews*, ii. 17. 9, vⅰ. 8. 1 ff.).—A literary
memorial of the views and hopes of the Zealots is the *Assumptio Mosis*,
which had its origin about that time (see Div. II. vol. iii. pp. 73–80),
which goes so far in the way of prophecy as to say that Israel will tread
on "the neck of the eagle," *i.e.* of the Romans (10. 8).

⁸⁴ Compare Josephus, *Antiq.* xviii. 2. 2, 4. 2, 6. 10 *fin.*—The period
during which the first three held office cannot be quite exactly determined.
That of the two following is fixed by the facts that Valerius Gratus was
in office for eleven years (Josephus, *Antiq.* xviii. 2. 2) and Pontius Pilate
for ten years (xviii. 4. 2). But Pilate was deprived of his office before
Vitellius was in Jerusalem for the first time, *i.e.* shortly before Easter
A.D. 36, as results from a comparison of *Antiq.* xviii. 4. 3 with xviii. 5. 3.
The period during which the last two held office is determinedly this,
that Marullus was installed immediately after the accession of Caligula
in March A.D. 37 (Josephus, *Antiq.* xviii. 6. 10 *fin.*).—Eusebius affirms
{*Hist. Eccl.* i. 9) that Josephus sets the date of Pilate's entrance upon office
in the twelfth year of Tiberius, A.D. 25 and 26, which is only so far
correct, that this conclusion may be deduced from Josephus.

⁸⁵ Josephus, *Antiq.* **xv**iii. 6. 5.—Tiberius' care for the provinces is also
witnessed to by Suetonius (*Tiberius*, 23 : "praesidibus onerandas tributo
provincias suadentibus rescripsit : boni pastoris esse tondere pecus, non
deglubere"). Tacitus also, in *Annals*, i. 80, iv. 6, speaks of the long
periods granted to governors.

⁸⁶ Philo, *De Legatione ad Cajum*, sec. 38, ed. Mangey, ii. 590 .

⁸⁷ Josephus, *Antiq.* xviii. 3. 1 ; *Wars of the Jews*, ii. 9. 2–3 ; Eusebius,
Hist. Eccles. ii. 6. 4.—According to Eusebius, *Demonstratio evangelica*, **viii**
p. 403, this story has also been reported by Philo in portions of his work
on the persecutions of the Jews under Tiberius and Caligula, which are
no longer extant (αὐτὰ δὴ ταῦτα καὶ ὁ Φίλων συμμαρτυρεῖ, τὰς σημαίας
Φάσκων τὰς βασιλικὰς τὸν Πιλάτον νύκτωρ ἐν τῷ ἱερῷ ἀναθεῖναι).

⁸⁸ Josephus, *Antiq.* xviii. 3. 2 ; *Wars of the Jews*, ii. 9. 4 ; Eusebius,
Hist. Eccles. ii. 6. 6–7.—The length of the aqueduct is given by Josephus,
Antiq. xviii. 3. 2, at two hundred stadia ; in *Wars of the Jews*, ii. 9. 4, at
four hundred ; so at least is it in our text of Josephus, whereas in his
rendering of the latter passage Eusebius (*Hist. Eccles.* ii. 6. 6) makes it
three hundred stadia. In any case, according to these measurements, there
can be no doubt that the reference is to the aqueduct from the so-called
pool of Solomon south-west of Bethlehem. From thence to Jerusalem
two aqueducts were built in ancient times, of which the ruins of the one
are discernible ; the other is still preserved in comparative completeness.
1. The former is the shorter, and runs upon a higher level ; it begins
south of the pool of Solomon in the Wady Bijar, then goes through the
pool, and thence without any further deviations straight to Jerusalem.
2. The one that is still completed is longer and lies lower ; it begins still
farther south in the Wady Arrub, passes then also through the pool, and
thence with great windings to Jerusalem. The latter conduit is certainly

the more modern ; for, on account of the more remote derivation of the
water, the aqueduct running on the higher level could no longer be used,
and so a new one had to be built. Its length, owing to the long windings,
reaches to about 400 stadia, although the direct line would measure much
less than half that distance. When it had become dilapidated, during
the Middle Ages, earthenware pipes were placed in it. In its original
form it was probably identical with the building of Pilate. Many, however, owing to the absence of any trace of the characteristics of Roman
building, hold it to have been still older than the time of Pilate, and
suppose that Pilate only restored it. But this theory is directly in
opposition to the words of Josephus. That the aqueduct of Pilate ran
along the course taken by this water conduit, may be regarded as highly
probable.—In the Jerusalem Talmud we find the statement that an
aqueduct led from Etam to the temple (*Jer. Yoma*, iii. fol. 41, in Lightfoot, *Descriptio templi*, c. 23, *Opera*, i. 612). In fact, Etam (עיטם), according
to 2 Chron. xi. 6, lay between Bethlehem and Tekoa, unquestionably at
the spring which is now called Ain Atan, in the immediate neighbourhood of Solomon's pool.

[89] Philo, *De Legatione ad Cajum*, sec. 38, ed. Mangey, ii. 589 sq.—That
the incident occurred in the later years of Pilate is probable from the
decisiveness of the tone of Tiberius ; for, according to Philo, *Leg. ad
Cajum*, sec. 34, ed. Mangey, ii. 569, Tiberius assumed a friendly attitude
toward the Jews only after the death of Sejanus in A.D. 31. Sejanus was,
according to Philo, an arch-enemy of the Jews. To his influence is
ascribed both the expulsion of the Jews from Rome in A.D. 19, and the
harsh treatment of Pilate in Judea.

[90] Josephus, *Antiq.* xviii. 4. 1.

[91] Josephus, *Antiq.* xviii. 4. 2. Pilate must have taken about a year
on his journey from Judea to Rome, for he did not arrive in Rome until
after the death of Tiberius (*Antiq. l.c.*). His subsequent fortunes are
not told by Josephus.—The Christian legend makes Pilate either end his
own life by suicide, or suffer death at the hands of the emperor as
punishment for his proceedings against Christ. 1. In regard to the story
about his suicide, Eusebius refers in his *Church History* to the Greek
chroniclers, who "have made a list of the Olympiads together with the
occurrences that took place in each " (*Hist. Eccl.* ii. 7 : ἱστοροῦσιν Ἑλλήνων
οἱ τὰς Ὀλυμπιάδας ἅμα τοῖς κατὰ χρόνους πεπραγμένοις ἀναγράψαντες).
In the *Chronicle* he mentions as his source "the Roman historians
(Eusebius, *Chronicon*, ed. Schoene, ii. 150 sq. : (*a*) According to the
Armenian : "Pontius Pilatus in varias calamitates implicitus sibi ipsi manus
inferebat. Narrant autem qui Romanorum res scriptis mandaverunt."
(*b*) According to Syncellus, ed. Dindorf, i. 624 : Πόντιος Πιλᾶτος ἐπὶ Γαΐου
Καίσαρος ποικίλαις περιπεσὼν συμφοραῖς, ὥς φασιν οἱ τὰ Ῥωμαίων συγγραψά-
μενοι, αὐτοφονευτὴς ἑαυτοῦ ἐγένετο. (*c*) According to Jerome, " Pontius
Pilatus in multas incidens calamitates propria se manu interficit. Scribunt
Romanorum historici "). The verbal agreement of the *Chronicle* with the
Church History (comp. *Hist. Eccl.* ii. 6 : τοσαύταις περιπεσεῖν . . . συμφο-

ραῖς . . . αὐτοφονευτήν) shows that on both occasions Eusebius used the same source. Cedrenus, ed. Bekker, i. 343, and Orosius, vii. 5. 8, are derived directly or indirectly from Eusebius. The legend of Pilate's suicide is further expanded and adorned in the apocryphal literature, e g. in the Mors Pilati in Tischendorf's Evangelia apocrypha, 1876, pp. 456–458 (the demons crowding around his corpse utter forth dreadful shrieks, so that the body is transported from Rome to Vienne on the Rhine, and thence to Lausanne, until at last the people of Lausanne "a se removerunt et in quodam puteo montibus circumsepto immerserunt, ubi adhuc . . . diabolicae machinationes ebullire dicuntur ").—2. According to another form of the Christian legend, Pilate was executed by Nero. So Malalas, ed. Dindorf, pp. 250–257 ; Johannes Antiochenus in Müller, Fragmenta historicorum Graecorum, iv. 574 (also in Fabricius, Cod. apocryph. N. T. iii. 504 sq.); Suidas, Lexicon, s.v. Νέρων ; Chronicon paschale, ed. Dindorf, i. 459. According to the apocryphal Παράδοσις Πιλάτου it was Tiberius who caused Pilate to be executed. See text in Thilo, Codex apocryph. N. T. pp. 813–816 ; Tischendorf, Evang. apocryph. pp. 449–455. According to this account Pilate dies as a penitent Christian.

92 Josephus, Antiq. xviii. 4. 3, says that it was at the time of a Passover feast.

93 Josephus, Antiq. xviii. 4. 3, xv. 11. 4.

94 Josephus, Antiq. xviii. 5. 3.

95 Philo, De Legatione ad Cajum, sec. 32 (Opera, ed. Mangey, ii. 580).

96 Josephus, Antiq. xviii. 7. 2 fin.:

97 Philo, Legat. ad Cajum, secs. 11–15 (ed. Mangey, ii. 556–561); Josephus, Antiq. xviii. 7. 2 fin., 8. 1, xix. 1. 1 ff. ; Dio Cassius, lix. 26, 28 ; Suetonius, Caligula, 22

98 Philo, In Flaccum, sec. 3 init., ed. Mangey, ii. 518 .

99 Philo, In Flaccum, secs. 3–4, Opera, ed. Mangey, ii. 518–520.—On the death of young Tiberius, see also Philo, Legat. ad Cajum, secs. 4–5, Mangey, ii. 549 sq. ; Dio Cassius, lix. 8 ; Suetonius, Caligula, 23. On the death of Nävius Sertorius Macro (after the overthrow of Sejanus, A.D. 31, praefactus praetorio, see Pauly's Real-Encyclopaedie, v. 402) ; Philo, Legat. ad Cajum, secs. 6–8, Mangey, ii. 550–554 ; Dio Cassius, lix. 10 ; Suetonins, Caligula, 26.—The death of Tiberius, according to Dio Cassius, l.c., occurred in A.D. 37 ; that of Macro in A.D. 38.

100 Philo, In Flaccum, secs. 5–6, ed. Mangey, ii. 521 sq.

101 Philo, In Flaccum, secs. 6–8, ed. Mangey, ii. 523–525.

102 Plundering of houses : Philo, In Flaccum, sec. 8, ed. Mangey, ii. 525 ; Legat. ad Cajum, sec. 18, ed. Mangey, ii. 563. — Massacre of the Jews : Philo, In Flaccum, sec. 9, ed. Mangey, ii. 526 sq.; Legat. at Cajum, sec. 19, ed. Mangey, ii. 564.—Destruction and profanation of the synagogues or proseuchae : Legat. ad Cajum, sec. 20, ed. Mangey. ii. 565.—The plundering, according to Philo, In Flaccum, sec. 11, ed. Mangey, ii. 531 init., extended to four hundred houses.

[103] Philo, *In Flaccum*, sec. 10, ed. Mangey, ii. 527–529.

[104] Philo, *In Flaccum*, sec. 11, ed. Mangey, ii. 529–531.

[105] Philo, *In Flaccum*, sec. 12, ed. Mangey, ii. 531, 532.

[106] Philo, *In Flaccum*, secs. 12–21, ed. Mangey, ii. 532–544.—The chronological data for the incidents above recorded converge upon the autumn of A.D. 38. Compare Lewin, *Fasti sacri*, n. 1534–1538. Agrippa arrived at Alexandria favoured by the trade-winds (ἐτήσιοι, *In Flaccum*, sec. 5, ed. Mangey, ii. 521), which blow from the 20th of July for the space of thirty days (Pliny, *Hist. Nat.* ii. 47. 124, xviii. 28. 270). The scourging of the thirty-eight members of the Jewish Gerousia took place on Caligula's birthday (*In Flaccum*, sec. 10, ed. Mangey, ii. 529), *i.e.* on the 31st August (Suetonius, *Caligula*, 8). The departure of Flaccus, which occurred soon after this, took place during the Jewish Feast of Tabernacles (*In Flaccum*, sec. 14 *init.* ed. Mangey, ii. 534); therefore in September or October.— The year 38 is obtained from the two following facts : (1) Agrippa returned from Rome to Palestine in the second year of Caligula (Josephus, *Antiq.* xviii. 6. 11). (2) The Jewish warehouses were plundered when they had been closed on account of the mourning for Drusilla, the sister of Caligula (Philo, *In Flaccum*, sec. 8, ed. Mangey, ii. 525). But she died in A.D. 38 (Dio Cassius, lix. 10–11).

[107] According to Dio Cassius, lix. 10, Caligula had appointed Macro governor of Egypt. But he, while still Flaccus was governor of Egypt, was compelled to commit suicide (Philo, *In Flaccum*, secs. 3–4, ed. Mangey, ii. 519). He therefore never actually entered upon his governorship.

[108] Josephus, *Antiq.* xviii. 8. 1.—According to Josephus the two embassies consisted each of three men ; according to Philo, *Legat. ad Cajum*, sec. 46, ed. Mangey, ii. 600, the Jewish embassy consisted of five men.

[109] Philo, *Legat. ad Cajum*, secs. 25–26, ed. Mangey, ii. 570 (Helicon) ; *ibid.* sec. 27, ed. Mangey, ii. 571 (the ambassadors of the Alexandrians) ; *ibid.* secs. 27–28, ed. Mangey, ii. 571 sq. (how the Jewish ambassadors vainly entreated Helicon to secure them an audience).

[110] Philo, *Legat. ad Cajum*, sec. 28, ed. Mangey, ii. 572 (the narrator here speaks evidently, in the first person, of himself).

[111] Philo, *Legat. ad Cajum*, sec. 29, ed. Mangey, ii. 573.

[112] Philo, *Legat. ad Cajum*, secs. 44–46, ed. Mangey, ii. 597–600.—In the narrative of Philo, it is remarkable that he speaks about the complaints of the Alexandrian and Jewish ambassadors in Rome without having made any mention of the sending of the embassies. Possibly there is some gap in the text that has come down to us. So Massebieau, *Le classement des oeuvres de Philon* [*Bibliothèque de l'École des Hautes Études, Section des Sciences religieuses*, vol. i. Paris 1889], p. 65 sqq. But this hypothesis seems to me quite unnecessary ; for Philo does not by any means propose to tell the history of this embassy, as one might suppose from the false title, which was not given by Philo himself. His theme is rather the same as that of Lactantius in his treatise, *De Mortibus Persecutorum* : that

the persecutors of the pious are punished by God. So correctly Masse-bieau. As with Flaccus, so also with Caligula—first of all his evil deeds are enumerated, and then the divine retribution ; only this second half of the treatise about Caligula is no longer extant. The Jews are here, there-fore, not the principal figures, but Caligula ; and so the Jewish embassy from Alexandria to Rome is quite a subordinate matter.

113 Josephus, *Antiq.* xix. 5. 2.

114 Philo, *Legat. ad Cajum*, sec. 30, ed. Mangey, ii. 575 sq.

115 According to Josephus, *Antiq.* xviii. 8. 2, two legions ; according to *Wars of the Jews*, ii. 10. 1, three. The former statement is the correct one ; for in Syria there were four legions (see above, p. 182). When therefore Philo, sec. 31, says " the half," this agrees with Josephus, *Antiq.* xviii. 8. 2.

116 Philo, *Legat. ad Cajum*, sec. 31, ed. Mangey, ii. 576–579.

117 Philo, *Legat. ad Cajum*, sec. 32 f., ed. Mangey, ii. 579–582 ; Jose-phus, *Antiq.* xviii. 8. 2 ; *Wars of the Jews*, ii. 10. 1–3.

118 Philo, *Legat. ad Cajum*, secs. 33–34, ed. Mangey, ii. 582–584. This correspondence does not occur to be identical with that spoken of by Josephus, *Antiq.* xviii. 8. 2 ; for the latter had taken place before the proceedings at Ptolemais.

119 Josephus, *Antiq.* xviii. 8. 3–6 ; *Wars of the Jews*, ii. 10. 3–5. The recall of the army is merely mentioned in *Wars of the Jews*, ii. 10. 5.

120 Philo, *Legat. ad Cajum*, sec. 35, ed. Mangey, ii. 584–586.

121 Philo, *Legat. ad Cajum*, secs. 36–41, ed. Mangey, ii. 586–594.

122 Philo, *Legat. ad Cajum*, secs. 42–43, ed. Mangey, ii. 594, 595. The projected journey to Alexandria is also mentioned in sec. 33, ed. Mangey, ii. 583, and in Suetonius, *Caligula*, c. 49.—A somewhat different account of Agrippa's intervention is given by Josephus, *Antiq.* xviii. 8. 7–8. According to him, on a particular occasion when Agrippa had won the special good will of the emperor by means of a luxurious banquet, Caligula demanded of the Jewish king that he should ask of him any favour that he desired, whereupon he besought the emperor for the revocation of the order to set up his statue in the temple of Jerusalem. The result, according to Josephus, was the same, namely, that the prayer was granted.

123 Josephus, *Antiq.* xviii. 8. 8–9 ; *Wars of the Jews*, ii. 10. 5.—Compare also, generally, the Jewish tradition in Derenbourg, p. 207 sq.

The order of succession in time of the different incidents recorded may be set forth in something like the following arrangement. It must be here presupposed that the transmission of news from Rome or Gaul to Jerusalem, and *vice versâ*, would ordinarily take about two months :—

Winter, A.D. 39–40 :   Petronius receives orders from Caligula to set up
                          his statue in the temple at Jerusalem, and goes
                          with two legions into Palestine.

April or May A.D. 40 :	When harvest was at hand, the negotiations were opened at Ptolemais. First report of Petronius to Caligula (Philo, *Legat. ad Cajum*, secs. 32–33 ; Josephus, *Antiq.* xviii. 8. 2 ; *Wars of the Jews*, ii. 10. 1–3).
June :	Caligula receives Petronius' first report, and answers him, urging him to make haste (Philo, sec. 34).
August :	Petronius receives Caligula's answer, but still puts off the final decision.
End of September :	Agrippa pays a visit to Caligula at Rome or Puteoli ; learns of what had happened, and intervenes. Caligula sends to Petronius the order to put a stop to the undertaking (Philo, *Legat. ad Cajum*, secs. 35–42 ; Josephus, *Antiq.* xviii. 8. 7–8).
Beginning of November:	Negotiations at Tiberias in time of sowing ; Petronius prays the emperor to desist from setting up the statue (Josephus, *Antiq.* xviii. 8. 3–6 ; *Wars of the Jews*, ii. 10. 3–5).
End of November :	Petronius receives the order to put a stop to the undertaking.
Beginning of January A.D. 41 :	Caligula receives the petition of Petronius to desist from setting up the statue, and sends him the order to take away his own life (Josephus, *Antiq.* xviii. 8. 8).
24th January A.D. 41 :	Caligula is murdered.
Beginning of March :	Petronius receives the news of Caligula's death.
Beginning of April :	Petronius receives the letter with the order for self-destruction (Josephus, *Antiq.* xviii. 8. 9 ; *Wars of the Jews*, ii. 10. 5).

This table may still be regarded as essentially correct, even if in some cases the time taken for a letter to travel from Italy or Gaul to Palestine, and *vice versâ*, might be somewhat shorter. On the average the time may be put down at between one or two months.

[124] Josephus, *Antiq.* xix. 5. 1 ; *Wars of the Jews*, ii. 11. 5.

Excursus. The so-called Testimony of Josephus to Christ.

[1] The equally ancient *Parisin.* 1419, which Gerlach, p. 107, designates the oldest manuscript, contains only the first ten books of the *Antiquities*.

[2] In several passages where Origen speaks of James, the brother of Jesus Christ, he mentions it as a remarkable circumstance that Josephus should have made favourable allusion to this man, although he (Josephus) did not believe in Jesus as the Christ. (1) *Com. in Matth.* tom. x. c. 17

(on Matt. xiii. 55): καὶ τὸ θαυμαστόν ἐστιν, ὅτι τὸν Ἰησοῦν ἡμῶν οὐ κατα-
δεξάμενος εἶναι Χριστόν, οὐδὲν ἧττον Ἰακώβῳ δικαιοσύνην ἐμαρτύρησε τοσαύτην.
(2) *Contra Cels.* i. 47: ὁ δ᾿ αὐτὸς καίτοι γε ἀπιστῶν τῷ Ἰησοῦ ὡς Χριστῷ
κ.τ.λ.—It is scarcely conceivable that Origen would have so expressed
himself, if he had known the famous passage.

§ 18. HEROD AGRIPPA I., A.D. 37, 40, 41-44.

[1] The New Testament, Acts xii., names him simply as Herod. By
Josephus, however, and on the coins, he is always designated Agrippa.

[2] As is evident from *Antiq.* xix. 8. 2, according to which he had
reached at his death, in A.D. 44, the age of fifty-four years.

[3] Josephus, *Antiq.* xviii. 5. 4.

[4] Josephus, *Antiq.* xviii. 6. 1.

[5] Μαλαθά or Μαλααθά is also several times referred to in the *Onomasticon* of Eusebius (ed. Lagarde, pp. 214, 255, 266). It lay fully 20 Roman
miles south of Hebron, probably on the site of the modern Tell-el-Milh.

[6] Josephus, *Antiq.* xviii. 6. 2.

[7] Josephus, *Antiq.* xviii. 5. 3 .

[8] Where Tiberius lived almost without interruption from A.D. 27
(Tacitus, *Annals,* iv. 67) down to his death.

[9] Josephus, *Antiq.* xviii. 6. 3.

[10] *Ibid.* xviii. 6. 4.

[11] Josephus, *Antiq.* xviii. 6. 5.

[12] Josephus, *Antiq.* xviii. 6. 6–7 ; *Wars of the Jews,* ii. 9. 5.

[13] Philo, *In Flaccum,* sec. 6, ed. Mangey, ii. 523.

[14] Josephus, *Antiq.* xviii. 6. 10 ; *Wars of the Jews,* ii. 9. 6 ; Philo, *In
Flaccum,* sec. 5 *init.,* ed. Mangey, ii. 520 sq. ; Dio Cassius, lix. 8.—From
the inscription at El-Muschennef (in Le Bas et Waddington, *Inscriptions
Grecques et Latines,* t. iii. n. 2211) we see that the territories of Agrippa
extended as far as what is now the Haurân.

[15] Josephus, *Antiq.* xviii. 6. 11 ; Philo, *In Flaccum,* sec. 5, ed. Mangey,
ii. 521.

[16] Josephus, *Antiq.* xix. 1–4 ; *Wars of the Jews,* ii. 11.

[17] Josephus, *Antiq.* xix. 5. 1 ; *Wars of the Jews,* ii. 11. 5 ; Dio Cassius,
lx. 8. Josephus expresses himself in such a manner as to imply that the
tetrarchy of Lysanias was now anew conferred upon Agrippa. But seeing
that he had already received that territory from Caligula, the statement
can only mean that now the gift was formally confirmed. It is in the
highest degree probable that Josephus found in the documents which he
used the statement that Agrippa, by the favour of Claudius, held possession
of the tetrarchy of Lysanias in addition to the whole territories of his
grandfather.

[18] Josephus, *Antiq.* xix. 6. 1.—The golden charms which, according to the Mishna, *Middoth* iii. 8, were hung on the curtain of the temple court, can scarcely be the same as are referred to here. See the contrary in Derenbourg, p. 209.

[19] Josephus, *Antiq.* **xix. 6. 1.**

[20] Josephus, *Antiq.* xix. 7. 3 .

[21] Mishna, *Bikkurim* iii. 4 : When the procession with the firstlings of the fruits of the fields reached the temple mount "every one, even King Agrippa himself, took his basket upon his shoulder, and went up until he came into the court," etc.—Here, as generally throughout the rabbinical traditions, it is not, indeed, quite certain whether Agrippa I. or II. is meant.

[22] Josephus, *Antiq.* xix. 6. 3.

[23] Josephus, *Antiq.* xx. 7. 1.—Epiphanes afterwards refused to fulfil his promise, and therefore the marriage was not consummated.

[24] At the close of each Sabbatical year, *i.e.* in the beginning of the eighth year, Deuteronomy had to be read at the Feast of Tabernacles (Deut. xxxi. 10 ff.; *Sota* vii. 8).

[25] Mishna, *Sota* vii. 8. The declaration of the people could also be vindicated in accordance with strictly Pharisaic ideas ; for when the Edomites (Idumeans) went over to Judaism, their descendants in the third generation became full members and citizens of the Israelitish commonwealth (Deut. xxiii. 8, 9).

[26] Josephus, *Antiq.* xix. 7. 3 .

[27] Josephus, *Antiq.* xix. 6. 3.

[28] Josephus, *Antiq.* xix. 7. 1.

[29] Frankel, *Darke-ha-Mishna*, p. 58 sq., regards him as identical with Simon, the reputed son of Hillel and father of Gamaliel I. But the existence of this Simon is more than questionable (see Div. II. vol. i. p. 363). Besides, the chronology does not rightly fit in, since Gamaliel I. was already head of the school before the time of Agrippa (Acts v. 34).

[30] Josephus, *Antiq.* xix. 7. 4.

[31] Josephus, *Antiq.* xix. 7. 2 ; *Wars of the Jews*, ii. 11. 6, v. 4. 2. Compare also Derenbourg, p. 218 f. The original forbearance of the emperor toward the building of the wall seems to have been purchased by Agrippa through the bribing of the imperial councillors. Compare Tacitus, *History*, **v.** 12 : "per avaritiam Claudianorum temporum empto jure muniendi struxere muros in pace tamquam ad bellum."

[32] Josephus, *Antiq.* xix. 8. 1.

[33] Acts xii. 1–19.

[34] Josephus, *Antiq.* xix. 9. 1.

[35] Josephus, *Antiq.* xix. 7. 5.—The favour shown to Berytus is explained by the circumstance that it was a Roman colony.

[36] Josephus, *Antiq.* xix. 8. 2.

[37] Josephus, *Antiq.* xix. 9. 1.

[38] On the inscription at Athens, *Corpus Inscr. Graec.* n. 361 = *Corpus Inscr. Atticarum*, iii. 1, n. 556, his daughter Berenice is called 'Ιουλία Βερενείκη βασίλισσα μεγάλη, 'Ιουλίου 'Αγρίππα βασιλέως θυγατήρ.—There is also evidence of other members of the Herodian family bearing the Gentile name of the Julians; by Agrippa II., from the inscription given by Le Bas et Waddington, *Inscriptions*, t. iii. n. 2112. Agrippa I. had a son-in-law called 'Ιούλιος 'Αρχέλαος (Josephus, *Antiq.* xix. 9. 1; *Against Apion*, i. 9). Probably also the Γάϊος 'Ιούλιος βασιλέως 'Αλεξάνδρου υἱὸς 'Αγρίππας ταμίας καὶ ἀντιστράτηγος τῆς 'Ασίας (Wood, *Discoveries at Ephesus, Inscriptions from the Great Theatre*, p. 50, note 5), referred to in an inscription at Ephesus, belonged to the Herodian family.

[39] The most complete form of the titles of Agrippa I. and Agrippa II. has been given us in the interesting inscriptions which Waddington found at Sī'a, half a league from Kanawât, on the western base of the Haurân (Le Bas et Waddington, *Inscriptions Grecques et Latines*, t. iii. n. 2365). It runs as follows:—

'Επὶ βασιλέως μεγάλου 'Αγρίππα Φιλοκαισαρος εὐσεβοῦς καὶ Φιλορωμα[ί-] ου, τοῦ ἐκ βασιλέως μεγάλου 'Αγρίππα Φιλοκαίσαρος εὐσεβοῦς καὶ [Φι-] λορωμαίου, 'Αφαρεὺς ἀπελεύθερος καὶ 'Αγρίππας υἱὸς ἀνέθηκαν.

The titles φιλόκαισαρ and φιλορώμαιος occur very frequently during that period. Numerous examples are given in the Index of the *Corpus Inscr. Graec.* p. 165.

[40] Keim in Schenkel's *Bibellexikon*, iii. 55.

[41] The rendering of the story of Eusebius, *Hist. eccl.* ii. 10, is in all essential points in thorough agreement with that of Acts and Josephus, although he changes the owl of Josephus into an angel.

[42] Josephus, *Antiq.* xviii. 6. 7.—On the owl as a bird of evil omen, see Pliny, *Hist. Nat.* x. 12. 34–35.

[43] Josephus, *Antiq.* xix. 9. 1–2; *Wars of the Jews*, ii. 11. 6.

§ 19. THE ROMAN PROCURATORS, A.D. 44–66.

[1] Josephus, *Wars of the Jews*, ii. 11. 6.

[2] Josephus, *Antiq.* xix. 9. 2.

[3] Josephus, *Antiq.* xx. 1. 1.

[4] Josephus, *Antiq.* xx. 1. 1–2. Compare xv. 11. 4.

[5] Josephus, *Antiq.* xx. 5. 1 = Eusebius, *Hist. eccl.* ii. 11.—The name Theudas is met with also elsewhere (*Corp. Inscr. Graec.* n. 2684, 3563, 3920, 5698; Wetstein, *Nov. Test.* on Acts v. 36; Pape-Benseler, *Wörterbuch der griech. Eigennamen, s.v.*). —Our rebel chief Theudas is well known from the reference made to him in Acts v. 36, where the allusion to him occurs in a speech of Gamaliel delivered a considerable time

before the actual appearance of Theudas. Indeed, according to the representation of the narrative of the Acts, the appearance of Theudas is placed before that of Judas of Galilee in A.D. 6. But as many are unwilling that so serious an error should be attributed to the author of the Acts of the Apostles, several theologians have assumed the existence of two different rebels of the name of Theudas. But such an assumption is not justified in consideration of the slight authority of the Acts in such matters.

[6] Josephus, *Antiq.* xx. 5. 2, xviii. 8. 1.

Compare in regard to this famine, besides *Antiq.* xx. 5. 2, also *Antiq.* iii. 15. 3, xx. 2. 6; Acts xi. 28-30.

[8] Josephus, *Antiq.* xx. 5. 2.—Tiberius Alexander served at a late period under Corbulo against the Parthians (Tacitus, *Annals,* xv. 28), was then made governor of Egypt (Josephus, *Wars of the Jews,* ii. 15. 1, 18. 7, iv. 10. 6; Tacitus, *History,* i. 11, ii. 74, 79; Suetonius, *Vespasian,* 6), and was the most distinguished and trusted counsellor of Titus at the siege of Jerusalem (*Wars of the Jews,* v. 1. 6, vi. 4. 3). His full name is given in an edict which he issued as governor of Egypt: "Tiberius Julius Alexander" (*Corpus Inscr. Graec.* n. 4957).

[9] Ventidius, according to Tacitus, *Annals,* xii. 54; in Josephus called only Cumanus.

[10] Compare *Wars of the Jews,* v. 5. 8; *Antiq.* xx. 8. 11.

[11] Josephus, *Antiq.* xx. 5. 3; *Wars of the Jews,* ii. 12. 1.

[12] Josephus, *Antiq.* xx. 5. 4; *Wars of the Jews,* ii. 12. 2.

[13] Josephus, *Antiq.* xx. 6. 1-3; *Wars of the Jews,* ii. 12. 3-7.—There is a divergence in regard to essential points between this representation of Josephus and that given by Tacitus, *Annals,* xii. 54. According to the Roman historian, Cumanus was only procurator of Galilee, while during the same period Felix had the administration of Samaria, and indeed of Judea also (Felix . . . jam pridem Judaeae impositus . . . aemulo ad deterrima Ventidio Cumano, cui pars provinciae habebatur, ita divisae, ut huic Galilaeorum natio, Felici Samaritae parerent). Felix and Cumanus were equally to blame for the bloody conflicts that took place. But Quadratus condemned only Cumanus, and even allowed Felix to take part in the trial as judge.—It is really impossible to do away with the contradiction between Tacitus and Josephus; for Josephus leaves no doubt of this, that, according to his understanding of the matter, Cumanus was the only governor in the territory of the Jews, and that Felix only went to Palestine as his successor. Compare especially the definite statement that the high priest Jonathan, who was in Rome at the time of the deposition of Cumanus, had besought the emperor that he should send Felix (see note 14). But it seems a matter scarcely to be questioned that the very detailed narrative of Josephus deserves to be preferred to the indeterminate remarks made by Tacitus.

[14] Josephus, *Wars of the Jews,* ii. 12. 6. Compare *Antiq.* xx. 8. 5.

[15] Josephus, *Antiq.* xx. 7. 1; *Wars of the Jews,* ii. 12. 8; Suetonius, *Claudius,* 28.

[16] Tacitus, *History*, v. 9 ; Suetonius, *Claudius*, 28.

[17] Antonius Felix, according to Tacitus, *History*, v. 9.

[18] Suetonius, *Claudius*, 28, gives prominence to it as something un-usual : " Felicem, quem cohortibus et alis provinciaeque Judaeae prae-posuit."

[19] *History*, v. 9 : " per omnem saevitiam ac libidinem jus regium servili ingenio exercuit."

[20] Suetonius, *Claudius*, 28, calls him *trium reginarum maritum*.

[21] Tacitus, *History*, v. 9 .

[22] As appears evidently from *Antiq.* xix. 9. 1, according to which Drusilla, the youngest of the daughters of Agrippa I., was six years old at the time of his death.

[23] Josephus, *Antiq.* xx. 7. 1.

[24] Josephus, *Antiq.* xx. 7. 2.   Compare Acts of the Apostles xxiv. 24.

[25] Tacitus, *Annals*, xii. 54 .

[26] This appears most distinctly from the account given in *Wars of the Jews*, ii. 13. 2–6, which is much more lucid and clear than that given in the *Antiq.* xx. 8. 5–6.

[27] *Wars of the Jews*, ii. 13. 2 ; *Antiq.* xx. 8. 5.

[28] Tacitus, *Annals*, xii. 54 .

[29] Josephus, *Antiq.* xx. 8. 10.

[30] Josephus, *Wars of the Jews*, ii. 13. 3 ; *Antiq.* xx. 8. 5.—The Sicarii are also referred to during the war, when they had in their possession the fortress of Masada. See *Wars of the Jews*, ii. 17. 6, iv. 7. 2, 9. 5, vii. 8. 1 ff., 10. 1, 11. 1.   The author of the Acts of the Apostles was also aware of their existence as a political party (Acts xxi. 38 : τοὺς τετρα-κισχιλίους ἄνδρας τῶν σικαρίων).—In Latin *sicarius* is the common desig-nation for a murderer.   Thus, for example, the law passed under Sulla against murderers is called " lex Cornelia de Sicariis " (Pauly's *Real-Encyclopaedie*, iv. 969, and generally the article " Sicarius " in the same *Encyclopaedie*, vi. 1. 1153 f.).   It also occurs in the Mishna in this same general sense : *Bikkurim* i. 2, ii. 3 ; *Gittin* v. 6 ; *Machshirin* i. 6.   In none of these passages is the term *Sicarii* used to designate a political party.   In the passage *Machshirin* i. 6 the story told is this, that on one occasion the inhabitants of Jerusalem hid their fig-cakes in water from fear of the סיקרים.   In the other passages a case is supposed in which a robber-murderer has violently appropriated to himself a piece of land. It is asked what is to be done in this case with reference to the taxes (*Bikkurim* i. 2, ii. 3), and whether one would be able by process of law to buy from the robber-murderer such a piece of land (*Gittin* v. 6).   In reference to this last point it is said that since the war, which here clearly means the war of Hadrian, it had been decreed that the purchase would be valid only when the property had been first obtained from the lawful possessors and then from the robber who had taken it by force, but not when it had been bought first from the robber and then from the legal owners.   Here we are to understand by the *Sicarii* rather non-

Jewish than Jewish robber-murderers. Compare generally : Grätz, *Geschichte der Juden*, iv. 422 f., who wrongly makes the *Sicarii* a Jewish political party ; Derenbourg, *Historie de la Palestine*, pp. 280, 475 sqq. ; Levy, *Neuhebräisches Wörterbuch*, iii. 518.—The correct form סיקרים = *sicarii*, is found in *Machshirin* i. 6 (*e.g.* in the Cambridge manuscript edited by Lowe). But it is deserving of remark that in the other passages the best texts, *e.g.* the Cambridge manuscript, constantly have סיקריקן, *sicaricon*, and that indeed as a mas. sing. = "the murderer."

[31] Josephus, *Wars of the Jews*, ii. 13. 4 ; *Antiq.* xx. 8. 6.

[32] Josephus, *Wars of the Jews*, ii. 13. 5 ; *Antiq.* xx. 8. 6 : ὁ δὲ Αἰγύπτιος αὐτὸς διαδρὰς ἐκ τῆς μάχης ἀφανὴς ἐγένετο. Undoubtedly the people believed in a wonderful deliverance and escape, and hoped for a return, to which even Acts xxi. 38 contains a reference.—Compare also Eusebius, *Hist. eccl.* ii. 21.

[33] Josephus, *Wars of the Jews*, ii. 13. 6 ; *Antiq.* xx. 8. 6.

[34] Josephus, *Antiq.* xx. 8. 8.

[35] Acts of the Apostles, xxiv. 24 f.

[36] Josephus, *Antiq.* xx. 8. 7 ; *Wars of the Jews*, ii. 13. 7.

[37] Josephus, *Antiq.* xx. 8. 9 ; *Wars of the Jews*, ii. 14. 1.

[38] Josephus, *Antiq.* xx. 8. 9 ; *Wars of the Jews*, ii. 14. 4.—The two representations of Josephus are inconsistent with one another in certain particulars. According to *Antiq.* xx. 8. 9, the ambassadors of the Jews of Caesarea did not go to Rome to make their complaint against Felix until after the entrance of Festus upon his office. According to *Wars of the Jews*, ii. 13. 7 *fin.*, however, the ambassadors of both parties had been sent by Felix himself to Rome, which is probable for this reason, that even according to *Antiq.* xx. 8. 9 the ambassadors of the Syrians were also in Rome.—According to *Wars of the Jews*, ii. 14. 4, it would seem as if the decision of the emperor had not been given before A.D. 66. But this is not possible, since Pallas, who died in A.D. 62 (Tacitus, *Annals*, xiv. 65), played an important part in the proceedings.

[39] Josephus, *Antiq.* xx. 8. 10 ; *Wars of the Jews*, ii. 14. 1.

[40] Josephus, *Antiq.* xx. 9. 1.

[41] Eusebius, *Hist. eccl.* ii. 23. 21-24 ; literally the same as Josephus, *Antiq.* xx. 9. 1.

[42] Origen makes reference three times to that passage in Josephus :— (1) *Comment. in Matth.* tom. x. c. 17 (on Matt. xiii. 55) : "So high was the reputation of this James among the people for his righteousness, that Josephus in his *Antiquities*, when he is explaining the cause of the destruction of the temple, says, κατὰ μῆνιν θεοῦ ταῦτα αὐτοῖς ἀπηντηκέναι, διὰ τὰ εἰς Ἰάκωβον, τὸν ἀδελφὸν Ἰησοῦ τοῦ λεγομένου Χριστοῦ, ὑπ᾽ αὐτῶν τετολμημένα. . . . Λέγει δὲ, ὅτι καὶ ὁ λαὸς ταῦτα ἐνόμιζε διὰ τὸν Ἰάκωβον πεπονθέναι." (2) *Contra Celsum*, i. 47 : Ὁ δ᾽ αὐτὸς . . . ζητῶν τὴν αἰτίαν τῆς τῶν Ἱεροσολύμων πτώσεως καὶ τῆς τοῦ ναοῦ καθαιρέσεως . . . Φησὶ ταῦτα συμβεβηκέναι τοῖς Ἰουδαίοις κατ᾽ ἐκδίκησιν Ἰακώβου τοῦ δικαίου, ὃς ἦν ἀδελφὸς Ἰησοῦ τοῦ λεγομένου Χριστοῦ, ἐπειδήπερ δικαιότατον αὐτὸν ὄντα ἀπέκτειναν.

(3) *Contra Celsum*, ii. 13 *fin.*: Τίτος καθεῖλε τὴν Ἱερουσαλήμ· ὡς μὲν Ἰώσηπος γράφει, διὰ Ἰάκωβον τὸν δίκαιον, τὸν ἀδελφὸν Ἰησοῦ τοῦ λεγομένου Χριστοῦ.— In the same style as Origen, *contra Celsus*, i. 47, and presumably following him, the passage is quoted in Eusebius, *Hist. eccl.* ii. 23. 20. From Eusebius are derived the short statements in Jerome, *De viris illustr.* c. 2 and 13; *adversus Jovinianum*, i. 39 (*Opera*, ed. Vallarsi, ii. 301). The Greek translation of Jerome, *De viris illustr.*, is reproduced by Suidas, *Lexicon*, *s.v.* Ἰώσηπος.

[43] Eusebius has preserved for us (*Hist. eccl.* ii. 23. 11–18) a literal transcript of the account given by Hegesippus. According to him, James was cast down from the pinnacle of the temple, then stoned, and at last beaten to death by a fuller (γναφεύς) with a fuller's club. The narrative concludes with these words: Καὶ εὐθὺς Οὐεσπασιανὸς πολιορκεῖ αὐτούς. Clement of Alexandria, in Eusebius, *Hist. eccl.* ii. 1. 4, and Epiphanius, *Haer.* 78. 14, base their statements upon Hegesippus. The close connection in time between the execution of James and the destruction of Jerusalem is also emphasized by Eusebius in his own exposition (*Hist. eccl.* iii. 11. 1): μετὰ τὴν Ἰακώβου μαρτυραν καὶ τὴν αὐτίκα γενομένην ἅλωσιν τῆς Ἱερουσαλήμ. Though much that is legendary is contained in the narrative of Hegesippus, it is nevertheless, from a chronological point of view, at least as deserving of consideration as the passage in Josephus, *Antiq.* xx. 9. 1, which is open to the suspicion of interpolation.—It should, however, be remarked, that the casting down from a height before the stoning, is a regular injunction of the Jewish law (Mishna, *Sanhedrin* vi. 4).

[44] The date of Albinus' entrance upon his office may be discovered from *Wars of the Jews*, vi. 5. 3. According to the statement given there, Albinus was already procurator when, at the time of the Feast of Tabernacles, four years before the outbreak of the war, and more than seven years and five months before the destruction of the city, a certain man, Jesus, son of Ananos, made his appearance, prophesying misfortune. These two indications of time carry us to the Feast of Tabernacles A.D. 62. Hence Albinus entered upon his office, at the latest, in the summer of A.D. 62.—Our Albinus is very probably identical with Lucceius Albinus, who, under Nero, Galba, and Otho, was procurator of Mauritania, and, during the conflicts between Otho and Vitellius, was, in A.D. 69, put to death by Vitellius' party (Tacitus, *History*, ii. 58–59).

[45] Josephus, *Wars of the Jews*, ii. 14. 1.

[46] Josephus, *Antiq.* xx. 9. 2; *Wars of the Jews*, ii. 14. 1.

[47] Instead of Ἀνάνου we should undoubtedly read Ἀνανίου. Compare *Wars of the Jews*, ii. 17. 2, 20. 4; Derenbourg, *Histoire de la Palestine*, p. 248, note 1.

[48] Josephus, *Antiq.* xx. 9. 3.

[49] Josephus, *Wars of the Jews*, ii. 14. 1.

[50] Josephus, *Antiq.* xx. 9. 2.

[51] Josephus, *Antiq.* xx. 9. 4.

⁵² Josephus, *Wars of the Jews*, ii. 14. 1.

⁵³ Josephus, *Antiq.* xx. 9. 4.

⁵⁴ Josephus, *Antiq.* xx. 9. 5.

⁵⁵ Seeing that Florus, according to *Antiq.* xx. 11. 1, had entered upon the second year of his administration when, in May A.D. 66 (*Wars of the Jews*, ii. 14. 4), the war broke out, he must have entered upon his office in A.D. 64.—The name Gessius Florus is also attested by Tacitus, *History*, v. 10. In the Chronicle of Eusebius it is corrupted into Γέστιος Φλῶρος (the Greek form as given in Syncellus, ed. Dindorf, i. 637; in the Latin rendering of Jerome [Eusebius, *Chronicon*, ed. Schoene, ii. 157], Cestius Florus); in the Armenian translation it is further converted into *Cestius filius Flori* (Euseb. *Chronicon*, ed. Schoene, ii. 156, on the 14th year of Nero).

⁵⁶ Josephus, *Antiq.* xx. 11. 1; *Wars of the Jews*, ii. 14. 2.

SUPPLEMENT. AGRIPPA II., A.D. 50–100.

¹ Josephus, *Antiq.* xix. 9. 2.

² Josephus, *Antiq.* xx. 1. 2; xv. 11. 4. Compare above, p. 225.

³ Josephus, *Antiq.* xx. 6. 3. Compare above, p. 227.

⁴ Josephus, *Antiq.* xx. 5. 2; *Wars of the Jews*, ii. 12. 1. Compare *Antiq.* xx. 9. 7: Ἐπεπίστευτο ὑπὸ Κλαυδίου Καίσαρος τὴν ἐπιμέλειαν τοῦ ἱεροῦ. There is indeed no mention of the conferring of the right of appointing the high priests, but only of the practical exercise of that right. Compare below, § 23. IV. That the gift of the kingdom was not made before A.D. 50, may be concluded from *Wars of the Jews*, ii. 14. 4, according to which Agrippa had reached the seventeenth year of his reign when, in the month Artemisios (Ijjar) of A.D. 66, the war broke out. His seventeenth year therefore began, if we count the reign of Agrippa II. as Jewish king, according to Mishna, *Rosh-hashana* i. 1, from 1st Nisan to 1st Nisan, on the 1st Nisan of A.D. 66, and his first year at the earliest on 1st Nisan A.D. 50, but probably somewhat later.

⁵ Josephus, *Antiq.* xx. 7. 1; *Wars of the Jews*, ii. 12. 8. To the tetrarchy of Lysanias undoubtedly belongs also Helbon, not far from Abila Lysanias, where the inscription referred to in note 1 was found. Of the ἐπαρχία Οὐάρου Josephus gives us an explanation in his *Life*, c. xi.; for the Varus there referred to, the Noarus of *Wars of the Jews*, ii. 18. 6, whom Josephus describes as ἔκγονος Σοέμου τοῦ περὶ τὸν Λίβανον τετραρχοῦντος, is most probably to be identified with our Varus. Then, again, his father Soemus will be no other than the Soemus who, at the end of A.D. 38, obtained from Caligula τὴν τῶν Ἰτυραίων τῶν Ἀράβων (Dio Cassius, lix. 12), which territory he governed till his death in A.D. 49, when it was incorporated in the province of Syria (Tacitus, *Annals*, xii. 23). It may therefore be assumed that to his son Varus a portion of the territory on the Lebanon had been left for a time, and that this is the ἐπαρχία Οὐάρου which Claudius bestowed upon Agrippa.—Seeing then that Agrippa

obtained the new territory in the thirteenth year of Claudius (that year including from 24th January A.D. 53 till the same day in A.D. 54), after he had ruled over Chalcis for four years (δυναστεύσας ταύτης έτη τέσσαρα), and seeing that further his fourth year, according to the reckoning we have accepted above, began on 1st Nisan A.D. 53, the gift must have been bestowed toward the end of A.D. 53.

⁶ Josephus, *Antiq.* xx. 8. 4 ; *Wars of the Jews,* ii. 13. 2. In the latter passage Abila is spoken of as still in Perea.

⁷ Josephus, *Antiq.* xx. 7. 3 ; Juvenal, *Satires,* vi. 156–160 : —

  " . . . . adamas notissimus et Berenices
    In digito factus pretiosior ; hunc dedit olim
    Barbarus incestae, dedit hunc Agrippa sorori,
    Observant ubi festa mero pede sabbata reges,
    Et vetus indulget senibus clementia porcis."

⁸ Tacitus, *Annals,* xiii. 7.

⁹ Acts of the Apostles xxv. 13, 23.

¹⁰ Josephus, *Antiq.* xx. 9. 4.

¹¹ This palace lay, according to *Antiq.* xx. 8. 11 and *Wars of the Jews,* ii. 16. 3, on the so-called Xystus, an open plain, from which a bridge led directly to the temple (*Wars of the Jews,* vi. 6, 2).

¹² Josephus, *Antiq.* xx. 8. 11.

¹³ Josephus, *Antiq.* xx. 7. 1, 3.

¹⁴ Derenbourg, *Histoire de la Palestine,* pp. 252–254 ; Grätz, *Monatsschrift,* 1881, pp. 483–493. Tradition names sometimes Agrippa's minister, sometimes Agrippa himself as the party in question.

¹⁵ Josephus, *Wars of the Jews,* ii. 15. 1.

¹⁶ On the meaning of the words of Agrippa in Acts xxvi. 28, see especially Overbeck on the passage. They were certainly not used ironically, but in thorough earnest. " The king confesses that with the few words that he had spoken Paul had made him feel inclined to become a Christian." But then his indifference is shown in this, that he does nothing further in the matter.—It should not indeed be left unrecorded that instead of γενέσθαι very good manuscripts (אAB) read ποιῆσαι, and instead of πείθεις one manuscript (A) has πείθῃ, which would give the translation : "With little thinkest thou to make me a Christian." But πείθῃ is too weakly supported, and unless we could adopt that reading the ποιῆσαι would be untranslatable.

¹⁷ Josephus, *Wars of the Jews,* v. 1. 5 ; *Antiq.* xv. 11. 3.

¹⁸ Josephus, *Antiq.* xx. 9. 6.

¹⁹ Josephus, *Antiq.* xx. 9. 7.

²⁰ Keim in Schenkel's *Bibellexikon,* iii. 59.

²¹ Josephus, *Wars of the Jews,* ii. 15. 1.

²² *Ibid.* ii. 17. 6.

²³ *Ibid.* ii. 18. 9, 19. 3.

²⁴ Further details regarding Agrippa's conduct during the war are given

in Keim, *Bibellexikon*, iii. 60–63.—Agrippa was not present in Palestine
during the interval between the defeat of Cestius Gallus and the advance
of Vespasian. He gave over the administration of his kingdom to a
certain Noarus or Varus, and, when this man began to indulge in the
most despotic and high-handed procedure, to a certain Aequus Modius
(*Wars of the Jews*, ii. 18. 6 ; *Life*, c. xi. and xxxvi., compare also xxiv.).—
Of the three cities named (Tiberias, Tarichea, Gamala), Gamala was of
special importance as a strong fortress. It was at first held faithfully for
the king by Philip, an officer of Agrippa (*Life*, c. xi.). But when Philip
was recalled by Agrippa the city went over to the side of the rebels (*Life*,
xxxv.-xxxvii. ; *Wars of the Jews*, ii. 20. 4, 6, ii. 21. 7). Agrippa then
ordered Aequus Modius to recapture Gamala (*Life*, xxiv.). But even a
seven months' siege failed to secure this end (*Wars of the Jews*, iv. 1. 2).
Another officer of Agrippa fought against Josephus (*Life*, lxxi.-lxxiii.).—
Agrippa remained in Berytus till the spring of A.D. 67 (*Life*, xxxvi., lxv.,
ed. Bekker, p. 342, 32), then waited in Antioch along with his troops the
arrival of Vespasian's army (*Wars of the Jews*, iii. 2. 4), advanced with
Vespasian to Tyre (*Life*, lxxiv.) and Ptolemais (*Life*, lxv., ed. Bekker, p.
340, 19–25, and c. lxxiv.), and seems now to have taken up his quarters
more generally in Vespasian's camp (*Wars of the Jews*, iii. 4. 2, 9. 7–8,
10. 10, iv. 1. 3).

[25] Josephus, *Wars of the Jews*, iii. 9. 7.

[26] *Ibid.* iv. 1. 3.

[27] Josephus, *Wars of the Jews*, iv. 9. 2 ; Tacitus, *History*, ii. 1-2.

[28] Tacitus, *History*, ii. 81.

[29] *Ibid.* v. 1.

[30] Josephus, *Wars of the Jews*, vii. 2. 1.

[31] Photius in his *Bibliotheca*, cod. 33, gives the following extract about
Agrippa from Justus of Tiberias : παρέλαβε μὲν τὴν ἀρχὴν ἐπὶ Κλαυδίου,
ηὐξήθη δὲ ἐπὶ Νέρωνος καὶ ἔτι μᾶλλον ὑπὸ Οὐεσπασιανοῦ, τελευτᾷ δὲ ἔτει
τρίτῳ Τραϊανοῦ.

[32] Josephus, *Wars of the Jews*, vii. 5. 1. Josephus there tells how that
Titus, on the march from Berytus to Antioch, came upon the so-called
Sabbath-river, which flows μέσος 'Αρκαίας τῆς 'Αγρίππα βασιλείας καὶ
'Ραφαναίας. A city therefore is intended which lay north of Berytus,
and so undoubtedly the same Arcae which according to the old itineraries lay between Tripolis and Antaradus, 16 or 18 Roman miles
north of Tripolis and 32 Roman miles south of Antaradus (18 *mil.
pass.*: *Itinerarium Antonini*, edd. Parthey et Pinder, 1848, p. 68 ; 16
mil. pass.; *Itinerarium Burdigalense*, edd. Parthey et Pinder, p. 275 =
Itinera Hierosolymitana, edd. Tobler et Molinier, i. 1879, p. 14; they
agree in giving the distance from Antaradus at 32 *mil. pass.*). The
name is retained to the present day in that of a village at the north
end of the Lebanon on the spot indicated in the itineraries. In ancient
times the city was very well known. The Arkites are named in the
list of peoples in Gen. x. 17 (עַרְקִי). Josephus, *Antiq.* i. 6. 2, calls it:

Ἀρχὴν τὴν ἐν τῷ Λιβάνῳ.

33 Josephus, *Antiq.* xvii. 2. 2. In the *Wars of the Jews*, iii. 3. 5, Batanea is reckoned as still belonging to the territory of Agrippa.

34 Even Titus' return to Palestine on receiving intelligence of Galba's death was ascribed by his defamers to his longing for the society of Berenice (Tacitus, *History*, ii. 2).

35 Dio Cassius, lxvi. 15 ; Suetonius, *Titus*, 7 : "Insignem reginae Berenices amorem cui etiam nuptias pollicitus ferebatur."—Berenice had even already publicly assumed the name of Titus' wife (πάντα ἤδη ὡς καὶ γυνὴ αὐτοῦ οὖσα ἐποίει, Dio Cassius, lxvi. 15). Any suspected of having intercourse with her were rigorously punished by Titus. Aurel. Victor, *Epit.* 10 : "Gaecinam consularem adhibitum coenae, vixdum triclinio egressum, ob suspicionem stupratae Berenices uxoris suae, jugulari jussit."

36 Dio Cassius, lvi. 18 ; Aurel. Victor, *Epit.* 10 : "Ut subiit pondus regium, Berenicen nuptias suas sperantem regredi domum . . . praecepit." Suetonius, *Titus*, 7 : "Berenicen statim ab urbe dimisit, invitus invitam." —Aurelius Victor and Suetonius speak only of a dismissal of Berenice after the enthronement of Titus ; for even in Suetonius "statim" can be understood only in this sense. But Dio Cassius clearly makes a distinction between the two occurrences : the involuntary dismissal before his succession to the throne, and the non-recognition of Berenice after that event.—On her travels between Palestine and Rome, Berenice seems to have gained for herself a certain position in Athens which the council and people of the Athenians have made memorable by the following inscription (*Corp. Inscr. Graec.* n. 361 = *Corp. Inscr. Atticarum*, iii. 1, n. 556 ; on the name Julia, see above, p. 162) :—

Ἡ βουλὴ ἡ ἐξ Ἀρείου πάγου καὶ
ἡ βουλὴ τῶν χ´ καὶ ὁ δῆμος Ἰου-
λίαν Βερενείκην βασίλισσαν
μεγάλην, Ἰουλίου Ἀγρίππα βασιλέως θυγατέρα καὶ μεγάλων
βασιλέων εὐεργετῶν τῆς πόλεως ἔκγονον . . .

37 Josephus, *Life*, lxv. ; *Against Apion*, i. 9.

38   Photius, *Bibliotheca*, cod. 33.

39 Whether he was married or not, we do not know. In the Talmud (*bab. Succa* 27a) the story is told of the steward of Agrippa putting a question to R. Elieser, which seems to imply that the questioner had two wives. Founding upon this, many assign to Agrippa two wives, assuming that the steward put the question in the name of the king. So, for instance, Derenbourg, *Historie de la Palestine*, pp. 252–254, and Brann, *Monatsschrift*, 1871, p. 13 f. There is, however, no sufficient foundation for such an assumption. See Grätz, *Monatsschrift*, 1881, p. 483 f.

§ 20. THE GREAT WAR WITH ROME, A.D. 66–73.

[1] Josephus, *Wars of the Jews*, ii. 14. 6–9, 15. 1.

[2] Josephus, *Wars of the Jews*, ii. 15. 2 ; comp. ii. 14. 4; *Antiq.* xx. 11. 1 (in the twelfth year of Nero). Though Josephus uses the Macedonian names of the months we are really to understand by them the Jewish months, which only approximately correspond to the months of the Julian calendar.

[3] Josephus, *Wars of the Jews*, ii. 15. 3–6.

[4] Josephus, *Wars of the Jews*, ii. 16. 1–5 ; comp. 15. 1.—The statistical details about the Roman empire which Josephus has woven into this speech of Agrippa, were probably borrowed from an official publication.

[5] Josephus, *Wars of the Jews*, ii. 17. 1.

[6] Josephus, *Wars of the Jews*, ii. 17. 2–4.—On the fortress of Masada, see below at the end of this section.

[7] Josephus, *Wars of the Jews*, ii. 17. 4–6.—The troops sent by Agrippa were ὑπὸ Δαρείῳ μὲν ἱππάρχῳ, στρατηγῷ δὲ τῷ Ἰακίμου Φιλίππῳ (*Wars of the Jews*, ii. 17. 4 *fin.*). Philip was therefore the commander-in-chief. He was grandson of the Babylonian Zamaris, who in the time of Herod the Great had founded a Jewish colony in Batanea (*Antiq.* xvii. 2. 3). Compare on him also, *Wars of the Jews*, ii. 20. 1, iv. 1. 10 ; *Life*, xi., xxxv., xxxvi., lxxiv.

[8] Josephus, *Wars of the Jews*, ii. 17. 7–8 ; comp. v. 4. 4.—The leader of Agrippa's troops, Philip, was subsequently called to account for his conduct (Josephus, *Life*, lxxiv.).

[9] Josephus, *Wars of the Jews*, ii. 17. 9.

[10] Josephus, *Wars of the Jews*, ii. 17. 10. Compare *Megillath Taanith*, § 14 : "On the 17th Elul the Romans withdrew from Judea and Jerusalem" (Derenbourg, pp. 443, 445 ; Hitzig, ii. p. 600).

[11] Josephus, *Wars of the Jews*, ii. 18. 1–8 ; *Life*, vi.

[12] Josephus, *Wars of the Jews*, ii. 18. 9–10, 19. 1.—Γαβαώ is the Gibeon often referred to in the Old Testament, identified with El-Jeb north-west of Jerusalem.

[13] Josephus, *Wars of the Jews*, ii. 19. 2.

[14] Josephus, *Wars of the Jews*, ii. 19. 4.—Scopus is also referred to in *Wars of the Jews*, ii. 19. 7, v. 2. 3, 3. 2 ; *Antiq.* xi. 8. 5 : εἰς τόπον τινὰ Σαφὶν [so the best manuscripts read] λεγόμενον· τὸ δὲ ὄνομα τοῦτο μετα-φερόμενον εἰς τὴν Ἑλληνικὴν γλῶτταν Σκοπὸν [so the best manuscripts] σημαίνει. צָפִין is the Aramaic form for צוֹפִים, as the place is called in Mishna, *Pesachim* iii. 8. Compare also Lightfoot, *Centuria Matthaeo praemissa*, c. 42 (*Opera*, ii. 202). From this point a beautiful view of the

city was obtained (*Antiq.* xi. 8. 5 ; *Wars of the Jews*, v. 2. 3).—The
suburb Bezetha is also referred to in *Wars of the Jews*, ii. 15. 5, v. 4. 2,
5. 8. It is the most northerly suburb included by the so-called wall of
Agrippa (*Wars of the Jews*, v. 4. 2).

[15] Josephus, *Wars of the Jews*, ii. 19. 5–7.

[16] Josephus, *Wars of the Jews*, ii. 19. 7–9.

[17] Josephus, *Wars of the Jews*, ii. 20. 1–3.

[18] Josephus, *Wars of the Jews*, ii. 20. 3–4 ; *Life*, vii. In the latter
passage Josephus is impudent enough to declare that the purpose for
which he was sent was to pacify Galilee (compare also, *Life*, xiv.).—As
had been already shown, the conduct of the revolt was in the hands of
the people of Jerusalem (τὸ κοινὸν τῶν Ἱεροσολυμιτῶν, *Life*, xii., xiii.,
xxxviii., xlix., lii., lx., lxv., lxx.), and as their representative the Sanhedrim
(τὸ συνέδριον τῶν Ἱεροσολυμιτῶν, *Life*, xii.).

[19] Josephus, *Wars of the Jews*, ii. 20. 5 ; *Life*, xiv.

[20] Josephus, *Life*, xii.

[21] Josephus, *Wars of the Jews*, ii. 20. 6 ; *Life*, xxxvii. Compare in
addition : Ritter, *Erdkunde*, xvi. 757–771 ; Robinson, *Biblical Researches*,
vol. ii. p. 387.—Among the above-named seven important places Sepphoris
never took the side of the revolution, but, so long as it was without
Roman protection, assumed a vacillating position, hence even expending
care on its fortifications ; and then, so soon as Roman troops were
available, taking sides with them. For further details, see Div. II.,
vol. i. p. 136.—Of the other six cities or fortresses, three, Tarichea,
Tiberias, and Gamala, belonged to the territory of King Agrippa, and in
part also joined the side of the revolution only after internal conflicts.
See particularly on Tiberias, Div. II. vol. i. p. 143 f. ; on Gamala, the
present vol. p. 242.—Gischala took up a distinct position of its own, for
there, John, son of Levi, the celebrated revolutionary hero of a later
period, assumed to himself the government. He was dissatisfied with
the lukewarm attitude of Josephus, and so refused to make over to him
the fortress of the city, but took the command of it himself (*Wars of the
Jews*, ii. 20. 6 ; *Life*, x., xxxviii.). See especially on the attitude of
Gischala, *Wars of the Jews*, ii. 21. 7. 10 ; *Life*, x., xiii., xvi.–xviii., xx.,
xxv., xxxviii.—All the seven places here mentioned will be again referred
to in the history of the rearrangement of Galilee by the Romans.

[22] Josephus, *Wars of the Jews*, ii. 20. 6–8.

[23] Josephus, *Wars of the Jews*, ii. 21. 1–2 ; *Life*, xiii.

[24] Josephus, *Wars of the Jews*, ii. 21. 3–5 ; *Life*, xxvi.–xxx.

[25] Josephus, *Wars of the Jews*, ii. 21. 6 ; *Life*, xvi.–xviii.

[26] Josephus, *Wars of the Jews*, ii. 21. 7 ; *Life*, xxxviii.–lxiv., especially
xxxviii.–xl., lx.–lxiv.

[27] Josephus, *Wars of the Jews*, ii. 21. 8–10 ; *Life*, xxxii.–xxxiv.—In
his autobiography (lxviii.–lxix.), Josephus relates that the πρῶτοι τῆς
βουλῆς of Tiberias once at a later period sent entreating Agrippa for a
garrison.—Tiberias, as might be expected from its mixed population, and

as is expressly declared in the *Life*, ix., was in its sympathies partly Roman, partly anti-Roman, so that it is found sometimes in league with King Agrippa, sometimes in league with John of Gischala. On its precise position, however, it is difficult to say anything with confidence, since the statements in Josephus' autobiography are all made with a purpose.

[28] Josephus, *Wars of the Jews*, ii. 22. 1.

[29] Josephus, *Wars of the Jews*, ii. 20. 1, iii. 1. 1.

[30] "Fato aut taedio occidit," says Tacitus, *Hist.* v. 10.—In the winter of A.D. 66–67, Cestius Gallus was still in the province. See Josephus, *Life*, viii., xliii., lxv., lxvii., lxxi.

[31] Josephus, *Wars of the Jews*, iii. 1. 2–3.—According to the common text of *Wars of the Jews*, iii. 1. 3, Titus was to have brought two legions from Alexandria, τό τε πέμπτον καὶ τὸ δέκατον. But of the return of Titus to Vespasian it is said, *Wars of the Jews*, iii. 4. 2 : καὶ ἐκεῖ (supply " to Ptolemais ") καταλαβὼν τὸν πατέρα, δυσὶ τοῖς ἅμα αὐτῷ τάγμασιν, ἦν δὲ τὰ ἐπισημότατα τὸ πέμπτον καὶ τὸ δέκατον, ζεύγνυσι καὶ τὸ ἀχθὲν ὑπ' αὐτοῦ πεντεκαιδέκατον. This can only mean that to the two legions which he found with his father, the 5th and the 10th, he added the 15th, which was with him. With this also agrees the fact that Titus, according to Suetonius, *Tit.* iv., was during the war commander of one legion (*legioni praepositus*), that is, of the 15th. Accordingly the corrected reading in *Wars of the Jews*, iii. 1. 3 will be : τὸ πεντεκαιδέκατον.

[32] Josephus, *Wars of the Jews*, iii. 2. 4.—Sepphoris had even before the arrival of Vespasian possessed a Roman garrison (*Life*, lxxi. ; *Wars of the Jews*, iii. 2. 4). Whether this garrison had meanwhile been withdrawn, or was now only relieved or strengthened, is not quite clear.

[33] Josephus, *Wars of the Jews*, iii. 4. 1 ; *Life*, lxxiv.—On Placidus, who had been in Galilee previous to the arrival of Vespasian, see also *Life*, xliii.

[34] Josephus, *Wars of the Jews*, iii. 4. 2.

[35] Josephus, *Wars of the Jews*, iii. 6. 2–3.

[36] Josephus, *Wars of the Jews*, iii. 7. 2.

[37] Jotapata appears in the Mishna in the form יודפת (*Arachin* ix. 6 ; the Cambridge manuscript has ירפת with *Resh*, but the *editio princeps* and the *cod. de Rossi*, 138 : יודפת, Jodaphath, also Aruch ידפת with *Daleth*). It is there spoken of as an ancient city, which had been, even in Joshua's time, surrounded with walls.

[38] Josephus, *Wars of the Jews*, iii. 7. 3.—Since, according to *Wars of the Jews*, iii. 7. 33 and 8. 9, the siege lasted forty-seven days, and according to *Wars of the Jews*, iii. 7. 36, it ended on the 1st of Panemos, the date 21st Artemisios cannot be correct.

[39] Josephus, *Wars of the Jews*, iii. 7. 4–36.

[40] Josephus, *Wars of the Jews*, iii. 8. 1–8.

[41] Josephus, *Wars of the Jews*, iii. 8. 9 ; Dio Cassius, lxvi. 1 ; Suetonius, *Vespasian*, c. 5. According to Zonaras, *Annales*, xi. 16, Appian also in the

twenty-second book of his *Roman History* tells of the saying of the Jewish oracle with reference to Vespasian.—Our older scholars have earnestly investigated the story of Josephus' prophetic gift. Compare Olearius, *Fl. Josephi de Vespasianis ad summum imperii fastigium advehendis vaticinium*, 1699 ; Strohbach, *de Josepho Vespasiano imperium praedicente*, Lips. 1748. There may be some truth in the story. Probably Josephus has wittingly construed a couple of general phrases into a formal prophecy. It is noteworthy the rabbinical tradition ascribes this same prophecy to Rabbi Jochanan ben Saccai. See Derenbourg, p. 282.— Upon this Holwerda (*Verslagen en Mededeelingen der koninkl. Akademie van Wetenschappen, Afdeeling Letterkunde, Tweede Reeks deel*, ii. 1872, p. 137 sq.) has made the remark that similar oracles were addressed to Titus and Vespasian by heathen priests. Thus Sostratus, the priest of Aphrodite at Paphos in Cyprus, revealed the future to Titus in secret conference when he inquired of the oracle there and sought for favourable omens (Tacitus, *Hist.* ii. 4 : "petito secreto futura aperit." Still more distinctly, Suetonius, *Titus*, c. 5 : "aditoque Paphiae Veneris oraculo, dum de navigatione consulit, etiam de imperii spe confirmatus est"). The priest Basilides on Carmel declared to Vespasian on the ground of the sacrificial signs : "quidquid est, Vespasiane, quod paras, seu domum extruere seu prolatare agros sive ampliare servitia, datur tibi magna sedes, ingentes termini, multum hominum" (Tacitus, *Hist.* ii. 78. Compare Suetonius, *Vespasian*, c. 5 : "Apud Judaeam Carmeli dei oraculum consulentem ita confirmavere sortes, ut quidquid cogitaret volveretque animo quamlibet magnum, id esse proventurum pollicerentur"). These heathen oracles, however, belong to a later period than the one referred to by Josephus.

[42] Josephus, *Wars of the Jews*, iii. 9. 1.

[43] Josephus, *Wars of the Jews*, iii. 9. 7–8.

[44] Ταριχέαι or Ταριχέα (both forms of spelling are met with) had its name from the curing of fish which was carried on there (Strabo, xvi. 2. 45, p. 764). It is first mentioned in the time of Cassius, who, during this first administration of Syria in B.C. 52–51, took the city by force of arms (Josephus, *Antiq.* xiv. 7. 3 ; *Wars of the Jews*, i. 8. 9), and, during his second administration, again visited it. He wrote to Cicero in B.C. 43, "ex castris Taricheis," *Cicero ad Familieres*, xii. 11. — According to Josephus, *Life*, xxxii., it lay thirty stadia from Tiberias ; according to *Wars of the Jews*, iii. 10. 1, it was situated upon the lake of Gennezaret at the foot of a hill (ὑπώρειος) ; according to Pliny, *Hist. Nat.* v. 15. 11, it lay at the south end of the lake (*a meridie Tarichea*). It is therefore to be sought on the site or in the neighbourhood of the present Kerak where the Jordan emerges from the lake.

[45] Josephus, *Wars of the Jews*, iii. 10. Suetonius, *Titus*, 4, ascribes to Titus the conquest of Tarichea and Gamala; the latter incorrectly.—After Tarichea had been taken by surprise, a portion of the inhabitants endeavoured to make their escape in a boat out upon the lake. Vespasian caused them to be pursued on rafts, and the fugitives all met their

death, either by the sword or in the water. It has been conjectured that this is the "Victoria navalis," which was celebrated by coins or medals, and in the triumphal procession was made noticeable by a ship (*Wars of the Jews*, vii. 5. 5 : πολλαὶ δὲ καὶ νῆες εἵποντο).

[46] Josephus, *Wars of the Jews*, iv. 1. 1.—Gamala (גַּמְלָא) is mentioned in the Mishna, *Arachin* ix. 6, among the cities which are said to have been surrounded with walls from the days of Joshua. Its existence is historically demonstrable from the time of Alexander Jannaeus (Josephus, *Antiq.* xiii. 15. 3 ; *Wars of the Jews*, i. 4. 8). According to the *Wars of the Jews*, iv. 1. 1, it lay opposite Tarichea in Lower Gaulanitis, therefore east of the Lake of Gennezaret.

[47] Josephus, *Wars of the Jews*, iv. 1. 2–10.

[48] Josephus, *Wars of the Jews*, iv. 1. 8.

[49] Josephus, *Wars of the Jews*, iv. 2. 1.

[50] Josephus, *Wars of the Jews*, iv. 2. 2–5.—Gischala is in the Hebrew Gush-Chalab, גוּשׁ חֲלָב, and is also mentioned in the Mishna among the cities which from the time of Joshua were surrounded with walls (*Arachin* ix. 6). Its name signifies "fat or rich clod." In fact, it yielded abundance of oil (Josephus, *Life*, xiii. ; *Wars of the Jews*, ii. 21. 2 ; *Tosefta Menachoth* ix. 5 ; *Bab. Menachoth* 85*b* ; Neubauer, *Géographie du Talmud*, p. 230 sq.). In the Jewish traditions of the Middle Ages it was famous for its graves of Rabbis and its ancient synagogue (Carmoly, *Itinéraires de la Terre-Sainte*, 1847, pp. 133 sq., 156, 184, 262, 380, 452 sq.).—It lay in the neigbourhood of the territory of Tyre (*Wars of the Jews*, iv. 2. 3 *fin.*), and is undoubtedly to be identified with the present Eljish in Northern Galilee, somewhere about the same geographical latitude with the southern end of the Merom lake. Of the ancient synagogue there are still ruins to be found there.

[51] Josephus, *Wars of the Jews*, iv. 3. 1–3.

[52] *Ibid.* iv. 3. 4–5.

[53] Josephus, *Wars of the Jews*, iv. 3. 6–8. Compare Derenbourg, p. 269.

[54] So Josephus names him here. But he is probably identical with the Joseph, son of Gorion, mentioned above at p. 250. So also Derenbourg, p. 270.

[55] Compare on him also : Josephus, *Life*, xxxviii., xxxix., xliv., lx. ; Derenbourg, pp. 270–272, 474 sq.

[56] Josephus, *Wars of the Jews*, iv. 3. 9.

[57] *Ibid.* iv. 3. 10.

[58] Josephus, *Wars of the Jews*, iv. 3. 12.

[59] *Ibid.* iv. 4. 1–4.

[60] *Ibid.* iv. 4. 5–7.

[61] *Ibid.* iv. 5. 1–3.

[62] Josephus, *Wars of the Jews*, iv. 5. 4.—Some have sought wrongly to identify this Zacharias with the one mentioned in Matt. xxiii. 35 and Luke xi. 51.

[63] Josephus, *Wars of the Jews*, iv. 5. 5, 6. 1.　　　[64] *Ibid.* iv. 6. 1.

[65] Eusebius, *Hist. eccl.* iii. 5. 2–3 ; Epiphanius, *Haer.* 29. 7 ; *de*

mensuris et ponderibus, § 15.- The migration took place κατά τινα χρησμὸν τοῖς αὐτόθι δοκίμοις δι' ἀποκαλύψεως ἐκδοθέντα κ.τ.λ. (Euseb. *Hist. eccl.* iii. 5. 3).

[66] Josephus, *Wars of the Jews*, iv. 6. 2–3.

[67] Josephus, *Wars of the Jews*, iv. 7. 3. 4.

[68] Josephus, *Wars of the Jews*, iv. 7. 4–6.

[69] ὑπὸ τὴν ἀρχὴν τοῦ ἔαρος, Josephus, *Wars of the Jews*, iv. 8. 1.

[70] Josephus, *Wars of the Jews*, iv. 8. 1.—On Corea, see present work, p. 98 . The other cities are well known.

[71] Josephus, *Wars of the Jews*, iv. 9. 1.—On Adida, see present work, p. 54 |—Gerasa cannot be the celebrated Hellenistic city of Decapolis, for it certainly continued faithful on the side of the Romans.

[72] Josephus, *Wars of the Jews*, iv. 9. 2.—See further details regarding the journey of Titus in Tacitus, *Hist.* ii. 1–4.

[73] Josephus always designates him υἱὸς Γιώρα. The form Βαργιορᾶς, Bargiora, occurs in Dio Cassius, lxvi. 7, and Tacitus, *Hist.* v. 12. Tacitus erroneously ascribes this cognomen to John. גִּיּוֹרָא is the Aramaic form for גֵּר, the proselyte.

[74] Josephus, *Wars of the Jews*, iv. 9. 3–8.

[75] Josephus, *Wars of the Jews*, iv. 9. 9.—On Gophna and Acrabata, see Div. II. vol. i. p. 158. On Bethel and Ephraim, see present work, p. 45 and p. 51.

[76] Josephus, *Wars of the Jews*, iv. 9. 10.

[77] *Ibid.* iv. 9. 11–12. Compare v. 13. 1.

[78] Josephus, *Wars of the Jews*, iv. 10. 2–6; Tacitus, *Hist.* ii. 79–81 ; Suetonius, *Vespasian*, 6. That the Egyptian legions were the first to proclaim Vespasian emperor is stated by Tacitus and Suetonius ; according to Josephus, the Palestinian legions had the precedence. The proclamation, in any case, was made in Palestine, according to Tacitus, "*quintum Nonas Julias;*" according to Suetonius, "*V. Idus Jul.*"— After his appointment as emperor he gave to Josephus a free pardon in thankful remembrance of his prophecy (*Wars of the Jews*, iv. 10. 7).

[79] Josephus, *Wars of the Jews*, iv. 10. 6, 11. 1; Tacitus, *Hist.* ii. 81–83.

[80] According to Josephus, *Wars of the Jews*, iv. 11. 5, Vespasian wished to march to Rome λήξαντος τοῦ χειμῶνος. According to Tacitus, he waited in Alexandria till the time of the summer winds, and till he had assurance of being able to make the voyage by sea (*Hist.* iv. 81 : "statos aestivis flatibus dies et certa maris opperiebatur"). On the route of his journey, see especially Josephus, *Wars of the Jews*, vii. 2. 1. He did not, however, reach Rome until after the middle of the year 70.

[81] Josephus, *Wars of the Jews*, iv. 11. 5.

[82] Josephus, *Wars of the Jews*, v. 1. 1–5 ; Tacitus, *Hist.* v. 12. See also Rabbinical traditions about the destruction of the collection of grain in Derenbourg, p. 281.

[83] Josephus, *Wars of the Jews*, v. 1. 6; Tacitus, *Hist.* v. 1.

[84] Josephus, *Wars of the Jews*, vi. 4. 3.

[85] Josephus, *Wars of the Jews*, v. 1. 6.

[86] As appears from **v. 3. 1** compared with **v. 13. 7.**—The elder Pliny held a position in the army of Titus, and was indeed ἀντεπίτροπος of Tiberius Julius Alexander, according to Mommsen's skilful rendering of the inscription of Aradus, *Corpus Inscript. Graec.* t. iii. p. 1178, n. 4536 [f]. With reference to this, Pliny, in the dedication of his *Natural History* to Titus, says : "nobis quidem qualis in castrensi contubernio."

[87] Josephus, *Wars of the Jews*, v. 2. 1-2.

[88] *Ibid.* v. 2. 4-5.

[89] Josephus, *Wars of the Jews*, v. 3. 1 ; Tacitus, *Hist.* v. 12 *fin.*

[90] Compare the designation in Josephus, *Wars of the Jews*, v. 4.

[91] The situation of the Acra and the lower city is the one point most disputed in the topography of Jerusalem. By a careful expression and estimation of the sources, however, it seems to me that the above statement may be accepted with certainty. Compare above, p. 27. The history of the siege by Titus confirms this. For Titus, who pressed on from the north, came into possession of the lower city only after he had taken the site of the temple, and so the lower city must have lain south of this. It reached as far as Siloah (*Wars of the Jews*, vi. 7. 2).

[92] On Bezetha, compare also this point, — p. 249.—Josephus says in *Wars of the Jews*, v. 4. 2 : Βεζεθὰ, ὃ μεθερμηνευόμενον Ἑλλάδι γλώσσῃ καινὴ λέγοιτ' ἂν πόλις. That is impossible. For Βεζεθά can be nothing else but בית זיתא, "Place of Olives." In the statement of Josephus therefore this much may be correct, that Bezetha was also called the New City.

[93] Josephus, *Wars of the Jews*, v. 6. 2-5 ; Suetonius, *Titus*, 5 : "duodecim propugnatores totidem sagittarum confecit ictibus."

[94] Josephus, *Wars of the Jews*, v. 7. 2.

[95] Josephus, *Wars of the Jews*, v. 7. 3-4, 8. 1-2.

[96] *Ibid.* v. 9. 2 ; comp. 11. 4.

[97] *Ibid.* v. 9. 3-4.

[98] *Ibid.* v. 10. 2-5, 11. 1-2.

[99] *Ibid.* v. 11. 4-6.

[100] Josephus, *Wars of the Jews*, v. 12. 1-2 ; Luke xix. 43. Similar circumvallations are often spoken of. The most celebrated is that of Alesia by Caesar (*Bell. Gall.* vii. 69 : "fossamque et maceriam sex in altitudinem pedum praeduxerant ; ejus munitionis, quae ab Romanis instituebatur, circuitus XI milium passuum tenebat." Also before an attempt was made to attack it, Masada was surrounded by such a wall (Josephus, *Wars of the Jews*, vii. 8. 2). Large remnants of it are to be seen to this day. It was erected of unhewn stones without the use of mortar.

[101] Josephus, *Wars of the Jews*, v. 12. 3, 13. 7, vi 3. 3. Compare *Aboth derabbi Nathan* c. 6 (in Derenbourg, p. 285). Well known is the tragical history of that Mary of Beth-Esôb, who was driven by hunger to devour her own child. See *Wars of the Jews*, vi. 3. 4 ; Eusebius, *Hist. eccl.* iii. 6 ; Hieronymus, *ad Joelem*, i. 9 ff. (*Opera*, ed. Vallarsi, vi. 178);

and the passages from the Talmud and Midrash in Grätz, Bd. iii. 4 Aufl. p. 537 (2 Aufl. p. 401).—A mother's devouring of her own child belongs to the traditional and customary descriptions of the horrors of war, as well in threatenings: Lev. xxvi. 29, Deut. xxviii. 53, Jer. xix. 9, Ezek. v. 10, as in history: 2 Kings vi. 28, 29 ; Lam. ii. 20, iv. 10 ; Baruch ii. 3.

[102] Josephus, *Wars of the Jews*, v. 13. 6.

[103] Josephus, *Wars of the Jews*, v. 12. 4.

[104] *Ibid.* vi. 1. 1–3.

[105] *Ibid.* vi. 1. 3–6.

[106] *Ibid.* vi. 1. 7–8, 2. 1.

[107] Josephus, *Wars of the Jews*, vi. 2. 1 ; Mishna, *Taanith* iv. 6 : בְּשִׁבְעָה עָשָׂר בְּתַמּוּז בָּטַל הַתָּמִיד.

[108] Josephus, *Wars of the Jews*, vi. 2. 1–6.

[109] *Ibid.* vi. 2. 7.

[110] *Ibid.* vi. 3. 1–2.

[111] *Ibid.* vi. 4. 1–2.

[112] *Ibid.* vi. 4. 3.

[113] Josephus, *Wars of the Jews*, vi. 4. 4–5.

[114] Josephus, *Wars of the Jews*, vi. 4. 6–7.—According to the account given above, the burning of the temple took place on the 10th Loos = Ab, as also Josephus in *Wars of the Jews*, vi. 4. 5, expressly states. The Rabbinical tradition places the destruction of the temple on the 9th Ab (Mishna, *Taanith* iv. 6 : בְּתִשְׁעָה בְּאָב חָרַב הַבַּיִת בָּרִאשׁוֹנָה וּבַשְּׁנִיָה), and indeed early on the evening before that day (*b. Taanith* 29a: ערב תשעה באב, Derenbourg, p. 291) ; that is, in our way of reckoning, on the 8th Ab. It therefore regards as the day of destruction the day on which Titus caused fire to be laid to the gates. According to Rabbinical tradition it was Sabbath evening, מוצאי שבת, when the temple was destroyed. Arachin 11b., and Derenbourg, p. 291. According to Dio Cassius, Jerusalem was destroyed ἐν αὐτῇ τῇ τοῦ Κρόνου ἡμέρᾳ.

According to the representation of Josephus, which we have followed, Titus had expressed a wish to spare the temple proper (*Wars of the Jews*, vi. 4. 3). Divergent from this is the narrative of Sulpicius Severus, *Chronicon*, ii. 30 : "Fertur Titus adhibito consilio prius deliberasse, an templum tanti operis everteret. Etenim nonnullis videbatur, aedem sacratam ultra omnia mortalia illustrem non oportere deleri, quae servata modestiae Romanae testimonium, diruta perennem crudelitatis notam praeberet. At contra alii et Titus ipse evertendum in primis templum censebant, quo plenius Judaeorum et Christianorum religio tolleretur : quippe has religiones, licet contrarias sibi, isdem tamen ab auctoribus profectas ; Christianos ex Judaeis exstitisse : radice sublata stirpem facile perituram." Orosius, vii. 9. 5–6, from a somewhat different point of view, ascribes the destruction to Titus. Seeing that Sulpicius Severus, as Bernays has proved, elsewhere bases his statements on Tacitus, Bernays has concluded that on this point also his statement rests on the history of Tacitus, which for this period is no longer extant, and served as model for Josephus, who wishes to free Titus from the *nota crudelitatis* (Bernays, *Ueber die Chronik des Sulpicius Severus*, 1861, pp. 48–61, in his *Gesammelte Werke*, ii. 159–181).

[115] Josephus, *Wars of the Jews*, vi. 5. 1–2. The greeting of Titus as Imperator : *Wars of the Jews*, vi. 6. 1 ; Suetonius, *Titus*, 5 ; Dio Cassius, lxvi. 7; Orosius, vii. 9. 6. On the significance of this procedure, see especially Suetonius, *l.c.* Titus was suspected of having fallen away from Vespasian, and of having wished to set up as an independent ruler of the East.

[116] Josephus, *Wars of the Jews*, vi. 6. 2–3.

[117] *Ibid.* vi. 6. 3, 7. 2–3.

[118] *Ibid.* vi. 8. 1–5.

[119] Josephus, *Wars of the Jews*, vi. 8. 5, 10. 1.

[120] *Ibid.* vi. 9. 2, 4, vii. 2. 1–2.

[121] Josephus, *Wars of the Jews*, vii. 1. 1–3.—Of the three gates of the palace of Herod, only one is preserved to the present day under the name of "David's Tower," commonly identified with Hippicus, but by Schick with Phasael. A minute description is given by Schick in *Zeitschrift des deutschen Palästina-Vereins*, i. 226 ff.

[122] Josephus, *Wars of the Jews*, vii. 1. 2–3.—The tenth legion in the time of Dio Cassius, in the beginning of the third century after Christ, still remained in Judea, Dio Cassius, lv. 23. Not until the time of Eusebius is it spoken of as the garrison at Aela on the Red Sea (Eusebius, *Onomasticon*, ed. Lagarde, p. 210). Inscriptions, in which it is referred to, have been found recently in considerable numbers in Jerusalem.

[123] Josephus, *Wars of the Jews*, vii. 2. 1.

[124] Josephus, *Wars of the Jews*, vii. 3. 1 : χρονιωτέραν ἐποιήσατο τὴν ἐπιδημίαν.

[125] Josephus, *Wars of the Jews*, vii. 5. 1–3.

[126] The arrival of Titus in Rome is set down "somewhere about the middle of June A.D. 71" by Chambalu, *Philologus*, xliv. 1885, pp. 507–517.

[127] Josephus, *Wars of the Jews*, vii. 5. 3–7 ; Dio Cassius, lxvi. 7. The Jewish spoils which were borne along in the triumphal procession are to be seen to the present day on the relief work on the Arch of Titus. Compare Reland, *De spoliis templi Hierosolymitani in arcu Titiano Romae conspicuis*, Ultraj. 1716. New edition by Schulze 1775. Also in Ugolini, *Thesaurus*, t. ix. An engraving and a description of the Arch of Titus, which was not erected *divo Tito* until after the death of Titus, is given by many ; among others, by Reber, *Die Ruinen Roms und der Campagna*, 1863, pp. 397–400. On the relief, see Philippi, "Ueber die römischen Triumphalreliefe und ihre Stellung in der Kunstgeschichte" (*Abhandlungen der philol.-hist. Classe der sächs. Gesellsch. der Wissensch*. Bd. vi. 1874, pp. 245–306 ; with illustrations : Tafel ii.–iii.).—In the inscription on the Arch of Titus (*Corpus Inscriptionum Latinorum*, t. vi. n. 945) no mention is made

of the Jewish war. But another Arch of Titus, destroyed in the fourteenth
or fifteenth century, which had stood in the Circus Maximus, bore the
following pompous and, so far as it deals with the earlier history of
Jerusalem, untrue inscription, bearing date A.D. 81, preserved in a manuscript at Einsiedeln : "Senatus populusque Romanus imp. Tito Caesari
divi Vespasiani f. Vespasiano Augusto . . . quod praeceptis patri(is) con-
siliisque et auspiciis gentem Judaeorum domuit et urbem Hierusolymam
omnibus ante se ducibus regibus gentibus aut frustra petitam aut omnino
intemptatam delevit" (Piper, *Jahrbb. für deutsche Theol.* 1876, pp. 52–54 ;
Corp. Inscr. Lat. t. vi. n. 944 ; Darmesteter, *Revue des études juives*, t. i.
1880, p. 35 sq. ; on its genuineness : Mommsen, *Berichte der sächs.
Gesellsch. der Wissensch. philol.-hist. Cl.* 1850, p. 303).—The coins of
Vespasian, Titus, and Domitian with the superscription : Ιουδαιας
εαλωκυιας, *Judaea evicta, Judaea capta,* and such like, are given most
fully in Madden, *Coins of the Jews,* 1881, pp. 207–229.

[128] Josephus, *Wars of the Jews,* vii. 5. 6 ; Dio Cassius, lxvi. 7.—Simon
was dragged to the place over against the Forum (*Wars of the Jews,* vii.
5. 6 : εἰς τὸν ἐπὶ τῆς ἀγορᾶς ἐσύρετο τόπου). Upon this statement Haver-
camp correctly remarks : "scil. carcerem, quem Livius dicit Foro im-
minere." The *carcer Mamertinus* lay near the Forum. There, and
indeed in its lower part, the *Tullianum,* were, *e.g.,* Jugurtha and the
Catilinian conspirators put to death. It was the common practice to
put prisoners of war to death there by strangling. Trebellius Pollio,
Tyranni triginta, c. 22 (in : "Scriptores Historiae Augustae, ed. Peter) :
"strangulatus in carcere captivorum veterum more."

[129] Josephus, *Wars of the Jews,* vii. 6. 1.

[130] Machärus in Greek : Μαχαιροῦς (so Josephus, Strabo, xvi. 2. 40, p.
763 ; Stephanus Byzant. *s.v.*) is in the Semitic languages *Mechawar,* מכוור
or מכבא. In the Mishna, *Tamid* iii. 8, the *editio princeps,* the Cambridge
Manuscript, and *cod. de Rossi,* 138, have מכוור ; *Aruch* has מכבר. Both
forms also occur elsewhere, but מכוור is more common. The pointing of
the word מְכַוֵּר, *Mechawar,* as in *cod. de Rossi,* 138, is confirmed by the
reading מכאוור, which a Munich Manuscript, *Joma* 39a, has. See Levy,
Neuhebräisches Wörterbuch, iii. 111 f. Also generally : Lightfoot, *Opera,* ii.
582. Besides this Semitic form, we have the following : Μαχαβέρως
(Parthey, *Hieroclis Synecdemus et Notitiae graecae episcopatuum,* 1866, p.
93) and *Machaveron,* as an accusative form, Tobler and Molinier, *Itinera
Hierosolymitana,* 1879, p. 326.—According to *Wars of the Jews,* vii. 6. 2,
Machärus had been fortified as early as in the days of Alexander
Jannäus. Gabinius demolished the fortress (*Antiq.* xiv. 5. 4 ; *Wars of
the Jews,* i. 8. 5). Herod the Great fortified it anew (*Wars of the Jews,*
vii. 6. 2). On its importance, see Pliny, *Hist. Nat.* v. 16. 72 : "Machaerus
secunda quondam arx Judaeae ab Hierosolymis."—It lay on the
southern border of Peraea (*Wars of the Jews,* iii. 3. 3), and in the time of
Herod Antipas is said to have belonged to the king of Arabia (*Antiq.*
xviii. 5. 1). Undoubtedly it is the modern *Mkaur,* east of the Dead Sea.

131 Josephus, *Wars of the Jews*, vii. 6. 1, 4.

132 On Masada, *i.e.* מְצָדָה, *mountain stronghold*, in Strabo, xvi. 2. 44, p. 764, corrupted into Μοασάδα, see especially the comprehensive monograph of Tuch, *Masada, die herodianische Felsenfeste, nach Fl. Josephus und neueren Beobachtungen*, Leipzig 1863, p. 4.—It had indeed been fortified even by the high priest Jonathan (*Wars of the Jews*, vii. 8. 3), and was spoken of as an important stronghold as far back as the time of Hyrcanus II. about B.C. 42 (*Antiq.* xiv. 11. 7 ; *Wars of the Jews*, i. 12. 1), and during the invasion of Palestine by the Parthians served as a safe retreat for the members of the family of Herod (*Antiq.* xiv. 13. 8 f., 14. 6, 15. 1 f. ; *Wars of the Jews*, i. 13. 7 f., 15. 1, 15. 3 f.). Herod the Great fortified it anew (*Wars of the Jews*, vii. 8. 3).—According to *Wars of the Jews*, vii. 8. 3, it lay near to the western bank of the Dead Sea ; according to *Wars of the Jews*, iv. 7. 2, it was not far from Engedi. So, too, Pliny, *Hist. Nat.* v. 17. 73 : " Inde (*scil.* ' from Engedi ') Masada castellum in rupe et ipsum haut procul Asphaltite." According to this, and according to the description which Josephus, *Wars of the Jews*, vii. 8. 3, gives of the locality, there can be no doubt that it is to be identified with the modern Sebbeh on the western bank of the Dead Sea south of Engedi, as Smith and Robinson were the first to recognise. The siege works of the Romans of A.D. 73 are still to be distinctly seen in that place.

133 Josephus, *Wars of the Jews*, ii. 17. 9, vii. 8. 1.

134 Josephus, *Wars of the Jews*, vii. 8. 1-7, 9. 1-2.—According to vii. 9. 1, the self-slaughter of the garrison of Masada took place on the 15th Xanthicus (Nisan, April). The year is not mentioned. But since in an earlier passage, vii. 7. 1, the fourth year of Vespasian is mentioned, which began on 1st July A.D. 72 (comp. Tacitus, *Hist.* ii. 79), the conquest of Masada must have occurred in the spring of A.D. 73.

135 Josephus, *Wars of the Jews*, vii. 10-11 ; *Life*, lxxvi.

136 Josephus, *Wars of the Jews*, vii. 6. 6 .

137 Josephus, *Wars of the Jews*, vii. 6. 6 .

Our Emmaus (*Wars of the Jews*, vii. 6. 6) is most probably rather to be identified with the New Testament Emmaus, Luke xxiv. 13, although the distance in the two cases, respectively 30 and 60 furlongs, are only approximately correct. It has been shrewdly conjectured that our Emmaus, in which Vespasian founded a Roman colony, is identical with the modern Culonie near Jerusalem.

138 Josephus, *Wars of the Jews*, vii. 6. 6 : Dio Cassius, iv. 8. 1.

§ 21. FROM THE DESTRUCTION OF JERUSALEM TO THE OVERTHROW OF BAR-COCHBA.

1 The name Judaea occurs, *e.g.*, on the military diploma of A.D. 86 (*Corpus Inscr. Lat.* t. iii. p. 857, Dipl. xiv.), on the inscription of Julius Severus (*Corpus Inscr. Lat.* t. iii. n. 2830), on the coin which celebrates Hadrian's visit to Judea (*adventui Aug. Judaeae*, in

Madden, *Coins of the Jews*, 1881, p. 231), on the inscription of an otherwise unknown "proc(urator) Aug(usti) provincia(e) Jud(aeae) v(ices)
a(gens) l(egati)" in *Corpus Inscr. Lat.* iii. n. 5776, and elsewhere. At
a later date, somewhere after Hadrian, the prevailing designation is *Syria
Palaestina*, which occurs even as early as in Herodotus (see Division II.
vol. ii. p. 193. Yet even then the name Judea had not altogether passed
out of use. The geographer Ptolemy sets both alongside of each other
(Ptolemy, v. 16. 1).

[2] Proofs of what is said above are given by von Rohden, *De Palaestina
et Arabia provinciis Romanis*, p. 30 sq.

[3] After Flavius Silva had conquered Masada he went back again to
Caesarea (*Wars of the Jews*, vii. 10. 1).—Tacitus also describes Caesarea
as *Judaeae caput* (Tacitus, *Hist.* ii. 78).

[4] Josephus, *Wars of the Jews*, vii. 1. 1 .

[5] The full name in Justin Martyr's *Apology*, i. c. 1 : ἀπὸ Φλαουΐας
Νέας πόλεως τῆς Συρίας Παλαιστίνης. Similarly : Eusebius, *Hist. eccl.* iv.
12.

[6] Josephus, *Wars of the Jews*, iv. 8. 1 : παρὰ τὴν Νεάπολιν καλουμένην,
Μαβορθὰ δὲ ὑπὸ τῶν ἐπιχωρίων.—Pliny, *Hist. Nat.* v. 13. 69 : *Neapolis
quod antea Mamortha dicebatur.*—Eusebius, *Onomasticon*, ed. Lagarde, p.
290 : Συχὲμ ἡ καὶ Σίκιμα ἡ καὶ Σαλήμ· πόλις Ἰακὼβ νῦν ἔρημος· δείκνυται
δὲ ὁ τόπος ἐν προαστείοις Νέας πόλεως. *Ibid.* p. 274, s.v. Λουζά· παρα-
κειμένη Συχὲμ ἀπὸ θ´ σημείου Νέας πόλεως ; instead of which Jerome gives
in his text more correctly : *in tertio lapide Neapoleos;* Epiphanius, *Haer.*
72. 23 : ἐν Σικίμοις τουτέστιν ἐν τῇ Νεαπόλει. So, too, *Haer.* 80. 1.—Jerome,
"Peregr. Paulae," in Tobler, *Palaestinae descriptiones*, p. 23 (=Jerome, *Opp.*
ed. Vallarsi, i. 703): "Sichem, non ut plerique errantes legunt Sichar,
quae nunc Neapolis appellatur."

[7] By Septimius Severus it was deprived of the *jus civitatis* (*Spartian.
vita Severi*, c. 9), but the same emperor at a later period again restored to
it that privilege (*Spartian. vita Severi*, c. 14 : "Palaestinis poenam remisit
quam ob causam Nigri meruerant"). Under Philip the Arabian, according to the evidence of the coins, it was made into a Roman colony.
Ammianus Marcellinus designates it as one of the greatest of the cities of
Palestine (*Ammian.* xiv. 8. 11).

[8] On the numerous extant coins, from Domitian down to the middle
of the third century, we meet with Serapis, Apollo, the Ephesian Diana,
and other deities. In regard to the temple on Gerizim, see "Damascius"
in Photius, *Bibliotheca*, cod. 242, ed. Bekker, p. 345b : ἐν ᾧ Διὸς ὑψίστου
ἁγιώτατον ἱερόν. Renan, *L'église chrétienne*, p. 222. On the earlier and
later history of the worship on Gerizim, see Eckhel, *Docr. Num.* iii. 434.—
The flourishing condition of Hellenistic culture and religion in Neapolis
is also proved by a marble basis of a tripod recently found there. On the
relief of this marble are represented the battles of the gods and the heroes,
especially of Theseus and Hercules. According to an inscription discovered there, the tripod, probably also the marble basis, had been

brought by the founder from Athens. See *Zeitschrift des deutschen Palästina-Vereins*, vi. 230 f., vii. 136 f.

[9] See the inscription of the time of Marcus Aurelius in Le Bas and Waddington, *Inscriptions*, t. iii. 2, n. 1620*b*, communicated literally and in full in Div. II. vol. i. p. 24.

[10] Compare the careful demonstration in Friedmann and Grätz, "Die angebliche Fortdauer des jüdischen Opfercultus nach der Zerstörung des zweiten Tempels" (*Theol. Jahrbücher*, 1848, pp. 338–371).—Against them : Friedenthal in Fürst's *Literaturblatt des Orients*, 1849, col. 328–322.— Against him again : Friedmann in *Literaturblatt*, 401, 433, 465, 534, 548. —In reply : Friedenthal, *Literaturblatt*, 492, 524, 573, 702.—Derenbourg, *Historie de la Palestine*, pp. 480–483.

[11] Clemens Romanus, c. 41 ; *Epist. ad Diognetum*, c. 3.

[12] Josephus, *Antiq.* iii. 9–10.

[13] Josephus, *Treatise against Apion*, ii. 23.

[14] Josephus, *Treatise against Apion*, ii. 6, *s. fin.*.

[15] The most deserving of attention is *Pesachim* vii. 2, where the question is discussed whether one should roast the paschal lamb on a gridiron. " R. Zadok said : Once Rabban Gamaliel spoke to his slave Tabi : Go and roast us the paschal lamb on the gridiron." Since a slave Tabi is elsewhere named as servant of Gamaliel the second, about A.D. 90–110 (*Berachoth* ii. 7 ; *Succa* ii. 1), it would seem that this later Gamaliel is the one intended in this place.

[16] *Edujoth* viii. 6.

[17] *Taanith* iv. 6. Compare what is said above, p. 269.

[18] *Pesachim* x. 3.

[19] *Rosh hashana* i. 4.

[20] *Rosh hashana* 31[b], *Pesachim* 72[b], *Sebachim* 60[b], in Friedmann and Grätz, *Theol. Jahrbücher*, 1848, p. 349 ff.

[21] Justin, *Dialogus cum Trypho*, c. 40 .

[22] Justin, *Dialogus cum Trypho*, c. 46 .

[23] In the statement about Gamaliel and his slave Tabi it is indeed Gamaliel I. that is intended, and the name of Tabi has crept in by mistake. It may, however, be conjectured that Tabi as a youth had served the grandfather and as an old man the grandson (so Derenbourg), or that the name Tabi had come to be hereditary in the family of the slave just as Gamaliel in the family of the master (so Friedmann and Grätz).

[24] On the suppression of the Sanhedrim, see also *Sota* ix. 11.

[25] *Shekalim* viii. 8 : " The Shekalim or tax of two drachmas and the Bikkurim or first-fruits of the produce of the fields were presented only while the temple stood, but the tithe of the grain and the tithe of the cattle and the first-born were presented all the same, whether the temple stood or not."—These three imposts are here mentioned only by way of example as the most important. There remained in force, *e.g.* also the Teruma (*Bikkurim* ii. 3) and the tax of the three pieces of the slaughtered

victims, namely, the right fore-leg, the cheeks, and the stomach (*Chullin* x. 1). Further details on all these imposts are given in Div. II. vol. i. pp. 230–236.—The priest's due of the right shoulder is witnessed to as a custom of his time by the Emperor Julian in Cyrill. *adv. Julian*, p. 306 A : καὶ τὸν δεξιὸν ὦμον διδόασιν ἀπαρχὰς τοῖς ἱερεῦσιν, where it is not to be translated as by Neumann (*Kaiser Julians Bücher gegen die Christen*, 1880, p. 39) "the right shoulder," but "the right fore-leg," for it rests not upon Lev. vii. 32, but upon Deut. xviii. 3. Compare also Friedmann and Grätz, *Theol. Jahrbücher*, 1848, p. 359 ff.

[26] *Baba kamma* viii. 6.

[27] *Sukka* iii. 12 ; *Rosh hashana* iv. 1, 3, 4 ; *Menachoth* x. 5. Derenbourg, *Histoire de la Palestine*, p. 304 sq.

[28] *Rosh hashana* ii. 8–9.—According to *Edujoth* vii. 7, once in Gamaliel's absence the year was declared to be an intercalary year, on the condition that he would confirm this opinion when he returned.

[29] *Kelim* v. 4 ; *Para* vii. 6. Compare also *Bechoroth* iv. 5, vi. 8 (how they were wont to do in Jamnia in making inspection of the first-born).

[30] *Sanhedrin* xi. 4 ; *Rosh hashana* iv. 2.

[31] *Sebachim* i. 3 ; *Jadajim* iii. 5, iv. 2.

[32] Josephus, *Antiq.* xiv. 10. 17 ; *Codex Theodosianus*, ii. 1. 10 : *ex consensu partium in civili duntaxat negotio.* Compare Div. II. vol. ii. pp. 263, 269.—According to *Edujoth* vii. 7, Gamaliel II. once made a journey to the governor (Hegemon) of Syria (it should be "of Judea") "in order to obtain a permission from him " (לטול רשות מהגמון בסוריא). It is possible it had to do with an investiture, or extension, or execution of legislative functions.

[33] Origen, *Epistola ad Africanum*, § 14, given literally in Div. II. vol. i. p. 173.

[34] Enforcement of the tax, Suetonius, *Domitian*, 12 ; prohibition of conversions to Judaism, Dio Cassius, lxvii. 14. Both passages are quoted in full in Div. II. vol. ii. p. 267.

[35] Eusebius, *Hist. eccl.* iii. 12 (Vespasian) ; *ibid.* iii. 19–20 (Domitian) ; *ibid.* iii. 32. 3–4 (Trajan) ; reference being made in all cases to Hegesippus.

[36] Eusebius, *Hist. eccl.* iii. 12 .

[37] Eusebius, *Hist. eccl.* iv. 2 : Ἔν τε γὰρ Ἀλεξανδρείᾳ καὶ τῇ λοιπῇ Αἰγύπτῳ καὶ προσέτι κατὰ Κυρήνην ὥσπερ ὑπὸ πνεύματος δεινοῦ τινος καὶ στασιώδους ἀναρριπισθέντες ὥρμηντο πρὸς τοὺς συνοίκους Ἕλληνας στασιάζειν. —With reference to the war in Egypt, the oldest witness, though very brief, is Appian, *Civ.* ii. 90. Appian there relates how that Caesar had dedicated a sanctuary at Alexandria to the memory of Pompey ; and then proceeds : ὅπερ ἐπ' ἐμοῦ κατὰ Ῥωμαίων αὐτοκράτορα Τραϊανόν, ἐξολλύντα τὸ ἐν Αἰγύπτῳ Ἰουδαίων γένος, ὑπὸ τῶν Ἰουδαίων ἐς τὰς τοῦ πολέμου χρείας κατηρείφθη.—Undoubtedly the reference is to this period in a fragment of Appian in which he tells how he had been obliged to flee from Egypt

at the time of the war with the Jews (*Revue archéologique*, Nouve Série, t. xix. 1869, pp. 101–110 = Müller, *Fragmenta hist. graec.* (v. 1, p. lxv.).

[38] Eusebius, *Hist. eccl.* iv. 2 ; *Chronicon*, ed. Schoene, ii. 164 sq. (at the eighteenth year of Trajan, 2131 Abr.) ; Orosius, vii. 12 : "In Alexandria autem commisso proelio victi et adriti sunt." Compare also Buxtorf, *Lexicon Chald.* col. 99, *s.v.* אלכסנדריא ; Derenbourg, *Histoire*, pp. 410–412 ; Wünsche, *Der jerusalemische Talmud* (1880), p. 125 f.—In the Chronicle of Eusebius it is remarked on the first year of Hadrian that this emperor restored Alexandria that had been destroyed by the Jews (or Romans ?). See Eusebius, *Chronicon*, ed. Schoene, ii. 164 sq., according to the Armenian : "Adrianus Alexandriam a Judaeis subversam restauravit ;" according to Jerome : "Hadrianus Alexandriam a Romanis [sic] subversam publicis instauravit expensis." The city must therefore have suffered severely, even though it might not have been, strictly speaking, "destroyed."

[39] Dio Cassius, lxviii. 32. Compare Orosius, vii. 12 .

[40] Eusebius, *Hist. eccl.* iv. 2 ; Dio Cassius, lxviii. 32.

[41] Eusebius, *Hist. eccl.* iv. 2.—According to Eusebius, *Chronicon*, ed. Schoene, ii. 164 sq.; Orosius, vii. 12, the revolt had also extended into the Thebaid.

[42] Dio Cassius, lxviii. 32.

[43] Eusebius, *Chronicon*, ed. Schoene, ii. 164 sq. (on the nineteenth year of Trajan, 2132 Abr.). According to the Armenian : "Salaminam Cipri insulae urbem Judaei adorti sunt et Graecos, quos ibi nacti sunt, trucidarunt, urbemque a fundamentis subverterunt." According to the Greek in Syncellus, ed. Dindorf, i. 657 : Τοὺς ἐν Σαλαμῖνι τῆς Κύπρου Ἕλληνας Ἰουδαῖοι ἀνελόντες τὴν πόλιν κατέσκαψαν.—Orosius, vii. 12 : "Sane Salaminam, urbem Cypri, interfectis omnibus accolis deleverunt."

[44] Dio Cassius, lxviii. 32.

[45] Eusebius, *Hist. eccl.* iv. 2 ; *Chronicon*, ed. Schoene, ii. 164 sq. (on the eighteenth year of Trajan, 2131 Abr.) ; Orosius, vii. 12 ; Dio Cassius, lxviii. 32 (who also gives many personal details about Quietus).—On Lusius Quietus compare also what is said above at p. 277. His name seems at an early date to have been corrupted in the text of the Chronicle of Eusebius, for Jerome has Lysias Quietus, and Syncellus (ed. Dindorf, i. 657), Λυσίας Κύντος. The correct form is given in Eusebius, *Hist. eccl.* ed. Heinichen, Dio Cassius, ed. Dindorf, and Spartian, *Hadrian.* c. 5.

[46] Eusebius, *Chronicon*, ed. Schoene, ii. 164 sq. (on the 1st year of Hadrian, 2133 Abr.). According to the Armenian : "Adrianus Judaeos subegit ter [tertio] contra Romanos rebellantes." According to Jerome : "Hadrianus Judaeos capit secundo contra Romanos rebellantes." According to Syncellus : Ἀδριανὸς Ἰουδαίους κατὰ Ἀλεξανδρέων στασιάζοντας ἐκόλασεν,

[47] Spartian, *Hadrian.* c. 5 : "Lycia denique ac Palaestina rebelles animos efferebant.

[48] Volkmar, *Theolog. Jahrbücher*, 1857, pp. 441–498, and especially, *Das Buch Judith* (1860), pp. 56 ff., 64 ff., 83 ff., 90 ff. Grätz, *Geschichte der*

Juden, iv. 439 ff. On the other side, see Lipsius, *Zeitschrift für wissenschaftliche Theologie*, 1859, pp. 81–111.

[49] Mishna, *Sota* ix. 14, and *Seder Olam. sub fin.* In both passages, instead
of the common reading of the text, פולמוס של טיטום, we should read : פולמוס
של קיטוס. See Grätz, *Geschichte der Juden*, iv. 439 ff. ; Volkmar, *Judith*, pp.
83–90 ; Lipsius, *Zeitschrift für wissenschaftliche Theologie*, 1859, pp. 97–104 ·
Derenbourg, *Histoire*, p. 404 f. ; Salzer, *Magazin für die Wissenschaft des
Judenthums*, iv. 1877, pp. 141–144.—In the Mishna passages קיטוס is the
reading in : (1) a manuscript of the Royal Library at Berlin (*MSS. Or.* fol.
567, previously in private hands ; it is the same to which Grätz had
referred). (2) The Cambridge Manuscript, edited by Lowe in 1883 (*University Additional*, 470. 1). In the passage from the *Seder Olam*, this same
reading is found in an old manuscript collated by Azariah de Rossi. See
Grätz in the work above quoted. In the latter passage this reading is also
required by the context ; for there are, according to it, fifty-two years to be
reckoned between the war of Vespasian and the war of the קיטוס, and
from that to the war of Ben-Cosiba (Bar-Cochba), 16 years. Also in the
Mishna passage the war of the קיטוס follows upon the war of Vespasian,
and then after that " the last war," *i.e.* that of Bar-Cochba.

[50] Derenbourg, *Histoire de la Palestine*, pp. 443, 446. On the forms of
the name טוריינוס, טיריון, etc., see Derenbourg, *Histoire*, p. 408.

[51] See Derenbourg, *Histoire*, p. 406 f. ; Grätz, *Geschichte der Juden*, iv. p.
445 ff. ; Volkmar, *Judith*, pp. 90–100 ; Lipsius, *Zeitschrift für wissenschaftl.
Theologie*, 1859, pp. 104–110.

[52] At the basis of the legend there may lie probably an obscure remini-
scence of the fact that Lusius Quietus, the oppressor of the Jews, was
recalled by Hadrian, and subsequently executed (Spartian, *Hadrian.*
5 and 7).

[53] *Bereshith rabba* c. 64. See the passage in the original text, and in a
French translation in Derenbourg, *Histoire de la Palestine*, p. 416 sq. Text
and Latin translation in Volkmar, *Judith*, pp. 108–111. German in
Wünsche, *Der Midrasch Bereschit Rabba* (1881), p. 307 f.

[54] So Volkmar, *Judith*, pp. 108 ff., 131 ff. ; Grätz, *Geschichte der Juden*,
iv. 138 ff., 442 ff. ; Derenbourg, *Histoire de la Palestine*, p. 412 sq. ; Neu-
bürger, *Monatsschrift für Geschichte und Wissenschaft des Judenthums*, 1873,
p. 433 ff. ; Hausrath, *Zeitgeschichte*, iv. 328 f. ; Salzer, *Magazin*, iii. 127 ff. ;
Hamburger, *Real-Encyclopaedie*, art. " Hadrian."

[55] The passages are collected in Münter, p. 64 f., and Volkmar, *Judith*,
pp. 131–134.

[56] The καί is given only in the *Sinaiticus ;* in all other texts it is wanting. The explanation given above, that the building was for heathen
worship, is supported, for example, by Lipsius in Schenkel's *Bibellexion*,
i. 371 f. The words have been understood of the aid given to the Jewish
building by the heathens, especially by Volkmar, and that indeed even before
the discovery of the *Sinaiticus*, resting upon the common reading without
the καί (*Theolog. Jahrbücher*, 1856, pp. 351–361, and elsewhere).

[57] Spartian, *vita Hadriani*, c. 22 (in the *Scriptores Historiae Augustae*, ed. Peter): sacra Romana diligentissime curavit. peregrina contempsit.

[58] Spartian. *Hadrian*. 14.

[59] Dio Cassius, lxix. 12.

[60] Compare Gregorovius, *Sitzungsberichte der philos.-philol. und hist. Classe der Münchener Akademie*, 1883, p. 499 ff. ; *Der Kaiser Hadrian*, p. 188 ff. In favour of Gregorovius' view one might refer to the state of the original documents. Dio Cassius, as well as Spartian, founds partly on the autobiography of Hadrian (see Dio Cassius, lxix. 11, ὡς ᾿Αδριανὸς γράφει ; Spartian, 1. 1, "in libris vitae suae Hadrianus ipse commemorat ; " 7. 2, "ut ipse vita sua dicit ;" comp. also 3. 3, and 3. 5). In Dio Cassius, however, the history of the Jewish war follows immediately upon the quotation from the autobiography, and may probably have been derived from it.

[61] Modestinus, *Digest*. xlviii. 8. 11, pr. : " Circumcidere Judaeis filios suos tantum rescripto divi Pii permittitur : in non ejusdem religionis qui hoc fecerit, castrantis poena irrogatur." This statement of fact is also corroborated by other witnesses. In the Syrian Dialogue on Fate, which is ascribed to Bardesanes, as a historical instance of the fact that ofttimes kings when they conquer foreign countries have abolished the native laws and introduced their own without the stars putting any hindrance in the way, this is advanced as pre-eminently applicable, that only shortly before the Romans, after the conquest of Arabia, had abolished the laws of that country, especially the law regarding circumcision (Cureton, *Spicilegium Syriacum*, 1855, p. 30 ; in the somewhat abbreviated text in Eusebius, *Praeparatio evangel.* vi. 10. 41, ed. Gaisford, the prohibition of circumcision is not mentioned). But the same author speaks immediately after of circumcision as an existing institution among the Jews. He witnesses, therefore, precisely to the condition of matters as determined by Antoninus Pius. A further witness for this is Origen, who distinctly says that only the Jews were allowed to practise circumcision, but that it was forbidden to all others on the pain of death (*Contra Cels.* ii. 13). The jurist Paulus, a contemporary of Origen, says, *Sent.* v. 22. 3–4 (in Huschke's *Jurisprudentiae antejustinianae quae supersunt*, ed. 5, Lips. 1886) : " Cives Romani, qui se Judaico ritu vel servos suos circumcidi patiuntur bonis ademptis in insulam perpetuo relegantur ; medici capite puniuntur. Judaei si alienae nationis comparatos servos circumciderunt, aut deportantur aut capite puniuntur." The prohibition, therefore, by no means applied especially to the Jews, but they rather were by Hadrian's immediate successor expressly excluded from its application.

[62] Compare Mommsen, *Römische Geschichte*, v. 549.—Hadrian strictly forbade castration; it was to be punished under the *lex Cornelia de sicariis*, *i.e.* it was treated as murder (*Digest*. xlviii. 8. 4. 2). That circumcision was treated in the same category as castration, is seen from the passage quoted above from Modestinus.

[63] Epiphanius, *De mensuris et ponderibus*, § 14.

[64] *Chronicon Paschale*, ed. Dindorf, i. 474.

[65] Eusebius, *Hist. eccl.* iv. 6.

[66] Dio Cassius, lxix. 12.

[67] This route is particularly described in Dio Cassius, lxix. 11-12.

[68] Compare generally: Dürr, *Die Reisen des Kaisers Hadrian*, p. 4 f. ; Gregorovius, *Der Kaiser Hadrian*, 3 Aufl. p. 468 ff.—On numerous inscriptions Hadrian is called σωτήρ, οἰκιστής, εὐεργέτης, κτίστης. See the texts in Dürr, p. 104 ff. On coins of Hadrian are found the following inscriptions : restitutori Achaiae, restitutori Africae, restitutori Arabiae, restitutori Asiae, restitutori Bithyniae, restitutori Galliae, restitutori Hispaniae, restitutori Italiae, restitutori Libyae, restitutori Macedoniae, restitutori Nicomediae, restitutori orbis terrarum, restitutori Phrygiae, restitutori Siciliae."

[69] On Tiberias, see Epiphanius, *Haer.* 30. 12 : ναὸς δὲ μέγιστος ἐν τῇ πόλει προὔπῆρχε· τάχα, οἶμαι, Ἀδριάνειον τοῦτο ἐκάλουν.— On Gaza, *Chronicon*, ed. Dindorf, i. 474: καὶ ἐκεῖ ἔστησεν πανήγυριν . . . καὶ ἕως τοῦ νῦν ἡ πανήγυρις ἐκείνη λέγεται Ἀδριανή.—The coins of Petra with the superscription : Ἀδριανὴ Πέτρα, in Mionnet, *Description de Médailles*, v. 587-589 ; *Suppl.* viii. 387 sq. ; De Saulcy, *Numismatique de la Terre Sainte*, pp. 351-353.

[70] Eckhel, *Doctr. Num.* vi. 495 sq.; Madden, *Coins of the Jews* (1881), p. 231 ; Cohen, *Médailles impériales*, ed. 2, t. ii. p. 110 sq. The coins were minted in Rome (S. C.).—There were similar coins for almost all the provinces.

[71] Pliny, *Hist. Nat.* v. 14. 70.

[72] From Dio Cassius, lxix. 12, it appears that the founding of Aelia occurred in the time of Hadrian's first visit to Syria, A.D. 130, but the outbreak of the rebellion after his second visit in A.D. 131, and so probably in A.D. 132. In fact, the Chronicle of Eusebius places the beginning of the rebellion in the sixteenth year of Hadrian, *i.e.* A.D. 132-133 (Eusebius, *Chronicon*, ed. Schoene, ii. 166 sq.).

[73] Χοχεβᾶς and Chochebas are the forms of the name in the Chronicle of Eusebius, and in Jerome, *ad ann. Abr.* 2149 (ed. Schoene, ii. 168 sq. ; the Greek form in Syncellus, ed. Dindorf, i. 660) ; so too in Orosius, vii. 13 (ed. Zangemeister). Βαρχωχέβας in Justin Martyr, *Apol.* i. 31 (ed. Otto), and Eusebius, *Hist. eccl.* iv. 6 (ed. Heinichen); the passage from Justin also in Eusebius, *Hist. eccl.* iv. 8. Barcochabas in Jerome, *Adv. Rufin.* iii. 31 (*Opp.* ed. Vallarsi, ii. 559).—In the rabbinical sources, on the other hand, we have בר כוזיבא or בן כוזיבא (Derenbourg, *Histoire de la Palestine*, p. 423 ; Lebrecht, *Bether*, p. 13).

[74] *Jer. Taanith* iv. fol. 68ᵈ (Cracow ed.) : " R. Simon ben Jochai said : R. Akiba my teacher expounded the passage : There shall go a star (כוכב) out of Jacob" (Num. xxiv. 17), as follows : ' There goes כוזבא out from Jacob.' When R. Akiba saw Barcosiba he said, This is the king Messiah. Then said to him R. Jochanan ben Torta : Akiba, the grass will grow out of thy jaw-bone, and yet the Son of David will not have come."

[75] Since Barcosiba or Bencosiba is the prevailing form, even in the mouths of such as esteemed him highly, like Akiba, it cannot have had a disrespectful meaning. Cosiba is either the name of his father (so in earlier days, Derenbourg, *Histoire*, p. 423, note 3) or of his home, כוֹבָא, 1 Chron. iv. 22=כּוֹזֵב, Gen. xxxviii. 5=אַכְזִיב, in the tribe of Judah, Josh. xv. 44; Micah i. 14 (hardly to be identified with אַכְזִיב in the tribe of Asher = Ekdippa, between Tyre and Ptolemais, as conjectured by Derenbourg, *Mélanges publiés par l'école des hautes études*, 1878, p. 157 sq.).—The rendering of it כּוֹזֵב, "Liar," makes its appearance first in the Midrash, *Echa rabbathi*, see Levy, *Neuhebräishches Wörterbuch*, ii. 312.

[76] Midrash on *Echa* ii. 2; *Gittin* 57ᵃ (in Derenbourg, *Histoire*, pp. 424, 433. See on Eleasar of Modein: Bacher, *Die Agada der Tannaiten* (1884), pp. 194–219.

[77] Ewald, *History of Israel*, viii. 291; De Saulcy, *Revue Num.* 1865, p. 44.

[78] See the passage quoted in note 83; also Bacher, *Die Agada der Tannaiten*, p. 291 f.

[79a] Jerome, adv. *Rufin.* iii. 21 (*Opp.* ed. Vallarsi, ii. 559). Jerome says there to his opponent Rufinus that he spits fire "ut ille Barchochabas, auctor seditionis Judaicae, stipulam in ore succensam anhelitu ventilabat, ut flammas cvomere putaretur."

[80] Justin Martyr, *Apol.* i. 31: Καὶ γὰρ ἐν τῷ νῦν γεγενημένῳ Ἰουδαϊκῷ πολέμῳ Βαρχωχέβας, ὁ τῆς Ἰουδαίων ἀποστάσεως ἀρχηγέτης, Χριστιανοὺς μόνους εἰς τιμωρίας δεινάς, εἰ μὴ ἀρνοῖντο Ἰησοῦν τὸν Χριστὸν καὶ βλασφημοῖεν, ἐκέλευεν ἀπάγεσθαι. Eusebius, *Chronicon*, ed. Schoene, ii. 168 sq. ad. ann. *Abr.* 2149. According to the Armenian: "Qui dux rebellionis Judaeorum erat Chochebas, multos e Christianis diversis suppliciis affecit, quia nolebant procedere cum illo ad pugnam contra Romanos." So, too, the Latin reproduction of Jerome in Schoene, and Syncellus, ed. Dindorf, i. 660. Compare also Orosius, vii. 13.

[81] Dio Cassius, lxix. 12. Compare Jerome, *Chronicon*, ad ann. *Abr.* 2148 (Eusebius, *Chronicon*, ed. Schoene, ii. 167): "Judaei in arma versi Palestinam depopulati sunt." The Armenian text of Eusebius has: "Judae rebellarunt et Palestinensium terram invaserunt."

[82] Chrysostom, *Orat. adv. Judaeos*, v. 10, speaks of an attempt at the rebuilding of the temple in the time of Hadrian. He endeavours there to show that the destruction of the temple had been brought about by the will of God. If the Jews had not made the attempt to build again the temple, then they might say: If we had chosen we might have built it again. Νυνὶ δὲ αὐτοὺς δείκνυμι, ὅτι οὐχ ἅπαξ, οὐδὲ δὶς, ἀλλὰ καὶ τρὶς ἐπιχειρήσαντας καὶ ῥαγέντας, namely, under Hadrian, Constantine, and Julian.—Georgius Cedrenus, ed. Bekker, i. 437, relates: ἐφ' οὗ στασιασάντων τῶν Ἰουδαίων καὶ τὸν ἐν Ἱεροσολύμοις ναὸν οἰκοδομῆσαι βουληθέντων ὀργίζεται κατ' αὐτῶν σφόδρα καὶ πολέμου γενομένου μεταξὺ ἀνεῖλεν ἐξ αὐτῶν ἐν ἡμέρᾳ μιᾷ μυριάδας νη΄. In the details of his statement this Cedrenus agrees so exactly with the statement of Chrysostom that it is apparent that he must have drawn his information either directly from Chrysostom, or else

from the sources which Chrysostom had used. Nicephorus Callistus also, in his *Eccles. Hist.* iii. 24 (Migne, *Patrol. Graec.* t. cxlv.), reproduces this report. The *Chronicon Paschale* asserts that Hadrian at the building of Aelia, after the suppression of the revolt, destroyed the Jewish temple (ed. Dindorf, i. 474 : *καθελὼν τὸν ναὸν τῶν Ἰουδαίων τὸν ἐν Ἱεροσολύμοις*).— Much weight cannot be laid upon any of these witnesses.

[83] Dio Cassius, lxix. 13.

[84] On the increasing of the strength of the troops : Eusebius, *Hist. eccl.* iv. 6. 1 ; *Chronicon, ad ann. Abr.* 2148.—Generals : Dio Cassius, lxix. 13 : *τοὺς κρατίστους τῶν στρατηγῶν ὁ Ἀδριανὸς ἐπ᾽ αὐτοὺς ἔπεμψεν.*

[85] *Corpus Inscr. Graec.* n. 4033 and 4034 (the former = *Archäolog.-epigraph. Mittheilungen aus Oesterreich-Ungarn*, ix. 118). In both inscriptions, which are almost literal copies of each other, it is told that Ti. (or P.?) Severus was commander of the *leg. IV. Scythica*, and administered Syria as commissary when Publicius Marcellus had left Syria on account of the outbreak of the Jewish revolt(*Σεούηρον . . . ἡγεμόνα λεγεῶνος δ' Σκυθικῆς καὶ διοικήσαντα τὰ ἐν Συρίᾳ πράγματα, ἡνίκα Πουβλίκιος Μάρκελλος διὰ τὴν κίνησιν τὴν Ἰουδαϊκὴν μεταβέβηκει ἀπὸ Συρίας*). Publicius Marcellus led a portion of the Syrian garrison, which consisted of three legions (Pfitzner, p. 187), against Judea, while Severus undertook as commissary the administration of Syria, presumably still retaining the command of his legion. The *leg. IV. Scythica* therefore probably remained in Syria.

[86] Eusebius, *Hist. eccl.* iv. 6. 1.

[87] *Bab. Taanith* 29a in Derenbourg, *Historie*, p. 422. Generally : Schoettgen, *Horae hebraicae*, ii. 953–957 ; Buxtorf, *Lexicon Chaldaicum*, col. 916 (*s.v.* טרן); Levy, *Neuhebräisches Wörterbuch*, ii. 149, *s.v.* טורנוס ; Bacher, *Die Agada der Tannaiten*, 1884, pp. 294–300 = *Monatsschrift für Geschichte und Wissenschaft des Judenthums*, 1883, pp. 303 ff. 347 ff.—The form טורנוס רופוס is indeed only a corruption of Tineius Rufus. In the Jerusalem Talmud the older editions (*e.g.* that of Cracow) have in several places, *Berachoth* ix. fol. 14b from below, *Sota* v. fol. 20c from below,טונוסטרופוס,Tunustrufus, where the *t* between the *s* and *r* seems to have been introduced as a modification in pronunciation, as in *Istrahel, Esdras*, and such like forms.

[88] Dio Cassius, lxix. 13.—That Julius Severus was recalled from Britain is shown by an inscription, *Corpus Inscr. Lat.* t. iii. n. 2830, which gives his entire *cursus honorum*.

[89] *Gittin* 57a, in Derenbourg, *Histoire*, p. 433 sq.

[90] (1) One Q. Lollius was "legatus imp. Hadriani in expeditione Judaica, qua donatus est hasta pura corona aurea" (Orelli-Henzen, n. 6500 = Renier, *Inscriptions de l'Algérie*, n. 2319 = *Corp. Inscr. Lat.* t. viii. n. 6706). The expression "legatus imp.," without any particularizing addition, can only be understood as designating a personal adjutant, who occupied the position of an immediate attendant upon the emperor. (2) On an inscription, certainly in a very fragmentary condition, but undoubtedly belonging to the later period of Hadrian's reign, very probably to

A.D. 134 or 135, it is said that he "(lab)oribus max(imis rempublicam ab ho)ste liberaverit" (Orelli-Henzen, n. 5457 = *Corp. Inscr. Lat.* t. vi. n. 974). Since the only event occurring in this later period is the Jewish war, the inscription would seem to refer to Hadrian's active participation in it. See Henzen's remarks. According to Schiller, Hadrian's presence at the seat of war is made certain from the fact that to Julius Severus were awarded only "ornamenta triumphalia," not "supplicationes" (*Corp. Inscr. Lat.* t. iii. n. 2830), "he was not therefore commander-in-chief."

[91] *Corp. Inscr. Graec.* n. 5906.

[92] Appian, *Syr.* 50 .

[93] Eusebius, *Demonstratio evangel.* vi. 18. 10, ed. Gaisford : the prophecy of Zech. xiv. 2, ἐξελεύσεται τὸ ἥμισυ τῆς πόλεως ἐν αἰχμαλωσίᾳ, was fulfilled in the time of Vespasian ; the other half of the city, *i.e.* of the inhabitants, was besieged in Hadrian's time and driven out, τὸ λοιπὸν τῆς πόλεως μέρος ἥμισυ πολιορκηθὲν αὖθις ἐξελαύνεται, ὡς ἐξ ἐκείνου καὶ εἰς δεῦρο πάμπαν ἄβατον αὐτοῖς γενέσθαι τὸν τόπον. Eusebius therefore does not speak of the destruction of the city, but only of the driving forth of the Jewish population after a siege had been conducted against the city.

[94] Chrysostom, *Adv. Judaeos*, v. 11 : τὰ λείψανα ἀφανίσας πάντα. — Cedren. ed. Bekker, i. 437 : καὶ τὰ μὲν παλαιὰ λείψανα τῆς πόλεως καὶ τιῦ ναοῦ κατερειπώσας κτίζει νέαν Ἱερουσαλήμ.—Nicephorus, *Callist. Eccl. hist.* iii. 24 : ὅσα γε μὴν τῇ πόλει περιελείφθη τῆς ἐκ πάλαι οἰκοδομῆς λείψανα ἐρειπῶσαι καὶ παντάπασιν ἀφανίσαι.—Hieronymus, *Comm. in Jes.* i. 5 (*Opp.* ed. Vallarsi, iv. 15) : "post Titum et Vespasianum et ultimam eversionem Jerusalem sub Aelio Hadriano usque ad praesens tempus nullum remedium est." *Idem*, in Jer. xxxi. 15 (Vallarsi, iv. 1065) : "sub Hadriano, quando et urbs Jerusalem subversa est." *Idem*, in Ezek. c. 5 (Vallarsi, v. 49) : "post quinquaginta annos sub Aelio Hadriano usque ad solum incensa civitas atque deleta est ita ut pristinum quoque nomen amiserit." *Idem*, in Ezek. c. 24 (Vallarsi, v. 277) : "post quinquaginta annos sub Hadriano civitas aeterno igne consumta est." *Idem*, in Dan. c. 9 *fin.* (Vallarsi, v. 696). *Idem*, in Joel. i. 4 (Vallarsi, vi. 171) : "Aelii quoque Hadriani contra Judaeos expeditionem legimus, qui ita Jerusalem murosque subvertit, ut de urbis reliquiis ac favillis sui nominis Aeliam conderet civitatem." *Idem*, in Hab. ii. 14 (Vallarsi, vi. 622) : "usque ad extremas ruinas Hadriani eos perduxit obsidio." *Idem*, in Zech. viii. 19 (Vallarsi, vi. 852). *Idem*, in Zech. xi. 4, 5 (Vallarsi, vi. 885).

[95] Mishna, *Taanith* iv. 6, enumerates five unfortunate events as happening on 17th Thammuz, and five unfortunate events as happening on 9th Ab. In reference to the latter it is said : "On 9th Ab sentence was pronounced upon our forefathers that they should enter into the country, and the temple was on the first occasion and on the second occasion destroyed, and Beth-ther was conquered and Jerusalem levelled down with the plough" (נחרשה העיר). The Babylonian Talmud, *bab. Taanith* 29a (Derenbourg, *Histoire*, p. 422), relates more particularly that it was the "turannus Rufus" (טורנס רופוס) who caused the plough to

pass over the site of the temple (it is there called הַהֵיכַל, not הָעִיר).—The whole passage is to be found quoted almost literally in Jerome, who expressly refers for authority to the Jewish tradition ("cogimur igitur ad Habraeos recurrere"), ad Zechar. viii. 19, *Opp.* ed. Vallarsi, vi. 852 : "In quinto mense, qui apud Latinos appellatur Augustus, quum propter exploratores terrae sanctae seditio orta esset in populo, jussi sunt montem non ascendere, sed per quadraginta annos longis ad terram sanctam circuire dispendiis, ut exceptis duobus, Caleb et Josue, omnes in solitudine caderent. In hoc mense et a Nabuchodonosor et multa post saecula a Tito et Vespasiano templum Jerosolymis incensum est atque destructum ; capta urbs Bethel [l. Bether], ad quam multa millia confugerant Judaeorum ; aratum templum in ignominiam gentis oppressae a T. Annio [l. Tinnio] Rufo."

96 That the plough should have been driven over Jerusalem as a sign of devastation and utter ruin is not probable, since, indeed, the building of a new city was contemplated. But this act may indeed have been performed at the beginning of the founding of the new city as a ceremony of initiation. The ceremonial act would be in either case the same ; see Servius on Virgil. *Aeneid,* iv. 212 : "cum conderetur nova civitas, aratrum adhibitum, ut eodem ritu quo condita subvertatur." An exact description of the ceremony is given in a passage from Varro quoted by Servius on Virgil. *Aeneid,* v. 755.

97 *Chronicon Samaritanum, Arabice conscriptum, cui titulus est Liber Josuae,* ed. Juynboll (Lugd. Bat. 1848), p. 47.

98 The name of the city is given by Eusebius, *Hist. eccl.* iv. 6, as Βίθθηρ (accus. Βίθθηρα), or according to some manuscripts, Βέθθηρ, Βήθθηρ ; in Rufinus, *Bethar.* In the Jerusalem Talmud, *Taanith* iv. fol. 68ᵈ–69ᵃ, where the name occurs frequently, it is almost constantly בֵּיתַּר, only very rarely בֵּיתָר. In the Mishna, *Taanith* iv. 6, the Cambridge and Hamburg manuscripts have בֵּיתַּר ; the *editio princeps* and *cod. de Rossi,* 138, בֵּיתָר ; a Berlin manuscript, בֵּתָר. The correct form is undoubtedly בֵּיתַּר, Beth-ther.—On the ground of the common printed text of the Mishna it is generally assumed that our Beth-ther is also referred to in *Challa* iv. 10. But, according to the context, the place there intended lies beyond the borders of the land of Israel, and the correct reading there is בֵּיתּוּר, Bê-jittur. — In other passages also, where it has been thought that our place was referred to, this is found to be extremely questionable. Thus in Josephus, *Wars of the Jews,* iv. 8. 1, where a village, Βήταρις, is mentioned as "in the midst of Idumea." We may also compare Βαιθήρ, which, according to some manuscripts of the Septuagint text of Josh. xv. 59, is named among the cities of Judah in the neighbourhood of Bethlehem (*cod. Vaticanus* has Θεθήρ, but *Alexandrinus,* Βαιθήρ ; so also read Jerome, *Comm. in Micham,* v. 2, *Opp.* ed. Vallarsi, vi. 490). Also Βαιθθήρ, which the text of the *cod. Alex.* 1 Chron. vi. 59 (vi. 44), names besides Beth-shemesh. In the passage in the Song of Songs ii. 17, בֶּתֶר is not *Nomen proprium* but *appellativum.*

[99] In determining the site many have allowed themselves to be led astray by adopting a wrong point of view. In the *Itinerarium Antonini*, and by the Pilgrim of Bordeaux, a Bethar is spoken about south of Caesarea on the road to Lydda ; and the rabbinical legends tell how that the blood of those slain in Beth-ther rolled away with it great masses of rock until it flowed into the sea (*jer. Taanith* iv. fol. 69ᵃ from above, text in Lebrecht, *Bether*, p. 45 ; French in Derenbourg, *Histoire*, p. 434 ; German in Wünsche, *Der jerusalemische Talmud*, 1880, p. 159). On the basis of these statements many have assumed that it lay in the neighbourhood of the coast, and was identical with that Bethar. But whoever will follow the rabbinical legend must follow it out fully. Now it expressly states that the blood flowed from Beth-ther into the sea, although Beth-ther was forty *mil. pass.* from the coast. See Derenbourg's and Wünsche's translations of the *jer. Taanith* iv. fol. 69ᵃ. Only by later writers, who found the statement too absurd, has the distance been reduced to four or one *mil. pass.* (see Derenbourg, *Histoire*, p. 434, note 4). That Bethar of the *Itineraries* cannot therefore be identified with our Beth-ther, because it lay in a predominantly heathen district, and on the plain, and was therefore certainly not an important military post in the Jewish war. The only certain point of view for determining the site is that offered by the statement of Eusebius, that it was not far from Jerusalem (*Hist. eccl.* iv. 6 : τῶν Ἱεροσολύμων οὐ σφόδρα πόρρω διεστῶσα). It is accordingly scarcely to be doubted that it is identical with the modern Bettir, some three hours south-west of Jerusalem. A steep ridge, which only in the south joins the mountain range, there breaks into the valley. The place is therefore admirably fitted for a stronghold, and indeed traces of an early fortress are still to be found there. Finally, from this to the sea the distance is just about forty *mil. pass.*, as mentioned in the Jerusalem Talmud ; as the crow flies, thirty-one.

[100] Eusebius, *Hist. eccl.* iv. 6.

[101] Mishna, *Taanith* iv. 6, and Jerome, *Comm. in Zech.* viii. 19, *Opp.* ed. Vallarsi, vi. 852 (see the passage quoted in note 93).—If we could give any credence still to this tradition it might be understood of **Ab of the** year 135 ; for the war was probably carried on into that year. The years of Hadrian's reign run from 11th August to 11th August (Spartian, *Hadrian.* c. 4). The 9th Ab would correspond to the end of July.

[102] Eusebius, *Hist. eccl.* iv. 6.

[103] The legends about the fall of Beth-ther are found principally in *jer. Taanith* iv. fol. 68ᵈ–69ᵃ and Midrash, *Echa rabbathi* c. ii.

[104] That " the government of Barcosiba" lasted three and a half years is stated in *Seder Olam* (in Derenbourg, *Histoire*, p. 413 : מלכות בן כוזיבא שלש שנים ומחצה ; the reading three and a half is certainly the correct one ; see Salzer, *Magazin für die Wissenschaft des Judenthums*, iv. 1877, pp. 141–144). Jerome also mentions it as the opinion of some *Hebraei* that the last week year of Daniel (Dan. ix. 27) covers the period of Vespasian and of Hadrian (*Comm. in Daniel 9 fin.* = *Opp.* ed. Vallarsi,

v. 696 : "tres autem anni et sex menses sub Hadriano supputantur, quando Jerusalem omnino subversa est et Judaeorum gens catervatim caesa "). In the Jerusalem Talmud the three and a half years are mentioned as the period of the siege of Beth-ther (*jer. Taanith* iv. fol. 68^d in Lebrecht, *Bether*, p. 44 ; Wünsche, p. 158) ; in the Midrash, *Echa rabbathi*, three and a half years are assigned to Vespasian's siege of Jerusalem and three and a half years to Hadrian's siege of Beth-ther (Derenbourg, *Histoire*, p. 431).— Although these witnesses do not carry any great weight, they are correct in saying that the war lasted about three and a half years. Later documents confound the continuance of the siege of Beth-ther with the continuance of the war. That the beginning is to be placed in A.D. 132 has been shown above in p. 299. The end is to be placed, according to Eusebius, *Hist. eccl.* iv. 6, in the eighteenth year of Hadrian = A.D. 134–135, and, indeed, in 135 rather than 134. For on inscriptions of the year 134 Hadrian does not yet bear the title (*Imp*)*erator II.*, which was given him in consequence of the Jewish war. The war was therefore then not yet ended.

[105] According to the *bab. Berachoth* 61^b, R. Akiba was put to a martyr's death by torture, his flesh being torn from his body with iron combs. But during his sufferings he prayed the *Shema*, and while he, proceeding with the repetition of it, lingered long over the word Echad (Deut. vi. 4), he breathed out his spirit. Then there sounded forth a *Bath Kol*, a voice from heaven, saying : "Blessed art thou, R. Akiba, that thy soul departed with ' Echad.'"—Elsewhere also in the older Midrash literature, and in the Jerusalem and Babylonian Talmud, casual reference is made to the martyr death of this and that rabbi. The gathering together of ten martyrs, on the other hand, makes its appearance first in the Midrashim of the post-Talmudic period. Jellinek, *Midrasch Ele Eskera*, edited for the first time, according to a manuscript of the Hamburg City Library, with dissertations, 1853, and in *Bet ha-Midrasch*, Bd. ii. 64–72 and vi. 19–35, gives some texts. Compare further : Zunz, *Die gottesdienstlichen Vorträge der Juden*, p. 142 ; Grätz in the *Monatsschrift für Geschichte und Wissenschaft des Judenthums*, 1851–1852, pp. 307–322 ; *Geschichte der Juden*, iv. 175 ff. ; Möbius, *Midrasch Ele Eskera, die Sage von den zehn Märtyrern, metrisch übersetzt*, 1854 ; Derenbourg, *Histoire*, p. 436 ; Hamburger, *Real-Encyclopaedie für Bibel und Talmud, Supplementalband*, i. (1886) pp. 155–158, art. "Zehn Märtyrer" (this last the relatively best statement). — Bibliographical hints are also given in Steinschneider, *Catalog. librorum hebr. in Biblioth. Bodl.* col. 585, n. 3730–3733.

[106] In this designation of Hadrian the title *Imp(erator) II.* is wanting in two military diplomas which are dated 2nd April and 15th September A.D. 134 (*Corp. Inscr. Lat.* t. iii. pp. 877 and 878, *Dipl.* xxxiv. and xxxv. ; the latter also, *Corp. Inscr. Lat.* t. x. n. 7855). Also, it is wanting on other inscriptions of A.D. 134 (*Corp. Inscr. Lat.* t. vi. n. 973, *Inscr. Regni Neapol.* n. 5771 = *Corp. Inscr. Lat.* t. ix. n. 4359). Particularly

decisive is the witness of the military diplomas, which in the designatory clauses are usually most precise.—Even from A.D. 135 (*Hadr. trib. pot.* xix.) up to a very recent period the title had not been proved. But perhaps certain inscription-fragments, on which the number xix. and the letters *teru* are found, should be expanded into *Hadr. trib. pot.* xix. *imp. iterum* (so Hübner, *Corp. Inscr. Lat.* t. ii. n. 478).—The title *Imp. II.* is certainly demonstrable for A.D. 136 (*Hadr. trib. pot.* xx.); see Orelli, *Inscr. Lat.* n. 813 and 2286 = *Corp. Inscr. Lat.* t. vi. n. 975 and 976 ; also on an inscription which bears this date (*Hadr. trib. pot.* xx.), but belongs probably to the very beginning of that year, namely, December A.D. 135, *Corp. Inscr. Lat.* t. xiv. n. 3577 = 4235 (the tribunicial year began then in December).—Hadrian therefore received the title *Imp. II.* in A.D. 135, undoubtedly in consequence of the successful ending of the Jewish war.

[107] On Julius Severus, see *Corp. Inscr. Lat.* t. iii. n. 2830 : "Huic senatus auctore imperatore Trajano Hadriano Augusto ornamenta triumphalia decrevit ob res in Judea prospere gestas." Julius Severus was probably the last upon whom this honour was bestowed.

[108] Dio Cassius, lxix. 14. Comp. Fronto, *De bello Parthico, s. init.* (ed. Mai, 1823, p. 200 = *Frontonis epistulae*, ed. Naber, 1867, p. 217 sq.): "Quid ? avo vestro Hadriano imperium optinente quantum militum a Judaeis, quantum ab Britannis caesum ?"

[109] Dio Cassius, lxix. 14.

[110] Jerome, *ad Zechar.* xi. 5 (Vallarsi, vi. 885); *ad Jerem.* xxxi. 15 (Vallarsi, iv. 1065); *Chronicon Paschale*, ed. Dindorf, i. 474.

[111] Dio Cassius, lxix. 12 ; Eusebius, *Hist. eccl.* iv. 6 ; *Demonstratio evangelica*, vi. 18. 10, ed. Gaisford.

[112] Justin, *Apologia*, i. 47 : ὅτι δὲ φυλάσσεται ὑφ᾿ ὑμῶν ὅπως μηδεὶς ἐν αὐτῇ γένηται, καὶ θάνατος κατὰ τοῦ καταλαμβανομένου Ἰουδαίου εἰσιόντος ὥρισται, ἀκριβῶς ἐπίστασθε. *Dialog. c. Trypho*, c. 16 ; 92. Aristo of Pella in Eusebius, *Hist. eccl.* iv. 6 : ὡς ἂν μηδ᾿ ἐξ ἀπόπτου θεωροῖεν τὸ πατρῷον ἔδαφος (comp. on Aristo, vol. i. pp. 69–72). Tertullian, *Adv. Judaeos*, c. 13 *init. :* " de longinquo eam oculis tantum videre permissum est," seems to be a conscious modification of the words of Aristo for the purpose of harmonizing them with Isa. xxxiii. 17. See Grabe, *Spicilegium patr.* ii. 131 sq. : Routh, *Reliquiae sacrae*, i. 104 sq. : "saltim vestigio salutare conceditur ;" Eusebius, *Demonstratio evangel.* vi. 18. 10, ed. Gaisford ; Eusebius, *Chronicon*, ed. Schoene, ii. 168, *ad. ann. Abr.* 2151 ; according to the Armenian : "ex hoc inde tempore etiam ascendere Hierosolymam omnino prohibiti sunt primum Dei voluntate, deinde Romanorum mandato ;" Jerome, *Comm. in Is.* vi. 11 sqq., ed. Vallarsi, iv. 100 ; *in Jerem.* xviii. 15, ed. Vallarsi, iv. 971 : "nullus Judaeorum terram quondam et urbem sanctam ingredi lege permittitur ;" *in Dan.* ix. *fin.*, ed. Vallarsi, v. 696 : "ut Judaeae quoque finibus pellerentur."

[113] Dio Cassius, lxix. 12 ; Ulpian, *Digest.* l. 15. 1. 6, and *Tabula Peuting.* (*Helya Capitolina*) gives the name in full, Aelia Capitolina. In

Ptolemy, v. 16. 8 and viii. 20. 18, the common printed text has in both
cases Αἰλία Καπιτωλιάς.—It was called Aelia after the family name of
Hadrian : Capitolina after the Capitoline Jupiter.

    [114] Ulpian, *Digest.* l. 15. 1. 6 : " In Palestina duae fuerunt coloniae,
Caesariensis et Aelia Capitolina, sed neutra jus Italicum habet."—Paulus,
Digest. l. 15. 8. 7 : *similes his* (namely, like the Caesariens who had not
the full *jus Italicum*) *Capitulenses esse videntur.*—A memorial inscription
which the courts of the colony set up in honour of Antoninus Pius is
given by De Saulcy, *Voyage atour de la mer morte,* ii. 204, with atlas, pl.
xxiv. n. 6 = Le Bas and Waddington, *Inscriptions,* iii. 2, n. 1895 = *Corpus
Inscr. Lat.* t. iii. n. 116 : " Tito Ael(io) Hadriano Antonino Aug. Pio P.
P. pontif(ici) Augur(i) d(ecreto) d(ecurionum).

    [115] *Chronicon Paschale,* ed. Dindorf, i. 474.

    [116] Jerome, *Chronicon, ad. ann. Abr.* 2152 (Eusebius, *Chronicon,* ed.
Schoene, ii. 169) : " Aelia ab Aelio Hadriano condita, et in fronte ejus
portae qua Bethleem egredimur sus scalptus in marmore significans
Romanae potestati subjacere Judaeos."—The figure of the swine was found
also upon a coin of the *leg. X. Fratensis* discovered in Jerusalem, which
De Saulcy has published (*Revue archéologique,* nouv. série, t. xx. 1869, pp.
251-260, and De Saulcy, *Numismatique de la Terre Sainte,* p. 83 sq., pl.
v. n. 3).

    [117] Dio Cassius, lxix. 12.—The figure of Jupiter often occurs on the
coins of Aelia.

    [118] Jerome, *Comm. in Jes.* ii. 9 (Vallarsi, iv. 37) : " ubi quondam erat
templum et religio dei, ibi Hadriana statua et Jovis idolum collocatum
est."—*Idem, Comm. in Matt.* xxiv. 15 (Vallarsi, vii. 194) : " potest autem
simpliciter aut de Antichristo accipi aut de imagine Caesaris, quam
Pilatus posuit in templo, aut de Hadriana equestri statua quae in ipso
sancto sanctorum loco usque in praesentem diem stetit."—Since, according
to this, the statue of Hadrian stood on the site of the Jewish temple,
where, according to Dio Cassius, the temple to Jupiter was erected, and
since it is mentioned by Jerome in the former passage along with the
figure of Jupiter, it must have stood in the temple of Jupiter. Compare
also, Chrysostom, *Orat. adv. Judaeos,* v. 11 ; Cedrenus, ed. Bekker, i. 438
(στήσας τὸ ἑαυτοῦ εἴδωλον ἐν τῷ ναῷ) ; Nicephorus Callistus, *Eccl. Hist.* iii.
24.—The Pilgrim of Bordeaux speaks of two statues of Hadrian (*Palaestinae
descriptiones,* ed. Tobler, p. 4 : " sunt ibi et statuae duae Hadriani ").

    [119] Eusebius, *vita Constantini,* iii. 26.   Constantine, it is well known,
caused a church to be built on that site.   According to the later legend,
which to Eusebius was still unknown, the cross of Christ was found upon
the excavation of the sepulchre in its neighbourhood (Socrates, *Hist. eccl.*
i. 17 ; Sozomenus, *Hist. eccl.* ii. 1, and others.   Compare Holder, *Inventio
sanctae crucis,* 1889 ; Nestle, *De sancta cruce,* 1889).

    [120] Jerome, *Epist.* 58 *ad Paulinum,* c. 3 (Vallarsi, i. 321) : " Ab Hadriani
temporibus usque ad imperium Constantini per annos circiter centum
octoginta in loco resurrectionis simulacrum Jovis, in crucis rupe statua
ex marmore Veneris a gentibus posita colebatur."—The difference of

statement between Jerome and Eusebius has its origin evidently in the legend of the finding of the cross. Socrates and Sozomen still speak, like Eusebius, only of a sanctuary of Aphrodite. On account of the story of the finding of the cross, however, they assumed that this was the site of the sepulchre as well as of the crucifixion. Jerome, on the other hand, endows each of the two holy places with an idol of its own.

[121] Derenbourg, *Histoire de la Palestine*, p. 430 .

[122] *Capitolin. Antoninus Pius*, c. 5 (in the *Scriptores Historiae Augustae*, ed. Peter): " Judaeos rebellantes contudit per praesides ac legatos."

———•———

Selected Bibliography (1900-1960)

Abbreviations

ARAST	Atti dell reale Accademia di scienze di Torino
BASOR	Bulletin of the American Schools of Oriental Research
BJPES	Bulletin of the Jewish Palestine Exploration Society
HZ	Historische Zeitschrift
HUCA	Hebrew Union College Annual
IEJ	Israel Exploration Journal
JAOS	Journal of the American Oriental Society
JBL	Journal of Biblical Literature
JJS	Journal of Jewish Studies
JPOS	Journal of the Palestine Oriental Society
JQR	Jewish Quarterly Review
JSS	Jewish Social Studies
MGWJ	Monatsschrift für die Geschichte und Wissenschaft des Judentums
PAAJR	Proceedings of the American Academy for Jewish Research
QDAP	Quarterly of the Department of Antiquities in Palestine
RB	Revue Biblique
REJ	Revue des études juives
RHR	Revue d'histoire des religions
ZDPV	Zeitschrift des deutschen Palästina-Vereins
ZNW	Zeitschrift für die neutestamentliche Wissenschaft

SELECTED BIBLIOGRAPHY
(1900-1960)

Abel, F. M., *Géographie de la Palestine*, I-II. Paris, 1933-38.

——, "L'ère des Seleucides", RB XLVII, 1938, 198-213.

——, *Les Livres des Maccabées*. Paris, 1949.

Aberbach, M., "The Conflicting Accounts of Josephus and Tacitus concerning Cumanus' and Felix' Terms of Office," JQR XL, 1949-50, 1-14.

Albright, W. F., "The Excavations at Ascalon," BASOR VI, May 1922, 11 ff.

——, *From the Stone Age to Christianity*. Baltimore, 1940.

Allon, G., "The Attitude of the Pharisees toward Roman Rule and the Herodian Dynasty," *Zion* III, 1935, 300-322 (Heb.).

——, "The Burning of the Temple," *Yavneh* I, 1939, 85-106 (Heb.).

——, "On the History of the High Priesthood at the Close of the Second Temple," *Tarbiz* XIII, 1941-42, 1-24 (Heb.).

Apfelbaum, S., "The Rebellion of the Jews of Cyrenaica in the Time of Trajan." "Three Additional Remarks on the Jewish Rebellion in Cyrene under Trajan." *Zion* XIX, 1954, 23-56; XXII, 1957, 81-85.

Aptowitzer, V., *Parteipolitik der Hasmonäerzeit in rabbinischem und pseudepigraphischem Schrifttum*. Vienna and Leipzig, 1927.

Auerbach, Moses, "Zur politischen Gechichte der Juden unter Kaiser Hadrian." *Festschrift zum 50-jährigen Bestehen des Rabbinerseminars in Berlin*. Hannover, 1924.

Avi-Yonah, M., *Biyme Roma u-Bizantion*. Jerusalem, 1946.

——, *A Map of Roman Palestine*. 2nd ed. Oxford, 1940.

——, "The City Boundaries of Roman Transjordan," BJPES I-II, 1943-44 (Heb.).

——, "The Battles in the Books of the Maccabees," *Hans Lewy Memorial Volume*. Jerusalem, 1949, 13-24 (Heb.).

——, "The Development of the Roman Road System in Palestine," IEJ I, 1950-51, 54-60.

——, "The Foundation of Tiberias," IEJ I, 1950-51, 160 ff.

——, "The 'War of the Sons of Light and the Sons of Darkness' and Maccabean Warfare," IEJ II, 1952, 1-5.

——, "The Missing Fortress of Flavius Josephus," IEJ II, 1952, 94-98.

Avi-Yonah, M., Avigad, N., a.o., "The Archaeological Survey of Masada, 1955-56," IEJ VII, 1957, 1-60.

Baramki, J., "Coin Hoards from Palestine," QDAP XI, 1944, 86 ff.

Baron, Salo W., *The Jewish Community*, I. Philadelphia, 1942.

———, *A Social and Religious History of the Jews*, Second Ed., I-II (Ancient Times). Philadelphia, 1952.

Bevan, Edwyn R., "Syria and the Jews." *Cambridge Ancient History* VIII, 1930, 495-533.

Bévenot, H., "Prolegomena to the Maccabees," *Bibliotheca Sacra* LXXXI, 1924, 31-54.

Bickermann (Bickerman), Elias, "Ein jüdischer Festbrief vom Jahre 124 v. Chr. (II Macc. 1:1-9)", ZNW XXXII, 1933, 233-254.

———, "La charte séleucide de Jérusalem," REJ C, 1935, 4-35.

———, *Der Gott der Makkabäer*. Berlin, 1937.

———, "Un document relatif à la persécution d'Antiochos IV Épiphane," RHR CXV, 1937, 188-223.

———, *Les institutions des Séleucides*. Paris, 1938.

———, "Les Herodéens." RB XLVII, 1938, 184-197.

———, "Héliodore au temple de Jérusalem," *Annuaire de l'Institut de Philologie et d'Histoire orientales* VII, 1939-42, 1-40.

———, "Une proclamation séleucide relative au temple de Jérusalem," *Syria* XXV, 1946-48, 67ff.

———, *The Maccabees*. New York, 1947.

———, "The Warning Inscription of Herod's Temple," JQR XXXVII, 1946-47, 387-405 (Cf. S. Zeitlin, JQR XXXVIII, 1947-48, 111-116).

Brand, Joshua, "The Temple of Onias," *Yavneh* I, 1939, 76-84 (Heb.).

Brandon, S. G. F., *The Fall of Jerusalem and the Christian Church*. London, 1951.

Braun, Martin, "King Herod as Oriental Monarch," *Commentary* XXV, 1958, 48-53.

Burrows, Millar, "On the Fortress Antonia and the Praetorium," *Biblical Archaeologist* I, 1938, 17-19.

———, *What Mean these Stones?* New Haven, 1941.

Chabot, J. G., ed., *Répertoire d'épigraphie sémitique*. Paris, 1900 sq.

Corbishley, Thomas, "Quirinius and the Census," *Klio* N. F. XI, 1936, 81-93.

Crawfoot, J., Kenyon K., and Sukenik, E. L., *The Buildings at Samaria*. London, 1942.

Dalman, Gustaf, "Der zweite Tempel zu Jerusalem," *Palestina Jahrbuch* V, 1909, 29-57.

Dancy, J. C., *A Commentary on I Maccabees*. Oxford, 1954.

Daniel, R., *M. Vipsanius Agrippa*. Breslau, 1933.

Dessau, Hermann, "Judaea und die Juden," in *Geschichte der römischen Kaiserzeit*. Berlin, 1930.

Enslin, M. S., *Christian Origins*, I, II. New York, 1938.

Fairweather, William, *The Background of the Gospels on Judaism in the Period between the Old and New Testaments*. 8th ed., Edinburgh, 1926.

Farmer, W. R., *Maccabees, Zealots, and Josephus*. New York, 1956.

Finkelstein, Louis, *The Pharisees, I-II*. Philadelphia, 1938.

Fischel, Henry A., *The First Book of Maccabees*. New York, 1948.

Fishman, J. L., "The Maccabaean Period in our Ancient Literature," *Sinai* II, 1938-39, 59-77 (Heb.)

Fuks, A., "The Jewish Revolt in Egypt (A.D. 115-117)," *Zion* XXII, 1957, 1-9.

Galling, K., "Die syrisch-palästinische Küste nach der Beschreibung bei Pseudo-Scylax," ZDPV LXI, 1938, 83 ff.

Gaster, Moses, *The Samaritans, their History, Doctrines and Literature*. London, 1925.

———, "Demetrius and the Seder Olam," *Simonsen Festschrift*, 1923, 243-252.

Ginsburg, Michel, *Rome et la Judée*. Paris, 1928.

———, "Fiscus Judaicus," JQR XXI, 1931, 281-291.

Glatzer, N. N., ed., *Jerusalem and Rome: The Writings of Josephus*. New York, 1960.

Glück, Nelson, "Nabataean Syria and Nabataean Transjordan," JPOS XVIII, 1938, 1-6.

———, *The Other Side of the Jordan*. New Haven, 1940.

———, *Rivers in the Desert*. Philadelphia, 1959.

Goodenough, Erwin R., *Jewish Symbols in the Greco-Roman Period*, I-VIII. New York, 1953 seq.

———, "The Political Philosophy of the Hellenistic Kingship," *Yale Classical Studies* I, 1928, 53 ff.

Grandjean, Georges, *La destruction de Jérusalem*. Paris, 1940.

Gressmann, Hugo, "Die Ammonitischen Tobiaden," *Sitzungsberichte der Berliner Akademie der Wissenschaften* XXXIX, 1921, 128 ff., 663-672.

Guignebert, Charles, *The Jewish World in the Time of Jesus*. London, 1939.

Gulack, Asher, "The Roman Method of Collecting Taxes in Palestine," *Magnes Anniversary Volume*, 1938, 97-104 (Heb.).

———, "Boule and Strategia: a Contribution to the Study of Roman Fiscal Administration in Palestine," *Tarbiz* XI, 1939-40, 119-122 (Heb.).

Hadas, Moses, *The Third and Fourth Books of Maccabees*. New York, 1953.

Haefele, L., *Geschichte der Landschaft Samaria*. Münster, 1923.

———, *Cäsarea am Meer: Topographie und Geschichte etc*. Münster, 1923.

Hamilton, R. W., "Excavations against the North Wall of Jerusalem 1937-38," QDAP X, 1942, 1-53.

Heinemann, Isaak, "Wer veranlasste den Glaubenszwang der Makkabäerzeit?" MGWJ, LXXXII, 1938, 145-172.

Herz, J., "Grossgrundbesitz in Palästina im Zeitalter Jesu," *Palestina Jahrbuch* XXIV, 1928, 98-113.

Hollis, F., *The Archaeology of Herod's Temple with Commentary on the Tractate Middoth*. London, 1934.

Holtzmann, Oskar, *Neutestamentliche Zeitgeschichte*. Tübingen, 1906.

Iliffe, J. H.,"Nabataean Pottery from the Negeb," QDAP VI. 1916, 61 ff.

Jeremias, Joachim, *Jerusalem zur Zeit Jesu*, I-II. Leipzig and Göttingen, 1923-1937.

———, "Die Einwohnerzahl Jerusalems zur Zeit Jesu," ZDPV LXVI, 1943, 24-31.

Jones, A. H. M., "The Urbanization of Palestine," *Journal of Roman Studies* XXI, 1931, 78-85.

———, *The Cities of the Eastern Roman Provinces*. Oxford, 1937.

———, *The Herods of Judea*. Oxford, 1938.

Juster, Jean, *Les Juifs dans l'Empire romaine*, I-II. Paris, 1914.

Kadman, L., "A Coin Find at Masada," IEJ VII, 1957, 61-65.

Kahrstedt, Ulrich, *Syrische Territorien in hellenistischer Zeit*. Berlin, 1926.

Kammerer, A., *Pétra et la Nabatène*. Paris, 1929-30.

Kanael B., "The Beginning of Maccabean Coinage"; "The Greek Letters and Monograms on the Coins of Jehohanan the High Priest," IEJ I, 1950-51, 170-175; II, 1952, 190-194.

———, "The Coins of King Herod of the Third Year," JQR XLII, 1951-52, 261-264.

———, "The Partition of Judea by Gabinius," IEJ VII, 1957, 98-106.

Kennard, J. Spencer, *Politique et religion chez les Juifs au temps de Jésus etc*. Paris, 1927.

———, "Judas of Galilee and his Clan," JQR XXXVI, 1945-46, 281-286.

Kindler, A., "Rare and Unpublished Hasmonaean Coins," "Some Unpublished Coins of King Herod," "The Jaffa Hoard of Alexander Jannaeus," "More Dates on the Coins of the Procurators," IEJ II, 1952, 188-189; III, 1953, 239-241; IV, 1954, 170-185; VI, 1956, 54-57.

Kittel, Rudolf, *Geschichte des Volkes Israel*, III. Stuttgart, 1929.

Klausner, Joseph, *Historia shel ha-Bayit ha-Sheni, III-V*. Jerusalem, 1952.

Klein, Samuel, *Jüdisch-palästinensisches Corpus Inscriptionum*. Vienna and Berlin, 1920.

———, "Das tannaitische Grenzverzeichnis Palestinas," HUCA V, 1928, 197-251.

———, *Galiläa von der Makkabäerzeit bis 67*. Vienna, 1928.

———, "A Chapter in Palestine Research Towards the End of the Second Temple," *Magnes Anniversary Volume*, 1938, 216-222.

———, *The Land of Judah from the Babylonian Exile to the End of the Talmudic Period*. Jerusalem, 1939 (Heb.).

Kolbe, Walther, *Beiträge zur syrischen und jüdischen Geschichte.* Stuttgart, 1926.

————, "Die Seleukidenära des ersten Makkabäerbuches," *Hermes* LXII, 1927, 225-242.

Kraeling, Carl H., ed., *Gerasa, City of the Decapolis.* New Haven, 1938.

————, "The Episode of the Roman Standards at Jerusalem," *Harvard Theological Review* XXXV 1942, 263-289.

Krauss, Samuel, *Synagogale Altertümer.* Berlin-Vienna, 1922.

————, "Die jüdische Siedlung in Samaria (Sebaste)," MGWJ LXXV, 1931, 191-199.

————, "Did Hadrian Prohibit Jews from Entering Jerusalem?" BJPES IV, 1936-37, 52-60 (Heb.).

————, "Roman Rule in Palestine," BJPES V, 1937-38, 14-26 (Heb.).

Lacheman, Ernest R., "The So-Called Bar Kokba Letter," JQR XLIV, 1953-54, 285-290.

Lagrange, M.-J., *Le Judaisme avant Jésus Christ.* Paris, 1931.

Laqueur, R., *Kritische Untersuchungen zum zweiten Makkabäerbuche.* Strassburg, 1906.

————, "Griechische Urkunden in der jüdisch-hellenistischen Literatur," HZ CXXXVI, 1927, 229-252.

Lewy, Hans, "Ein Rechtsstreit um den Boden Palästinas im Altertum," MGWJ LXXVII, 1933, 84-99, 172-180.

Lichtenstein, Hans, "Megillat Taanit: Die Fastenrolle etc.," HUCA VIII-IX, 1931-32.

Lieberman, Saul, *Greek in Jewish Palestine.* Philadelphia, 1942.

————, *Hellenism in Jewish Palestine.* New York, 1950.

Macalister, R. A. S., *The Excavations of Gezer,* I. London, 1912, 211 f.

Mahler, Eduard, *Handbuch der jüdischen Chronologie.* Leipzig, 1916.

Maisler (Mazar), Benjamin, "The House of Tobiah," *Tarbiz* XII, 1941-42, 109-123 (Heb.).

Marcus, Ralph, *Josephus: Jewish Antiquities, Books XII-XIV.* London and Cambridge, Mass., 1943.

Mathews, Shailer, *New Testament Times in Palestine.* New York, 1933.

Meyer, Eduard, *Ursprung und Anfänge des Christentums,* II. Stuttgart and Berlin, 1921.

Meyshan (Mestschanski), J., "The Coinage of Agrippa the First," IEJ IV, 1954, 186-200.

Momigliano, Arnoldo, "I Tobiadi nella prehistoria del moto maccabaico," ARAST LXVII, 1931-32, 165-200.

————, "Herod of Judaea," "Roman Government of Palestine," "The Jewish Rebellion," "The Campaigns of Vespasian," "The Siege and Fall of Jerusalem." *Cambridge Ancient History,* X, 1934.

Montgomery, James A., *The Samaritans, the Earliest Jewish Sect.* Philadelphia, 1907.

Moore, George Foot, *Judaism in the First Centuries of the Christian Era,* I, II, III. Cambridge, Mass., 1927-1930.

Morison, Frank, *And Pilate Said: A New Study of the Roman Procurator*. London 1939.

Morr, Joseph, "Die Landeskunde von Palästina bei Strabon und Josephus," *Philologus* LXXXI, 1926, 256-279.

Narkis, Mordecai, *Coins of the Land of Israel, I-II*. Jerusalem, 1936-38 (Heb.).

Niese, B., "Eine Urkunde aus der Makkabäerzeit," *Orientalische Studien Th. Nöldeke gewidmet* II, 1906, 817-824.

Oesterley, W. O. E., *A History of Israel*, II. Oxford, 1932.

——, *Jews and Judaism during the Greek Period*. London, 1941.

Otto, Walter, *Herodes. Beiträge zur Geschichte des letzten jüdischen Königshauses*. Stuttgart, 1913.

——, "Hyrcanos," in Pauly-Wissowa-Kroll, *Realencyclopädie* IX, 1916, 527-534.

Perowne, Stewart, *The Life and Times of Herod the Great*. London, 1956.

Pfeiffer, Robert H., *History of New Testament Times*. New York, 1949.

Poidebard, O., *La trace de Rome dans le desert de Syrie, I-II*. Paris, 1934.

Rankin, O. S., *The Origins of the Festival of Hannukkah*. Edinburgh, 1930.

Reifenberg, A., *Ancient Hebrew Arts*. New York, 1950.

——, "Unpublished and Unusual Jewish Coins," *IEJ* I, 1950-51, 176-178.

——, *Israel's History in Coins*. London, 1953.

Reinach, Th., "L'empereur Claudius et les Juifs," *REJ* LXXIX, 1924, 113-144.

Reinhold, Meyer, *Marcus Agrippa: A Biography*. Geneva, N. Y., 1933.

Ricciotti, G., *Storia d'Israele* II, Turin, 1934.

Romanoff, Paul, *Onomasticon of Palestine*. New York, 1937.

——, "Jewish Symbols on Ancient Jewish Coins," *JQR* XXXIII and XXXIV, 1942-43 and 1943-44.

Rostovtzeff, M., *Studien zur Geschichte des römischen Kolonates*, Leipzig and Berlin, 1910.

——, *Social and Economic History of the Hellenistic World*. Oxford, 1941.

Rosenthal, J., "Bar Hebraeus and a Jewish Census under Claudius," *JSS* XVI, 1944, 267 ff.

Roth, Cecil, "The Jewish Revolt against Rome"; "Simon bar Giora, Ancient Jewish Hero." *Commentary* XXVII, 1959, 513-522, and XXIX, 1960, 52-58.

Roth, Otto, *Rom und die Hasmonäer*. Leipzig, 1914.

Rowley, H. H., "The Herodians in the Gospels" *Journal of Theological Studies* XLI, 1940, 14-27.

Saliternik, D., "Observations on the Third Wall," *BJPES*, 1934-35, 13-19.

Schalit, Abraham, *Roman Administration in Palestine*. Jerusalem, 1937 (Heb.).

——, *King Herod: Portrait of a Ruler*. Jerusalem, 1960 (Heb.).

Schlatter, A., *Geschichte Israels von Alexander dem Grossen bis Hadrian*. Stuttgart, 1906; 3rd ed., 1925.

Schulten, A., "Masada, die Burg des Herodes und die römischen Lager," *Zeitschrift des deutschen Palästinavereins* LVI, 1933, 1-185.

Schunk, K. D., *Die Quellen des I. and II. Makkabäerbuches*. Halle, 1954.

Schwabe, Moshe, "A Contribution to the History of Tiberias," *Hans Lewy Memorial Volume*. Jerusalem, 1949, 200-251 (Heb.).

——, "Two Jewish-Greek Inscriptions Recently Discovered at Caesarea," *IEJ* III, 1953, 127-130, 233-238.

Sellers, O. R., *The Citadel of Beth-zur*. Philadelphia, 1933.

Smith, George Adam, *Historical Geography of the Holy Land*. 25th ed. London, 1932.

Sonne, Isaiah, "The Newly Discovered Bar Kokeba Letters," *PAAJR* XXIII, 1954, 75-108.

Stern, M., "The Death of Onias III," *Zion* XXV, 1960, 1-16.

Stinespring, Wm. F., "Hadrian in Palestine 129-30 A.D." *JAOS* LIX, 1934, 360-365.

Strathmann, K., "Der Kampf um Beth-Tar," *Palestina Jahrbuch* XXIII, 1927, 92-173.

Sukenik, E. L., *The Ancient Synagogues in Palestine and Greece*. London, 1934.

——, "More About the Oldest Coins of Judaea," *JPOS* XV, 1935, 109 ff.

——, "A Hoard of Coins of John Hyrcanus"; "Some Unpublished Coins of Aelia Capitolina," *JQR* XXXVII, 1947, 281-284; XXXVIII 1947-48, 157-159.

Sukenik, E. and Mayer, A. L., *The Third Wall of Jerusalem*. Jerusalem, 1930.

Swain, Joseph W., "Gamaliel's Speech and Caligula's Statue," *Harvard Theological Review* XXXVII, 1944, 341-349.

Täubler, Eugen, *Imperium Romanum*. Leipzig, 1913, 157-187, 239-254.

——, "Palestina in der hellenistisch-römischen Zeit," *Tyche*. Leipzig and Berlin, 1926.

——, "Jerusalem 201 to 199 BCE," *JQR* XXXVII, 1946-47, 1-30, 125-137, 249-263.

Taylor, Lily Ross, "Quirinius and the Census of Judaea" *American Journal of Philology* LIV, 1933, 120-133.

Tcherikover, Victor, "The Documents in the Second Book of the Maccabees," *Tarbiz* I, 1930, 31 ff. (Heb.).

——, "Palestine under the Ptolemies," *Mizraim* IV-V, 1937, 9 ff. (Heb.).

——, "The Third Book of Maccabees as a Historical Source of the

Augustan Period," *Zion* X, 1945, 1 ff. (Heb.).

——, *Hellenistic Civilization and the Jews.* Philadelphia, 1959.

Tedesche, Sidney, tr., *The First Book of Maccabees.* New York, 1950.

——, *The Second Book of Maccabees.* New York, 1954.

Teicher, J. L., "Documents of the Bar Kochba Period," JJS IV, 1953, 132-134.

Thackeray, H. St. John, tr., *Josephus: The Jewish War*, 2 vols. London-Cambridge, Mass., 1927.

——, *Josephus the Man and the Historian.* New York, 1929.

Thomsen, Peter, *Palästina und seine Kultur in fünf Jahrtausenden.* Leipzig, 1909.

——, *Die griechischen und lateinischen Inschriften der Stadt Jerusalem.* Leipzig, 1922.

Torrey, C. C., "Three Troublesome Proper Names in First Maccabees," JBL LIII, 1934, 31-33.

——, "The Letter Prefixed to Second Maccabees," JAOS LX, 1940, 119-150.

Tracy, S., "Aristeas and III Maccabees," *Yale Classical Studies* I, 1928, 239-252.

Vincent, H., "L'Antonia et le Praetorium," RB XLII, 1933, 83-113.

Vincent H. and Abel, F. M., *Jérusalem* I-II. Paris, 1926.

Watzinger, Carl, *Denkmäler Palästinas*, II. Leipzig, 1935.

Weber, Wilhelm, *Josephus und Vespasian.* Berlin, Stuttgart and Leipzig, 1921.

Willrich, Hugo, *Urkundenfälschung in der hellenistisch-jüdischen Literatur.* Göttingen, 1924.

——, *Das Haus des Herodes.* Heidelberg, 1929.

Wolfson, H. A., "Philo on Jewish Citizenship in Alexandria," JBL LXIII, 1944, 165-168.

——, *Philo: Foundations of Religious Philosophy in Judaism, Christianity and Islam*, I-II. Cambridge, Mass., 1947.

Wruck, W., *Die Syrische Provinzialprägung von Augustus bis Trajan.* Stuttgart, 1931.

Yeivin, Samuel, *Milhemet Bar Kokhba.* 2nd ed. Jerusalem, 1952.

Zeitlin, Solomon, *Megillat Taanit as a Source for Jewish Chronology etc.* Philadelphia, 1922.

——, *The History of the Second Jewish Commonwealth: Prolegomena.* Philadelphia, 1933.

——, "The Tobias Family and the Hasmoneans," PAAJR IV, 1933, 169-233.

——, "The Assumption of Moses and the Revolt of Bar Kokba," JQR XXXVIII, 1947-48, 1-45.

——, "Bar Kokeba and Bar Kozeba," JQR XLIII, 1952-53, 77-80.

Zucker, Hans, *Studien zur jüdischen Selbstverwaltung im Altertum.* Berlin, 1936.

INDEX

417

296
ScH 3
1961
C.2

LINCOLN CHRISTIAN UNIVERSITY

132100

3 4711 00227 4068